The Bigod

Book Four

Hugh

A Medieval Novel by
Martin P Clarke

Copyright © 2017 by Martin P Clarke

First published in Great Britain in 2017 by Martin P Clarke

ISBN 978-0-244-95174-0

Although every attempt has been made to place the
actual characters within historical events,
this novel remains a work of fiction.

The Bigod Chronicles

Book One   Ilger
Book Two   The Order
Book Three   William
Book Four   Hugh

"One should see the world, and see himself as a scale with an equal balance of good and evil. When he does one good deed the scale is tipped to the good - he and the world is saved. When he does one evil deed the scale is tipped to the bad - he and the world is destroyed."

Maimonides 1177

Additional Main Characters

Thomas Becket	*Archbishop of Canterbury*
Richard le Breton	*knight of King Henry*
Ned Bonham	*knight of Hugh Bigod (fictional)*
William Albini	*son of Wills Albini*
Matilda St Hilary de Harcourt	*wife of William Albini*
Roger Bigod	*son of Hugh Bigod*
Earl of Leicester	*joint Justicar of England*
Richard de Lucy	*joint Justicar of England*
Marcus Tyler	*squire to Hugh Bigod (fictional)*
Ralph le Broc	*castellan of Haughley Castle*
Jacques de Exmes	*commander of the Ramleh garrison*
Henry Malache	*steward to Count Thierry of Flanders*
Bertrand de Blanchefort	*Grand Master of the Templars*
Arius	*Christian scholar/delegate Council of Nicea*
King Amalric	*King of Jerusalem*
Maimonides	*physician/advisor to Saladin*
Robert de Beaumont	*Earl of Leicester*
Petronella	*wife of the Earl of Leicester*
Queen Eleanor	*wife of King of France/King Henry II*
Reginald FitzUrse	*knight of Henry II*
Hugh d'Morville	*knight of Henry II*
William de Tracy	*knight of Henry II*
Marshall Bryce	*Marshall to King Henry II*
Baruch	*Jewish scholar*
Wilhelm de Mandeville	*Earl of Essex*
Vizier Shawar	*Emir of Egypt*
Marie the Countess of Champagne	*wife of Count Henri*
Chrétien de Troyes	*patronage to Marie of Champagne*
Simon de Moorslede	*aide to Count Philip of Flanders(fictional)*
Odo de St Armand	*Grand Master of the Templars*
Thomas Martin	*Norfolk antiquarian*
Thomas Payne	*mentor to Tom Paine*

Book Four

Hugh

Eight Years Later…

1164-1177

'Nothing is hidden that will not be made known,
or secret that will not come to light.'

Jesus Christ   Luke 8:1

Chapter 1

Clarendon Palace
Salisbury
1164

After two days of posturing by fretful bishops, councillors and lawmakers, the air of desperation hanging over the great hall of Clarendon suddenly lifted. Having weathered the bitter cauldron of argument and counter argument, all the earls and nobles began to relax and breathe again.

Under pressure from his bishops, Archbishop Thomas Becket had reluctantly given way to the king and the conflict between the church and the crown had been averted. He had submitted to the sixteen articles of the Constitution of Clarendon and everyone in the great hall felt that all was well with the world again.

While waiting for d'Cheney, Hugh settled into a window seat and absorbed the faces of those around him. At the age of sixty-eight, it dawned on him that only a handful of his contemporaries were still alive, and although many sons had inherited the titles of their noble fathers, few seemed to exude the same qualities.

While he was no longer perceived as a pariah, his unfortunate habit of being on the wrong side at the wrong time had gained him few friends and as a consequence his true loyalties appeared questionable. In the eyes of many, only his longevity seemed to gain him any respect.

Hugh would be the first to admit that his temperament had mellowed with age but not to the extent where he was ready to roll over and die. Ever since the second King Henry had confiscated his castles, he had put a lid on his anger and no one was more impressed by his new found tolerance than his wife Gundred. But like any lid on a boiling pot, the liquid would occasionally boil and hiss and she was not blind to the raw loathing that Hugh felt towards the young king. Like a hardened scab there was an urge to scratch, until the blood ran free.

Gundred had become his new-found soul mate and sympathised with his enduring anger. She could hardly blame her husband, for she also resented the king's punitive taxes. In addition, all of King Henry's vassals were ordered to pay an annual scutage in lieu of military service and this proved to be a financial millstone around the neck of many barons, especially those with a large number of knights.

Now aged thirty-one, Gundred was also a good mother to his baby son Hugh, born in their first year of marriage. As for being a stepmother to Roger, she had always treated him as her own.

Without his natural power base of Framlingham Castle, Hugh had to work tirelessly to levy taxes from his estates. He squeezed every penny he could from peasant and Lords alike, and those that could not pay were threatened with forfeiture or expelled from his land. His ruthless tactics were paying off and soon he would be in a position to retrieve Framlingham Castle. But first, he would have to persuade the king to agree to the sale, and that opportunity was yet to present itself.

Across the hall, Hugh spied the English Master of the Knights Templar leading his men towards the west door. Their white tabards emblazoned with red crosses glowed brightly in the dull light. Apparently, they had persuaded Thomas Becket to accept Henry's terms in good faith, and as a reward for their good council, Henry had bestowed the Order with gold and additional estates.

Hugh never understood how a supposed wise king could be parted so easily from his hard earned wealth. Only a few days earlier, he heard that the king's brother William had donated a church and estate near Dover. Hugh wondered if he was the only one who was at odds with a religious Order that showed a greater regard for money and land than for the souls of men.

The sudden appearance of 'Wills' Albini made Hugh sit up. They had not spoken for many years and it was obvious that fate had continued to smile upon Albini's good fortune. Only a few years younger than Hugh, he had grown into a formidable character. The hatred between them had dimmed, only to be replaced by a stubborn resentment. Time and distance had healed some of the rift and perhaps the acrimony that had pricked like a thorn over the decades, now began to feel a little remote and indistinct.

Throughout his life, Wills Albini had been a stalwart defender of the kingdom and was an established member of the king's inner circle of royal stewards. The king made no secret of his appreciation and favoured the earl above all the other barons.

Jealous of his accumulated wealth and innumerable estates, Hugh reflected that Wills would never have to scrape the bottom of his coffers to pay his scutage, nor complain of his fees for one hundred and fifty knights.

Among the throng of the Albini entourage, he recognised William, the son of Wills Albini. How quickly the boy had grown into a man and Hugh guessed his age to be about twenty. For a moment, his heart missed a beat as he saw in young William a fleeting resemblance to his long passed brother. The flash of guilt that churned in his stomach diminished as quickly as it had come as he remembered that the mother of Wills Albini had been his older sister Maud. There was little doubt that Bigod blood now ran in the Albini family. At least the neutral stance between the two families in recent years, had enabled young William to visit his ageing grandmother right up to her death and Hugh remembered how much she appreciated seeing him.

Hugh called over to Ned Bonham, one of his Suffolk knights, and once he was seated, he signalled a servant to bring a platter of mussels and a flagon of wine for the two of them. Hugh had taken a shine to Bonham. His family was relatively rich and had not blanched when Hugh was in need of a substantial loan some five years earlier. That favour had brought Bonham within his inner circle. Aged nearly forty years, his dry wit and debonair looks sometimes reminded Hugh of Robert Picot. The very thought jarred his senses.

Picot.

Of all the grievances that had scarred his troubled life; none ached more than the sickening death of his friend. The man responsible was the late Earl William of Norwich, who duped the king into believing that Picot was assembling a gang of Flemish assassins at Walton Castle.

When Hugh received news that Earl William had died a slow and painful death on an obscure battleground in Aquataine, Hugh dared to believe for once that God was on his side. He even went as far to say a grateful prayer when he heard that the king knelt by the earl's side, only to puke up at the sight of his entrails spilling over his groin.

Good riddance to the bastard.

Though Hugh was morbidly gratified by the bloody demise of William of Norwich, there were other consequences to his death. As Earl of Norfolk, Hugh could have expected Norwich to be granted into his custody, but if truth be told, he realised long ago that the king's mind had been poisoned against him, no doubt by the likes of Wills Albini. Not surprisingly, the king decided to hold the city for the crown rather than yield Norwich to him.

The other significant consequence was the fate of Williams widow, Lady Isobel de Warenne, now the richest widow in all Christendom and at the age of thirty, still considered very attractive.

Beauty and wealth proved to be a heady mix and when the king learnt that his brother, William FitzEmpress, had fallen in love and desperately wanted to marry Isobel, he announced their betrothal thereby quelling the attention of other prospective suitors.

So why after a year, were they were still unmarried? With a keen eye for such anomalies, Hugh smelt a whiff of conspiracy and sought to pry a little deeper into the mystery.

Bonham gave Hugh a nudge and nodded to his left. 'As you requested, d'Cheney brings Richard le Breton to see you.'

Hugh stood up and greeted the knight, offering the seat next to him. 'Please join me in celebrating this good day.'

Le Breton sat down and took a goblet of wine, wondering why he was being honoured in the presence of Earl Bigod. Sensing his unease, Hugh relaxed and chatted casually for a while, keeping the wine flowing, before he broached the subject of his choosing.

'I am told your liege lord, William FitzEmpress holds you in high regard, as a close confidant. As it happens, I have a close relationship with the Warenne family and normally it would be indiscreet for me to bring the matter up directly, but it appears that the plans for a wedding have stalled?'

Bolstered by the strong wine, Le Breton gave an enthusiastic explanation. 'There were some initial concerns over consanguinity but in all truth, they are but distant cousins and fall outside the rules. My lord simply awaits the final dispensation of the Archbishop of Canterbury. Of course his grace is fully aware of their genuine love for each other.'

Hugh gazed thoughtfully into the bottom of his cup. 'So, as far as FitzEmpress is concerned, the love of his life hangs on the word of the Archbishop Becket. Would you like me to put in a good word for your Lordship?' he asked nonchalantly.

Richard le Breton was surprised by the offer. 'I am sure Lord FitzEmpress would welcome any support you are willing to give.' Slightly baffled by the encounter, Le Breton thanked Hugh then wandered back to his companion, de Morville.

Hugh sat for a while staring into space, envisaging his next move, no less complex than a game of chess. He beckoned d'Cheney to his side. 'Could you get me an audience with Becket before he leaves?'

D'Cheney sighed heavily. 'He is very busy but I will try. You had better warn me of any mischief you have in mind, my lord?'

'It's nothing really. I think it is time I repaid him a small debt.'

A single lamp spluttered ineffectually on a large table, making it difficult for Archbishop Becket to read the rolls of parchment. Three clerks hovered like crows, busily fussing over his every movement. There was a knock at the door and Becket looked up and frowned at Hugh as he was led into the dimly lit antechamber.

'Earl Bigod, what can I do for you on such an auspicious day? As you can see, I am afraid I have little time to give.'

With a solemn expression, Hugh sat opposite Becket. He noticed how his face was gaunt and aged compared to the last time they had met. 'My lord Archbishop, I have grave news of the day's events of which I am honour bound to tell you.' He looked up at the clerks. 'In private, if you please.'

Becket sighed heavily, and then dismissed the two clerks, who walked quickly from the chamber. 'Osborn is my chancellor and he shall remain at my side, if you please. Now what have you to say?'

Hugh edged forward and leant on the desk so he could keep his voice low. 'You are probably wondering why the Bishop of Norwich was so vociferous in wanting a speedy acceptance to the king's constitution. Indeed I spoke to him myself about his flagrant breach of decorum.'

Becket was fully aware of the bishop's over enthusiasm. 'Please go on,' he said, looking down his long nose, irritated by Hugh posing as a conspirator.

'I have heard of grave allegations. Quite simply, the bishop was placed under duress to find a speedy solution, along with a number of other bishops that also sided with the king, to use all their powers…to persuade you to accept the proposals.'

Osborn gasped out loud while Becket remained impassive. 'Do you have the names of the bishops in league with the king?'

Hugh could see Becket's face begin to redden with anger. 'No, not yet. I can let you have the names later today, but listen…there is more.'

With steel in his eyes, Becket looked up at Osborn and asked him to stand guard by the door.

Hugh struggled to keep his face straight. 'The king was heard to pour scorn on your inability to come to a decision on his brother's marriage to Lady Isobel. After repeatedly promising William FitzEmpress of a favourable outcome, he would if necessary compel you to agree to the marriage before the end of the week.'

Becket's face flinched. His hand was shaking and he curled it into a fist, slamming it on the table, sending parchments into the air.

Hugh was startled by the reaction. 'My lord archbishop, I am sorry if this news angers you so, but I felt it was my duty to…'

'Yes, yes…I know,' Becket interrupted. He stood up and walked around the table. He stared at the small wooden crucifix on the wall then sat down next to Hugh. 'You have never shown the church or me any sense of duty before. Why should I trust you now?'

Hugh was prepared for that very question. He took a small bag of coins from his pocket and placed it on the table. 'You trusted me once before. I believe it was fourteen silver coins.'

The memory of their first meeting flashed across Becket's face. He took the bag and counted the coins. 'Indeed there are fourteen coins present. So is all this just a display of duty and trust?'

'My lord, I confess you have seen right through me, for I do have an embarrassing favour to ask in return.'

Becket smiled knowingly, pleased at his ability to see inside the minds of simple men.

Hugh sucked in a lungful of air. 'I have need of some financial assistance to help me buy back Framlingham Castle.'

Becket raised his eyebrow. 'Is that all?'

Hugh stood up and held the shoulder of the archbishop. 'I am not as young as I used to be. Unlike many of your so-called supporters, I am not in the pocket of the king and I pray you will accept my support in my twilight years. Let me have the means to rest with my family in peace with the dignity my title deserves and I shall give you the names of the bishops that have so blatantly deceived you.'

Becket sat back down in his chair. 'Osborn shall approve a loan this afternoon. In the meantime, I shall think on your words and see you after Nones this afternoon. God be with you, Earl Bigod.'

Becket never arrived at Nones and Hugh discovered from an aide that he had already departed to Canterbury. He reckoned the Archbishop was clever enough to unearth the rogue bishops without any further help. The aide handed a sealed letter confirming the loan would be in place within the week. Hugh smiled broadly.

By all accounts, the king flew into a temper when told of Becket's departure and was still in a foul mood when dawn broke the next day. He called his court to appear at Winchester Palace.

As Hugh prepared to join the vast entourage on the one-day march, he reckoned the first phase of his plan to have Becket and the king at each other's throats had gone well enough. But nothing could prepare him for the dire consequences to come.

Only a week had passed at Winchester when the terrible news broke throughout the court. William FitzEmpress, the brother of the king was dead.

The only person in a rage rivalling that of the king's was the knight Richard le Breton. Striding into the king's chamber, he bowed then handed his petition to King Henry's Justicar, who placed it on his table without a glance.

'My Lord King, I beseech you. I was a vassal and close friend of William FitzEmpress. The petition states that I, as well as his entire household, blame none other than Archbishop Thomas Becket for your brother death.'

King Henry did not react. He sat still in his seat, taking a gulp of wine and studied Richard's face.

Richard caught his breath and continued his pleading. 'Lord FitzEmpress was a good man, a kind man, who loved Lady Isobel more than anything in the world. The denouncement on consanguinity given only days ago by Becket was the act of a sick and evil man, not a man of God.' Tears welled up but his anger spurred him to finish his words. 'Your brother never fought the fever that struck him down. With no hope of marriage, he quickly ailed and in the end gave up the ghost. He died of a broken heart. The same heart that Becket deliberately ripped asunder.'

The king sat without emotion, his face set in a grimace. 'The death of my brother has stricken many good people and left a hole in all our lives. Your grief is heartfelt and etched deep on your face. He obviously gave your support much credence, so I think in his honour I would like to welcome you into my council. As for now, I thank you for your petition.'

Richard opened his mouth to speak but words failed him. He was escorted from the chamber, confounded by what the king had said. Behind the closed door, Richard could hear a cry of anger then the sound of a wine jug smashed to the floor. His escort nudged him on and in the dimly lit corridor; he nearly bumped into Earl Hugh Bigod walking towards him.

Hugh quickly changed his expression to appear solemn. 'Oh Richard. I heard the sad news of the death of your liege lord. No doubt, the king is distraught at the loss of his brother.'

'Yes…and I was not afraid to tell him what I thought of Becket.'

'That was brave of you but do not worry, for you have my unfailing support.' Hugh walked on and nodded to the guard to knock on the door.

Eventually a voice asked him to enter and judging by the mess, the contents of the king's table had been smashed and thrown across the floor.

King Henry was pacing with fists clenched; then he saw Hugh stood at the door. 'Earl Bigod! If you have come to argue over Norwich, it is not a good time and you can leave now before…'

'Nothing is further from my mind, my lord king.' Stepping boldly into the room, Hugh bowed.

The king could not contain his anger and with a sweep of his hand, a wad of scrolls flew across the table onto the floor. 'All this is Becket's doing! Petitions and claims and counter-claims from everyone who has a yea or nay for that…that malevolent protagonist.' Henry picked up a parchment and waved it in the air. 'I even have a petition from Becket claiming you are retaining lands that belong to Pentney Monastery. I pray you will not be relinquishing those lands just to satisfy his appetite.'

The malicious streak on the king's face gave Hugh no option. 'As you so wish my lord king.'

The king sat down, his body still as taut as a bow. 'Then what is it you want?'

'After I heard the terrible news of your brother, my first thought was to offer my heartfelt condolences.'

The king breathed in deeply. 'Very well, but time is pressing.'

Hugh looked at the floor and picked up a broken flagon. 'To feel such anger to someone as callous as Thomas Becket is quite normal.'

The king stared through steely eyes. 'Tread carefully with your criticisms. No one knows Becket as well as I do.'

11

'My apologies my lord king. I know little of the man...then again, I am not deaf to what I hear.'

'Then tell me what it is you hear.'

Moving closer, Hugh leant on the table so as the Justicar could not hear. 'It may be nothing, but apparently when Becket was told of your brothers death, he said, "God willing, that is one thorn out of my side." I believe a servant reported the words…'

'He said what!' the king bawled. His burnished hair seemed to stand up and match the colour of his face. He slammed the table with his fist and paced back and forth.

Intent on timing his coup-de-grace to perfection, Hugh waited, as the king boiled in his own anger. 'My lord king, that is not all I have learnt. I have a duty to warn you that Becket is set to repudiate the articles of Clarendon.'

Now the king stood still, staring at Hugh as his broad chest heaved in and out. 'How can he! He has only just agreed to them!'

'Perhaps I have said too much, so I will leave you to discover the truth for yourself.' Hugh pulled a sealed scroll from his tunic and placed it on the table. If I am right, you may look favourably upon this authority to sell Framlingham Castle.'

The king seemed not to hear. 'What…yes, I shall look into it. Now leave me in peace for I have much to consider.'

Hugh stood up and bowed respectfully before walking slowly to the door.

The king called after him. 'Earl Bigod, thank you for the warning.'

Many within the court tried to council restraint but failed as the king's anger began to spiral out of control. He insisted his methodology was simple. If he could not make Becket see reason, he would fight him in the courts.

By the time Hugh attended court again at Northampton, he was amazed at the list of lawsuits that had been compiled against the Archbishop. The charges included perjury, embezzlement, heresy and treason thrown in for good measure. Upon hearing such an extended litany of charges, Becket was left in no doubt. The tide had turned and Henry was intent on his ruination.

Sensing his moment of weakness, some of the kings supporters saw the archbishop as a traitor. The Earl of Leicester and Richard de Lucy held the office of Justicar jointly, and while Becket was still at court they confronted him. 'The king commands you render all your accounts!' de Lucy demanded.

Becket forcefully repudiated the authority of the court and declared it had no jurisdiction over him. With the accusing words of de Lucy ringing in his ears, he took his leave, beating a hasty retreat.

Again, the king vented his fury at Becket's unauthorised departure, resulting in another charge of contempt in his absence. The office of Justicar stipulated that all his property and goods were subject to forfeiture by the crown and fearing that Becket would flee the country, the king instructed the ports to be watched.

But Becket was clever enough to evade capture and secured passage across the channel from an obscure jetty in Kent.

While all the bishops and barons throughout the land could only see more trouble arising from the debacle, Hugh Bigod was quietly satisfied at the outcome. The ecclesiastical rift had distracted both Archbishop Becket and King Henry. Now Becket was in exile, his loan was as good as his to keep.

Given they still had to retrieve Framlingham from the crown, his wife Gundred was too cautious to celebrate. Hugh remained quiet until they left the precincts of Northampton, then he could not contain his joy any longer. He unfurled the bill of sale for Framlingham Castle and she screamed with delight, leaping from her horse to hug him. She declared it his finest hour.

Chapter 2

Bilbeis
Egypt

Over his formative years, Saladin had nurtured a great admiration for his uncle. As a boy, he remembered being frightened by his battle-worn face with only one eye and even though he was short and quite rotund, he always appeared wild and fearsome. As a great tactician, he was respected by all his men .

It had always been Muzawi's intention that Saladin should learn more of military matters from his Uncle Shirkuh. Now in his late twenties Saladin fulfilled that obligation by accompanying the General on an important mission.

General Shirkuh had observed the steady collapse of the Egyptian Caliphate over a few years and the once mighty regime was now led by a succession of failed Viziers. One such Vizier named Shawar had promised Nuradin ten chests of gold if he would support his claim to the throne of Egypt. Unable to refuse such a huge amount, Nuradin sent a small army into Cairo led by General Shirkuh, with the intention of establishing Shawar as the new Caliph.

Once Shawar had been installed as the governing power, the army left Cairo with the chests of gold. Stopping on the way back, an aide from the treasury was busy counting the gold coins when he noticed each chest was short by a third. Shawar had underpaid the agreed sum.

Unable to return to Nuradin with such an obvious deficiency of gold, Shirkuh was at pains not to lose face. Just twenty-five miles north east of Cairo, he entered the town of Bilbeis and proclaimed by messenger to Shawar that he would not leave until he had received payment in full.

The months passed slowly while Shirkuh waited for a reaction from the Egyptian vizier but none was forthcoming. Then without warning, King Amalric arrived from Jerusalem with a sizeable army and started to besiege Bilbeis. Using the same money he owed Shirkuh, Shawar had bribed Amalric to besiege Bilbeis. Shawar had played his most treacherous strategy ever, causing even more embarrassment to befall General Shirkuh.

After three months under siege, his patience was wearing thin.

The General's men began to resent their hardship as the food supply dwindled. Even the local population of Coptic Christians became nervous as the occupying force began to grow restless.

High above the town, Saladin paced the walls of Bilbeis, watching the full moon as it rose above the dark blue horizon. Looking out across the surrounding wasteland, he sighed at the sight of the enemy camp fires that flickered along the skyline. Now he began to speculate on the wisdom of Nuradin and his uncle.

A familiar voice alerted him and he stood to attention as General Shirkuh walked up the steps to greet him. He looked more jovial than usual, his crooked smile exaggerated by the missing eye.

'This is your first siege. Don't look so disillusioned. The general gave a smile.

Saladin frowned. 'It is a waste of three months. It is not my idea of warfare.'

'But it is sometimes necessary in order to achieve what you want. You will be pleased to know the siege is over. We have reached a peace with both King Amalric and Shawar. We will leave Bilbeis with the full payment and the Christian army led by Amalric will leave with nothing.'

Saladin was surprised and at the same time delighted. 'How on earth did you persuade King Amalric to leave without payment?'

Shirkuh handed his nephew a letter. 'We have received a message from Muzawi. I think it explains everything.'

Reading the words by lamplight, Saladin began to smile. When he finished, he gasped in disbelief. 'So Muzawi convinced Nuradin to attack a fortress that protects Antioch, knowing that King Amalric would have to hurry north to save Antioch from falling to Nuradin.'

Shirkuh nodded. 'Read on, there is more.'

Turning the page, Saladin's face dropped as he looked up from the letter. 'Muzawi wants us to meet him in Tanis, in two days time. Why?' He carried on reading. 'We are to proceed to a grotto at the site of a temple that is guarded by the Knights Templar.' He handed the letter back to Shirkuh and spat on the ground. 'Good. The more dead Templars the better.'

Shirkuh was fully aware of his nephew's hatred of the notorious Order of Knights. 'This is not an assault. The small garrison of Templars have received a fake message telling them to retire immediately to their new quarters in Bilbeis. Better to keep our movements clandestine. So, our escort will comprise of only two Turcomen horse archers, while the rest of the army returns as agreed.'

Saladin was not convinced. 'But even so, people will see what we are up to.'

Shirkuh looked up from the papyrus. 'Look, Muzawi says all eventualities will be taken care of. You should have more trust in his judgement. Come, we must prepare to leave at once.'

Saladin felt a twinge of guilt at not trusting Muzawi implicitly. He should have known the shaman would have thought of everything.

The ruins of ancient Tanis jutted out from the ever-changing desert landscape. Saladin and Muzawi finished the loin of water-buck and shaded his eyes from the glare of the morning sun under the shade of two lone palms. A respectable distance away, two horse archers quarrelled over a fire as they cooked the inferior cuts of meat. Their hunting skills over the last three days had proved invaluable, though the water they had carried from the nearby lake tasted foul.

Shirkuh joined Muzawi and surveyed the amount of sand they had excavated around the stone blocks of the temple walls. Wiping his eye cavity with a cloth, he shook his head. 'Tell me again, why are we here in this hell-hole; removing desert sand to reveal old stones?'

Even Muzawi found it difficult to hide his disappointment. 'My spies in Jerusalem told me that the Templars insisted on guarding this place but no one seemed to know why. It intrigued me. Was it simply a strategic stronghold or perhaps they sought something much more important?' He left the question hang on the thin breeze. 'The city of Tanis was an important delta city for thousands of years, indeed, it replaced Thebes as the main city of Egypt but it was abandoned when the lake silted up all access.'

Turning to Saladin, Muzawi gestured across the sand. 'This plain in front of us hides the royal tombs of many Pharaohs. Including that of your ancestor, Pharaoh Shishak.'

Saladin raised his head at the casual mention of the name carried by his father and for a moment he gazed wistfully across the desert as if looking for a sign. 'So tell me again what we have found and what we are looking for.'

Muzawi looked upon the walls that protruded from the sand in a rectangle of two hundred by one hundred and fifty paces. 'You see the stele and the obelisks we have uncovered inside the walls. The writing tells us this was the Temple dedicated to Amun and Horus. That in itself is interesting but not the reason why we are here.' He grimaced from the heat as he took another drink from his water skin. 'Somewhere nearby is the Temple of Astarte that dates from the time of Baal. I do not need to tell you the importance of that temple.'

Saladin was well aware of the significance of finding such a rarity dedicated to Astarte, but Shirkuh was not convinced.

He stood up and faced Muzawi. 'So it could be anywhere. I am afraid I am not the right person for this exercise. I must return to Damascus in the hope of leading another army into Egypt. My friend, I hope you understand that military matters must come first.'

Muzawi could not admit his failings but was beginning to wish he had prepared their mission more carefully. He stood up and turned to Shirkuh. 'Of course you are right. In fact I agree that any further digging could prove a waste of our time...'

Just then he froze as he spied the dust rising on the horizon as horsemen approached. They all stood to follow his gaze. 'They are Templars and they are coming here at speed. It appears they are not aware of our presence.'

Shirkuh immediately took charge.'There are only four of them, each with a squire. We will ambush them before they know we are here.' He ordered the archers to keep the horses hidden and find strategic positions as Saladin took up a forward position.

Muzawi ducked his head behind a wall. 'Kill the squires but make sure you leave one of the Templars alive. We need to question him.'

In a flurry of dust and hooves, the four Templars and squires rode inside the ancient walls, oblivious to the danger around them. As they dismounted, the archers fired and shot two arrows each into the chest of two of the horsemen. Rising like a leopard from his hiding place, Saladin pounced onto the third Templar and slit open his skull with a single blow of his mace. He looked to his right to see that Shirkuh had the forth Templar on the ground with a sword at his throat.

Two of the squires decided to run for their lives and Saladin called out to the archers. A flurry of arrows felled them as they ran. Cowering on the ground the other two begged for mercy. While he manoeuvred behind them, Saladin was surprised at how young they were. Little more than boys. As servants to the hated enemy, they deserved no compassion and he ran them through with his sword. Turning to the last Templar, he looked upon his prey with eyes that were filled with hatred.

Muzawi stood on front of Saladin and could feel the intensity of his rage searing into his back. 'I shall tie him up for interrogation.'

For half an hour, Muzawi let the archers have their way as they skilfully sliced into the flesh of the Templar. He was a young nobleman named Lambert and his handsome features were now a passing memory. With little care for the agony they were inflicting, they rubbed salt into his wounds before applying a heated blade of a sword to his groin.

It was time for Muzawi to take charge. 'Hold him still,' he ordered. He then proceeded to draw a deep slice down the man's penis, being careful to avoid a major blood vessel. In between his screams, Lambert begged for a merciful death.

Leaning over the knight, Muzawi placed his arm around his shoulder and holding him close to his chest, he whispered into the Knight's ear. 'But we have only just begun to enjoy ourselves. Look at the faces of my men. They see no difference between the pleasure of physical violence and sexual violence. They miss their wives back in Damascus. How can I deny them the pleasure they intend to have in sodomising you all night, before they slice off your face?'

Exhausted and bereft of willpower, Lambert felt his heart sink into a pit of despair. He begged again for a quick death.

Muzawi whispered a promise. 'Tell me what I need to know and I shall finish you quickly with my own hand.'

Panting like a wounded animal, Lambert nodded.

Muzawi gave him a drink of wine and let him take his fill. 'So tell me why the Knights Templar are interested in these particular ruins.'

Over the next hour, Lambert put the terrible pain to one side and confessed everything he knew about Tanis. All the while Muzawi supported his back, sometimes gently stroking his head, encouraging him to say more.

Eventually satisfied that all his questions had been answered, Muzawi took his dagger and drew it silently across Lambert's throat, taking care not to spill any blood onto his robe.

Watching from the shade of a palm tree, Saladin sat up, surprised and disappointed by the Templars sudden demise. 'We should have staked him out to bake in the sun.'

Muzawi washed his hands and took a drink of foul water. 'Or we should have simply slit his throat. Besides, he was already dying and time is of the essence.' He told the archers to bury Lambert's body and prepare to leave. 'Saladin, you will return to Damascus with Shirkuh. In the meantime, I shall go to the library in Alexandria to try and piece together what I have been told.'

Saladin looked surprised. 'So after all that, he did not tell you the location of the temple.'

'All I can say it is imperative we find the site of the Temple of Astarte before more Templars arrive. I will contact you as soon as I require your assistance.'

Saladin wanted to speak out but caught sight of Shirkuh preparing to leave. He bowed respectfully to his mentor, knowing deep inside that his destiny lay with the shaman.

Muzawi directed the activity around him as they quickly packed up their provisions to go their separate ways. Muzawi dismissed the need for an escort and they wished each other well as he proceeded on his journey west across the Nile.

Shirkuh decided his most expedient route with Saladin was to ride north to Pelusium where they could hire a dhow to the Syrian coast. On their journey, Saladin mulled over the mystery of Tanis. At times, he thought the sensation was almost tangible. Of all that was certain, he knew that one day he would be returning to find out.

It was the first time Jacques de Exemes had ridden up the new track from Ramleh to Lydda. He had a brief recollection years ago, of a steep rock-strewn road but after the landslip, the whole landscape had radically changed. Now a track led gently uphill, winding around the remains of some rocky outcrops that were the only evidence of the once precipitous escarpment.

His recent appointment as Commander of the Ramleh garrison meant he would see less of Jerusalem but in some respects that was not such a loss. The recent disastrous Egyptian campaign had cost the lives of many Templars and had widened the rift between King Amalric and the Grand Master, each blaming the other.

Jacques sympathised with the Grand Master, Bertrand de Blanchefort. After being captured by Nuradin eight years ago, he had spent three years imprisoned in Aleppo and now in his mid-fifties, he had no wish to be incarcerated again. Given the dire fate of most captured Templars, Bertrand considered himself spared by God.

Jacques rode through the gate into Lydda. The earthquake had left the two pillars undamaged though the Church of St George had not fared so well. No one seemed interested in repairing the damage. He crossed the square, keeping to the road leading north.

Out of the town he reached a crest and peered into the distance. He could see the horse farm of William Bigod. He was met by a foreman from the farm, who led Jacques to the main house beyond an extensive spread of barns, paddocks and stables.

As a senior captain of the Order in Jerusalem, Jacques had often overseen the delivery of horses from Lydda and he reckoned he had met William twice before, though many years ago. As he tried to imagine how he would look now, he saw a man on the shaded terrace outside the house. He was busy writing in a journal but when he saw Jacques, he stopped and closed the book.

Holding out his hand in greeting, William stood up from the table and leant to one side to compensate for his awkward gait. With a full head of hair and a short grey beard, the years had treated William well, looking younger than his seventy years.

Smiling broadly, he greeted Jacques and at the same time gave orders to Gerash, his long serving foreman, using a stick to reinforce his ill-defined speech. 'My men will ensure your squire is well fed and watered; almost as well as your own fine horse,' he jested.

Given the loss of his tongue many years ago, Jacques was astounded at William's ability to speak at all. Some words were obviously affected but once familiar with his limitations, most of his words were coherent.

Before sitting back down on the terrace, William placed the loose pages of parchment into his book and wrapped it into a leather folder before giving it to his servant Gerash to take back into the house.

'You must have many fine memories to record,' Jacques said conversationally.

'Oh, just the ramblings of an old man,' William replied, calling to a servant to bring wine. 'One day I shall do what all old men should do before they die. Sit on my terrace and make my peace with God. This journal will help.'

'And will you write of all the cruelty and injustice in the world?' Jacques questioned.

'Everything.'

Overlooking the paddocks, they enjoyed a meal of lamb stew and vegetables, and Jacques brought William up to date with the news from Jerusalem.

It came as no surprise that the Templar Grand Master and the king had fallen out again. 'King Amalric has an unhealthy appetite for Egypt,' William observed dryly. 'Should have learnt from Baldwin.'

Jacques nodded. 'He also has an unhealthy appetite for all things edible. He is so fat he struggles to mount a horse and when fatigued, he has to be carried in a litter like some bloody Sultan! He made a pigs ass of trying to overthrow the Fatimid Caliphate. He fails to realise that he cannot raise two armies at the same time. But that is not the worst of it.' Jacques took a gulp of wine. 'Twelve Templars were arrested for supposed desertion. They were guarding a small stronghold near Tanis and they were fooled by a false message to rejoin the army at Bilbeis. Sultan Shawar captured them but mercifully handed them over to Amalric. Accusing the men of desertion, he executed them without a trial. They were willing to give their lives for the city of Christ but instead he hung them like dogs from the walls.'

A broody silence fell between them at the wasteful loss.

Gerash cleared away their platters then excused himself for the evening, wishing them both a good night.

'You have a fine life here,' Jacques observed. 'Do you truly miss anything of your previous life?'

'This is my home and my life.' The words were few but his thoughts filled the cavernous silence between them. Taking his time over a long sip of wine, William eventually spoke again. 'I heard Count Thierry of Flanders is in Jerusalem for a fourth pilgrimage.'

'You are well informed my friend, 'Jacques confirmed. 'He has joined Amalric and as we speak he is on the road to Antioch. From there, the count will return to Flanders. I don't think his heart or his health is up to another long campaign.' Another moment of silence passed awkwardly as William sensed that Jacques had more to say.

Jacques cleared his throat. 'I have some sad news that you will not have heard. Count Thierry's wife, Sybille, died at the Abbey of Lazarus in Bethany.'

With just a thin grimace of emotion, William stared into his cup. 'When?'

Jacques swallowed hard. 'I am sorry William, but I believe it was about six months ago.'

William finished his cup and his gaze lifted into the distance.

Jacques grappled with his words. 'She was installed in the abbey some eight years ago. It was said...at the time...that Thierry suspected her of having an affair. In a rage he questioned his steward, Henry Malache...well actually he tortured him and knocked out three of his teeth with a single blow. But Henry maintained all along that he did not know who the culprit was. He was ordered back to England, never to return to the Holy Land. I know all this because I escorted him to the coast. He wanted to divert to Lydda to see you, but I was under strict instruction not to allow any detour. From what he said, I assumed that you must have had something to do with...the affair.'

'And you tell me this now because Thierry will soon leave the Holy land for the last time.'

Jacques nodded guiltily. 'Thierry suspected it was you from the start, but Bertrand de Blanchefort insisted that as a retired Knights Templar, your character was beyond reproach. He gave the count implicit orders not to question you.'

William sighed and shook his head in sorrow 'Strange you should call it an affair. Yes, we kept our brief liaison a secret but it was all to no avail. Countess Sybille wanted to see me but her cause was not borne out of love or lust. Fate entwined us with a common purpose.'

'But later, you went to the abbey to see her.'

'No, not to see her. Again, that was God weaving His threads of the tapestry.' William twisted in his chair, straining to make his words clear. 'We were worlds apart, but always destined by the hand of God to share something special. God looked kindly on her but once my part had been played, He punished her for her adultery. We were never destined to become anything more than puppets.'

'I believe God did forgive her,' Jacques said leaning forward. 'She went on to become abbess of one of the most respected abbeys in the Holy Land and when Queen Melisende died, she was asked to take the regency. King Amalric was on a campaign and she personally held the kingdom together in his absence.'

William smiled but remained tight lipped.

'Can we talk some more tomorrow?' Jacques asked.

'I think it is better to let my thoughts rest in my journal.'

Jacques nodded. He knew that deep down the recollections had wounded William. As he stood up and stretched his limbs, William pointed his walking stick towards the stables. 'As for tomorrow, I have a young mare to show you. It is the most splendid horse I have ever bred.'

'And what do you call her?' Jacques enquired.

'Adelice. After my mother.'

Chapter 3

Framlingham Castle
Suffolk

Young Roger Bigod moved silently through the rushes that lined the lakeside. The flattened reeds meant he was on the right track and confirmed he was close to his prey. He had high hopes that he may suddenly surprise them and at best catch his friend with his britches down around his ankles.

Then came the strangest sounds he had ever heard. Grunting and moaning interspersed with a light giggle then followed by a deeper moan. The circumstances that could create such varied sounds baffled him and bizarre visions flashed instantly through his mind. He prayed hard he had actually caught them having sex.

Prising apart the last few reeds before a clearing, he gazed upon the sight of William Albini laid on his back while his nubile wife Matilda sat astride his groin, with her lavender skirt hitched above her waist. Her body rode up and down, her breasts bouncing with each beat of her loins. With her head stretched back, her face became contorted as her climax was imminent. Suddenly her body stiffened, her movement slowed to an ecstatic thrust that made her stomach muscles harden, and her breasts heave one last time.

Roger waited to see what would happen next. He spied her long hair covering William's naked groin and thinking she about to sleep upon his lap, he coughed loudly and walked boldly out into the grassy opening next to water's edge. Her head shot upright and then he saw Williams erect prick leave her open lips.

The horror on her face turned to deep embarrassment. Pulling her skirt back around her legs, she bustled up the embankment before sitting down. 'Roger, you bastard...'

William frantically scrambled for his britches but could not see them. 'What the fuck do you think you're playing at...' he shouted breathlessly. 'You gave my heart a bloody spasm.'

Roger's face cracked and he gave an inane laugh at William's taut prick as it wavered with a will of its own.

William leapt to his feet and wrestled him to the ground and they rolled as one into the shallow waters. Dragging themselves back onto the grass, Roger took off his filthy shirt and britches and laid them on the bank to dry.

William's wife goaded him. 'Call yourself a wrestler. You are five years older than him but I do believe the boy could whip you...'

'Oh you think so do you?' William grabbed Roger around the waist and they held each other in a bear hug while Matilda settled back to enjoy the contest.

Hugh Bigod rode over the drawbridge alongside Bonham and into the bailey of Framlingham Castle. Shouting for the stable boys, he dismounted hurriedly and stormed towards the grand hall. In the foulest of moods, he unbuckled his belt and sword and threw them at the feet of his servant. 'Clean them well...no get me a bloody drink first. Fuck! Its bloody hot and I have ridden all day.' His temper was rising as the servant nervously stumbled over his belt and buckle. Marcus Tyler, one of his squires, stepped forward from the shadows and took the belt and sword from the servant.

Hugh was livid. 'Where the fuck is everyone! Someone get me some fucking food and something to drink!'

'I shall see to it my lord,' Marcus said and ran to the kitchen.

Gundred appeared on the stairs, clucking at the servants like a mother hen. She walked over to Hugh and kissed him on the cheek before leading him up the staircase. She signalled to the nanny to take baby Hugh away while she sat down on the bed to observe Hugh. He stretched his arms and groaned out loud.

'Oh dear, what is it now that troubles you. It must be bad, for you have already scared away two servants and a made baby Hugh cry.'

Hugh made no attempt to appreciate Gundred's light sarcasm. 'Our illustrious King Henry does not trust me. I would not believe it without seeing with my own eyes…'

Now Gundred was alarmed. 'Tell me what he has done now.'

Hugh paced the floor. 'I will tell you what. No sooner do I buy back Framlingham and Bungay Castles; both of them legitimately, he starts to build a castle at Orford…apparently to keep me in check!'

Even Gundred found it hard to believe. She shook her head. 'So the rumours were correct. Have you seen it with your own eyes?'

Marcus appeared at the door with a tray of food and a jug of wine, and placed them on the table before closing the door behind him.

'I thought he was your groom,' Hugh queried.

'He is clever enough to do two jobs.'

Gazing out of the window towards the lake, Hugh was not listening. 'There are ten or twenty surveyors mapping the ground…but that is only the half of it. The man in charge was that bastard Sisland, one of King Henry's royal stewards. I watched for half a day while he pranced around, ordering his minions…as if he has any idea how to build…a castle…what the fuck…!' Staring out of the window Hugh froze in mid-sentence, then stormed angrily towards the staircase and disappeared, his footsteps quickly receding.

'Hugh! What is it?' Gundred rushed to the window trying to see the cause of his abrupt departure but the opening was too high for her to see anything other than sky. Exasperated, she lifted her skirt and followed her husband down the staircase.

Hugh marched across the bailey and glanced across to the stables. Now he saw the horse of the visitor. Quickening his step over the drawbridge, he left a trail of mystified servants and guards in his wake. By the time he had stomped around the moat to where the lake began to broaden, he had worked up a lather of sweat. Muffled shouts and cries were coming from the bulrushes and he paused to gather his bearings. The voices came from a clearing to his right and when he parted the rushes, the full spectacle of horror greeted him. His son Roger was laid on his hands and knees, clothed only in muddy underwear and sat astride his buttocks was young William Albini, virtually naked. Roger was struggling and crying out while William rode him like a horse.

The moment Roger glanced out of the corner of his eye and saw his father, his face fell. William followed his gaze and immediately tried to unravel himself, but his calves were trapped around Roger's legs and he fell forward.

Before he could extract himself, Hugh had grabbed William Albini by the hair and arm and pulled him off his son. A crashing blow to his head sent William reeling to the waters edge and while he lay dazed, propped up on his elbows, Hugh kicked him in the ribs.

'Stop it! Father, stop it!' Roger cried out, trying to pull his father back. At fifteen, Roger was tall for his age but not strong enough to prevent his father from kicking William again.

There was a scream from behind but Hugh only saw the veil of red mist and only listened to the voices clamouring in his head. Without a care, he pushed Roger away. It was then he saw the young lady stand up and plead for him to cease his attack.

Hugh shook his head. 'What the fuck is going on here?' He looked down at William. 'You were on top of my son, you bastard?'

William gasped for air and held out his arm trying to prop himself up to speak.

'We were playing!' Roger shouted indignantly. 'We had been swimming and were wrestling.'

Hugh was yet to be convinced. Then he watched the female wipe

William's bloody lip. She was about twenty, well dressed and had been sat on the bank. 'And who is she?'

Holding his ribs, William got to his knees, gulping mouthfuls of air. 'That is my wife, Matilda St Hilary de Harcourt. She was acting in judgement of the winner.'

The apparent innocence of the incident began to dawn on Hugh and his temper cooled, just as Gundred appeared followed by Bonham with a sword in his hand and Marcus holding a spear. They stopped in their tracks as soon as they realised the fighting was relatively harmless.

Gundred apologised to William and helped him up, while glaring at Hugh. 'What on earth are you doing, you fool. I agreed yesterday that William and his wife could be our guests.'

'I thought…I thought it was something else,' Hugh stammered.

Roger walked back to his pile of clothes. He looked at his father with nothing but contempt. 'How could you?'

Hugh tried to ignore the accusing stares. His blustered face reddened and he gave William a fleeting look. 'That's right, get some bloody clothes on, both of you.' Without apologising, he turned on his heels and walked back to the drawbridge.

Gundred was distraught at her husband's behaviour. 'William, I am sorry for the Earl's conduct. It is no excuse but he has just received some bad news and his mind is in turmoil.'

Roger would not meet her gaze. He finished dressing and then propped William up as Matilda helped him with his britches.

In the awkward silence, Gundred followed them back to the drawbridge and was lost for words as she watched them go to the stables.

That night Hugh thrashed about on his mattress as the night terrors from his boyhood returned. The years had not depreciated the sickly emotions he felt that night, as he laid spread-eagled over the altar of St Mary's Church. Images of sordid fornication and pain were seared into his nightmare, as vivid and frightening as ever. He could taste the sweat on his face, unable to move, and terrified of what was to come. Bishop Herbert pulled on his arms and licked his lips in anticipation as he gave the order to commence the punishment.

The first few strokes were the worst as the flesh was pink and fresh but by the time he counted to six, the unseen hands rubbed a salve into the stripes that took the pain away and made him feel light-headed. The numbness set in and the attack on his buttocks became more intense.

'Confess to me boy; where are the relics?' The bishop's voice was full of menace and seemed disconnected from reality.

Ten, eleven, twelve strokes. It wasn't stopping. Now the numbness wore off and a fire of pain spread from his waist down his legs to his knees. The relics…what about the relics…he didn't know! Each swipe was harder than the last…his back was arching in agony and he spat out the strap to scream, only to be threatened with more punishment if he screamed again. Then the bishop was no longer in his field of view. More lotion was rubbed into the welts and then a nervy hand offered him a sip of white poppy juice. The pain disappeared quite quickly and his vision blurred in a haze of white light.

A few moments of respite followed but he dare not move. The hissing sound in his ears mingled with the disjointed whispers of those behind him. He tried to lift his head and see who was there but all he saw was a blur of constant movement around the altar; the voices sounding muffled, as if underwater.

Then came a different form of discomfort…he felt something press against his buttocks then came the pain, deep inside, followed by more soothing oil and another sip of poppy juice. Someone was grunting and thrusting from behind again and again, but he was helpless. 'Please stop,' he gasped. 'Please stop.'

Daring to open his eyes, he turned his head and looked at a face in the distance partially obscured by the flicker of the candles. It was his brother's face. Why was he doing nothing to help him? Through watery eyes, he saw his brother in the confessional. He flashed a wicked smile before dropping his head onto the naked lap of Abbot Bund.

As if recovering from a trance, Hugh turned away. He did not want to watch. As his eyes drifted in and out of focus, Hugh spotted a familiar face high up in the newly erected scaffolding. He knew who it was. Then came the irate voice of the bishop and the face faded. His body was turned onto its side and plied with wine and sweet biscuits. His bloody welts were dabbed and cleaned.

The bishop spoke more angry words, but they were aimed at others who stood behind him. There followed more sweet biscuits then a litany of hell raising threats from those around him resounded relentlessly in his ears, telling him what would happen to his family and friends he were tell anyone of the dark secret that no one must know about. 'They will never believe your scrawny word against that of the church. In return for your lies, they will only punish you more.'

Just then, the bishop grabbed his arm. 'And you are sure the others know nothing of the relics?'

By now, Hugh was quite lucid. 'I am sure they know nothing.'

The bishop let go of his arm and Hugh ran towards the door, desperate to escape his living hell.

Hugh woke wide-eyed and panting as rivulets of sweat poured down his face. He strode from his bed to the window taking mighty gulps of air then hung onto the window side.

Gundred feared he was about to die and tried to shake some

words from his white lips. 'Speak to me. Are you in pain?' she pleaded.

Hugh splashed water on his face and caught the breeze from the window. His breathing settled and he pushed his torment to the back of his mind, trying to find the words to speak. 'Just a nightmare. Go back to sleep.'

She brought him a cup of wine. 'Is it to do with today?

'Why do you ask?' he replied.

'Well it was very upsetting for everyone. Poor Roger is distraught.'

Hugh grunted. 'He will get over it.'

Gundred persevered. 'While Wills Albini is away in France, William felt a little footloose and came to show off his new wife. She is with child, just a few weeks though. We are related you know.'

Hugh grunted again. 'Oh, I know that much.'

Gundred ignored his sarcasm. 'Roger is not back yet. I don't suppose we will see him till morning.'

'Has he gone off with William?'

Gundred nodded. 'Please don't go after him. You will only make more of a fool of yourself.'

Hugh still stared out of the window. At the other end of the corridor he could hear baby Hugh sobbing.

Gundred could see he was troubled and softened her voice. She came a little closer. 'Hugh, why do you prolong the bad feeling with the Albini family?'

'I don't want to prolong any bad feeling. It's just…too difficult to explain.'

'Is it to do with your brother, William?'

Hugh spun around. 'Why do you say that? Who has been slandering me?'

'No one slanders you. But neither have I been deaf to the rumours and gossip over the years.'

'They are all lies,' Hugh said emphatically.

'Then tell me once and for all; what ails you now? They were just wrestling, so why would you attack them?'

'I think William Albini is a little old to be wrestling with a boy of only fifteen.' His rebuke was not heartfelt and Hugh continued to stare into the darkness for an answer. But there was little comfort to be had in the darkness. Demons lay hidden and spawned painful memories from long ago. Memories barely visible in the murky depths of his soul.

Perhaps it was time to share his pain. 'I have torrid nightmares from when I was a small boy at school. I was...whipped and beaten by the bishop who was supposed to mentor us.'

Gundred put her hand to her mouth in shock.

'On one particular occasion I was singled out for questioning over some hidden relics. When he had finished with me, he threatened to give the same treatment to my brother William, and Wills Albini. Christ, he was only eight or so at the time. I pleaded with the bishop not to touch them.' He dare not look at Gundred. But now the lance was boiled he wanted to tell everything. 'I swore to keep everything a secret. But they were right, if I had told anyone, no one would have believed me. I used to lie about everything...like a defensive measure.'

Gundred spoke softly. 'And what of your brother?'

Hugh closed his eyes, his breathing laboured. 'He was two years older than me and could have stopped it...but he did nothing. I saw him with Abbot Bund, in the confessional. He stared...he actually smiled, as if he was enjoying it....'

Without warning, Hugh lashed out and his fist hit the wall. His face was fixed in a grimace of anguish. 'I was drugged!. To ease the pain...I don't know what was happening...'

Gundred put her arm around his waist and hugged him. 'Hugh, are you sure it was William?'

'It is more than fifty years…the details become blurred but I fear the loathing will never diminish. The following months, he was forever fawning in the company of the bishop or his monks. Nothing else would make any sense, would it?'

'And Wills?'

Hugh turned away from the window and sat next to Gundred on the bed. 'Wills was a few years younger than me, but even so we were good friends until our twenties. Then my brother turned him against me and we barely spoke again. And he never appreciated what I did to save him from the hands of Bishop Herbert…

'But surely he never realised what had happened and was too young to understand. Did he even suspect anything was wrong?'

'Of course he did. I remember seeing his little face, perched half way up some scaffolding. It's all so hazy…like looking through a snowstorm, but I swear he saw everything. And I protected him…'

Gundred touched him tenderly, wanting to banish his inner demons. 'And what happened to the bishop?'

Hugh sighed then took a breath. 'I was twenty-three when I killed him.'

Gundred jolted and crossed herself.

'I was not as brave as it sounds. He was on his deathbed anyway. As for the abbot and the priest, they died at the hands of their God…in a fire.'

She held him closer and felt the tension drain from his body. 'Well I think you were brave to have lived with this ordeal. There now, all nightmares are better for having been exorcised.' She kissed him on the lips. Again, she kissed him, this time a little harder and more passionate. 'Come back to bed and I will make you feel better.' Her hand pressed into his groin and his prick instantly appreciated her delicate touch.

Hugh smiled and for a fleeting moment, the bitter burden he had carried for a lifetime lifted from his shoulders. In the glow from the window, his wife never looked more fair and alluring. Her eyes narrowed and her breasts began to glisten with sweat from the quickening of her breath. The chamber seemed unusually bright and Hugh broke from the passionate embrace to look over her shoulder.

Gundred also looked to the window and said the words they most feared. 'Please God, tell me it is not a fire?'

There were shouts of alarm coming from the household staff and the sound of neighing horses from the stables began to fill Hugh with dread. With a nimbleness that belied his years, Hugh jumped to the window. The sky to the south was lit up and but he could not see the source. 'I don't know what it is, but we had better go outside now.'

Once in the bailey, they quickly established there was no fire in the castle. Drawn like moths to a candle they climbed the steps of the castle wall to stare at the bright ball of light in the sky. They stood alongside others who trembled in fear and muttered prayers for God to protect them. Mothers screamed and hid the faces of the children but Hugh could not tear his eyes away from the terrifying spectacle. He held his wife close to his chest and waited for the moment when the Hand of God would strike the earth with impunity.

Chapter 4

Haughley Castle
Suffolk

After the bizarre incident with his father, Roger felt no compunction to stay the night at Framlingham. He joined William and Matilda who were due to go to Haughley Castle less than two hours ride west and William assured him they would all be welcome.

'Ralph le Broc has been a good friend of our family for many years. I am sure he will be delighted to meet my new wife,' William explained.

Whether expected or not, Roger took the comment in good faith but doubted he would receive a welcome.

It was a hot and steamy ride with little relief from the oppressive heat as the sun sank behind the massive mound and keep that was perched high above the village of Haughley.

Le Broc greeted them warmly. As the king's castellan of Haughley, he was a man who seemed to give little care for his rugged, down to earth appearance. Aged about fifty, he looked happy with his lot and they assumed he had little ambition to better himself.

After a brief introduction to his wife Gwen, the maids whisked Matilda away by to her chamber to freshen up. Le Broc's wife was delighted that her monotonous day had been interrupted and longed to catch up on all the news and gossip. No doubt, the actions of his wayward father would be the first topic of conversation, thought Roger.

When William introduced Roger Bigod, le Broc could not hide the frown on his face. 'Well young man, I can honestly say your father and I have never seen eye to eye...'

William could see Roger begin to redden with embarrassment and quickly intervened with a wide grin. 'Fear not Ralph, the lad is innocent of his father's behaviour and I can vouch that he is house-trained.'

Everybody laughed at the witty remark and le Broc ordered food and wine from the kitchens. He revelled in the company of such noble guests and while they relaxed in the hall, he told bawdy stories over the flow of wine and juicy venison.

The sound of footsteps drew their attention to the spiral staircase and a demure young girl cleared her throat, trying to catch her father's attention.

Le Broc walked over to his daughter. 'Anna, what is it you want my girl?'

'Mama said I should formally greet our guests.' The self conscious thirteen year-old stepped forward and gave a perfect curtsy.

Ralph laughed, eager to please his daughter. 'Oh of course, where are my courtly manners. Noblemen of Norfolk and Arundel, may I introduce Anna le Broc, the second lady of my castle. Anna, this is William Albini, son of Earl Wills Albini of Arundel and Sussex. And this young man is Roger Bigod, son of Earl Hugh Bigod of Norfolk.'

William acknowledged the girl with a brief nod and smiled broadly. Roger stood up and took a step towards Anna, bowing graciously as a flash of red filled her rosy cheeks.

More jugs of wine arrived from the kitchen and le Broc was quick to usher his daughter back upstairs. 'Well done Anna, but you should really retire now and practice some more of your etiquette.'

She curtsied again and Roger gave an appreciative clap as she disappeared back up the stairs, her face bright red and flustered.

Le Broc enlightened them as he poured wine into his best goblets. 'Bless her; she is taken by this new notion of chivalry, imported into the royal courts by the likes of Queen Eleanor from the troubadours and minstrels of Aquataine, I am told.'

With a stomach full of good food and wine, Le Broc gradually slipped into a drunken stupor. His snoring became oppressive and William asked a servant to gently take him to his chamber.

The dark of night had brought little relief from the heavy heat of the day and William and Roger took to the path outside that led to the ramparts above the moat. Dwelling on the earlier events of the day, their conversation was laboured and they sat in awkward silence throwing pebbles into the water.

Eventually William spoke. 'I hope you don't get into trouble for coming with us to Haughley.'

Anger over his father still rankled with Roger 'Father won't give a shit where I am. Anyway, I told my groom where I was going.'

'And what of your mother?'

'She is not my mother! My real mother ran off to Flanders with another man, the year I was born.' Roger did not hold back his irritation when others spoke of Gundred as his true mother.

William apologised and calmly observed the petulance of the young teenager wondering if the boy had inherited some of his father's traits after all.

Roger had never understand the bad blood. 'Why is my father so at odds with your family? He seems to have forgotten that the two of us are related. You are my uncle aren't you?'

William smiled at the innocent error. 'As near as dam it, I suppose. Your Aunt Maud, God bless her soul, was married to my grandfather.'

'Is he the one who is buried at Wymondham Abbey?' he asked.

'Indeed, my grandfather founded the abbey. Just as your grandfather, Roger Bigod founded Thetford Priory. They were both great men in their time.'

Roger shook his head. 'Then why this stupid feud?'

William hoped the easiest explanation would suffice. 'A few years ago, I asked my father the same thing. When they were younger, they were the very best of friends. But when your father began to behave without honour, they parted on bad terms.'

'But surely, that cannot explain everything that has happened since?'

William thought hard before continuing. 'Your father had a brother who was on the White Ship.'

'I know. His name was William', Roger acknowledged. Although the tragedy happened nearly forty-five years ago, the tale of the sinking of the king's ship was one of folk legend that was well known throughout the land.

'Well for some reason, my father believes that William survived the wreck...and your father knows it to be true, but denies it.'

Roger looked shocked. 'But why would your father believe such a thing? Everyone knows only the Rouen butcher survived the wreck of the White Ship.'

Before Hugh could ask another question, William held up his hand.

'It's no good asking more questions; I simply do not know the answer. However, there are many people throughout the land that say Hugh Bigod has spent a lifetime hell bent on treachery and rebellion, whereas my father has given a lifetime of loyal service and good council to the crown. As we speak, my father is on a mission for the king. He accompanies three important bishops to France to ask King Louis to give up Thomas Becket and have him return to England to stand trial. Just ask yourself, whose word would you trust.'

Roger went quiet and stared down at the water in the moat, biting his lip. He often heard the whispers in the corridors that confirmed William's indictment, for there was no denying his father was disliked by many of his peers. But could it really be true that his father would deny his brother, just to further his own ambitions?

William stood up and stretched his legs. 'Well, though it is a wonderful night, I have a beautiful wife waiting for me in my chamber. I am sure a servant will have laid you a mattress in the hall and I shall see you after dawn. I think it best I send an escort with you back to Framlingham at first light. On top of everything else, I don't want to pick another fight with Earl Bigod.'

Just as they were standing up, they both turned their attention to the glow of light coming from the south. Like a false dawn, the sky became brighter, except the intensity began to waver.

'Is it the night lights?' William asked out loud.

But the light began to take shape and a ball of intense radiance illuminated the land, shedding shards of fiery debris in its wake. Slowly it carved its ominous path across the sky.

'What is it?' Roger asked, not knowing whether to be afraid or excited by the spectacle.

'Saints preserve us! It must be a fireball sent by God Almighty!' William exclaimed, his eyes wide open in wonder.

Behind them, they heard the clamour of screams and shouts as the grooms and servants ran outside, many fearing for their lives. The ball of fire began its excruciating, silent descent towards the horizon then suddenly speeded up until it became one with the earth. The screams and prayers from the household mingled with an air of dread and awe as the trail of the fiery glow stretched across the sky, and began to slowly diminish.

Roger gazed open-mouthed at William, his mind full of questions and the excitement still evident on his face.

Then William turned to make his way back to the house and above the shouts he called to Roger to follow him. With a sparkle in his eye, he was determined to satisfy his curiosity. 'After I have made sure Matilda is settled, how do you fancy an adventure?'

William had assumed the fireball had struck only five or six miles away and by the time he and Roger had ridden through Ipswich and Colchester he began to realise how wrong he had been. They rode south for two hours as the townsfolk gathered along the route, all pointing in the same direction, warning the two young noblemen that they were riding towards the wrath of God. Eventually they reached the shoreline near Maldon, overlooking Osea Island.

A large crowd in sombre mood had congregated on a sandbank, overlooking the estuary towards the small island. Although less than a mile away, no one was in any hurry to leave the shore and investigate the disaster that had befallen the poor inhabitants of the island. Apart from the occasional prayer, everyone looked on in silence.

Flames could still be seen licking over the smouldering ruins of the houses and there was little doubt in the minds of those watching, that the islanders must be guilty of unfathomable sins in order for the hand of God to strike so mercilessly.

'Do not intervene against God's will,' an old priest proclaimed solemnly.

'There may be demons and witches walking amongst the flames,' spoke an anonymous voice.

The swell of opinion affirmed it was ill advised to take to the boats until the full light of day. As the prayers of the priest rang in their ears, the crowd wandered reverentially back to their homes.

No one heard the splash of oars come from the other side of the sandbank. William pulled on one oar while trying to follow the indecipherable instructions from the fisherman on the other oar. He said he was the only fisherman who knew the way across the sandbanks to the channel that ran to the island jetty. He was also the only one willing to row to the island for a silver coin.

William was facing Roger and noticed his apprehension. 'I don't believe in all this hogwash about demons. Don't worry, we will be there in no time.' His words of comfort belied his own concerns.

Under the light of a watery moon, they nudged nervously amongst the sandbanks and all three of them were relived when they tied up to the wooden jetty on the isle of Osea.

A long track wound its way towards the only inhabited area on the island and they had only walked a few paces down the track before the full extent of the devastation became apparent. Every house on both sides of the road were burnt to the ground. As far as the eye could see, the crops had been scorched and lay flattened and smouldering. Animals had been incinerated where they were stood and the stench of burnt flesh filled the air.

A few villagers were huddled watching a man trying to help a woman from her house. One look was enough to see they had all suffered badly in the fire and were still in shock. The fisherman ran off to tend to some relatives, while William and Roger approached the villagers.

'Where did the fireball hit the ground?' William asked.

One man walked forward. 'It didn't hit the ground, my lord. The whole sky just burst into flames…a thousand fires fell from the sky. The whole island was covered; houses, barns and fields. Nothing was spared.' The man fell to his knees and Roger could see the clothes on his back had been scorched through to his skin.

'Where does the lord of the island reside?' William asked.

The man pointed to the far end of the road.

'We will return after we see the lord.' He and Roger ran up the track.

The once beautiful manor house had burnt out and just a one wall and a few glowing timbers were left standing. They called out into the night and a thin voice replied on the breeze.

The man was laid on his back next to his burnt mattress. A few paces to his right lay a blackened body that was probably his wife. Burnt beyond recognition, William thought it best that he could not see her remains.

'My wife was calling me. Please find her...she is injured,' he begged in a croaky voice.

Roger let him drink from his water skin, and then saw William nod to the man's legs. One was crushed to a pulp and the other was still trapped under a smouldering timber.

'Are you the lord of the manor?' William asked as he heaved on the timber.

'I am a knight from the Holy Land, living out my days with my wife. Please, you have to save her, for the love of God...' He winced in pain as William heaved the burning timber aside. What was revealed made Roger feel sick. Neither of them had ever seen so much damage to a living person.

The knight cried out as he glanced down at his body below the waist. 'Tell me the truth young man.'

William crouched down next to the knight. 'I can offer you no comfort. My friend and I will pray that a priest offers you absolution before the sun rises. I am afraid your wife is dead, God bless her soul.'

Closing his eyes, the knight gave a silent prayer and seemed to accept his fate.

They tried to make him comfortable but the blood seeping from his thigh was unstoppable and he would soon be dead.

'Please tell me your names, young sirs.'

'I am William Albini and this is Roger Bigod.'

The knight was quite still; his eyes were fixed far into the distance, his voice sounding far away. 'William, my friend, I am so sorry...but they forbade me to go to Lydda. I was told only today of her death...poor Sybille. She was a good woman, so badly treated. And now my wife struck down without mercy. Oh God, are my sins so great. By His grace…my punishment is complete…'

As the knight slipped away into his private purgatory, they looked at each other, baffled by his dying words.

William closed the knight's eyes. 'Why did he call me his friend?'

'And where is Lydda supposed to be?' Roger asked.

'Maybe he means Lydd, near Romney Marsh,' William replied still puzzled. 'Even though I have never been there.'

They walked back to the street and soon the strange words of the mysterious knight were forgotten. The least injured inhabitants were gathering the wounded together. All of them were suffering from burns; some of them hideously scarred for life and others unlikely to see the light of day.

William looked across at Roger. 'We seem to be the only able bodied men on the island. For a start, we can tear our shirts into bandages to treat the burns and then somehow collect water and food. Are you game?'

Roger returned the smile and took off his tunic. 'Some adventure this turned out to be.'

A squire came running from the direction of the ruined manor. 'Have you found his Lordship?'

William broke the news. 'I am afraid your lord is dead. Who was he anyway?

'I suppose he won't mind me saying now. Lord Henry Malache was steward to Count Thierry of Flanders who banished him from the Holy Land. But in his defence, he was wronged…'

'Yes, I am sure he was. Now please help us find a well and help us bring clean water.'

The squire looked at the injured people nearby. Finally, the shock became to much and the squire broke down in tears.

Chapter 5

Westminster
London

King Henry beckoned Hugh over to his table and made a space for him to sit down. This show of camaraderie surprised Hugh and the usual raucous noise of the banquet dulled a little as the king leaned over to speak. He chose his words quietly and carefully. 'Hugh, I have been meaning to thank you for the information you gave me. Your sources proved to be authentic and I was able to prepare myself for Becket's betrayal.'

Under the scrutiny of a dozen pairs of eyes, Hugh spoke with equal deliberation 'My lord King knows he can rely on my support'.

'I am pleased to hear that. Are you are happy to be back in residence at Framlingham?'

'I consider it to be my home, as granted to my father by your grandfather, the first King Henry. I believe it was a reward for his loyalty and wise council.'

The king nodded and those watching were impressed by the accord between them. The atmosphere relaxed once more.

Deep inside, Hugh was seething. He hated the young king who had achieved so much in so little time. He almost spat the wine out as he calculated Henry's age at only thirty-one. It left a bitter taste in his mouth and made his next words tumble awkwardly from his mouth. 'Why are you building a castle at Orford?'

For what seemed an age, the king looked into his goblet. Hugh sat back, hoping the king felt as uncomfortable as he did.

Eventually he spoke. 'I must admit, I know little of the castle at Orford. Lord Sisland suggested it and he agreed to supervise its construction. It is his project, you understand.'

Hugh was completely thrown by the answer. The king would never give such a carte-blanch authority to anyone without the strictest of controls, and that included Sisland. The king must be lying.

The awkward silence continued.

Hugh looked up and cursed silently at the approach of the Earl of Leicester to the king's table. The earl was not afraid to rile Hugh at every opportunity. Many years ago he to had been a witness to the death of the first King Henry and had listened to the oath Hugh had sworn on that fateful day: that the king had named Stephen as his successor. Time and again, he would taunt Hugh over the oath; though would never accuse him of perjury to his face.

Leicester had been amply rewarded for his loyal support of the king and at the age of sixty, he believed he had done well for himself. At the end of the civil war, Leicester was appointed Joint Chief Justicar with Richard de Lucy and together they ruled England in the king's many absences across the channel.

Leicester whispered something in the king's ear and they both smiled as the king quickly left the table.

Hugh watched him join the Queen Eleanor and they disappeared up the stairway.

Leicester jabbed Hugh in the ribs. 'I hope you understand Hugh, but the king has an appointment with the Queen in the solar.'

'As needs be,' Hugh muttered.

'If truth be told, I thought for a moment you were going to quarrel with the king…again. It's bad enough listening to him ranting and raving over Becket without you providing more fodder for his temper.'

As Leicester sat down, Hugh took a deep swig of his wine and poured another cup. 'It's bloody Sisland,' he hissed venomously.

'Ah, Sisland. How many times have I heard that said.'

'So why is he not here tonight,' Hugh snorted.

'I suppose he must still be at Orford.'

Hugh leaned closer. 'Tell me, why would the king allow Sisland to build a castle without due process and supervision.'

Look Hugh, let me be honest. No one here likes Sisland but the king finds him useful…for the awkward jobs.'

'Like hacking my friend to pieces…'

'Hugh we were all outraged to hear what had happened at Walton Castle, all those years ago. Even the king was distressed.'

'He never apologised.'

Leicester looked down at his goblet and shook his head. 'Hugh, you of all men should know that kings do not apologise. Sisland thought he was carrying out royal orders; but I admit his judgement was grossly amiss.'

'Then perhaps when Sisland takes charge of a impregnable castle, the king would wish he had learnt his lesson.'

Leicester became aware of too many pricked ears. 'Please Hugh keep your voice down. Listen to me. We will meet tomorrow in my office at Terce and we will talk more of your concerns.'

Hugh watched Leicester walk off and returned the stares of those watching his every move. His mind was as taught as a siege engine. He finished his goblet and took a deep breath as he recalled the invitation to meet with Leicester. Perhaps unwittingly, he had sown some seeds of sympathy and tomorrow he would try to cultivate his unexpected crop.

At morning prayers, the corridors of Westminster palace were empty and Hugh entered the office of the Justicar, to find the Earl of Leicester, sat with his son, also named Robert. They were joined by Richard de Lucy. Cautiously, Hugh took his seat at the small table, glad that Bonham was stood close by in the corridor.

Leicester spoke first. 'Hugh, I thought your concerns so grave that I thought it best to let my son and de Lucy come to our rendezvous. I hope you do not mind.'

Hugh quickly countered his initial concerns. 'Well all three of us must be near on seventy, so I suppose you have brought your son to keep us from falling asleep.' They all chuckled, glad that the tense atmosphere had eased.

Robert chortled holding out his hand to greet Hugh. 'Well I suppose forty must appear to be a babe-in-arms in this company. I am honoured to meet you again, Earl Bigod and a long time since we last met.'

Leicester raised his hand for quiet. 'Down to business. Let me first say that nothing of this meeting should be relayed to any other party. Agreed?'

They all agreed.

Leicester continued. 'I think we can establish that Lord Edmund Sisland is no friend of anyone around this table. However, more importantly, I believe him to be a possible threat to the king. There is evidence he has been acting deliberately contrary to the king's orders, favouring an interpretation that benefits only his own ends.'

De Lucy interjected. 'I have often thought of warning the king of Sisland's misconduct but with the king's obsession with Becket, the time is never right.'

'Indeed,' Leicester confirmed. 'But now Earl Bigod has brought to our attention yet another grave matter. One of possible rebellion and treason.' He looked to Hugh to comment.

Hugh was speechless. He had no idea Sisland was so universally disliked by the powerful barons sat around the table. He turned his hesitation inwardly, as if pondering a great question. 'It shocks me to say this...but surely the very fact that we are having a clandestine meetings must in itself be evidence enough. What hold does this...this steward has over the realm. The king must be advised to condemn his actions before it is too late.

De Lucy leant forward. 'But do you think him capable of rebellion?'

'He builds a castle as if it were his own project. Only last night, those were the words of the king.' Hugh was beginning to enjoy the limelight.

'The king is too trusting,' Leicester agreed. 'Bastards like Sisland will turn on him when he least expects it.'

De Lucy nodded and stroked his grey beard. 'But we need proof of wrong-doing, not speculation.'

Hugh was deep in thought. 'Can you tell me when Wills Albini and the delegation of bishops are due to return from Normandie?'

'We have received word that they were due to have an audience with King Louis of France yesterday. Therefore, the earliest return to Dover will be the day after tomorrow, weather and tides permitting.'

Hugh slapped the table and looked at Leicester. 'In that case I can get you all the proof you need.'

For six interminable days, Earl Wills Albini had been nursemaid to the bishops and their clerks, and in the end it was all to no avail. Louis had played them for fools, keeping them waiting for three days without reason. When they eventually met with the French King, he denied giving Becket anything, least of all asylum.

As they deliberated, Wills swore he could almost smell Becket nearby but he dare not say anything. After just an hour at the table, King Louis abruptly stood up and left the meeting. Another hour passed before a servant appeared to say King Louis did not appreciate the tone of the accusations and that the conference was over.

The bishops were infuriated at the blatant display of lies, but they could do nothing to vent their anger other than return to England.

All the way to Dover, they fumed over the way they had been treated. The constant rain added to the misery and tempers were inevitably frayed by the time they sailed into the harbour.

They agreed to send a report to King Henry immediately upon landing, recommending that the next step was to send an even larger delegation of bishops and priests to Rome and plead the case against Becket to the pontiff.

Earl Wills Albini waited with his delegation of bishops under a wet tarpaulin at the Dover quayside and silently cursed that the royal messenger he had ordered was late.

Through the downpour, he eventually spied a horseman on a mare riding at speed towards them and Wills held up his hand to attract his attention. As he approached, Wills looked for the king's coat of arms but one was not evident. 'Who are you? Are you a royal messenger or not?'

The horseman did not dismount. 'No my lord, I am acting on behalf of Lord Edmund Sisland. I am here to meet a French delegation. Is that you sire?' Wills was baffled. 'What do you mean, you are from Lord Sisland?'

'I apologise for my error sire.' The messenger turned his horse and hurried off, disappearing through the rain a few moments later.

Wills had no time to absorb what had happened before the true royal messenger, in all his heraldry, rode up offering his profuse apologies for his tardiness. There was no time for a reprimand and he handed the messenger a container of sealed documents for the urgent attention of the king, then sent him on his way.

The Bishop of London looked out from under the tarpaulin. 'For God's sake, we need to get out of this rain. We can wait at the priory for our coffers to be delivered.'

Earl Wills looked at the sodden delegation comprised of the realm's ecclesiastical leaders and agreed to make haste to the priory.

Failure on any account was always a source of disappointment, but the manner of this particular confrontation with Louis had preyed badly upon Wills. But even with everything that had gone before, only one matter now nagged him to distraction. What the hell was Sisland doing and why would he send an envoy to meet a mysterious delegation of Frenchmen at Dover?

After some rest, Wills Albini arrived at Westminster Palace where the king was waiting for him. Reading his mood was always difficult, but seeing his stony face, Wills assumed he had read his report and was none to happy.

'Earl Albini I am happy to see you return in one piece from your failed mission.' It was the closest Wills had ever received to an admonishment and he speculated how close the king was to losing his temper.

The king stood up and paced the floor, holding the report in his hand. 'I have done as you suggest and emboldened the bishops cause with even more of their Brethren. They are on their way back over the sea to Sens, albeit under duress. I pray this time the pontiff will be impressed by the delegation and will look favourably upon my demands.'

Wills chose his words carefully. 'I also pray that the enhanced delegation will be successful. However, I fear our words will fall on deaf ears. I believe that Pope Alexander will already have met Becket and made up his mind in his favour.'

The king continued to pace the floor, muttering to himself and leaving a trail of torn and crumpled parchment in his wake.

Against his better judgement, Wills knew this was the wrong time to bring up bad news. But his duty was to keep the king informed. 'My lord, I need to speak with you in private over a grave matter.'

From experience, the king knew such a request would be meaningful and he nodded at Wills to follow him to his private office.

Clasping his hands together, the king sat opposite Wills. 'Well, what has bloody Becket done now?'

'It is not Becket my lord.'

'Well I suppose that is a relief. Go on.'

'It may be nothing; but I had a curious encounter at Dover.'

Wills explained the strange turn of events and true to his fears, King Henry exploded with fury, slamming the table and kicking out at anything not fixed to the floor. Opened the door, he shouted for the Earl of Leicester and de Lucy to attend his office at once. They both appeared quickly and closed the door behind them.

They listened intently to Wills as he repeated word for word, the arrival and disappearance of the mysterious herald who said he was acting on behalf of Lord Sisland. Wills reinforced the story. 'And the Bishop of London was a witness to the whole conversation.'

They sat quietly digesting the story before de Lucy spoke up. 'My lord King, we have to report to you that this only adds to our own suspicions about Sisland.'

'What are you saying. Spit it out!'

De Lucy knew he was probably the only one strong enough to resist the infamous rage of the king. He detailed every complaint held against Sisland as if he was reading out a list of indictments, leaving the building of the castle at Orford till last.

The king stared at his most senior advisors. 'Are you telling me Sisland is capable of siding with Louis?'

'Yes my lord king.'

'And this is the opinion of you all?'

Even Wills felt compelled by the evidence to agree with Leicester and de Lucy.

The king stiffened. 'Very well, I shall sign a warrant for his arrest. Have a troop go to Dover and try and catch him in the act,' ordered the king.

'But my lord, Sisland is here in the palace.'

'But you said he was at Dover…'

De Lucy interrupted. 'No my lord. You recall he sent an envoy.'

'For God's sake just arrest him and throw him in the tower while I think!' the king cried out. 'What in hells name have I done to deserve such disloyalty. First Becket and now Sisland.'

They left the king in his office to mull over the fate of his steward while Wills told the others of his plans. 'I made a promise to visit my estates in Norfolk for a few days, to see my son and his wife. My soul has taken a battering of late and I need a break from the royal court.'

De Lucy nodded. 'You must be very proud of your son. I understand he is acclaimed as quite a hero in Essex.'

Wills looked puzzled.

'Have you not heard? Only a few days ago your son William and young Roger Bigod saved the lives of many townsfolk from a fire on Osea Island.'

'Good God! Is he unharmed?'

'I am sure he is fine, however they say the island was burnt to a charred cinder by an act of God.'

Wills called to his squire to prepare the horses.

Leicester sidled next to him. 'So what think you of Sisland, in case the king asks?'

Irritated by the distraction, Wills gave Leicester a cursory glance. 'I care not for any man who betrays the king. Let the man be dammed. He will be no loss to anyone.' He marched off to the stables thinking only of his son.

As Leicester and de Lucy walked upstairs to the shared apartments of the Justicar, they could hear laughter on the other side of the door. Inside, Hugh Bigod was sharing a jest with Leicester's son Robert.

Their faces dropped as they waited for de Lucy to speak. 'Sisland is being taken to the tower as we speak while the king deliberates on his fate.'

Hugh raised his goblet and toasted loudly. 'Here's to justice. I hope the bastard rots in hell.'

De Lucy looked down his long nose with barely a flicker of appreciation. 'Well of course, the whole incident is unfortunate and hardly a cause for celebration. Besides, I thought you would be in Norfolk, seeing your son.'

'Why, what has he done?'

De Lucy repeated the story he had heard earlier that morning.

'What the fuck is he doing with William Albini? Roger is only fifteen.'

De Lucy was confused. 'I thought you would be proud of your son. We have just told Wills Albini and he has left for Norfolk eager to...'

Hugh suddenly stood up, riled by the mention of the Albini family. He called out to Bonham. 'We shall leave now for Suffolk. There is nothing more I can do here.'

Chapter 6

The Tower
London

When they heard the footsteps coming from the staircase, the two guards on duty at the tower dungeon looked at each other suspiciously. The bell for middle night had sounded. No one had any cause to be visiting so late. They stood up as one, startled at the sight of the masked executioner enter the guardhouse. Immediately they challenged him. 'What is your business here at this hour?'

'I am here on the orders of the king.' His voice was muffled but full of authority. He handed the guards an order with the king's seal. 'I need to see the prisoner to measure him up for the noose. The king wishes for a dawn execution.'

They first guard handed back the order. 'Why do you wear the mask?'

The executioner stepped forward menacingly, so as the guard could feel his breath. 'Because one day I might have to hang your son or your daughter and I don't want pillocks like you trying to hunt me down. Now open the fucking cells.'

The guard hesitated then opened the main door to the cells. He took a torch from the wall sconce and led the way down the corridor to the end cell. He turned the lock and opened the door grill.

'Now leave me to my work,' ordered the voice behind the mask.

The guard walked away and the executioner placed the torch in the wall sconce and closed the grill behind him.

Spread-eagled with chains against the wall, Sisland looked a sorry sight. His rich clothes were soiled and his face was bloodied and bruised. Most of his teeth were missing and his jaw appeared broken.

Drained of all energy he could barely raise his head. When he saw the executioner standing before him, he let out a deep groan. 'Please have mercy, let me speak with the king.' He watched as the mask was raised to reveal the face of the executioner and fell silent at the face before him. 'You! How did you get in here? Please this is a mistake...' A fist smashed into his mouth and his words became incoherent.

'It is time to pay the reaper, Sisland.' The sword fell with a whoosh, detaching his right arm above the elbow. The shock left Sisland flailing as he pulled ineffectually on his chains. The second blow failed to sever his left leg completely and although the bones were smashed, it still dangled by a few strands of muscle.

Pulling his sword from the flesh, the executioner hissed into Sisland's ear. 'I am not a butcher so I will make this quick. When you are in hell, give Picot my regards.' The next sword thrust pierced the heart and Sisland was dead in an instant.

Hugh pulled the mask back over his face before carefully wiping the blood from his sword. Marching back out of the cell, he pushed his way past the guards without missing a step. 'Let him rest, for he will meet his maker soon enough.' He climbed the stairs and opened the big wooden door to the outside world. Discarding the mask, he breathed in deeply and saw Marcus Tyler his newly appointed squire, holding his mare only twenty paces away.

The opportunity to rid the world of Sisland was too much for Hugh to miss. Only Marcus and his four loyal knights knew of his clandestine visit to the Tower. The whole court had deliberately informed of his immediate departure for Suffolk.

Nothing was said of why he was at the Tower and Marcus knew better than to ask.

Hugh was keen to be as far away as possible and half an hour later, they rendezvoused three miles away with four knights and squires. The small troop set off into the night heading north east on the Colchester roman road.

Upon reflection, Hugh was happy with the way Marcus had handled himself. Once a groom for his wife, he was proving a good squire and leaving d'Cheney at Framlingham had proved a wise decision. While weakened with a painful stomach, he was restricted to light clerical duties.

At Colchester, they stopped to eat at a roadside tavern and Hugh sat in the corner with a bowl of thick porridge. Marcus approached formally, saying there was a young man waiting to see Hugh. 'He says he knows your son, my lord.'

Hugh studied the man standing behind Marcus and beckoned him forward. The colours he wore were unfamiliar to Hugh. 'My lord Earl Bigod, my name is Trelaw of Osea Island, squire to Henry Malache, lord of the island who died in the fire-storm. I had the honour of tending to the wounded with Roger your son, and I would be honoured if you would consider taking me into the service of the Bigod family.'

Hugh looked at the nervous young man and carried on eating. 'I have squires coming up to me all the time…'

'Your brother William met with my lord briefly in the Holy Land and he seemed…'

Hugh began choking on his oatmeal. 'The man you saw was not my brother, do you hear me?' he hissed, looking around to who was listening.

Trelaw was taken aback. 'I am sorry my lord, I just assumed he was your brother...from the name.'

'Listen to me, young man. You may ride next to me to Framlingham and tell me, in confidence, everything you know of this…this impostor.' Hugh signalled to Marcus to take the squire outside but to let him ride with them to Framlingham.

On the road, Hugh asked Marcus to bring up Trelaw to ride with them. Through gritted teeth he listened to the story of the man from Lydda who called himself William Bigod. A man who had lost his tongue but learnt to speak again. A man who became a horse farmer, breeding fine steeds for the noblemen and Knights Templars of Jerusalem.

Hugh listened but questioned nothing. When Trelaw had finished, he thanked him, saying the information was useful in tracking down the charlatan who had stolen then abused the good name of Bigod.

A few moments later, Hugh spoke alone with Marcus. 'There is little point in bringing Trelaw to Framlingham. You heard what he had to say...bloody cheeky sod. I don't want him spilling his lies to all and sundry, so make sure you persuade him otherwise.' Hugh rode off in a huff. 'I don't want to see him again.'

When Wills Albini arrived at Buckenham, he was delighted to see his son practicing his horse and sword skills on the quintain. As soon as William saw the earl, he dismounted and left his horse with a squire. 'Father, it is good to see you. Did you have any success in France?'

The earl looked his son up and down. 'Never mind my tales of woe, what has become of you in my absence? No less than five good men and women have told me I have a hero for a son. Either that or a saint.'

'It wasn't just me, father. Look who I had to help me.'

Another horse rode towards them and came to a stop. The earl screwed up his eyes trying to recognise the horseman as he dismounted. 'By God's breath...Roger Bigod! I thought it must be you, but the last time I saw you...you came up to my waist. Now look at you.'

Roger gave a short, respectful bow. 'Lord Albini, it is a great honour to see you again.'

'That is good of you to say so. Now let us go inside out of this interminable heat and you can tell me all about the exciting events on

Osea Island.'

Inside the manor house, the earl called for a change of clothes and some wine. William's wife, Matilda came across the hall to greet the earl and he kissed her affectionately on the cheek. 'You are looking prettier by the day, I actually envy my son. But you must excuse an old man who needs a bath and a jug of wine.'

They gathered outside an hour later in the relative cool of the shaded courtyard and after the earl had dealt with a few domestic and legal matters with his steward, he listened eagerly to William as he told the story of the fireball that swept across Osea Island. He beamed with pride as his son described how they succumbed to the need to help the injured and the dying and like everyone else, the earl was fascinated by the manifestation of a divine act.

'So did it leave a hole when it hit the ground?' he asked.

'We arrived about two hours after the event but the fireball burst and the covered the island with burning cinders. Everything was consumed in just a few moments,' William recalled.

Roger continued the story. 'There were twenty or thirty people injured and we just felt this overriding need to help. We sought bandages and water and even set broken limbs. Then at daybreak, some more people came across the water, including two monks who were physicians...oh and a priest. They blest us saying we had saved many lives.'

The earl looked awkwardly at Roger, still finding his presence round his table difficult to accept. 'Well I must say how proud I am...of both of you. So who was the lord of the island and what of his fate?'

'His name was Henry Malache from the Holy Land. He and his wife died next to each other,' William said sadly.

'He spoke to William as if he knew him,' Roger added.

William shook his head. 'You mean he muttered something about Lydd or Lydda and that Sybille was dead. He was delirious.'

The earl pricked up his ears. 'You say Lydda?' He wondered where he had heard the name before.

Roger put his goblet down. 'I can remember every word he said. *"William my friend, they forbade me to go to Lydda. Today, I was told of the death of Sybille."* I 'm not saying it makes any sense.'

The earl's mind seemed far away. 'How strange.'

Roger continued. 'And then his squire said his lord had been steward to Count Thierry of Flanders who banished him, but he had been badly wronged.'

The earl appeared startled. 'Say that again.'

Roger repeated the words of Trelaw the squire.

The earl slapped the table. 'Well I never. While in France, I heard that Sybille, the wife of Count Thierry of Flanders, died in the Holy Land. And now I know the name of Lydda. It is a town near Jerusalem, mentioned frequently in the scriptures. It is also said to be where St George was martyred and buried.'

William was impressed by his father's agile memory. 'But it doesn't explain why he called me his friend, as if he knew me.'

'No I suppose not. But I have met the Knights Templars from Jerusalem and if our paths cross again, they may throw some light on the subject. The stories that emanate from the Holy land never fail to surprise me.' The earl brought his attention back to Roger. 'Have you spoken to your father yet, about all this?'

The beaming smile on Roger's face suddenly fell away. 'I haven't seen my father for days, not since the day he attacked William…'

The earl was shocked. 'What do you mean…attacked?'

William quickly intervened. 'He saw us wrestling and his mind was addled by what he thought he saw. He simply pulled us apart…'

'More that that,' Roger explained. 'It was this senseless feud between our families. I know the cause goes back many years…' Roger left his words hanging, embarrassed at having said too much.

Memories of good times and bad suddenly came flooding back to

Wills Albini. His wounded heart made it impossible to give a simple answer. A lifetime of deceit had emanated from the fractured soul of Hugh Bigod. Should he now let loose a litany of grief in front of his son, whom he hardly knew?

He poured another goblet of wine and took a long drink before facing Roger. 'This is not the time or place to discuss the wayward life of your father. You are still young and there will be time enough for reconciliation. It has been good to see you and I pray that in the years to come, our families can look forward to better times. As for now, I think it best you return in the morning to Framlingham, to your family.'

Roger shrank into his chair and nodded sheepishly.

The next day William escorted Roger back to Framlingham. The mood was quiet as they both dwelt over recent events.

To break the silence, Roger posed a question. 'Your father says he has met the Knights Templars.'

'Yes, he spoke with them at Westminster, quite recently.'

'My father hates the Templars. *"The richest beggars ever to wear God's robes,"* he calls them.'

William tried to offer a crumb of comfort to his friend. 'After what you did on the island, I am sure your father will be proud of you.'

'I don't really care. Why should I take pleasure in pride from a man who I have grown to hate?'

Roger continued to indulge in his sulky mood until they approached Framlingham Castle and witnessed a commotion inside the bailey. About six or seven peasants were crowded around a cart and two guards aided by d'Cheney were trying to disperse them. A priest was stood on the cart appealing for calm as Roger and William dismounted at the stables.

Looking pale and exhausted, d'Cheney greeted Roger and

acknowledged William with a cursory nod of the head.

On closer inspection, Roger could see a body lay under a blanket on the cart. Only one thought entered his head. 'Where is my father?'

'Don't worry, your father arrived back from London yesterday. Your mother...I mean Gundred, is with him inside the castle.' D'Cheney looked to the cart. 'A man was found this morning with his throat cut in a ditch on the main road. He has been stripped and robbed. These buggers found him and now they expect a reward because they think he is from the castle. I sent for the priest to offer absolution for his soul but I fear it is too late.'

The guards prodded the disgruntled peasants back over the drawbridge as d'Cheney watched William walk to the cart.

'Gundred has been worried about you,' d'Cheney remarked, 'though I told her you would be fine. His Lordship told us of your exploits on Osea Island and she nearly had a fit. She prays for your safety in the chapel. Thank God she has been spared seeing the body of this poor wretch. I take it you are unscathed?'

Roger nodded then saw the expression of shock pass over William's face as he lifted the blanket from the top half of the body. Open mouthed, he turned to face Roger and d'Cheney.

'What is it?' d'Cheney asked.

William looked again to confirm what he knew to be true. 'How can this be? It's Trelaw, the squire from Osea Island.'

There was little to be gained from venturing from Framlingham Castle and Hugh was quite content to stay behind his walls while the repercussions of Sisland's death continued to rattle out of London. Despite the distance from London, he could almost feel the rage emanating from the mouth of the king.

Hugh tensed up whenever the sound of horses echoed from the inner bailey. But on this occasion he was relieved to see his son Roger had suddenly arrived unannounced. As Hugh walked over to welcome his Roger, he noticed William Albini stood with the horses near the stables.

Hugh smiled; relieved to see his son was looking well. 'Roger. It is good to see you. Are you going to tell me where you have been all this time? I hear you were quite the hero at Osea. You must tell me...'

Roger was agitated. 'That was days ago and is not the reason I have come this way to see you.'

The smile disappeared from Hugh's face.

Roger stared at his father. 'What do you know of a body left to rot in a ditch on the London road?'

'I don't know what you mean. What body do you speak of?'

'He was a brave squire who was murdered on the day you rode up from London.'

Hugh remained impassive though Roger thought he detected a flicker of emotion. 'I did not see anything nor do I know of what you speak.' He was becoming irritated by the questions from his son but took a conciliatory stance. 'Look Roger, I am pleased to see that you are in good health. Gundred has been praying over your absence. She was in the chapel just now...go and see her...'

Roger was wrong to take his tone as a sign of weakness. 'Swear to me you had nothing to do with this murder,' he interrupted.

Hugh's face suddenly turned thunderous as his temper flared. 'I don't have to swear anything to you.' Hugh looked across to William Albini who was listening intently. 'Is this an example of the poison you feed my son?' He turned back to Roger and stepped a little closer. 'Do you realise how disrespectful you sound, interrogating your father like some common criminal.'

Suddenly Roger noticed the embarrassed faces of everyone staring back at him. 'I'm...I'm sorry. I just thought...' His voice trailed off and he dropped his head.

Hugh forced a grin, trying to make light of his outburst. He placed a mollifying hand on his son's shoulder. 'Go and see Gundred, there's a good boy.' Hugh turned away stiffly to walk back to the main door of the castle.

William walked over to Roger. 'Well, that looked very uncomfortable. Why on earth were you so confrontational? Ask yourself; what possible motive could your father have for killing someone like Trelaw anyway?'

Roger kicked the ground, annoyed at himself for behaving like a fool. 'I don't know what the hell I was thinking. It's just too much of a coincidence. And he never answered me when I asked him to swear.' Roger looked up to see Gundred waving from the steps of the main hall and he swore under his breath as he walked off to meet her.

Shaking his head, William hoped that young Roger's attitude would soon mature, before his mouth caused even more trouble.

While Roger and Gundred were in upstairs, Hugh called for Marcus to join him outside. He checked they were alone before he spoke. 'Well, are you going to tell me what the hell happened to that fucking squire?' he asked sternly.

Marcus raised his eyebrows, displaying an air of innocence. 'You said you never wanted to see him again.'

'You fucking idiot, you killed him didn't you?' Hugh hissed angrily, not wanting to be overheard.

'He was threatening you…he kept going on about your brother…'

'Shut up about my brother. William is dead.' Hugh knew he had to control the fury deep inside. He paused before quietly asking the question. 'Well…did you kill Trelaw or not?'

Marcus kept his silence and looked to one side, not daring to meet Hugh's wild stare.

His continued silence confirmed his guilt. Hugh persisted. 'So, did anyone see you?'

Marcus shook his head. 'I killed him because he threatened you.' Hugh was unmoved. 'Never do anything like that again, without consulting me first. Is that understood?'

Marcus looked down at his feet. 'I did not discuss it with you…because you could then deny any involvement,' he muttered.

Hugh saw his logic but remained stoic. 'Then the whole matter shall remain our secret. Agreed?'

Nodding his head, Marcus smiled to himself and wondered how many dark secrets the earl kept to himself?

Chapter 7

Alexandria
Egypt

Muzawi rubbed his eyes from the strain of reading the scrolls stacked high upon the countless shelves of the Alexandria library. He sat down at his table to take a drink of fresh water and cursed for a moment. The destruction perpetrated by Julius Caesar more than a thousand years ago, when most of the library was engulfed in flames, would surely go down as one of the worlds greatest crimes. Then again, perhaps it was fortunate that at least some of the thousands of ancient texts and manuscripts had survived the roman fire ships.

The library had became his home; his obsession. Consuming every hour of the day, every day of the week; studying page after page of Latin, Arabic and Carthaginian texts. He ate on a rickety table and slept fitfully on the floor. The darkest hours were filled with pungent smell of two large oil lamps balanced on each end of the reading table.

After the torture of Lambert, the Knights Templar, Muzawi was confident he had revealed all he knew. But still he needed the location of the Temple of Astarte before he could confirm what secrets lay under the sands of Tanis.

His first task was to find the earliest copies of texts relating to the Pharaoh Smendes who lived more than two thousand years ago. As a descendant of both Pharaoh Khufu and Pharaoh Shishak, Smendes chose to make Tanis his ruling city where he built extensive palaces and temples, all of which now lay in ruins.

Carefully Muzawi opened the next jar. As expected, the papyrus scrolls were dedicated to Smendes but as he transcribed the hieroglyphics he sensed he was on the right course. The first scroll referred to an account given by a sea captain who referred to a letter of accreditation from Smendes. The letter gave permission for his boat to go to Baalbek to procure the highest quality of Lebanese cedar wood in order to build a 'special altar' dedicated to Baal, in the Temple of Astarte. Many documents supported the notion of this cedar wood being used in the construction of a sacred coffer, including the one stolen by Moses.

Reading the second scroll his heart began to beat a little faster. He reread the text again before sitting back to take a sip of water. Recalling the words of the knight Lambert, the Templars were under orders to secure the tomb of a Pharaoh. Now the scroll confirmed the name. In the ruins of Tanis, in the Temple of Astarte, lay the royal tomb of Pharaoh Shishak. According to Lambert, two more names were linked to the tomb and Muzawi moved on to another room, now anxious to confirm the truth.

Another day passed before he found the next clue. It was the enigmatic story of Arius, from a letter written in Greek. Wiping away the sweat from his face, he deciphered the parchment.

At the age of seventy, Arius was one of the delegates at the Council of Nicea, convened some three hundred years after the death of Christ. Not long after the council, Arius was mysteriously denounced for his heretical views and he left for Egypt in disgrace. First he came to Alexandria then he went to Tanis, seemingly obsessed by the ruins. He personally directed the excavation of the ancient Temple of Astarte.

Muzawi turned up the flickering lamp and held up the first page, praying to Baal that it would reveal the whereabouts of the Temple. His perseverance was rewarded.

'...the map in the catacombs proved correct...three steps lead to a hollowed out niche on a floor of granite. Placed on an altar of marble, a perfectly preserved cedar wood coffer, no more than my arm in length. I *opened the coffer and found what I was looking for. Two perfect spheres...at times translucent then shining like pearls, held in place by strange metal claws...'*

Many of the words at the bottom of the page were impossible to translate but they suggested that Arius was determined to keep the 'two spheres' as far apart as possible.

A smaller page made from a different papyrus was attached by a wooden splint at the top. He separated the page and began to read the words written by Eusebius the Bishop of Caesarea. He was a friend and colleague of Arius and supported him at the Council of Nicea. Muzawi recognised his name as a renowned author of his day. Eusebius had drawn a map of the entrance to the catacombs, only two miles away.

Muzawi was breathless with excitement as he read the words. *"Kom el Shoqafa hides the secret of Shamir."*

'Shamir. The Stone from heaven,' Muzawi repeated, awestruck by the discovery.

Outside, in the dazzling light of the midday sun, Muzawi screwed up his eyes and called for his servant who ran towards him and stood to attention.

'Ishmael, send a messenger to Saladin to come to Alexandria at once. Then assemble the men with picks and shovels. Today we search for Shamir.'

Within sight of the mighty pyramids, the battle was about to commence and crucially time was running out for the Christian army. The Grand master of the Templars, Bertrand de Blanchefort, decided he would deal with the king personally and approached his tent demanding that he should be woken. King Amalric's bodyguard blocked his path.

Bertrand was furious. 'I am the Grand Master of the Knights

Templar. We are in danger of being overrun by General Shirkuh You must wake the king now!'

Stumbling out of his tent, Amalric contradicted the Grand Master. 'Master Bertrand, you fret like an old woman. We are not in danger of being overrun.'

Bertrand's face remained set with anger. He could not believe this fat boor of a king who was responsible for the deaths of many of his men, now seemed determined to continue his reign of stupidity. 'My lord king, I must insist…'

'You must insist!' Amalric interrupted. 'You do not insist on anything?'

Bertrand was seething and had to bite his tongue to keep his temper in check.

With a forced smile, Amalric breathed in deeply and his mood changed. 'What I mean to say is that the saints are on our side this day. I have had a glorious vision, courtesy of Bernard of Clairvaux.'

Bertrand was sure that the mention of Abbot Bernard was a deliberate ploy to rile him. With fists tightly clenched, it was difficult to keep his peace.

Amalric fingered the fragment of the true cross dangling from a chain around his neck. 'I was told I must be strong, and worthy of carrying a piece of Christ's own cross. Today I will lead the attack and Shirkuh and the army of Nuradin will be defeated.' The king's armourer brought his chain mail and shield while his horse was readied.

Bertrand was waiting for his captains to assemble when his Marshal rode up on his destrier with news of the Syrian army. 'Grand Master, the right flank advances under General Shirkuh, and the one called Saladin commands the baggage train in the centre.'

Bertrand spun round his eyes wide open. 'Are you sure it was him.'

'I have seen him with my own eyes, Grand Master. It is Saladin.'

Bertrand thought for a moment. 'It is too obvious. Saladin will be bound to yield his ground, to lure us into a trap. Shirkuh is the real threat. We will counter his attack quickly and decisively. Inform the captains.' He looked up the steep slope where Shirkuh was still advancing. 'Order the ranks to start the attack.'

After the first charge, the Templars were proving so effective Bertrand was optimistic they could break Shirkuh on the right. Then he looked on in utter dismay as King Amalric led his men headlong against the soft centre commanded by Saladin.

True to form, Saladin feinted a withdrawal and the sandy slope worked against Amalric as his attack wallowed in a maelstrom of ox and baggage carts.

From his vantage point, Bertrand held his breath as he watched Saladin come around the other side of the slope cutting off the king's infantry and many of his knights. Then the slaughter began in earnest. Amalric was surrounded and was saved only by the heroism of his own bodyguard who bravely sacrificed themselves while he escaped.

An hour later, Amalric was safely back in camp and was quick to praise his vision of Bernard as his saviour. He rounded on Bertrand. 'You see, even against impossible odds I have eluded the enemy. In the eyes of a saint, I have proved myself worthy of a piece of the true cross.'

Gazing up the slope, Bertrand could count at least thirty of Jerusalem's best knights strewn in pieces across the battlefield. Marshalling his own men at their assembly point, he swore under his breath that never again would his Order be party to the whims of the imbecile they had for a king.

Shirkuh and Saladin had no time to congratulate themselves. Although victorious in battle they were still outnumbered by the combined armies of Shawar and Amalric. As they discussed which route they would take back to Damascus, a messenger arrived asking Saladin to come immediately to Alexandria. It was from Muzawi.

'What reason does he give?' Shirkuh asked reasonably.

'Muzawi does not have to give a reason,' Saladin replied 'but he has promised the city gates will be opened for us.'

Shirkuh shook his head in dismay. 'You realise Shawar and Amalric will follow and we will be trapped within the walls.'

Unconcerned, Saladin shrugged his shoulders. 'Well are you coming with me or not?'

Shirkuh forced a smile. 'Your father would never forgive me if I returned without you.'

True to his word, the citizens of Alexandria gave free passage to Saladin and Shirkuh to enter the city, though Saladin suspected any army was preferable to that of Shawar.

While Shirkuh invested his time wisely with the defence of the city, Saladin joined Muzawi in the library. After weeks of sleepless nights, the shaman looked exhausted. Dotted around his room were half-eaten loaves and the floor was covered in vermin, though Muzawi seemed not to notice.

Saladin was worried for his mentor. His demeanour did little to disguise his inexplicable behaviour as he walked amongst the aisles of books, filled with endless reams of scrolls, while talking without pause and making little sense.

Muzawi held Saladin by the shoulders and stared into his eyes. 'All the pieces are in coming into place.'

Saladin pulled away. 'I don't understand, I thought you brought me here to tell me of your success.'

'I have succeeded, more than I could possibly have imagined,' he insisted. 'But first, it was necessary to confirm what was so important about the Temple of Astarte at Tanis.'

Saladin sighed then sat down.

Muzawi looked around to make sure they could not be overheard. He started by telling the story of Arius. 'Arius was a learned Christian scholar and was quite capable of discovering the whereabouts of the two spheres at Tanis and the power they held. Through fear alone, he knew to keep them apart. The first sphere he left in place then took the second one to Jerusalem. Once there, Arius begged Helena, the mother of Emperor Constantine, to bury the sphere under the tomb of Christ, safe from evil intent. This meeting was dutifully recorded by Helena's clerk and I believe the Templars have read the same document. Now believe this. It seems that Helena's clerk did not record the whole story. The truth is that Helena refused to accept the sphere, saying she would not have the tomb of Christ tainted by a pagan relic. The second sphere was never deposited in Jerusalem. So where did it end up?'

Muzawi took a gulp of wine but was too excited to sit down. He swept his hand over a pile of dusty scrolls. 'The answer lay in these letters. Arius was so demented by the sphere, he never let it leave his body. He kept it under his clothes, tied in a bag around his waist. His friend, Eusebius, could see Arius was becoming sick, no doubt acerbated by the resentment of his contemporaries. He escorted Arius to Lydda, where he received protection from Aetius, the Bishop of Lydda, who had also declared support for Arius at the Council of Nicea. While in Lydda, Arius made an agreement with the bishop. In the crypt of a small derelict church built around the time of Christ, he disposed of the sphere in a pool of poisonous water. The bishop agreed to rebuild the church, thereby sealing the pond within consecrated ground.'

Muzawi began pacing the floor again, perspiring heavily in the heat. 'Now with the support of two bishops, Arius was authorized by the Emperor Constantine to be restored to communion in Constantinople. But his health failed rapidly and the day before he was due to appear before all his peers, he died in the most exceptional circumstances.' Picking up the page written by Eusebius, Muzawi pointed to the notes in the margin. 'This commentary refers to a letter by Socrates Scholasticus that describes the death of Arius in detail.' He gave Saladin the letter from Socrates.

'...*on the way to Constantine's forum...amid a mass of supporters he collapsed...his bowels vacated and then his intestines protruded as he writhed in agony...later in his throes of death, his stomach, liver and other organs were seen amid the copious volumes of blood and offal.*'

Wide eyed with astonishment, Saladin reread the passage. 'So what killed him?'

'The curse of the spheres killed him. Naturally, Eusebius thought Arius had been poisoned by his rivals. In secret, he brought his body back to Lydda and colluded with the Bishop of Lydda to have the body interred in a marble sarcophagus, inside the crypt of the restored church. It would lay directly over the entrance to the poisonous chamber below. In death, Arius was to protect the world from the sphere he feared so much.'

Saladin interjected. 'But it is well known that Saint George was buried in the crypt, in a carved marble tomb.'

'Yes, Saint George was probably martyred at Lydda. A misguided mason mistakenly believed the sarcophagus contained his remains and dedicated the sarcophagus with elaborate engravings.'

Saladin gazed into the distance. 'So one sphere is at Tanis and the other is in Lydda. Tell me again. Why do we waste our time looking for these cursed spheres, if we cannot find the two sceptres. You told me, we need both.'

'When we possess both spheres then the sceptres will reveal themselves. And the sceptres contain the power of Shamir.'

'Shamir?'

'They are the 'stones from heaven' and give the sceptres a mighty, unstoppable force. But we must act fast, before the Knights Templars get there first.'

Saladin remained quiet, absorbing everything but still unsure.

Muzawi still had a glint in his eye. 'I guarantee Jerusalem shall fall. Imagine…the power to build Temples that reach the stars or to destroy cities with a single blow. The world will fall to my will…'

Saladin's face dropped. 'Your will?'

'You must listen to me, Saladin. Just remember that your father Shishak failed at Baalbek…'

'Yes…he was killed by the knights,' Saladin said grimly.

'All I know is that he failed,' Muzawi said honestly. 'I am a descendant of the Shaman of Baal and it is my sworn duty to act as mentor to the descendants of Baal. Like my father Tammuz, my prime responsibility is that of guardian…'

Saladin frowned. 'Guardian ?'

'To be guardian of the two spheres, of course.'

'And where is my place in this great plan?'

Muzawi placed his hand on Saladin's shoulder. 'One day you will be master of the world and you will be feared as a demon or a God.'

'What if I don't want to be seen as a demon?'

Muzawi blinked. 'No…no, it is just that men have always been suspicious of the latent powers of your forefathers. At the 'time of promises', we…you shall test that power to the limit.'

For the first time, Saladin was deeply troubled by the words of Muzawi. He stared at the endless rows of leather bound texts. 'I think you have spent too long buried underground with these old scrolls. I just need an army…'

'I know where to find the map to the Temple of Astarte and the location of Shamir,' Muzawi interrupted. 'My men are clearing the entrance to Kom-el- Shoqafa.'

' You mean the catacombs of Alexandria? They are a myth.'

'They *were* a myth. This last six days, while you were playing soldiers, I found the entrance near a massive Roman column.'

Saladin had little enthusiasm for searching airless catacombs.

'Shirkuh will not approve of any of this.'

'Then we will say nothing until we have found the map. And with two of us, it will take half as long. Compared with your powers of perception, I am a just a blind man stumbling around in the dark. I am sure the general will demonstrate his worth in other ways.'

Later in the day Shirkuh joined them at the entrance to the catacombs and reproached them both for not considering the fate that awaited them. 'The city is under siege and starving and you are wandering an underground wilderness. Listen, I am taking a raiding party for food and supplies. I should be back within seven days.' In the glow of the sunset, he glanced at the mounds of debris around the entrance and shook his head before mounting up. 'Saladin, don't let this outlandish task distract you and cloud your judgement. Remember, the walls must not be breached.'

Saladin nodded. 'Do not worry for our sakes.'

The great shaft was surrounded by a steep staircase and Saladin was amazed at the depth of the structure. After three weeks of digging, the workforce had excavated to a depth equivalent to the height of twenty men.

'Like in Rome, the catacombs were used to store the dead,' Muzawi explained. 'The bodies were lowered down the shaft while the living walked down the stairs.' Near the foot of the stairwell an entrance to a passageway had been revealed. He ordered the men to clear the last of the debris, while he lit two lamps, giving one to Saladin.

'Are you ready?' he asked.

They crouched down and crept into the passageway that opened into a rotunda. Muzawi walked into a large chamber to the left. So far they had seen only a few carvings with Egyptian-like embellishments on the walls, but nothing that looked like a map.

Muzawi reappeared shaking his head. 'We are going to need more lamps and torches.'

The next compartment led to the top of some steep steps and holding their lamps high, they proceeded downwards only to find the stairway blocked by a rock fall. They looked at each other.

'It's not as bad as it looks..perhaps one day, maybe two...' Muzawi said optimistically.

Saladin took the delay as a sign to heed Shirkuh's words of warning. 'I need to speak to my officers on the wall while you decide the best course to take.'

He left Muzawi and climbed back up the stairs to the surface. After briefing his men, he slept a few hours then at sunrise he descended back into the catacombs. The blocked stairway had been fully excavated and when he reached the final steps he was handed a torch by Muzawi's bodyguard.

'Take care, my lord. The floor here is wet and muddy,' Ishmael warned him. 'Follow me closely.'

The water and silt eddied around his knees and made walking very tiresome. They reached some more steps leading upwards to a junction.

Ishmael pointed behind them. 'Just as well the fall did not come this far or we would not have made it through to the royal chamber.'

'The royal chamber!' Saladin exclaimed, dragging his feet up the steps. He held up his torch and gasped at the unbelievable sight in front of him. Carvings of Medusa and her serpents flanked either side of the entrance to the burial chamber and a row of columns supported massive lintels. It resembled a mixture of Egyptian and Roman lore, thought Saladin. A lamp appeared from the far side of the chamber and he saw the unmistakable outline of Muzawi stood next to Ishmael.

'Well. What do you think,' Muzawi asked, proud of his discovery.

Saladin could not tear his eyes from the walls. 'I was not expecting to see such carvings. But have you found the map yet?'

'There is a piece of plaster hiding some…'

Suddenly a large stone dropped from the ceiling and cracked sharply on the floor, making Saladin jump backwards. All eyes stared at the ceiling. One of the diggers in the shaft emerged shouting from the swirling water. 'My lord, water is coming fast. We must all leave now.'

Saladin stumbled back down the steps into the water. He gave a backward glance to see Muzawi stood with Ishmael, shouting from the top of the steps. 'I will stay…don't worry I shall...'

Before he had no time to finish his sentence, the roof above Muzawi began to cave in.

Saladin was pulled by the digger into the water and back to the shaft. By the time they had climbed half the stairwell, the water had completely filled the passageway to the ceiling, then abruptly stopped.

'I wonder if it was designed to do that,' Saladin muttered to himself. He turned to the digger. 'What is your name?'

'Hussein, my lord'.

'You have earned my gratitude, Hussein. Now go to the others and tell the best swimmer amongst you that I have a hundred dinars for the first man who can reach Muzawi.'

Hussein looked at Saladin and the muddy water that churned below. 'God willing, air is trapped in the shaft at the bottom of the rotunda. I will swim to Muzawi, my lord.' He took a deep breath then suddenly he was gone.

Eight days later, Shirkuh returned with three carts loaded with food. Saladin was surprised the general had succeeded again in obtaining a truce with Amalric.

'On the condition that both armies leave Egypt with immediate effect,' Shirkuh confirmed.

Saladin's face fell. He told Shirkuh of the rock fall in the tomb and presented Hussein, telling him of his bravery in swimming underwater to where Muzawi was trapped. He was adamant. 'We can still talk to Muzawi. We cannot leave while he is still alive.'

But this time Shirkuh was equally insistent. 'No you are wrong. We must keep to the terms of the agreement or the Christian army will enter the city…and you know what that means.'

'Yes. They will kill everyone,' Saladin said grimly.

Hussein spoke up. 'My lord, I will stay in the shaft where no one will see me. There is a small hole in the rubble through which I can keep Lord Muzawi supplied with food and water, until you can negotiate another truce to free him.'

Shirkuh looked pleased with Hussein and slapped him on the back. 'Give this brave man some money and let us prepare to leave now. I have a feeling Muzawi will fare better than most.'

Saladin handed the young man a bag of coins. 'I shall give you a hundred dinars now. If you succeed in freeing Muzawi, you will be rewarded with a hundred more, I promise.'

The scrawny looking digger bowed and kissed Saladin's robe. 'Allah be praised my lord. I shall not let Lord Muzawi down.'

Hussein scurried like a rabbit back to the shaft, with a parcel of food wrapped in a waxed robe, praying that none of Shawar's men had seen him as they entered the city.

Muzawi was relieved when he heard Hussein return. Through a tiny gap between two massive stones, the digger passed some fruit, bread and a water skin. Although the walls of the tomb ran with tiny rivulets of water that leaked from the ceiling, Muzawi did not intend to drink from the damp, slimy pools. 'At least we shall not starve. Did you bring oil for the lamp?' he asked.

'Only this spare torch, my lord. Tell me how is Ishmael? Is he conscious yet?'

A faint croaky voice answered. 'I can hear you Hussein.'

Relieved to hear Ishmael's voice, Hussein had to hold back the urge to cry. 'You sound in pain.'

Ishmael looked down at the smashed bones protruding from his flesh. 'My leg is broken. But do not worry for it will mend. Can you see a way out from your side?'

Looking around the blockage, he saw immediately it would be fruitless. 'The stones are too big. You must find a way out from your side.'

Muzawi answered. 'I have looked down all the passageways and they are filled with chambers and niches for the dead. There is no way out.' He put his face closer to the stones. 'Hussein, listen carefully to me. Go back into the town and get some more lamp oil. When you return have a look around the annex to the rotunda. There may be a secret door or a hidden passage. I will look again from this side.'

'Yes my lord. I will go now and return before nightfall, I promise.'

Muzawi heard him take deep breaths before he slid into the water. Then silence.

Climbing up the staircase Hussein reached the surface and walked only a few paces before being disorientated by the glare of the sun. He heard voices close by and turned in the opposite direction, stumbling noisily to the ground.

Before he knew what was happening, he was surrounded by soldiers shouting at him. Moments later they had a rope around his arms and marched him away for interrogation.

Chapter 8

Bungay
Suffolk

Roger de Beaumont sank his teeth into the succulent duck and took a swig of ale. 'I wonder what my father would say if he knew I was in Bungay with you.'

Hugh was sat opposite the future earl of Leicester. 'Oh, and why is that? ' he asked innocently. 'I thought your father was the master of secret meetings these days.'

'If truth be told, my father and Richard de Lucy have little fondness for you. But you must know that.'

'I know they only sit at my table when it suits them to do so,' Hugh replied caustically.

The barbed comment did not go amiss on Robert. 'I do not wish to appear disingenuous, but no one can change what has gone before. I genuinely believe we have more to gain by acting together than you think.'

Hugh asked Marcus to have the table cleared and dismiss the servants for the night. He showed Robert to the chairs near the fireplace and ordered they should not be disturbed. 'It is quieter here than at Framlingham. Not so many ears to the door. Better to talk now, while your wife accompanies Gundred at the priory; though I must admit, Petronella did not seem too happy about praying with the nuns.'

Robert laughed. 'Feisty isn't she. She will not give them any peace if the wine is not to her taste. By the way, I have not seen your steward this evening.'

'He is unwell and has taken to his bed at Framlingham.'

'Oh, well I suppose he is somewhat aged. Nevertheless, I hope his health improves soon.' Robert leaned forward. 'My father will not live forever and I have to consider my position as earl, when the time comes...'

Hugh shook his head and chuckled. 'You may not have noticed, but I am eight years older than your father.'

Robert looked hard at Hugh. Apart from the slight balding of the hair and the lines on his forehead, Hugh did not look much older than fifty, though he calculated he must be over seventy. Somehow, there was always more to Hugh Bigod than met the eye. 'My lord, I am one of those who believe that men like you were born to be virtually immortal. I just assume you have made a pact with the devil that ensures your longevity.'

Hugh stared at Robert, then both their faces cracked into laughter.

'I shall take that as a compliment,' Hugh chortled. Deep inside he believed himself to be still young at heart, but questioned if he wanted to spend his twilight years in the company of over-ambitious men like Robert.

'Forgive my ill-chosen words,' Robert apologised. 'But seriously, have you not noticed that while Becket wallows in exile, the king has found cause to re-establish his grip on our lands? The knight's fees and scutage are increased without consultation, crippling all but the richest of noblemen.'

Hugh nodded impassively.

'He places a stranglehold around any baron whose only fault is ambition. Look to your own stronghold. Through any number of cohorts, the king holds Norwich, Eye, Walton, and Thetford, and now the mightiest castle of all will be built at Orford. He will squeeze until you have nothing left...'

Hugh lifted his head and was quick to correct Robert. 'No you are wrong. Orford Castle was Sisland's project.'

'Hugh, my friend, I have come to tell you the king has taken you for a fool. It was always his intention to build Orford, to take away your supply line from the sea and tighten the noose until you squirm. All this time, he lied to you about Sisland's intention.'

Hugh felt his chest tighten and his heart race. He lifted the wine goblet to his lips but most of it spilt. He wanted to speak but the anger inside prevented any coherent words from forming.

Robert noticed the impact he was having and paused to pour another drink. 'If you want confirmation then go to Orford. The foundations are finished and the second course of walls are ready to infill…by the king's engineers.'

Hugh stood up and even though the hall was warm enough, he threw more wood upon the fire. The simple action gave him pause for thought. He leaned against the fireplace. 'So what were you saying about Becket?'

'I used to liken Becket to a swarm of bees. No matter how much the king flailed his arms in a rage, he would always get stung. His obsession with Becket meant he gave little thought to anything else. We need a bold move that will bring Becket back to the fore and distract the king from making both our lives a misery.'

Hugh stared into the flames of the fire. 'Everyone knows that Becket has gone to ground in France, but under which stone?'

'What would you say if I knew which stone to turn over?'

Hugh basked in the heat from the fire, churning over Robert's words.

Robert had gauged his argument well. 'Look at yourself Hugh. You sit safely in your castle playing happy families. Where is your spirit…where is your infamous guile? Is this yearning for obscurity truly the way you want to end your days?'

Through the emotional turmoil, the same painful truth kept nagging Hugh.

The king has taken you for a fool.

They heard footsteps and Petronella stormed into the hall,

slamming the door behind her. Her shrill accent pierced the air. 'If I have to listen to another fucking prayer I shall go mad.' Taller than most men, she marched across to the fireplace and poured some wine from a jug. She turned to Hugh. 'I hope this tastes better than the crap in the priory. Where are your servants? I can't eat any of the bloody gruel they serve over there.' She put down her cup and placed her ample frame on a chair in front of the fire. Sweeping back her unkempt hair, she wiped her mouth on her sleeve.

Moments later, Gundred opened the door and took off her muddy boots.

Petronella's voice crossed the hall. 'Ah, here is the lady of the house! These two have left us nothing to eat and I am starving. Can you see to getting some proper food on the table, my dear?'

The colour in Gundred's cheeks reddened and for a moment she looked fit to burst but she held her temper. Without a murmur she opened the kitchen door and disappeared, calling out loudly for a cook.

Hugh stood up and walked towards the kitchen door. 'Unfortunately I have dismissed the staff for the night but I am sure we can find you some scraps.'

'I'm not a bloody dog,' Petronella shouted after him, indignantly.

'That is true. But even dogs know what time to eat, my dear.' Hugh went through the door not caring if she had heard or not.

Gundred was pacing the kitchen, her fisted clenched at her side. 'I cannot believe the way that woman behaves.' She was barely able to conceal the vehemence in her voice. 'God forgive me, how I loathe that arrogant charlatan. For everyone's sake get her out of here.'

Hugh had never seen his wife look so angry. 'Don't fret. They are leaving tomorrow.'

'Thank the Lord for that small mercy. The last thing I want is that witch tangling with the servants. It is just as well poor d'Cheney is in Framlingham.'

Gundred relaxed her shoulders a little and turned away from Hugh. 'I think I shall stay a few days longer. The priory does give me some comfort...and I always have baby Hugh. He is such a darling and you hardly spend any time with him.'

Hugh grunted. 'I'm sure when he is a little older...'

'Oh no matter. In any case Roger is in Buckingham and he did say he would come and visit.'

Hugh was aware that Roger gave many promises that he never kept and while his wife sought comfort in God, he thought it best not to complain. 'Don't concern yourself about Roger. The boy is fine.'

She kissed Hugh on the cheek. 'I fret because he is no longer a boy. I am going to bed. Make my excuses to that...that woman.'

Hugh was about to say he had decided to go to France to see Becket but thought better of it. His news could wait another day.

Always impatient, Hugh waited for the spate of bad whether in the channel to clear. Twice he had been denied a crossing due to rough seas and had to return to Framlingham. He had never been so secretive about his movements before, and Gundred tried again to discover why it was so imperative for him to go. 'I had hoped your days of crossing that treacherous water had gone,' she mooted.

All the waiting was making him anxious. 'I am afraid it is a clandestine mission and I don't want anyone to know that I am in Normandie. If anyone asks, you must say I am on the south coast, visiting Arundel or something.'

'And you are taking Marcus with you, not d'Cheney.'

Hugh nodded. 'How is the old sod today?'

For a fleeting moment, Gundred considered using d'Cheney's bad health as an excuse to keep her husband in Framlingham. 'He is no better,' she replied honestly, biting her tongue.

Hugh looked absently out of the window. 'I was looking to

promote Marcus as my steward.'

'It seems like only yesterday you took him from my stable to be your squire. Be careful for I see too much ambition in his eyes,' Gundred warned.

Hugh ignored her words and looked to the clearing skies. He sensed the wind was dropping. 'I think it is looking a little more promising. Hopefully, this time I shall be sailing.' He turned around to see Marcus standing by the door and ordered him to prepare the horses. 'We shall leave for the coast in the morning.'

They arrived at Sandwich only to be disappointed yet again. The currents around the inlet were notorious and Hugh had to wait again at the tiny seaport for favourable conditions. He had learnt from Becket's escape from England that the tiny harbour attracted little attention from the king's men as it was still under the stewardship of the cathedral.

The captain of the ship was as anxious as Hugh to sail, often moaning that he made no money from being moored to the jetty. Hugh ensured he was well paid for his discretion.

They settled into an inn for a second night in a row. Apparently, everything was set for a dawn sailing though Hugh knew the best of intentions could be spoilt by a subtle change in wind and tide.

While they waited, he took the opportunity to get to know Marcus better. Since the Trelaw incident, neither of them had mentioned the unfortunate misunderstanding, but if truth be told, Hugh took some comfort from Marcus being beholden to him. The unspoken secret would safeguard his loyalty in the future.

Marcus came from a well-respected family near Warwick, and like many of the second and third sons of noblemen, his background was ecclesiastical, providing him with the ability to read and write. Fortunately, his manner remained unsullied with any religious fervour. As a groom, he had impressed Gundred since she was a teenager and for more than five years, he had effortlessly tended to

Hugh's demands as his senior squire. More frequently of late, he had helped the ailing d'Cheney with his administrative tasks.

It made sense that Marcus was a potential candidate to take over from d'Cheney. His only reservation was his age. At thirty-two, was he too young to appreciate the complex politics of the day?

Hugh struck up a conversation. 'Well, you are probably wondering why we are sailing from a jetty in Sandwich.'

Marcus immediately brightened up. 'My lord, I assume we are embarking on a covert mission. Otherwise, we would have sailed via Portsmouth. I believe Thomas Becket has taken up residence in France. But before we can look for him am I right in thinking we should first obtain consent from King Louis?'

'And how would you go about obtaining that consent?'

'Well, if we went to the palace in Paris we could be kept waiting a week or more. So much better if we had an ally with the ear of Louis, in order to expedite matters.'

Hugh was impressed as he climbed onto his mattress. 'We depart at dawn. Make sure the guards do their job…no prying eyes.'

The crossing to Boulogne was swift and while Hugh and his men waited on the quayside for the horses to disembark, a troop of horsemen appeared.

Two noblemen dismounted and walked boldly up to Hugh. More than ten years had passed since the murder of Robert Picot at Walton castle but Hugh was able to recognise Philip, the son of Count Thierry.

'Earl Hugh Bigod, you look well. I pray these are better times than when we last met.' He turned to the other nobleman. 'This is my brother Matthew, the Count of Boulogne.'

The young count looked disinterested and gave Hugh a condescending smile. 'My brother Philip has told me of the high respect he has for you. I give you safe passage through my lands as does King Louis.' Matthew looked to the skies, obviously keen to return to his castle. 'Anyway, I am pleased we have met and now I shall leave you in the capable hands of my younger brother. If I can be of further service…' His words were left hanging in the wind as he rode off taking his marshal and half his escort with him.

Hugh turned to Philip. 'So, can tell me what the hell is going on.'

'Sorry for all the subterfuge, but King Louis was expecting you. He has spies everywhere. He asked me to help you, in the hope that your actions would prove an inconvenience for King Henry.'

'You know the whereabouts of Becket?' Hugh asked.

'King Louis and the Pope have installed him in an abbey south of Paris. However, a boatload of Becket's relations have just landed in Caen and are making for the 'not so secret' location.'

As the escort gathered around them, Philip watched his brother ride up the slope from the harbour towards his impressive castle. 'My apologies for my brother's offhand behaviour. Unfortunately, the recent news of our mother's death in Bethany still affects him badly, though he would be the last to admit it. Now our father has just arrived back from the Holy Land and I am afraid his health is failing.'

Though Hugh had never met Countess Sybille, he was reminded of the brief encounter with Count Thierry of Flanders many years ago. Over the years, the Count and his wife had become famous for the service they had given in the Holy Land, both in battle and pilgrimage. He had little understanding of what drove nobles like them to travel across the world time and again, in search of thinly disguised salvation.

While Hugh feigned interest in the Count's family, Marcus was avidly listening to every word. He absorbed every nuance, every scrap of information; piecing together the fragments of the dramatic lives of those who succumbed to the lure of the Holy Land and those that died there.

Chapter 9

Pontigny
France

A chill wind whistled through the cloisters of Pontigny but Thomas Becket did not feel the cold. Gone were the fine silks and furs that used to adorn his body, but he did not mourn their passing. By now, he was immune to the chaffing of the filthy sackcloth, riddled with lice that relentlessly consumed his flesh every hour of the day and night.

He revelled in his ration of bread and bitter water and relished the occasional mix of oatmeal and gruel. Every day in the infirmary, he would tend the sick and wash the feet of the poor, handing out alms to those he considered most in need. Every night he would gladly scourge himself before Christ's Cross then walk with his feet bared back to his tiny cell to pray for God's forgiveness. For Thomas was determined to rid himself of a lifetime of pride and find true humility in the eyes of the Almighty.

The grey sky was darkening when a message from the abbot called him to his house. Opening the door he was surprised to see Earl Hugh Bigod and a young noble stood with the abbot. He quickly surveyed the room and there appeared to be nothing threatening about their behaviour.

The abbot introduced Hugh and Philip to Thomas, explaining that they were his guests but had specially asked to see Thomas, in the name of peace.

Becket acknowledged Hugh with a wry smile. They settled down in front of his fireplace and the abbot served a jug of wine before politely taking his leave.

Hugh was astonished at the change that had come over Thomas Becket and wondered a moment for his sanity. The great statesman of the English court had become a bedraggled beggar. How could any sane man give up everything in the name of God?

Thomas held his head high, revealing the aging skin that hung from his gaunt face. 'Do you come with word from King Henry?'

'It would be useless to try and mislead you, my lord Archbishop,' Hugh explained. 'We come on our own accord, but with both our interests at heart. Since you have been in exile, the scale of injustice has become commonplace in England. The king only listens to the evil protagonists that whisper schemes in his ear. He has confiscated all your property and expelled all your relations, friends and servants in an orgy of reprisal. No one, including myself, is safe from his temper. For as sure as day turns to night, he will destroy the church hierarchy and all the barons in his great design?''

Becket listened impassively as Hugh carried on listing all the bishops and members of the king's household who were rallying against the archbishop. He continued his dire litany. 'As we speak Richard de Lucy walks the corridors of your castle at Saltwood and the king's cronies ravage all of Kent, turning it into a wasteland.'

Becket's head dropped. 'You say de Lucy turns against me?'

Hugh looked at the archbishop's tonsure. 'The whole court follows the king blindly into oblivion, and only you can stop them. But in exile you are of little use to anyone.'

Thomas hesitated then stood up. 'You have come a long way for such a short pilgrimage. If there is nothing else, I shall go now to pray and seek guidance from God.'

Hugh was surprised at the sudden dismissal, but before he could say any more, Becket had gone through the door to the chapel.

Hugh looked bewildered at Philip; sure of the unmitigated failure of their mission.

Outside the abbots house Hugh heard a commotion and rushed

outside with Philip. Disembarking from a cart were about five families comprising some twenty men, women and children. They looked cold and frightened and under the supervision of the abbot, the monks ushered them quickly into the refectory.

'Did I hear right?' Hugh asked the abbot, 'that they are relatives of Becket, banished by King Henry?'

The abbot was distraught. 'Yes and there are thirty more arriving tomorrow. This is impossible...where is Thomas?' He scuttled off into his house, shouting orders to his monks as he went.

Hugh smiled at Philip. 'True to form, de Lucy has stirred up a wasps nest at court.'

The next morning the abbey was in chaos. Nearly fifty fugitives from England were wandering aimlessly around the abbey buildings, looking for food and a mattress to sleep on.

The abbot tried to keep order in the refectory and could not hide his distress. He led Hugh into a corridor, away from the bedlam. 'My lord earl, I am so sorry for all the mayhem but we are in serious trouble. King Henry has exiled all the relatives and servants of Archbishop Becket. An hour ago, a messenger arrived with a sealed letter from the king telling me that if I fed and housed any citizens he had banished, then he would seize the assets of the Cistercian abbeys in England. I cannot believe even his warped mind would do such a thing but I cannot risk such a disaster. I have my duty to God to consider. Archbishop Becket is no longer welcome at this abbey. I am sorry.' He rejoined the throng of people and was quickly surrounded by his anxious monks.

The abbot asked for Becket to be brought to him.

Hugh and Philip smiled in self-congratulation. 'We could not have planned this any better,' Hugh grinned. 'The timing of the messenger from England was better than perfect.'

Philip nodded warily. 'I think we had best depart before anyone connects our presence here to this unsightly fiasco.'

Pleased with the events in France, Hugh stopped for a meal and an overnight stop at his usual tavern in Colchester, situated midway between London and Framlingham. After swilling more than a few ales with Bonham and his men, Hugh took to his bed, pleased that he would soon be back at Framlingham.

Suddenly a violent shaking woke him from his drunken sleep and he stared up at the timbers in the ceiling above his head, hoping they would stay secured. Covered in dust he ran outside, only to see the horses being led from the stables just as the roof collapsed.

A cry of agony came from a stable lad and then only silence. Bonham ran to his side, joined by others who quickly gathered around Hugh and watched as the boy was pulled from the wreckage, his legs crushed to a bloody pulp.

Satisfied that his men and horses had escaped injury, Hugh ordered everyone to mount up. The boy was declared dead and he threw a small bag of coins to the tavern master and professed his sorrow at his loss.

Soon they were heading north into the glow of dawn. The morning sun was still hidden in low cloud as they approached Framlingham he sensed that all was not well. He ordered two of his men to go on ahead and organise an immediate inspection of the castle walls and the town.

As he approached the entrance to the castle, a young groom intercepted him. With his head hung low, he could not look Hugh in the eye. 'My lord, her Ladyship says she will meet you at your steward's house in the town.'

D'Cheney would never have gone to his house unless his condition was serious, thought Hugh.

'His end is in sight my lord earl,' the groom answered, his voice shaking in distress.

Hugh was saddened but not overly surprised by the news as his steward had been ill for some time. Now it seemed he had taken to his old family abode, to pass his last days in the house where he was born.

Solemnly, Hugh dismounted then with Bonham in attendance, they followed the groom a few streets away to a small peasant's hovel. Upon entering through a small door, the unmistakable scent of death added to Hugh's distaste of the building. The chamber was even worse.

Standing next to d'Cheney's bed, a priest was muttering the last rites and was startled by the sudden arrival of Earl Bigod. 'My lord earl, the omens are bad.'

In the dark of the small room, Hugh could barely make out the bed. 'Is there nothing the physician could do?'

The priest clasped his hands. 'His fate does not lie in the hands of others. God is displeased with his humble minions and he tests the faith of us all. The sinners of Osea Island were punished in a fireball, and now He shakes the very earth beneath our feet, causing the houses of the ungodly to fall at a stroke.'

Hugh had felt the effects of the earth moving and considered such random acts had little to do with God. Such sanctimonious drivel annoyed him intently, but he held his tongue out of respect for his dying friend. He gazed upon his face of and saw the sunken features and the deathly pallor. Taking to a chair, he quietly kept vigil at d'Cheney's side, listening to each futile gasp of air that senselessly prolonged the inevitable.

An hour passed when a shaft of light from the door shattered the darkness as Gundred entered the room. She held young Hugh by the shoulders and cajoled the boy forward to be at his father's side. Hugh smiled at his son as the eight-year-old placed a wooden toy horse in d'Cheney's hand.

'Is he going to die soon, Papa?' young Hugh asked with the true voice of innocence.

'Yes, my son, d'Cheney will die soon.'

'And will he go to heaven?'

Hugh looked across to Gundred, who looked at the priest. 'Yes, he is sure to go to heaven. Let us go now back to the castle.' He left the room with Gundred and his son.

It disappointed Hugh that his first son Roger had not responded to his message to pay his final respects to d'Cheney. The rift between them was inexorably widening and now he felt he hardly knew him. D'Cheney had been a good mentor to Roger and probably more like a father than he had ever been. Roger should have shown him some respect.

Hugh ate a bowl of soup and bread before continuing his vigil at his steward's bedside. The day dragged by and the priest seemed content to mutter psalms and prayers to pass the time.

Hugh wondered how much d'Cheney had paid the priest to pray over bed in his final hours and to absolve him of his sins.

Clutching the toy horse, d'Cheney's hand began to shake. Then without warning, the door burst open and a tall young man was silhouetted against the bright outside light.

Hugh could hardly believe how much his son had grown up. The awkward adolescent stance had gone, to be replaced by a well-built young man.

Ignoring his father, Roger discarded his mantle and walked solemnly to the bed, followed closely by Gundred. 'Am I too late?' he asked breathlessly.

The priest was sprinkling holy water over the bed. 'His time is close,' he replied in a hushed voice.

Roger knelt down on the opposite side of the bed to his father and closed his eyes as he recited the Lord's Prayer, followed by a psalm. 'Though I walk through the valley of death, I shall feel no evil...'

With a clatter, the toy horse fell from d'Cheney's hand onto the floor, resonating around the room and mingling with the rattle of his last breath.

The priest closed d'Cheney's eyes then pulled the blanket gently over his face. He nodded to Hugh then left the room. Outside he was heard to ask the servants to bring the coffin from the hallway.

Roger looked at his father. 'I am sorry I was late, but I was in Normandie when I got the message.'

'With William Albini, no doubt.' Hugh could not hide the bitterness in his voice.

Before Roger could reply, Gundred moved next to him and gently held his arm. 'I am pleased you were here at the end. I am sure it is what d'Cheney would have wanted. Such a shame he had no living family.' She put her arm around Roger and gently comforted him then turned to look at Hugh. 'There is a messenger waiting to see you but I thought you should remain undisturbed. He has been outside for an hour.'

'Yes, of course,' Hugh said, still shaken by the death of his steward and the sudden appearance of his son. He walked down the four steps into the tiny entrance and acknowledged the messenger who was standing next to Marcus. He signalled him to come over. Due to his fine clothing, Hugh assumed he was from the king then Hugh suddenly realised he was wearing the colours of the Archbishop of Canterbury. Sweat was running down his face of the messenger and his hand trembled as he nervously handed the scroll towards Hugh.

'You can hand that to my new steward.'

Marcus looked at Hugh and gave a short bow. 'Sire.' He unfurled the parchment and turned into the light, reading out loud. 'My lord, your name appears on a list…the document is addressed to a number of recipients. The archbishop declares under the authority invested in him by Pope Alexander…oh by God's breath…'

Out of the corner of his eye, Hugh noticed the messenger had discretely exited the house and remounted his horse, the hooves speeding over the cobblestones.

'Well speak up man. What does Becket have to say?' Hugh demanded.

Marcus stuttered, his face turning bright red. 'You have been excommunicated by Thomas Becket, the Archbishop of Canterbury.'

The scroll fluttered innocently in the breeze as the two men stared at each other in disbelief. Hugh turned his back to hide his fury.

Marcus continued reading. 'The list is long, my lord; it includes the Archbishops of York and London and Salisbury as well as all those that participated in the coronation of the king's son. But aside your name, he says he has sought Gods guidance...and while you have done nought but deceive God and kept hold of lands belonging to Pentney Abbey.'

Hugh cried out. 'Pentney! That God forsaken stinking church and pond that calls itself a monastery.' He snatched the scroll from Marcus and read the detail himself. 'Of course, I remember now. I was due to give a hundred acres to the monastery but the king insisted otherwise. I had to rescind the order on his say so.' Hugh handed the scroll back to Marcus. 'But there is more to this than Pentney. I was mistaken to think that Becket could be so easily led.'

From the steps of the house, Roger emerged with Gundred having overheard much of the shouting. Roger called out accusingly. 'I wonder why I am not surprised that my own father is guilty of fuelling discord between the king and his archbishop.'

Hugh's face broke into a grimace. 'Do not flatter me with such cunning and deviousness. Believe me, the king made the biggest mistake of his life the moment he made Becket Archbishop. Everything that followed that one blunder, would have happened anyway, with or without my say.'

For a moment, they faced each other, both of them aware that the next words spoken would dictate the outcome of their relationship for years to come.

Hugh took a breath and opened his mouth, but it was Gundred who spoke first. 'Roger, please stay a while. We have so much to talk about...'

Roger faced his father; close enough to feel his breath. 'There is nothing to keep me here. Let me leave you to your scheming. It is what you do best.'

At a stroke, Hugh saw their future crumble into pieces. 'Marcus, my son's horse is being fed and watered on the green. Will you please accompany him to collect his steed.'

Whatever words were trapped on Roger's lips, they remained unspoken. He turned sharply and followed Marcus without a backward glance.

Walking to the green, they were within sight of the groom who was waiting patiently with his horse. No one else was close enough to hear Marcus as he suddenly stopped to speak, catching Roger by surprise.

'I think it is time you know something of the truth about your family. Do you remember a few years ago, the death of that squire Trelaw from Osea island?'

Roger blinked, trying to regain his composure. 'Why do you ask? Do you know who killed him?'

Marcus looked around the green, making sure they could not be overheard. 'No, I don't know who killed him, except for those peasant morons who found him. But I did have an interesting conversation with Trelaw on the day he was killed. He told me your father's brother is named William Bigod and he did not die on the White Ship.'

Roger could not hide his shock. 'How the hell do you know that?'

Marcus continued, pleased with the reaction. 'He swore that

William has lived for many years in the Holy Land. That he had a secret tryst with the Countess Sybille, witnessed by lord Henry Malache, who was sent into exile to Osea Island…'

Roger had heard enough of the revelation. Everything began to fall into place. 'After all this time…William is alive.'

He looked back towards the castle, and realised any further confrontation with his father would be a waste of time. Denial would follow any accusation. He had heard enough secrets and lies to last a lifetime. Smouldering with resentment, he leapt onto his horse. 'Mark my words squire Marcus, if this is true my father will burn in hell and you would be wise to keep your thoughts to yourself lest you join him.'

Roger rode off without looking back. Now he wanted nothing to do with his father. Waiting for him at Haughley Castle was the love of his life and he was simply wasting his time with his so-called family in Framlingham.

Marcus smiled as he watched Roger leave, satisfied that the secret told by Trelaw had more than a whiff of truth. Earl Hugh Bigod of Norfolk was no more the true earl than he was.

Chewing over his thoughts he spied the blacksmith riding alongside the green on its way to the castle.

'Where the hell have you been?' he rebuked. 'We have horses at the castle waiting to be shod for three days.'

'I was delayed at Orford. The ground tremors caused a lot of damage and they needed my help to prop up buildings…and suchlike.'

At the mention of Orford, Marcus was suddenly interested. 'Really. What sort of damage?'

'The blacksmith took a swig from his water skin and spat on the ground. He did not appreciate the likes of Marcus taking him to task. 'Whole place was like bloody Jericho. Them foundations were the height and depth of two men and all of them had cracks, wide enough to put my fist through. They'll have to start again I reckon.'

Marcus smiled to himself and hurried back to the manor house. Moments later he saw Hugh walking with his wife across the bailey.

'Did you see my son leave?' Hugh asked.

Marcus recounted faithfully. 'I saw him leave the village at speed, my lord.'

'Good. My trust in him has gone the same way.'

'My lord, while you are rightly saddened by these events this day, I have just learnt the most inspiring news. I know well of your lack of faith in the Lord, but God himself seems to have smiled upon you.' Marcus told him word for word, what the blacksmith had said about the damage to Orford Castle.

Hugh smiled. 'That is good news. It gives us more time to re-think our strategy. As my steward, in future, I expect to rely on your loyalty.'

Gundred dwelt on the angry departure of Roger and she sensed that deep down, Hugh was concealing his true feelings for his wayward son. She was thankful that the news of Orford Castle had distracted him and as they walked back to the hall, she thought it time to speak openly. 'Hugh, you brood too much on your bitterness. Better to think on matters that can still be accomplished. A simple choice lies ahead. You can attempt a full rebellion, but only with sufficient support. That leaves just one other option. For the time-being, let fate take a hand. Be close to your friends but be closer to your enemies. When the time is right, you must decide to make your peace with the king and regain his trust.'

Hugh thought over his wife's well-considered words. It was not the first time she had offered a wise perspective of events. Reluctantly he nodded, knowing he would have to take care in choosing the right time for reconciliation.

Chapter 10

Kom el Shoqafa
Alexandria

On the first day of his incarceration, Muzawi had found a plastered patch on a wall of the tomb that was different from its surroundings. Once he had removed the plaster with his knife, the eight hundred year old map giving the location of the Temple of Astarte in Tanis was revealed. At last he could find the first sphere.

He memorised the simple directions as painted by Arius then wandered the catacombs looking for a route out. But the walls were solid and the days that followed slid inexorably into a twilight world. Then the lamp died.

Days passed into weeks and the dreadful sensation of solitude was replaced by the weight of oppressive blackness that was so heavy, it dragged him to the ground. Confused by what was up and down he was barely able to move. The greenish algae had dried up long ago, along with the faint trickles of water. Time lost its meaning. The only certainty was a long and painful death.

Then he heard the Voice. And it told him to stand up.

Using the last of his energy, Muzawi swayed to his feet, deciding to keep his eyes shut. That way he could see through his mind's eye. The Voice said he should eat and drink, and he did.

Muzawi said he was cold and the Voice told him to feel for the clothes in front of him. Revitalized by the food and liquid, the conversations grew longer and although he could not see the Voice, he sensed it was never far away.

His new world was no longer one of fear and blackness: it had become full of vivid shapes and blinding light: a world void of time.

Stroking his long beard and humming ancient mantras, he sometimes laughed and every so often he cried, but always he marvelled at the revelations around him.

In a world where the line between reality and dreams merged into one, he gazed at buildings so high they touched the sky and silent lines of crackling fire that carried through the air.

A lone figure cloaked in black climbed the steps of a massive stone monument. When he reached the top, the figure stood behind a sacrificial altar and turned around, his robes fluttering in the breeze. Looking through the same eyes, Muzawi gazed across a vast horizon of wonders, where cities were lit at night and water was pumped from rivers and lakes into the fields. He lusted to be part of it; to touch, to hear and smell the magic all around him. All his learning and all his wisdom now began to make sense but it was not enough. He needed to understand. He demanded more.

The Voice obliged.

The Sky God's came and went, creating mighty descendants that walked the earth as Kings and Pharaoh's. Over the aeons , the son's of Gods fought amongst themselves and great civilisations rose and fell as the world succumbed to incessant acts of destruction. Behind the thrones of the demi-gods were the shaman; the viziers, those whose forefathers had worked tirelessly to offer guidance and instruction.

Pharaoh Khufu was just one in a long line of the great and powerful. Guided by his grand vizier, his vain attempt at ever-lasting glory culminated in the building of the great pyramid. Ultimately, the power he held within the coffer so terrified the people, they believed the true legacy to be a terrible curse. They hurried to bury it deep inside the heart of the structure, alongside their dead Pharaoh.

When the Hebrews departed Egypt no one could have foreseen them stealing the coffer containing the spheres. Each subsequent Hebrew king defied the curse, leading to floods, earthquakes and fires on a massive scale.

Ancient writings described the ebb and flow of each 'time of promises'. Some devoted their lives to a force for good; but most sought a darker purpose.

Empowered by his high priest, Pharaoh Shishak attempted to retrieve the spheres held within the coffer. His failure resulted in the destruction of Jerusalem and the slaughter of its inhabitants.

The next 'time of promises' occurred during the reign of the Roman Emperor Hadrian. With the influence of his female shaman, the emperor pulverised Judea but again the coffer remained hidden. Hadrian became just another blood-soaked Roman Emperor.

'Which descendants benefit most from the 'time of promises'', Muzawi asked.

'There is no discrimination. Some choose to build a future for the good of Man. Or the lowliest wastrel can become a king who indulges in war and mindless violence. There is always a choice.'

Muzawi was prompted to remember Saladin's true father. Given the enormous potential to increase his powers, the man called Lugermann failed miserably. Yes, he could control the minds of those around him and evidently make certain receptive subjects see events through his own eyes. Precious time was wasted on the miscreant who lacked the intelligence to realise his true potential. Abandoning his efforts, Tammuz waited for the son of Lugermann to be born.

The smile returned to Muzawi's face as he remembered Shishak. The young man had so nearly proved his worth, but his mother made an even bigger impression. She fell into the role of the Goddess Astarte, unfortunately distracting Tammuz from his guardianship of the two spheres. Their mission failed but ironically they succeeded in fulfilling one of the great ancient Babylonian epics. The story of Gehenna and the underworld, as told by the demi-god Gilgamesh.

Given the unswerving support of Tammuz, Shishak should have succeeded, but no one could have foreseen the opposing forces that railed against them. From the bowels of the Christian priesthood, the Knights Templar had proved themselves to be a most potent enemy.

Muzawi spent many days drawing on his memories; scrutinizing the sad procession of the disobedient and the ignorant who had gone before.

Then there was Saladin.

For some years, he had been reconciled to life without an heir and perhaps with a whiff of desperation he had believed in Saladin more than he should. But as the 'time of promises' drew near, doubts began to prey on his mind.

'What about Saladin?' Muzawi asked the Voice. 'Is he the one?'

'His strength is diminishing. This is how it happens sometimes.'

'Does he need my help…?'

'He is no longer at one with Sharur. You should take it from him.'

Of course, the Voice was right. Saladin had become ineffectual in channelling the power of the mighty mace. Other weaknesses confirmed his suspicions. No longer could Saladin see the thoughts nor manipulate the will of others; nor could he perceive the true path of Baal. But one flaw above all others convinced Muzawi that Saladin had lost his way. Stood next to him at Tanis, he had failed to see where the Temple of Astarte lay under the sand. There was no better demonstration of his waning powers.

Muzawi sought the advice of the Voice. 'If I am no longer to be the guardian of the spheres, then what is to become of me?'

'You should take his place.'

Muzawi was silent and cowered a little in the dark. Fearing he had misheard, he dare not ask another question.

Many hours passed before he dared to speak again. 'Are you Baal?' he asked humbly.

'You know who I am.'

'You are a God...'

'I am the conscious thought of the first man to walk the earth, and I shall be the manifestation of the last. I have always been here. I am the choice between the shining light of revelation and the darkness of the bottomless pit.'

Muzawi curled up into a tight ball.

'You should not fear death, for you will be reborn.'

'How shall I be reborn?'

'It is foretold…at the End of Days.'

Muzawi felt a tinge of relief. His mind drifted to a timeless universe where he would attain the power of the stars for himself. Now, his final destiny was clear. He would be the one to gather the two spheres and the sceptres. He would be the one to hold apart the two sceptres, each bearing a fragment of Lapsit Exillus, the Stone of Heaven created at the beginning of time. Though the green gems carried many names, they were known throughout history as Shamir, another legacy of the Sky Gods.

The incessant gnawing from his insides subsided. The meat was long gone. Pacing endlessly around the tomb, he scratched at the slime on the walls and drank from the tiny pools of water on the stone floor. He begged the Voice to speak.

'Be patient. Your inner strength is equal to a hundred ordinary men. The 'time of promises' will come. Prepare for your deliverance.'

Upon his unexpected release from prison, Hussein had no idea what to do. They had interrogated him for months before charging him as a spy, saying he would never again see the light of day. Then for no reason they let him go. They had even given him a few dinars for some food.

All the time he had been in his cell, he prayed that Ishmael would forgive him for his stupidity. For so long, they had kept their love a secret.

At the market he spent all his money on an oil lamp and torches and found himself at the entrance to the catacombs. At least he could pray at the site to show his love one last time and pray that Allah would always look after his soul. At the bottom of the stairwell, he looked into the shaft where the water still remained. He crouched down and entered the first passageway, keeping the torch and oil lamp dry. Reaching the rotunda he remembered the words of Muzawi from long ago, telling him to look for any hidden doors. The large, square annex to the left led nowhere, but he placed the lamp on a shelf at the far end and holding a torch, inspected the walls.

He was about to give up when he accidentally banged into a statue in a large niche, nearly knocking it over. It was left leaning at a peculiar angle and although he tried pulling it back, the statue would not straighten up. So, he pushed it again and with each thrust he heard the unmistakable sound of large stone moving. An opening had appeared at the rear of the niche.

His heart was thumping as he clambered inside and slid down a steep slope cut into the rock. Moments later he scrambled out of another niche into a chamber that led into a long corridor with more burial tombs.

An atrocious smell assaulted his senses and all he could hear was his own footsteps and the pounding of his heart. He neared a central area that was surrounded by even more tombs. A large opening appeared on his right and suddenly he realised where he was. He had reached the other side of the massive chamber that housed the main tomb, where he had left Ishmael and Muzawi to die.

Falling to his knees, he cried out loud for the soul of his friend. Holding up the lamp, he could see the debris of the rock fall. He recoiled at the sight of a crushed leg bone protruding from a large stone slab. Turning around, he saw the remains of a skeleton scattered about the floor.

Kneeling at the side of a ribcage, the horror became clear. Something had dissected the flesh and chewed on every bone. There was no time for grief, for the urgent need to escape from the predator was overpowering. The last thing Hussein saw was the yellow-eyed creature moving towards him and his scream was to no avail as the blade descended between his eyes.

Grateful for the promised deliverance, Muzawi ate the food as presented to him. Afterwards he slept so well he did not want to wake up. The dreams were as vivid as ever, giving every pleasure imaginable to his weakened flesh.

Time had no meaning but long after the meat had all gone a thought entered his head.

Now was the time to leave.

He removed the rags from around his frame and dressed himself afresh in clean clothes. Finding the new entrance was easy for all he had to do was sniff like an animal and follow the draft of clean air.

The pain in his eyes at the foot of the stairwell made him stop. It would be some time before he could face daylight again, so he waited for darkness to fall.

That night he moved silent and unseen amongst the shadows, his body feeling as light as a feather and as strong as a lion. Stealing a horse was easy for he was able to exorcise the fear it felt from within.

On the way to Tanis, Muzawi entered Bubastis, a city built by Pharaoh Khufu. For thousands of years it was infamous for its world-renowned annual orgies. On the first day of the Nile inundation, thousands of ordinary people would arrive in the city and offer their bodies solely for the purpose of wanton sexual pleasure. It was recorded one year that as a tribute to the Gods, seven hundred thousand people indulged in their sexual pleasures.

Since the destruction of the city by the Persians, the orgies had diminished to only a few gratuitous souls that met every year in a nearby town.

Although in his early seventies, Muzawi felt like a hot-blooded teenager. As if to honour the great Khufu, he relished the idea of putting his newfound virility to the test. Afterwards, there would be time to enter Tanis and follow his path to immortality.

Chapter 11

Tanis
Egypt

His diversion to Bubastis had gone better than expected but only because he had exulted in such carnal pleasures he had never thought possible. Never in his previous life had he felt such a desire to immerse himself in unlimited depravity. The days of lust turned to weeks of mortal sin, and much to his dismay his sex slaves became difficult to replace as word of his ritual practices circulated.

There were ways to dispose of bodies that only he could appreciate and find enjoyment. Inevitably the death of three young women and a young boy had brought suspicion upon himself and it was time to leave. In the future he would have a city of willing slaves and an personal army to protect him from those that offered resistance or opposed him.

He cut his beard short and his shaved head glistened in the sun. As a result of his existence in the timeless world of the dark, his irises had turned jet black against the pure yellow eyeballs. To some his appearance was startling. Those who looked close enough were mesmerised by the eyes. Others found only the dark promise of things never thought possible.

When he finally reached Tanis his thoughts returned to the task in hand. He took to wearing a black Berber's robe that covered most of his body and hid much of his face. He explained to the Coptic Christians that he was a simple monk who sought out Christian relics. For assisting in his excavations, he would pay well for recruits to his cause. The tactic was sound and he could now re-start his excavations without fear of reprisal.

Ten willing men volunteered their services and he led them across the sands to the temple ruins. He walked amongst the fallen columns and blocks of granite and told them to clear away the sand from the outer wall of the Temple of Amun. Once the south west corner was exposed, he was able to re-imagine the map and pace out the distance to the Temple of Astarte.

In the cool of the evening light, they started digging and soon the first wall began to show itself. They worked thorough the night, uncovering two large statues, before coming to an altar in front of the eastern end of the structure. He paid the immediate circle of workers and dismissed them. Then with the help of just two men he set about digging out the altar.

Another day passed before the altar was fully excavated within its recess and Muzawi was able to inspect the intricate symbols and patterns upon its surface. Brushing aside the sand with his fingers, he revealed the carving of the high priest, stood with the two elongated sceptres placed on either side. The ominous spheres hovered above each spectre and in the middle the crescent moon cradling the newborn sun. He fingered the pendant hung around his neck. Now there was no doubt..

Using a small hand spade, he was able to take out the last few handfuls of sand from the base of the altar and found what he was looking for, exactly in the place described in the scrolls.

According to the dimensions recorded in the ancient tomes, the coffer was smaller than the one at Baalbek and he hoped it was light enough to carry. Coated in precious cedar wood and carved with the faces of the Gods, it looked as though it had been placed there that day. He wiped his forehead and tentatively opened the lid, squinting in anticipation as the interior was revealed for the first time since Arius had closed it.

Exactly as expected, he saw the sphere in the grip of its metal claw. On the opposite side of the coffer was another claw and it was empty. In between were strange wires attached by mechanical means to the claws, none of which made any sense and appeared to be of little consequence.

A small tablet lay on the floor of the coffer and he was able to make out the engraved shape of two monoliths.

Where had he seen these before.

Touching the precious sphere, he felt a tingling sensation and perceived an inner glow on the ultra smooth surface. Closing the lid, he was secure in the knowledge that when the time was right, everything would be made clear to him.

Climbing out of the trench, Muzawi walked to his horse and placed the coffer into his saddlebag. Around the perimeter he was surprised to see a crowd had gathered, with more arriving from the town all the time. This was unexpected, and unfortunate that so many were witness to his discovery, not forgetting the treasure hunters who would descend into the tomb the moment he was gone.

While staring at the crowd, he noticed two horsemen ride up and he overheard them ask questions of the men gathered. They had ridden from Bubastis and were looking for a murderer. He pulled his hood over his face and edged closer to his horse trying to hear the accusations.

'…and he did more than rape them. Two of the women were torn to pieces. One survivor said he gorged himself on the heart of one while it was still beating then drank the blood of another before slicing her into pieces…' The reaction of the crowd drowned out the words.

Then one of the braver women spoke out from under her hajab and pointed at Muzawi as he made his way out of the trench. 'The stranger arrived last night from Bubastis.'

All eyes turned to Muzawi and he smiled and bowed respectfully to his accusers. Inside his heart was thumping and his stomach was churning with fear.

He had not prepared himself for this.

Holding only a spade, he bent his back to exaggerate his age. 'I am just an old, simple-minded monk who leads a blameless life searching for the relics of Christ.'

'Then you won't mind if you pull down your robe to reveal your chest,' called out one of the horsemen.

'I do mind. How dare you accuse me…'

The horsemen looked determined and drew swords as they dismounted. In a flash, they pulled the robe from Muzawi's shoulder, exposing the pendant round his neck.

Muzawi hung his head low.

This was not supposed to happen.

The mêlée that followed was full of confusion. The two horsemen from Bubastis untied his saddlebag, then argued whether to take him back straight away but then decided to wait until the morning. They tied his hands and led the way into the town where they seconded a merchant's shop and cellar and settled down for the night.

The hours passed by and in the pitch black of night, Muzawi breathed in the cool air of the night. The trials and tribulations of the late afternoon were long gone and now he took pleasure in the earth around him. His initial panic had been replaced by the anticipation of what was to come. The darkness enveloped him and gave him comfort. There was no need to call for the Voice, for now it was within him and spoke to him whenever he wanted. The fools who had decided to hold him in the cellar overnight had made the biggest mistakes of their measly lives.

Closing his eyes in concentration, he settled his body close to the earth, feeling as one with nature, fingering the soil around him.

The Knights Templars refused point blank to enter into another campaign against Egypt. In their absence, the Hospitallers demanded that Egypt should be the obvious target and the newly arrived force under the Count of Nevers agreed. Under pressure to act, King Amalric led his forces across the River Nile expecting to find little resistance.

Shawar could not believe the news that the Christians had broken the truce and were camped once again outside the gates of Bilbeis. Shawar's inexperienced son commanded the garrison but refused to let the army enter the city.

Inexplicably, the Count of Nevers died suddenly that night and chaos ensued. In the confusion, his knights suspected the Egyptians of murder and refused to wait for negotiations to start. With no one to calm the situation, they attacked the walls and after three days of vicious fighting the Christian army broke through into the city.

The inhabitants were comprised mainly of Coptic Christians who detested Shawar, considering cruel and oppressive. If anything, many of the Coptic leaders believed the Jerusalem King to be an honest ally and had cautiously welcomed their arrival in Bilbeis; however, their trust was badly misplaced.

Fired up by the strength of the opposition, the army was in a bloodthirsty mood. While the newcomers were demanding total retribution, as was their right, the Hospitallers were out to prove they were a better Order than the Templars. The time was too late for dialogue and the devil licked his lips in anticipation.

Many of the knights and soldiers who entered the gates that day had revelled in the stories of the massacre of Jerusalem some seventy years before. Many had harboured the same dark desires to experience the realms of a pure blood lust. It was an invitation to piss on the morals of convention and virtue. As if affected by an unknown force, some would even admit to hearing the voices that encouraged them to leave their souls behind and to enter the gates of hell. To taste the blood of the desolate one.

To lose your soul proved so effortless that many lost their sanity and never survived the return journey to the west.

There was no one to ask for mercy, no one to shield the innocent as the rivers of blood ran through the gutters, washing the streets in honour of the evil of which man was capable. Without mercy, they cut the throats of the babies and children and hung them by the feet from the windows of the houses while the mothers were raped and mutilated in the streets below.

Thousands of men were led to the city square and beheaded. The slaughter continued into the night, until the inhabitants of Bilbeis were no more.

But it wasn't enough. The wanton indulgence in the atrocities tasted good. Never before had the army experienced such a craving that had to be sated.

No one knew why Bubastis and Tanis were chosen as the next targets. Some heard stories from the Hospitallers describing heretical practices going back thousands of years. More likely were the rumours of untold wealth and riches held within the walls of Tanis.

The leaderless army of death divided and rampaged through the streets of both towns sweeping away all in its path.

Muzawi heard the fear in the streets and he sat up to listen though a grate at the muffled voices of the men gathered in the street above the cellar.

'The Jerusalem army have entered Bilbeis,' a voice cried out. They are murdering everyone; the women and children as well.'

'I heard they have taken Bubastis and now there are boats coming towards Tanis. We must leave…' the footsteps ran down the street in sheer panic, shouting at everyone to flee.

While the city was in a state of dread, Muzawi knew he must collect his saddlebag from the soldiers upstairs before they escaped on their horses. The door was old and it opened easily with one push of his shoulder.

Reaching the top of the staircase, the two soldiers stared at him in disbelief. Between them they carried the coffer and quickly they realised that their swords were out of reach. They dropped the coffer but it was too late. Muzawi picked up one of the swords and effortlessly decapitated one and slashing the ear and cheek of the other. Under the spray of blood he lifted the coffer away from the men and placed it on the table. They had filled it with a bag of gold coins and loose gems they had extorted from the Coptic community.

'Have mercy on me,' whimpered the soldier on the floor. His neck was bleeding badly but it was not a fatal wound. Muzawi thought for a moment, then smiled. He took the sphere from the coffer and holding it in the thick cloth, he walked towards the cowering soldier.

'Have mercy, master have mercy,' he begged.

Holding the shining surface against his gashed ear, he watched intently to see what would happen. Immediately, the skin turned red and the man screamed. Then miraculously the blood stopped and the lesion began to cauterise and heal over.

'What is your name?' Muzawi asked placing the sphere back in the coffer.

'Edom…they call me Edom,' he replied wiping his neck in disbelief. 'Master, I owe you my life. Please do not waste it.'

Muzawi was impressed by the logic of the remark. He picked up the sword and held the point in front of Edom's face. 'Tell me why I should not run this blade through your eyeball, into your skull?'

His answer was swift and fluent. 'Because I am your servant, and you need me to carry your treasure to pay for more servants.'

The sword moved in a blur and Edom closed his eyes. When he opened them, the hilt was prodding his arm.

'Take it. The sword is yours,' Muzawi said. 'But I warn you, do not be fooled by my craggy face. Compared with you, I have the power of a hundred men.'

Edom stood up, still unsure of his new master. 'Are you a God or a Devil?'

Muzawi smiled and gave an enigmatic answer. 'I am neither; but as a one-year old baby, I was saved by one of them.'

An overpowering sense of awe compelled Edom to kneel and kiss the feet of Muzawi.

'Take the coffer to the horses and secure it onto my mare,' Muzawi ordered, 'then put the gold in your saddlebags.' Outside, panic reigned as everyone was running, but going nowhere.

'They scuttle like headless chickens,' Muzawi remarked. 'We ride south east towards Cairo'.

Crossing the sands on horseback, they rode past the trench where he had found the coffer. Looking down, Muzawi scowled at the desecration. 'The robbers will pay for this,' he promised looking back towards the city. The sounds of screaming drifted on the night breeze, as if his threat had come to light.

Edom stood high in his saddle. 'The murdering dogs from Jerusalem. Why do they slaughter innocent fellow Christians? The Coptic's were no threat.'

'Do dogs care where their next meal comes from? They have tasted blood and will have their fill again before this day is out.'

'But I hear that some dogs are prepared to take blood money. I heard that a Jewish rabbi has secured the lives of all the Jews in Bilbeis with a hefty ransom paid to Amalric.'

Muzawi flinched, his expression turning cold. 'Yes I heard. And one day he will atone for what he has done. Amalric is a fool, but at the moment he is a useful fool.'

'Where to now, master.'

Muzawi had considered his next move many times.

He must maximise his powers to be ready for the exact moment of the 'time of promises'. There was the second sphere to find in Lydda as well as solving the biggest mystery of all. The whereabouts of the two sceptres. But first there were scores to settle. The roads directly east to Jerusalem were full of Christian soldiers out for blood and were best avoided.

'The 'time of promises' affects many with its power. We head for the old city of Fustat. There we will witness the fall of Shawar.'

Edom shook his head. 'Shawar will never let his city fall to the Christians.'

'That is a truer statement than you could ever have imagined,' Muzawi replied wistfully. He was pleased with Edom and the way he had quickly accepted his pliant role as his servant, though his trust and loyalty were still to be tested.

It took three days and nights to reach Cairo but Muzawi was in no particular hurry. They entered the city and paid to sleep on the roof of an Auberge to ensure a good view to the south, overlooking the old city of Fustat.

The timing was impeccable as only a few days later, they heard the news that Amalric was poised outside the walls of Fustat and ready to storm the city.

That night Muzawi wrapped himself against the cold and stared to the south.

'Surely, we need to get out of Cairo before the Christian army beats down our door,' Edom warned.

Muzawi did not answer for he seemed to be concentrating. Suddenly a burst of flame lit up the sky followed by a series of explosions that rocked the Auberge.

Naphtha pots exploded and covered everywhere in a liquid hell that burned; never be extinguished. Soon the refugees began to flood the streets into Cairo.

'Shawar has gone mad!' a man shouted at his neighbours. 'He told us all to run for our lives and leave behind all our money and property. I thought it was just a ruse so he could steal everything, until I saw a hundred wagons full of naphtha. His men have placed the pots on every street corner. Thousands and thousands of pots, enough to burn the city ten times over. A madman I say…an absolute madman.' He ran towards the safety of Cairo city.

As the wind blew, the conflagration at the centre turned into a fire-storm; the exploding pots extending the raging fires in all directions. The flames became so bright, the night sky was banished into a permanent sunset.

While Muzawi was happy to stay in Cairo and watch Shawar's city burn, he decided to put the time to good use. The swarms of angry and disillusioned refugees proved to be such a good source of recruitment to his cause. By speaking to each one he was able to distinguish those with potential loyalty, devotion and most important the fanatical ones that would sacrifice themselves as and when required.

Satisfied with his small band of recruits, Muzawi rested and let them enjoy the spectacle of the fire. After a few more days, he took Edom aside and to plan his strategy.

Nearly eighteen months had passed since he had left Muzawi to die and Saladin still carried the grief and guilt over the appalling episode.

Six weeks after they had left Alexandria, Muzawi had still failed to reappear. Shirkuh had dispatched his best agent to evaluate what had come of the shaman. His report was far from good, and was especially distressing for Saladin.

Apparently, the digger who had been charged to aid Muzawi had been caught and arrested as a spy on the first day and was unlikely to be released from prison.

Despite this setback, the agent was sent again on numerous occasions but could not secure any more information. Sensing this was his final attempt, the agent used his initiative to gain entry to the the catacombs and after bribing a local captain he paid a guide to take him underground.

They reached the rock fall just as Saladin had once described and he was able to peer through the gaps in the massive stones. Solemnly, he reported back, that in the chamber on the other side he could see two sets of human skeletons, badly displaced by the attention of the rats, that apparently grew to the size of dogs.

The impossible had happened. Muzawi was dead and so was his servant Ishmael.

Saladin's disbelief turned to anger, and his antagonism knew no bounds. He locked himself away, refusing to see or speak to anyone. Then after three days, he opened his door and received Shirkuh.

'You must get over the loss of Muzawi,' his uncle warned. 'Your grief will cloud your judgement and then you make bad decisions.' He wondered if Saladin was even listening.

Deep in thought, Saladin apologised. 'I am sorry my lord. It won't happen again.'

In Damascus, Nuradin read of the reports from refugees of the needless slaughter of tens of thousands that had ended with the army drifting back into the Holy Land with the spoils of pillage and extortion.

Then came news that the city of Fustat was engulfed in flames for fifty days, until there was nothing left to burn. Though a spent force, Shawar still held on to power in Cairo but was thought unworthy of any further alliance.

To rid himself of Shawar, Nuradin agreed to arm General Shirkuh with eight thousand horsemen and a massive war chest to finish the job once and for all. He would accept nothing less than the full conquest of Egypt and the death of the wayward Emir.

Arriving in Cairo a few days later, Shirkuh and Saladin were surprised to see Shawar still ensconced in his palace with all the trappings of wealth and power. Rather than fight, he was quick to distribute food and money to the Syrian army as well as rich gifts to the generals.

Shirkuh was taken off his guard and graciously accepted the gifts. After they had banqueted throughout the evening and night, they were led to the palace guest apartments.

Saladin was unhappy at the cordiality with which his uncle had so readily accepted the situation. 'Your willingness to leave Shawar in power does nothing for our cause. By rights he should be just a memory by now. He must be stopped once and for all.' Saladin thought for a moment, stroking his short beard. 'Shawar burnt down his own city. We could exploit his guilt…by suggesting he seeks forgiveness for his sin.' Saladin wandered onto the balcony looking into the distance. 'There is a tomb of the Imam As-Shafii in Fustat. Ask him to join you in a short pilgrimage, on foot. Tell him he has a duty to ensure the tomb is undamaged and we will call on Allah for his mercy.'

Shirkuh did not question if Saladin had an ulterior motive. He called for his clerk to make the arrangements.

The walk did not suit Shawar. He only had a thin recollection of the tomb of the Imam but thought it best to agree to their request. Walking alongside Shirkuh and Saladin, they soon reached the burnt suburbs of Fustat before coming to a halt.

Saladin turned to his aides. 'This is where we leave our retinue behind. We cannot truly appear in front of the tomb with all the luxury of a travelling palace.'

Reluctantly, Shawar agreed, though he spoke to his captain to go on ahead and ensure there would be no unforeseen difficulty. Stumbling through the desolation of the old city, Shawar remained in good spirits. The three of them were chatting amicably, when without warning Saladin drew his sword and pushed Shawar to the ground. He was in shock but managed to scramble to his knees.

Shirkuh was equally surprised and told Saladin to stand back and immediately apologise. Saladin looked at Shirkuh. 'You don't understand.' The curved blade swung through the air and neatly sliced off Shawar's head at the neck. 'Now Egypt is ours.'

Shirkuh looked on in horror then looked around nervously. 'You fool! What about the captain...'

Saladin pointed to his side at the body of the captain lying in a shop doorway. Stood next to the body, Shirkuh recognised the assassin as one of Saladin's Mameluke bodyguards.

Rather than vent his anger, Shirkuh could only think of their safety. 'We will be held guilty of murder. There will be reprisals.' 'Tell the aides and the guards that Shawar has died unexpectedly then direct them to pillage his palace. That should divert attention away from us long enough to take control of the government. My bodyguard will hide the bodies. I have more agents in place ready to persuade those that do not agree with the changes. Last night I sent messages to your immediate family telling them of our take-over. They are at your command and ready to move into whatever positions you will grant them.' Saladin waited for a reaction. Smiling to himself, he wiped his blade before retuning it to his scabbard. 'You must agree, I have thought of everything. By tomorrow, you will be vizier of Egypt. By next week, you will be crowned regent.'

Shirkuh was still in shock and as he stared at Saladin, he inexplicably felt a pang of fear. But he also knew Saladin well enough; that everything he said was likely to come true.

At the news of Shawar's assassination, chaos reined in the royal court of Jerusalem. Recriminations followed and the blame fell squarely between the newcomers from the west and the ineffectiveness of the Hospitallers. Many barons compared them unfavourably to the Templars and questioned the lack the military skills and resolute courage of the Order.

Over the next weeks, Amalric sent a string of envoys abroad, begging for help in forming another Army of God from the west. As he pondered the future of the Kingdom of Jerusalem, there came news that immediately gave him some much needed relief.

The messenger could hardly contain himself. 'General Shirkuh is dead.' The entire court was so stunned the messenger repeated. 'My Lord King, Shirkuh is dead...apparently from over-eating, though there are consistent rumours he was poisoned.'

King Amalric sank onto his couch and immediately ordered all the bells in Jerusalem to be rung. The next day, confirmation was received that all of Shirkuh's titles had passed directly to his younger and inexperienced nephew, Saladin.

'Well he won't last long! At last, we have an advantage,' Amalric declared to his council. 'The death of Shirkuh will bring about chaos throughout Egypt.'

But wiser men than Amalric drew little comfort from Saladin's surprising rise to power. This relatively unknown Damascus general had abolished the Fatimid Caliphate at a stroke and was now, by all accounts, the undisputed ruler of Egypt.

Chapter 12

Framlingham Castle
Suffolk

Ever since his abortive attempt to force Becket to return from exile, Hugh was content not to interfere again, but to keep a close watch on how events unfurled. Becket had pleaded his case to King Louis who under Papal influence, agreed that the archbishop could move from Pontigny to the royal abbey in Sens.

From his new base, Becket was keen to display fresh support from the pope with the implicit threat of excommunicating King Henry and placing England under interdict.

Hugh mused at the damage that Becket could inflict even in exile. Ironically, throughout the period of ill-tempered exchanges, the main casualty appeared to be the king's marriage. For too long, Queen Eleanor had endured both of Henry's obsessions. One was his open affair with his young mistress and the other was his enduring preoccupation with his archbishop. The pretty mistress she could understand and put up with. As for Becket her contempt for him held no bounds. As she returned alone to Aquataine, no one in her company was left in any doubt as to which obsession she considered the worst. .

Then to Hugh's alarm, he was told that the building of Orford Castle had recommenced with even more builders and engineers. He immediately responded by building a new keep and larger walls at Bungay Castle, as well as reinforcing his defences at Framlingham. Deep down he knew it would have little effect but it was good for the moral of his men.

Unfortunately, while remaining neutral in East Angles, Hugh felt out of touch with some of his fellow protagonists. Upon the death of Count Thierry of Flanders, the title passed to his son Philip who now concentrated his efforts allying himself with King Louis.

Only a month later, Robert of Leicester was surprised by his father's untimely death and became the next Earl of Leicester; a little earlier than he had expected.

Disillusioned at the endless quarrels between King Henry and Thomas Becket, Robert did not take up his fathers office of Justicar but took his leave of the king's council, deciding to let the dispute run its course. Privately, he surmised it was akin to watching two ill-tempered boys throwing stones at each other across a pond, occasionally calling each other names.

Desperately looking for another stone to throw, the king announced another insult. 'The French Royals have a practice of crowning the eldest son as king during his own lifetime. I shall do the same with my son, Henry the Younger.'

The coronation took place in York, under the authority of the Archbishop of York. Many believed the entire ceremony was designed simply to offend Becket, rather than impressing everyone by crowning his fifteen-year-old son.

Whether by design or not, Becket felt the insidious pang of betrayal; as if all his power as archbishop was being drained away. Reluctantly, he agreed to meet with the king on the Normandie coast.

By now Henry felt exhausted by the thought of further argument and had reached a stage where he was willing to agree to anything in order to have Becket back in England. A settlement was agreed that Becket's estates would be restored and that he had the right to punish those who had defied him at the York coronation.

The king sent messengers informing his court of the reconciliation and Becket's imminent return from exile. When news of the agreement reached Hugh, he was astonished to hear that a painless concord had been reached and many secretly questioned if it was true.

The archbishop landed at Sandwich and was met by his supporters, though most of the crowd were curious to see the man who had defied the King of England for near on a decade.

An eyewitness report from one of his knights was even harder for Hugh to believe. Dressed in all his most expensive regalia, Becket led a procession all the way to Canterbury. Thousands of citizens lined the streets, cheering and offering him their prayers on his return from exile. By the time he reached Canterbury, Becket fell to his knees in supplication, as every bell from every tower, rang out to celebrate his return.

Richard le Breton had given many years of loyal service to the king's brother, William FitzEmpress and as promised by the king, he was seconded to the court. He soon proved himself to be a useful addition to the council and became one of the king's inner circle, witnessing much of the kings inner turmoil at the hands of the traitorous Becket.

The king assembled these men and all his barons at the hunting lodge of Bur le Roi near Bayeux; one that he often used in memory of the knights who swore their oaths to King William before setting sail to invade England, a little more than a hundred years before.

The Bishops of London and York, newly arrived from England, joined the gathering and it took no time at all for Richard le Breton to transform the drunken debate into a vitriolic attack upon one common enemy.

Becket.

As for Hugh's presence, the king seemed too drunk to care one way or the other. But everyone else knew that Hugh had been added to the list of those excommunicated and now considered him as one of their own. Delighted to revel in such a thinly disguised badge of honour, Hugh observed with relish the malicious words carelessly banded about the court and was happy to pour oil onto the flames of discontent. Bonham stood at his side to bolster his self-confidence.

Through a drunken haze, he beckoned over Richard le Breton who was loudly proclaiming his love for the king. Hugh had to shout to make himself heard. 'Richard, you remember upon your master's tragic death, when I said I would give you my full support?'

Le Breton's voice was slurred and he struggled to keep his wits about him. 'Yes, Earl Bigod, I remember your sympathetic words after I had seen the king.'

'I ask you about Becket. How much evil has passed the lips of this supposed man of God since we last met. I left England only yesterday and heard reports of the latest vile words from the pulpit of Canterbury. Christmas day no less, and he named the Bishops of London and York as "priests of Baal and were nought but false prophets." Can you believe such immoral words from an Archbishop.' Hugh pulled Richard closer and hissed in his face. 'Above all others, you have the ear of the king, so listen closely to what I have to say. I have heard it said that the men who lined the streets to his Cathedral…now form a secret army. An army not of the king's making but one that follows the command of King Louis and his cohort Becket.'

Shaken by the impact of the words, Le Breton staggered backwards. His manner quickly changed to one of sobriety and he thanked Hugh before rounding on his friends to follow him onto the small terrace outside.

Hugh looked at Marcus whose expression gave little away. He waited patiently knowing the next few moments would determine any number of possibilities. Hopefully there would be a call for a war with France, thereby allowing Hugh free rein in England. On the other hand, there may be another reconciliation and the king would continue to squeeze Hugh into a corner until all his land and power was gone.

The crowd of rowdy dissidents stood in front of the king. Hugh could not hear the words, but the king swung his head and stared in his direction. The expression was deadly and Hugh feared the worst. He took a long sip of wine. At the age of seventy-four, he was in no mood to make an undignified exit, just yet.

With his knights and bishops gathered around him, the king was informed of what Hugh Bigod had reported and was left in no doubt of the ill feeling they felt towards Becket. No longer wishing to be party to the king's anger, Hugh wondered soberly if he had gone too far. Moving discretely around the throng of distraught nobles and court officials, he reached the door.

Marcus checked the way was clear and Hugh followed him outside as the anguished, drunken voice of the enraged king rang loud in his ears.

'You wretched, impotent knaves that surround me and simply watch as a lowly clerk makes me endure such painful humiliation, in the eyes of my subjects. Why do you quake at the very mention of his name, while he tramples on the rights of your king? Not one of you is man enough to rid me of this burden…this troublesome…?'

Without knowing the full outcome of the king's venomous tirade, Hugh quickly made his way that night back to the coast. The danger was obvious. If the king had thought him as an agitator who persisted in spoiling the status quo, then his very presence at Bayeux could have turned the full imperial fury against him. In that heated environment, it would have been an end of him.

The inclement weather had moved north and hiring the first available boat they crossed the English Sea. By the time he landed at Portsmouth he was so fearful of the potential threat of ambush, he sent Bonham ahead with a messenger to muster some twenty knights to escort him back to Framlingham.

At first Gundred was simply happy to see her husband return safely from Normandie but the immense pressure he was under soon became apparent. She had delayed the Christmas festivities until his return but all her preparations were soon forgotten. The uncertainty of the days ahead put a great strain upon their relationship and her questions promptly spilled over into arguments.

Day by day, the mornings became colder and the stillness of a frosty dawn was broken by the arrival of a knight and squire at the gates of the castle. The squire carried the king's colours and Hugh was immediately woken from his slumber. The knight was brought into the hall to be greeted by the sight of Hugh alongside a phalanx of four of his loyal knights, led by Bonham, his boldest knight. To one side Marcus skulked in the shadows, preferring to observe from a distance.

The stranger unwrapped his face of the thick scarf and through the mist of heavy breath, Hugh immediately recognised the face. Richard le Breton begged to stand by the fireplace as he let slip his cloak. Underneath, his face was ashen as though he had witnessed some great terror.

Hugh turned to his guards. 'Someone bring a hot broth; can you not see he wears the king's colours.'

Le Breton's body shook with the cold and his blue lips trembled but he still managed a respectful bow of the head. 'My lord earl, forgive my ineptness but I have ridden through the night with news of a great horror. Since we last spoke of Becket there has been a catastrophe.'

Hugh stiffened, for now it had become clear the man had something of import to say. 'Well, say what you must. Do you have a message from the king or not?'

Le Breton's eyes narrowed and looked around at the knights and household. 'I carry no message from the king. But apart from a priest, you are the only mortal of which I can trust with my confession.

Please give me that honour.'

Hugh hesitated then nodded to those gathered around the hall to leave except for Marcus and Bonham. Gundred entered from the staircase. She had taken the bowl of steaming broth from a servant and laid it on the table. Le Breton slurped greedily as they settled close to his side so as the voices would not carry.

'Well...tell me what has happened.'

Wiping his dripping nose on his sleeve, Le Breton's eyes began to water and his voice dropped to a hoarse whisper. 'Between God and myself, I know my soul is vanquished and will spend eternity in purgatory. Three days ago, we left Dover and rode at haste to Canterbury. There were four of us...all king's knights. The king said...he said he wanted rid of Becket. You said yourself how traitorous Becket had been. The king has never been so...so distressed.' He face was white as he stumbled from the table and vomited the broth into the fireplace. Staring into the flames, his chest heaved with the effort of catching his breath. 'The devil himself squeezed my heart with hatred, then whispered in my ear. "Becket must pay for the death of lord William." We murdered him. All of us. God help us, on the altar of Christ we murdered Becket.'

The words hung on the air so still, no one dare breathe or say a word. Hugh stared at le Breton as though struck by an unknown force. Everyone within hearing was stunned.

Gundred broke the silence, forcing herself to ask the question. 'So...did the king order you and the three other knights to kill him?'

The answer was so quiet they were nearly drowned by the crackle of flames. 'I believe in my heart...at the time...that is what he wanted. Back then, everything was so clear...but now, for the love of God I don't know.' Le Breton sank to his knees, his face screwed up with an inner turmoil. 'I could not believe the other three knights were laughing and bragging about the deed. I left them, but in my heart I know we will all burn for eternity.'

Shaking himself from the shocking news, Marcus felt it was his duty to advise the earl. 'My lord, you cannot give this man any sanctuary. It will be seen as...'

Suddenly the knight thrust his arm deep into the fireplace amidst a shower of glowing red-hot cinders. Gundred and Hugh leapt up, transfixed as the smell of burning assaulted the nostrils.

Bonham was the closest and he leapt forward to pull le Breton's arm from the fire.

Gundred spun round and poured a flagon of wine over the smouldering flesh and although he did not cry out, the pain was etched on his face.

Hugh did not know which way to turn.

Marcus called for a servant. 'There is a physician in the bailey; tell him someone is badly burnt. Get him here at once.'

As one of the maids dabbed at the blistered skin, Gundred took Hugh to one side. 'Le Breton is in torment; as if the devil claws for his very soul. He needs a priest not an earl. If you allow him to stay here, then you are party to the conspiracy. You know he cannot stay, don't you.' It was a statement not a question.

Hugh shook himself and tried to absorb everything that had been said and done, then slowly he nodded his head. 'He must leave. Now.'

Chapter 13

Haughley Castle
Suffolk

Roger Bigod seemed to spend more time than ever at Haughley. He could not deny his love for Anna le Broc any longer. It was the most wonderful feeling he had ever known.

Now nineteen years old, her body had filled out with firm high breasts and rounded buttocks. On a few wild occasions they had run to his lodgings, tearing off her clothes as they clambered onto his bed. Roger ensured his landlady was paid enough to keep their stolen passion a secret.

While they found it difficult to control the call of young love, both of them were aware of her family's religious devotion and would be horrified if they were discovered by her parents, prior to wedlock. Which strangely made everything all the more exciting.

Her family were happy for them to marry and had pressured them to do so for near on six months. It even crossed Roger's mind that secretly they knew of their covert liaisons and wanted to avoid the risk of a scandal. But before they could marry, he wanted everything to be just right and he was afraid his father might embarrass everyone by opposing the marriage. The bad blood between them hung over him like a dark shadow.

At times, his father had made enormous errors of judgement throughout his long and turbulent life and was loathed by any number of nobles throughout the land. And yet, when he studied the lives of those who were critical, he found in many cases they had done far worse deeds. His father had never needlessly slaughtered, he had never been abusive to him and although Gundred was not his mother it was evident they truly loved each other.

Roger stood on top of the keep, his eyes stretching for miles over the Essex countryside. He held Anna's hand tightly and she kissed him on the cheek.

Anna did not wish to interrupt his thoughts when his mind wandered for she knew much of his inner turmoil regarding his father and felt it best not to interfere. She had led a sheltered life in the castle with a relatively strict upbringing. The village was small and isolated and over the years, her friends were few and had moved to the cities.

She reminisced back to the age of thirteen, when she had caught the eye of a young confidant boy of fifteen to whom she curtsied and when he bowed so graciously back; she had instantly fallen in love. They met time and again over the next few years, each occasion he gave a wonderful smile as he bowed. When they talked, she knew their love was destined and that marriage would follow when the time was right.

Roger squeezed her cold hand and she looked to the south. The sight of a fifty horsemen riding at speed towards the castle made her heart miss a beat and she shivered as a sudden cold wind blew. She had learnt that a horse was only ridden hard when the news was bad.

Roger recognised the colours. 'It is Wilhelm Mandeville, the Earl of Essex. I wonder what he wants here?'

Anna thought for a moment, recalling what she had learnt about the status of noblemen from England and Flanders. 'He was brought up with Philip, the new Count of Flanders and spent his childhood in Flanders court. That is why he prefers the name Wilhelm.' She looked to Roger hoping he was impressed with her knowledge.

But Roger was more intent on studying the other colours present in the approaching troop. 'He rides with William Albini but…my God…they ride with his father, old Wills Albini.' He turned to her. 'You had better run to your parents…to expect the Earl of Arundel.'

Anna blanched. 'Heavens above, my mother will have a fit.' She ran for the steps praying she would have time to change into her best gown and head dress.

William Albini waited for his father to climb the steps into the keep of Haughley Castle. On their ride to Haughley, he had pleaded with his father. 'I honestly believe the king can fight the Irish without you. For a man of your standing and advanced years, to ride to the Welsh coast and then sail on a winter sea to Ireland. It is madness.'

His father 'Wills' grimaced as he climbed the steps to the main door. Aged sixty-eight years, his left leg was ailing badly. But he made light of his son's remark. 'Lord Almighty, I can barely mount my horse these days, never mind fight. But in truth, the king will require my council in these difficult times.'

William shook his head as he helped his father through the door. 'I don't understand why he wants to invade Ireland anyway.'

'All the more reason why he will need my council. In any case, you must look to your own assignment.'

Inside the doorway, Ralph le Broc and his wife were waiting and shook hands with the earl and his son. Having no time at all to prepare for their illustrious guests, they knew they both looked in a sorry state.

Making his way from the reception, the earl put them at ease. He had seen it all before. 'We expect no hospitality. My men have brought pack-horses with enough food and wine to feast for a week!' He laughed heartily, trying to hide the pain written on his face. 'Young Earl Wilhelm will join us shortly. He feels he has to put his horse to bed personally.' This time everyone joined in the laughter.

Ralph nervously opened the doors into the grand hall just as the servants carried the stock of food down to the kitchens.

Roger Bigod was stoking the fireplace with more logs and he

strode confidently over to Earl Wills and bowed his head before shaking his hand.

'So young Bigod, William said you would be here.' The earl slumped into a chair, relieved to be off his feet. 'Now where is the lovely Anna I have heard so much about.'

Lady Broc opened a side door and called a servant.

Anna arrived a moment later with a long flowing gown made from expensive layers of silk. She curtsied in front of the Earl of Arundel just as Earl Wilhelm of Essex entered the hall, dressed elegantly in the style of the Champagne courts. He bowed graciously to Anna and spoke in a heavy accent. 'You must be the lovely daughter of the family that I have heard so much about. How lucky of Roger to be your betrothed. Or am I mistaken?'

An awkward silence followed before Roger spoke. 'There is no mistake my lord. We are betrothed.' The voice was steady and with conviction.

Wilhelm gave Roger a cursory glance before returning his gaze to the red faced Anna. 'My dear, is it true you have an ear for the troubadours and poets. I just happen to have brought a poem from Troyes...'

Earl Wills coughed to interrupt. 'I am afraid we have no time for poems this night. Lady Broc, I am afraid after we have eaten, we must ask you to retire to your apartments as we have important matters to discuss.'

Gwen Broc immediately understood and ushered Anna to the kitchens to hurry along the food. After everyone had filled themselves with a hearty meal of pheasant and duck, Gwen and Anna excused themselves and retired for the evening.

Earl Wills had everyone's attention. 'I am glad you are here Roger for a great furore is sweeping across the land and I want to be able to rely on your loyalty to the king. There is no easy way of saying this. Thomas Becket, the Archbishop of Canterbury has been murdered on the altar of his cathedral.'

The shock rippled over everyone in the hall. Ralph and Roger crossed themselves, muttering a prayer.

'My son William has been charged with chasing down the four knights responsible and bringing them to account. Roger, I want you to accompany him.'

At first, Roger Bigod was shocked by the tragic news of Becket. Now he was bewildered. 'My lord, I am honoured by your trust in such a mission, but why would you choose me?'

'Richard le Breton, one of those four knights, was last seen on the road to Framlingham Castle. Perhaps your father could explain why he offers sanctuary to a murderer.'

'How do you know it was Le Breton?'

Wills ignored the question. 'The murderer's made no secret of their identities, but let me tell you this. No matter how it is construed, the king gave no such order to have Becket killed.' He lowered his voice to a whisper. 'Le Breton was seen to strike the fatal blow to the head. So insanely powerful a stroke, it snapped his sword in two. There is even a possible charge of devilment against Le Breton.' He lowered his voice to explain. 'As Becket lay dying, he walked back to his body and with his broken sword he poked out the brains of the archbishop and dashed them about the altar floor, saying he did it for the love of William, the kings deceased brother.'

Ralph le Broc shuddered and shook his head in disbelief. 'You have to find these men and bring them to justice.'

Wills nodded. 'Public opinion agrees with you Lord Broc. As we speak, hundreds of pilgrims enter Canterbury Cathedral, many claiming that miracles are healing the sick. The Archbishop died a martyr and no doubt, one day a Saint. In the meantime, we must pick up the pieces. The king has decided to prepare for a campaign in Ireland. Earl Wilhelm and I will help with the preparations and accompany him. William and Roger will go to Framlingham and track down the traitors who murdered Becket. As a show of strength, you shall have the King's Marshal with twenty knights as an escort, carrying the King's colours. I shall pray for your success.'

The meeting broke up and as Roger gathered his mattress in front of the fireplace, he pondered on the dramatic events of the last few days. But above all, he wondered what kind of welcome he would receive at Framlingham.

Chapter 14

Framlingham Castle
Suffolk

Hugh was furious, kicking a stool out of his path as he strode across the grand hall. 'Be careful of who and what you accuse,' he warned his son.

Roger stood his ground impassively. Towering over his father, he no longer felt threatened, especially as his father's old age seemed to exaggerate all his shortcomings. 'I am simply asking why you took it upon yourself to give sanctuary to a murderer.'

'I can give sanctuary to anyone I like. I am the Earl of Norfolk and one day my first son will inherit my title.' Hugh looked towards Gundred and she noticed a flicker of concern.

Loathing every moment of the confrontation, Gundred stepped in-between them. 'Let me speak,' she said loud enough to for both men to stop their quarrel. 'Roger, a knight named Richard le Breton stopped here two nights ago. My husband insisted that he should leave.'

Before Roger could reply, the king's marshal stepped forward. He had been stood near to Marcus and quietly listening to the proceedings from the behind the row of knights and servants. He stepped forward with enormous authority and everyone turned to listen. 'My name is Bryce, the king's marshal and as such, his most senior representative. My lady, I find your description of events rather interesting. For instance, did you provide refreshments from your kitchens for the fugitive?'

'Well of course, but at the time we had no idea...'

'So you admit you are guilty of harbouring a murderer.'

Hugh tried pushing the marshal away from confronting his wife, before he realised how unyielding the younger man was.

Bonham took a step forward to protect the earl but Hugh waved him away.

'In what direction did he go?' Roger asked, wanting to move on and leave the awkward situation as soon as possible.

'North,' she answered. 'As soon as he confessed his crime, I decided he must leave.'

'You took his confession?' the marshal said, raising his eyebrows.

'Well yes...we heard him confess then he injured himself...'

The marshal loomed large in front of Gundred, then turned to face Hugh, a look of disbelief on his face. 'The man who murdered the Archbishop of Canterbury was invited into your midst where you fed and wined him, listened to his confession, and once you had dressed his wounds, this enemy of the crown left on his own accord...and you did not even think to follow him. It appears you must take some responsibility...'

Hugh thumped the table with his fist. 'Enough of this!' At last he had everyone's attention. 'As a sign of good faith, I shall ride with you to find the four fugitives.'

Marshal Bryce turned back to stare at Gundred, his innermost thoughts distracted by the slim body of the feisty, mature woman before him. 'Very well, we shall stay the night.' He slipped off his belt and sword and the relief in the hall was palpable.

Having overheard every part of the confrontation, Marcus breathed a sigh of relief and quickly ordered the servants to their various duties. With the rush of sudden activity, Hugh failed to notice the eyes of the Marshal roam over Gundred's ample curves.

It was late and by the time they had eaten, William and Roger along with the other knights, were all ready to retire for the night. All except Bryce.

He topped up his goblet with some more wine. 'It is unusual that you do not have a keep, Lord Bigod. How are you supposed to survey the countryside from such small buildings?'

Hugh was often asked the question. 'The high walls are the key to everything,' he explained. 'I prefer to keep them permanently manned and it is preferable to have the guards separated from our domestic arrangements. Also a keep is very expensive to build these days.'

'But have you seen Orford Castle recently. A magnificent keep, you must agree.'

Hugh wished he could wipe the smirk off Bryce's face. 'With unlimited funds anything is possible,' he replied.

The marshal turned to Gundred and smiled. 'And what do you think, Lady Bigod.'

Gundred was lost in her thoughts and the question caught her off her guard. 'My pardon sir, I am afraid I was not listening.'

'It was nothing. Perhaps you would be good enough to show me to my sleeping quarters,' he asked.

Hugh butted in. 'My servants will take you upstairs…'

'No, I shall do it,' Gundred interrupted, still feeling embarrassed. Taking holds of a oil lamp, she walked up the staircase and the marshal followed. On the first floor, Gundred nodded to one side of the corridor. 'This is your room, next to ours. I am sorry if it is smaller than you are used to. If you want to pray, the chapel is outside, a little to the east.'

Bryce towered menacingly over her frail frame 'Do you think my soul needs prayer? I will wager a woman such as you could twist any man into the devil's arms.' He pushed her gently against the wall of the corridor and placed his hands gently on her left breast. She jumped a little but remained calm. His hand moved inside her inner tunic and his fingers dwelt over her nipple as his head began to lower for a kiss.

'Take your hands off me now or I will scream,' she threatened.

His mouth was only a breath away. 'I can have you arrested and thrown in prison for what you have confessed this night. You will not scream.' His lips pressed against hers but she refused to open her mouth. His right hand moved down to the hem of her finest flowing gown and in an instant he had pulled the dress up above her knees. His hand moved roughly up between her legs, prising apart her thighs, causing Gundred to gasp in shock.

Instinctively she kept her legs closed, refusing him access to her innermost lips but she dare not cry out. He grunted and began to force an opening. His strength was overpowering and she felt herself give way. Again, his mouth pressed hard against hers, forcing a little gap to appear. In the same moment of weakness, his finger entered the moist walls of her vagina. With a final effort, she pulled away. Her breasts heaving, she tried to regain her composure.

The thud of footsteps made them both turn towards the staircase. Slowly, Bryce released her from his grip then lustfully took in the smell of her sex upon his finger. Staring into her eyes, he drew the finger across her lips, pressing it down to emphasis the meaning of silence. She recoiled at the musky smell, just as Hugh appeared on the top of the staircase.

Marshal Bryce slipped into his chamber and Hugh was none the wiser for the encounter. Inside their chamber, Hugh noticed his wife was trembling. 'Are you cold,' he asked.

'Yes…just a little,' she said with a quick smile.

Hugh frowned. 'I have spoken to Marcus and he appears concerned for your safety. He said he would stay here with you.'

'Do you suspect something is wrong?'

'No, but it is likely I shall be away for some time. Damn it, I hate being manipulated by the king like this.'

Led by Earl Hugh and Marshal Bryce, the troop set off towards

Cambridge and soon they joined the old Roman road that ran north to Lincoln. Hugh rode to the fore with Bonham and five of his best knights, while his son Roger and William Albini took up the rear, thus avoiding any unnecessary contact between the two parties.

From town to village, agents of the king would report on the movements of strangers, and William was pleased that a man fitting the description of Richard le Breton had passed only two days before. They kept to a steady pace, stopping only as fatigue forced them to rest at taverns in Cambridge and Lincoln.

Throughout the next few days, it became clear that Le Breton was still heading north. Eventually they reached York and to their surprise, they were told that Richard Le Breton had rejoined with the other three fugitive knights, Reginald FitzUrse, Hugh d'Morville and William de Tracy. All were reported to be still heading north, with one town burgher swearing he had overheard them talk of Scotland.

Unsure of how far they were to take the pursuit, William and Roger took the news ambivalently. The marshal reminded them that the king had given them leave to find the four men at all costs and that would include entering Scotland. They all turned to Hugh, silently seeking his agreement.

'Well I have no wish to enter Scotland,' he declared. 'At my age, the wet and the cold do not agree with me.'

Marshal Bryce spoke up. 'Out of all of us, you have the most sway with the King of Scotland. I would not like to question your loyalty to the crown but if you returned now, I think others would look dimly upon your decision. Besides, I believe King Henry would find your assistance worthy of a reward.'

Hugh bristled with indignation. He deliberately turned to his son Roger. 'Do you think I would do this for the king's coin. What do you think I am, some fucking surf looking for a handful of pennies to be thrown at my feet?'

Roger was caught off guard. 'No my lord...' he stammered.

'I will come with you if only to show my loyalty to King Henry. Not because this conniving bastard Bryce wants me to. Is that understood.' Hugh turned his horse. 'To Scotland it is then.'

Hugh smiled to himself. In just a few moments, he had become the leader of the mission to bring the four murderers to justice. Naturally, if he succeeded he would probably be offered money, land and probably another castle. But he would have only one demand. The city of Norwich would be his price.

That night they slept in an inn and Roger was woken by the sound of horses leaving on the road south. He ran downstairs to confront the senior groom and was told that the marshal had left with three of his knights. 'He was suffering with a bout of sickness and decided against a prolonged search in the north. He said we were capable of completing the mission without him.'

William Albini had joined Roger and they both thought the story was unlikely. More than likely the marshal had a pressing engagement elsewhere, that he preferred to keep to himself. Neither of them had liked the brooding marshal and were quietly pleased that the success of the mission was now back in their hands.

Hugh appeared in the door, still wrapped in a blanket. 'What the fuck is going on? And who rode off?'

They told him what had happened and he grunted.

'Didn't like the bastard anyway,' he said, speaking for all three of them as he took a pee into a basin. 'Let's get a move on or we will never catch those murdering bastards.'

Celia the nanny burst into the solar while Gundred was playing with young Hugh, her face a picture of girlish joy. 'My lady, horses are approaching the castle.'

The smiling maid took Hugh from Gundred and they went to play into her room while Gundred ran down the staircase, delighted that her husband had returned so soon. She reminded herself to instruct the kitchens to bone two capons and tonight they would have a feast. She entered the hall at the same time as the main door opened. Her heart broke at the sight of Marshal Bryce.

'Where is Earl Bigod and his son?' she asked calmly, her head held high in a dignified manner.

Bryce walked to the fireplace and took off his boots and sword. 'Well if they continue to follow the trail of the errant knights, then they are well on their way to Edinburgh. For that is where the king advised them to hide. Now get me something to eat and drink.' His eyes narrowed and he stared at Gundred with a glint in his eye that sent a shiver up her spine. '

Looking to the door, she heard footsteps. 'There are six knights within the precincts,' she warned trying to maintain her authority.

The door opened and in walked one of the marshal's men. 'My lord, we have apprehended four of the earl's knights and locked them in the storerooms.'

'Apparently you missed the other two. Kill them if they resist.'

Gundred took a step towards him. 'Are you mad…you cannot come here and kill…'

Bryce stood up sharply. 'Shut up you whore!' he slapped her hard across the face.

A trickle of blood seeped from her cut lip. Using every ounce of pride in her body, she stood rigid and faced her tormentor.

He raised his arm again to strike her and she cowered instinctively to shield herself from the blow. But it never came. Lowering his arm, he sat back down. 'That's more like it, ' he growled. 'Priggish boars like you are all the same. All pride and no fight. Now go and get the food and wine.'

They ate quietly, though all the time Gundred was thinking how to save herself from whatever ill fortune awaited her. Surely, this could not be happening. Not in her own castle, surrounded by her maids and servants…and her young boy. She prayed that Celia had shut herself safely in Hugh's room.

Hugh would kill her if anything happened to his son.

And where on earth was Marcus, she wondered. She had not seen him all day.

Bryce burped loudly and sat back satisfied at his capon and expensive red wine. I know what you are thinking. Why am I persecuting you when you have done nothing wrong.'

Gundred nodded hoping for an answer.

'I shall tell you. As a representative of the king I am duty bound to arrest those guilty of conspiring to aid the murderers of the archbishop.'

'But I don't understand, 'Gundred protested. 'You said the king told them to escape to Edinburgh.'

'The king was in a quandary and due to go to Ireland and as always the safety of the realm was his priority. I convinced the king that Bigod could easily be persuaded to follow the miscreants north, while the king decided on their fate. Yes, it was agreed they would go into hiding. And yes, the manhunt is just a sham. But sometimes the king must play on both sides of the same fight to keep the barons in check. But you did not know that when you helped Le Breton.' He stood up and towered over her. 'I am taking you to London to stand trial.'

A look of sheer horror swept over her face. Should she beg or plead for mercy. Her lips trembled and a tear fell down her face.

Sitting on the table edge, Bryce stroked her cheek and wiped away the tear. 'Of course, all this could be avoided if you give me what I want.' His hand caressed her throat then meandered lower until inside her tunic. He wrapped his palm around her breast and squeezed. 'This time we will not be interrupted.' Standing up, he undid his breeches and pulled her head down onto his groin.

This time Gundred accepted her fate. Totally helpless, she knew the best way of escape was to make the man spill his seed as soon as possible, before he committed rape or became violent. Without hesitation, she took his prick in her mouth and gently pulled and sucked as expertly as possible. He accepted her gratefully and his breathing quickened.

Only a few moments passed before Bryce rolled his head back and ejaculated in her mouth. Slowly his breathing returned to normal. 'As I thought, you are just a whore. The night is still young. I think we should retire for the night.'

Tears stung her eyes at the brazen audacity of the marshal when she realised he intended to sleep with her in her husbands bed. Reluctantly she was pulled up the staircase and into her bedroom. She cried out for Marcus to come to her aid but to no avail.

'He is the last person you will see coming to help you.'

He slapped her again and threw her onto the bed. 'Be quiet and take off all you clothes.'

'You are mad if you think you can get away with this.'

Bryce stripped off his tunic and breeches. 'I hear the dungeons at the tower are particularly cold and wet this time of the year. But the guards will keep you warm though…by raping you every day…then charging their friends to rape you every night.'

Gundred removed all her clothes and sat modestly on the bed, praying he would soon tire.

Just then, a scream was heard outside the door and Gundred recognised it as Celia. Her heart jumped, for she had left young Hugh with her.

Bryce leapt to his feet and called to his captain. 'Get the maid in here quickly.' Entering the chamber, the captain pushed Celia in front of him. She was still holding Hugh wrapped in his nightgown.

'Put the kid on the floor for God's sake and get her on the bed. I take it you have brought the elixir.'

The sergeant was about twenty, tall and well built. Apart from his tunic opened to the waist, he was naked.

Celia fell onto the bed next to Gundred.

'She has had her dose,' said the sergeant nodding to Celia. He looked lustily at Gundred.

Seeing his large member beginning to become aroused, she feared the worst. In his right hand, he held a small bottle and took a swig before passing it to Bryce. He too drank just one mouthful. 'Your turn my dear.'

'My son...'she stammered looking at the poor forlorn face of Hugh as he sat on the floor.

Bryce forcibly held Gundred down and put the bottle to her mouth while holding her nose. 'Drink!' he shouted.

She coughed and caught her breath, accidentally gulping at the liquid. She emptied the bottle but for a few drops.

'My God, you are a greedy bugger. You are going fuck like a animal.'

Little Hugh started crying and held out his arms towards Gundred. Bryce dipped his finger in the bottle and put it in the boy's mouth. Wrapping in his blanket he left him in the corner of the room. Gundred tried to see to him but her head was spinning and she lay back down. A warm luscious feeling spread through every muscle of every limb, and all she could do was smile.

Bryce pulled off his breeches. 'The little runt won't be disturbing us for a while.'

Gundred turned her head to look at Celia and took a sharp intake of air as she felt the delicate stroke of a woman upon her breasts. Her stomach seemed to glow as if touched by a thousand butterflies. There was an urge to widen her legs, as she felt something warm probing deep inside. Looking down, all she could see was the top of Bryce's head.

Her mouth was prized open, making her gag at first until she relaxed. Moaning loudly as the first rapturous wave swept over her;

she could only imagine what depravity was being exercised upon the rest of her body.

As the sweet smell of Celia's hair filled her nostrils, she gagged then swallowed a salty load before wrapping her lips around an engorged nipple. There was no compunction to stop the pleasure. In fact, her craving became more intense as all misgivings were swept away and her body demanded more, becoming entwined in an abundance of sweaty flesh.

Chapter 15

Blois
Loire Valley

Twenty-three years ago, young Henri, the Count of Champagne had joined the second army of God as a boy and returned a man. The people and the church had respected his brave exploits 'for one so young' and although Nuradin defeated the army at Damascus, he had received genuine and lasting support, ever since his return.

At the time of his father's death, he had inherited his title, and his younger brother Theobald ruled the territory of Blois as Theobald V.

Privately, he admitted to his closet family and friends that while the nightmares persisted, he would never return to the Holy Land. The inhuman death of his friend Earl Warenne had scarred him for life and tested his belief in all that was good and Holy. He found the remains of the earl after the evil Turks had sliced him open and attached his intestine to the leg of a terrified goat; no doubt to the delight of those who watched.

Seven years ago, everyone thought his marriage to Marie, the daughter of King Louis of France and Eleanor of Aquataine, to be the perfect match. Now in her early twenties, she was beautiful and charismatic, while he was handsome and intelligent and aged nearly twenty years more than his wife.

In the same year, either by an astonishing co-incidence or as many believed by design, his brother Theobald had married Alix, the younger sister of Marie and the second daughter of the King of France. The marriages left no one in any doubt of the alliance between the royal house of France and the houses of Champagne and Blois.

From the start, Henri was determined to make Champagne the most profitable territory outside of Louis's France and after twenty years of rule, most people agreed that he had succeeded. The triumph of the trade fairs instigated by Count Hugues, two generations ago, had brought wealth to the region on an unprecedented scale. With his wife Marie at the helm, the court of Troyes had become the most cultured in all the land, where the halls and corridors celebrated the troubadours, poets and performers from across the land, and the talk was of chivalry and courtly love.

But while Henri and Marie indulged themselves in commerce and culture, his brother Theobald found he was not capable of achieving anywhere near the same level of success.

Henri and Theobald had a younger brother Stephen Count of Sancerre and only a year ago there was great excitement when a delegation arrived from Jerusalem asking Stephen to consider marrying Sybilla, the daughter of King Amalric of Jerusalem.

Theobald had persuaded him to go, enticing him with the promise of the Kingdom of Jerusalem. Theobald remained ever hopeful that such an exotic marriage could only improve his own fortunes in trade and commerce.

Ironically, Theobald was rich enough but never seemed to have any money. Only a few months ago, he had been renovating the walls of Chartres, but now he had to call a halt to the work as he had nothing to pay the masons. Surrounded by councillors, the wealth of the province seemed to fritter away and all he had left were excuses and debts. And as for his wife Ali, she was the biggest culprit for wasting money.

Theobald rode into Blois from Chartres and discovered to his horror the city was suddenly gripped in the throes of rampant anti-Semitism. Angry at seeing the mob on the streets he demanded his councillors to assemble and report immediately.

Once in his palace, his chaplain Cranston stepped forward. 'My lord, while you were away a terrible event occurred. A Christian servant of the mayor reported a terrible act of violence had been perpetrated. As he was watering the mayor's horse by the River Loire, it was suddenly startled by the appearance of a Jew on horseback. This Jew threw the body of a small Christian boy into the river. So shaken was the horse, it refused to drink. In fear for his own life, the servant ran back to his master and told him what he had seen. He swore the boy's skin was so pale; his blood must have been drained. We suspect blood-letting and ritualistic murder.'

The gasp of horror from a number of councillors did not go unnoticed by Theobald and the mood of his council was self-evident. Someone muttered the same had happened in the English city of Norwich, some twenty-five years earlier to a boy called William and that he was now blessed as a saint.

Theobald felt himself being manipulated so before he would pronounce any opinion or judgement, he insisted that he would question the servant and master the next morning.

The dilemma raised a number of consequences for the count to consider, not least one of money. The province of Blois was deep in debt and most of the money was owed to Jewish moneylenders.

That evening he retired to the chapel for God's guidance, whereas in truth, he was about to meet a Jew who happened to be his largest lender and financial advisor.

As he prayed at the altar, he heard the feather light footsteps enter the antechamber next door. He crept out of the chapel and into the dimly lit chamber, closing the door behind him. Stood in front of him there was no mistaking the outline of Pulcelina, his secret lover. She rushed into his arms and kissed him passionately on the lips.

'Theobald, you must stop what is happening about this so called "ritual killing". You know the story is a nonsense...a complete fabrication.'

Theobald extracted himself from her grip. 'That is easy for you to say, but the evidence is…'

'The evidence does not exist. There is no missing child and there is no corpse. But tomorrow the council will tell you to make arrests but you know why they will try to convince you. All of them; including the mayor are in debt to the Jews.'

Theobald held her gently in his arms.

Again, she kissed him pulling him closer and taking his hand to her breasts. 'Please…please make love to me,' she pleaded. He pushed her against the table and tugged at the layers of expensive material before slipping his hand between her welcoming legs.

Listening outside the door to the grunts and groans of the lustful union was his chaplain, Cranston. He had heard enough and went back to the inner hall to report on his findings.

Conspiring quietly in the hall he found Theobald's wife Alix and the chancellor and two of his stewards. Cranston told them what was happening and although her cheeks turned red and a trembling voice betrayed her inner rage, Alix remained outwardly calm. 'Gentlemen, we must ensure tomorrow that the Jewess Pulcelina is arrested and kept away from my husband at all costs. Once we have convinced him of the correct course of action, we do not want him changing his mind under her evil influence.'

The next morning Theobald, was put under pressure from his wife Alix and his council to make a decision but he insisted he would not act hastily.

The time had come for Alix to present her hand and she took him to one side and whispered. 'You have been indiscreet, my husband. If you do not do as I wish, it is I who will have to act decisively. I suggest you feint outrage at the accusations and order the arrest of all Jews now.'

Theobald looked to the faces of those who schemed against him. He was left with no choice. With an appropriate amount of indignation, he ordered all the Jews of Blois to be rounded up and imprisoned.

As if a coiled spring was released, the palace garrison and courtyards burst into activity as soldiers and guards shouted their orders and assembled. Everything seemed pre-planned and he no longer felt in control.

Nervously, Theobald looked around for Pulcelina but she was nowhere to be seen. Then, in an attempt to take back control, he ordered that the mayor's servant be severely interrogated to see if he was lying about the encounter with the Jew. His council reluctantly agreed and while they awaited the outcome of the questioning, there was news of a delegation arriving from Troyes to plead the case on behalf of the Jews. A ripple of shock and consternation ran around the court when it became known who was leading the delegation.

Rabbi Jacob ben Meir.

For many years, his name had become synonymous with the Jews of Troyes and many of the courtiers recognised his name as a great and aged spiritual leader of the Jews.

But a few of the more senior councils of law understood the true significance of his attendance in Blois as they recalled when he had famously defended the Jews in Norwich, who stood accused of the same crimes of ritual murder. Twenty-five years ago, Jacob was just practicing law. Now he was a founder of the famous Troyes Council, regularly attended by over one hundred and fifty rabbis.

Waiting in the small reception hall of the palace, Rabbi Jacob sat stroking his long white beard and sighed at the wasted opulence of the court interior. At the age of seventy-one, it never failed to surprise him how much greed was wrapped up in the material wealth of the Christian nobles.

He gazed across at his clerk Ephraim and his protégée Baruch and could not resist a comment. 'A coat is worn to keep you warm. But these people have to have it lined with gold and trimmed with expensive gems and laces and all manner of unnecessary adornments. The coat becomes desirable and spreads envy amongst those who gaze upon its richness and in turn, they desire coats that are more expensive. But in the end, it is still a coat.'

They both nodded in agreement at Jacob while Ephraim wrote down a few words using a fine lead stick.

A few courtiers passing by, paused to hear his words.

Jacob recalled his last dealings with a riotous crowd. 'I remember being saved from a mob by two English Lords. Lord Peverel and Earl Warenne, no less.' Jacob held up his palms to show the tell-tale marks of the nail. 'They were not false or grandiose and neither did they fear the fervour of the mob. They were brave and fearless men and I was proud to be their friend. Pray that this day, such men still exist.'

Some passing courtiers hung their heads and gave each other awkward glances. Jacob heard a call echo down the corridor and they followed a servant into the inner hall. Count Theobald did not stand but smiled and waited patiently as Jacob settled into a chair alongside Ephraim and Baruch.

'I hope your journey has not been wasted. Do you wish to defend your community against the charges?'

Jacob cleared his throat. 'How can I defend against those who only believe in evil for their own gain?'

'Your point is what exactly?' Theobald countered.

'The myth that Christian blood is spilt from young boys at Passover is a lie spread by those who have ulterior motives. But I will not waste my time on semantics nor on the iniquity of the charges. In my stead, I shall let my protégé Baruch speak for my people.'

In his early thirties, Baruch was slim with a kindly face though his hooked nose detracted from his good looks. His thick black hair was swept from his face and he always took good care of his teeth.

Since he was an adolescent, he had studied at the famous yeshiva in Troyes, where he liked to think himself as a favourite of Jacob, and blushed with pride when he was described as a protégé. The dynasty of Rabbis that were related to Jacob was legendary, and association with Jacob assured Baruch's place in the line of academic succession.

Opening a satchel, Baruch took out ten bags of heavy coins. 'You hold forty Jews in prison and I have collected one thousand pounds for their release. This is a down payment of two hundred pounds.'

The count had been expecting an offer of money and the amount was impressive and certainly more than he thought they could have raised in so short a time. He pursed his thin lips and held his fingers to his chin as if deep in thought. 'Very well, I shall take the two hundred in good faith. But I cannot release any of them until I receive the balance.'

Baruch glanced at Jacob but he could offer little assistance. 'At least you can agree to release some of them,' he suggested. Both parties suddenly felt they were floundering not really knowing the course they should accept or deny.

The count whispered towards one of his advisors. 'I should really let some of them go.'

The young man did not want to disagree with the count. 'Perhaps the children, my lord.'

Theobald was relieved and nodded to his advisor to take the bags of money. 'Of course, the children can be released. A further decision regarding the others will be made at the trial tomorrow. Now if you would like to visit the refectory I am assured you will find something to eat.'

The count stood up and pointed them through a door, while he stepped up the staircase to his apartments.

Chaplain Cranston was waiting in the count's chamber with Alix and watched as the advisor dropped the bags of coins onto the table. 'We cannot accept the money. You must take it back to the negotiating table now.'

The count stared at the chaplain as if he were mad. 'What do you mean. We can make a thousand pounds…'

'I do not want to rot in hell for taking their money on top of everything else.' Alix interrupted.

The count sighed and nodded to the baffled advisor to take the bags back. 'Well I suppose at the trial we can always insist on full payment as a fine.'

Alix lent over to her husband and gave him a gentler kiss. 'Do not worry, my love. None of this should be your concern.'

'I must admit, all this worry has given me a frightful headache,' he complained, rubbing his forehead and sitting on the side of his bed.

Alix looked at Cranston. 'We will leave you to rest, my love.' They quickly disappeared down the staircase and out into the courtyard.

Theobald called for his servant and asked quietly. 'Have you seen Pulcelina?'

'No my lord, I have not.'

Theobald lay down, his head throbbing.

In the current climate she must be keeping out of the way.

Jacob had barely registered the count's departure. 'What has happened? Is he coming back?'

Ephraim and Baruch helped him down a few steps that led past the kitchens. The table had been laid with bread and boiled eggs and they sat down to eat. A serving girl smiled as she poured the wine. The courtesy of a meal was totally unexpected.

After the meal, Baruch wrapped three loaves of bread into a cloth and handed them to Ephraim. 'See if you can find out where the people are being held, and ensure they are in good health. It is the least we can do.' Ephraim nodded and went back up the staircase.

Jacob finished his wine. 'You have done well today, Baruch. There are many people who should be grateful for your efforts.'

'Was it like this in Norwich?' Baruch asked.

'It was far worse. They were rioting in the streets, howling like animals for our blood. But the family was saved from certain death...at a cost of course. I don't suppose this will be the last time such persecution will raise its ugly head.' Jacob took another sip of wine. 'You remember I told you of a similar instance in Egypt a year or two ago.'

Baruch remembered the story. 'yes, when the Christian army massacred the inhabitants of Bilbeis. A Rabbi collected a ransom from all the Jewish communities and negotiated with King Amalric to pay for their release. I found the story inspiring.'

Jacob smiled. 'Well I found out who the man was. None other than Rabbi Maimonides.'

Baruch did not look too surprised. 'The man is very talented and he will be a great scholar of the Torah one day. It does not surprise me that his first thought was to protect the lives of others.'

'I see many similarities in both of you. I am an old man now, whereas you and Maimonides are in your early thirties. You are the next generation of Talmudic authority and after all this is over, I want you to go to Egypt and join forces with him. Together you can fight the evil that seems to come so naturally to the gentiles. And just think what you could learn from each other.'

Baruch was surprised at the suddenness of the proposal. His mentor had obviously put some thought into the idea.

Suddenly the silence was broken when Ephraim ran back inside the refectory, panic etched across his face. He was carrying the bags of silver and gold. 'They have returned the money and everyone has gone except for a few servants. Quick, we must leave.'

Even Jacob was perplexed. 'I don't trust the count. He does not seem to be in control. Where are all his councillors?'

As Ephraim led Jacob outside to the courtyard, Baruch ran to the stables to find anyone who could help.

Jacob was becoming agitated and Ephraim tried to calm him. 'Don't worry yourself. We will find them and plead for their safety.'

Baruch came running out of the stable doors, shouting. 'Ephraim, quick get on your horse! They have taken everyone to the house of Pulcelina, a mile from here. We must ride hard.' He turned to Jacob. 'Rabbi you must stay here by the stables where you will be safe.'

Galloping out of the palace gates, Jacob shook his head and walked over to the shade of the stables, wiping the dust from his eyes.

In the glow of the afternoon sun, the scene at Pulcelina's house was becoming a dark nightmare from which she could not extract herself.

Her right leg was chained to her door-jamb and on the road outside the soldiers held back the children who screamed as their families were pushed inside the house.

Behind the children, were a crowd of onlookers and Pulcelina noticed a woman sat quietly on an ox cart. Her face was partly covered by a cowl but somehow she looked familiar.

Inside she could hear the raised voice of Cranston the chaplain, demanding the Jews relinquish their faith and convert. Twisting her head around the door, she winced at the scene inside. A Rabbi lay curled up in a foetal position as a young soldier stabbed him in the back and sides with a short knife. His malevolent eyes filled her with fear as he stabbed again and again, repeating the word, 'convert...convert...' The blood ran freely though his gown and onto the earthen floor.

Another soldier was punching a woman about the head until her jaw broke and a splatter of blood curdled from her mouth. Anonymous screams were coming from behind the door as unknown atrocities were being performed, though the sound of lustful grunting told her that maidenhoods were being taken.

About six women were led from the house swearing they would convert. They had been tortured and beaten and knew that a sympathetic God would not blame them. As they were led towards the church, she wondered when faced with the decision, would she be brave or stupid. More importantly, could she tell the difference.

The beatings eventually came to a halt, leaving numerous victims scattered about the floor. The soldiers emerged covered in sweat, followed by the chaplain. His habit was stained with blood and he wore a hood to mask his face in a vain attempt to hide his identity. The soldiers went to the cart, returning with bundles of faggots and thorn bushes and placed them against the walls of her house. A gasp of anticipation lifted the crowd who were slowly warming to the spectacle that until now had been mostly out of sight.

Suddenly two horsemen rode in front of the crowd. Angrily they decried what was happening and for a moment, she experienced the hope of release. Then she saw they were Jews. The soldiers pushed them back into the crowd and threatened them with the blade of a sword if they caused any more commotion.

Without warning, a soldier walked up to Pulcelina and ripped open her expensive gown. Then he tore at her inner tunic until her chest was laid bare down to her navel for all to see.

The eyes of the men in the crowd widened as they edged forward for a better view. Picking up a branch of thorn bush, the soldier wafted the thorns against her face and throat, teasing out the first trickles of blood.

He turned to the expectant audience. 'Go on then,' came the voice of one wide-eyed peasant. 'Do it.'

Standing back a little, he swung the branch with force against her breasts. The shock of pain did not hit her until the second blow. Instinctively she turned her torso away and the thorns pulled across her skin, ripping open her flesh. Again and again, he thrashed her

157

until her agonising screams began to fade until the only sound she heard was her own voice silently pleading. Looking across the faces of the baying crowd, she watched the woman sitting passively in the cart and detected the faintest of smiles.

Inside the house, three Rabbis' were dragged across the floor and tied to the central pillars and more faggots were placed about their feet.

Using the last of her strength, Pulcelina cried out. 'I convert. So help me God, I shall convert.'

The soldier looked to the chaplain who shook his head. 'Too late you whore of Satan.' He reached out and pulled at the remains of her gown to reveal her nakedness. Nodding to the solder, he broke off a piece of thorn bush then he told him to pull her legs apart. 'Let the thorns of Christ cleanse your blood.' He stuffed the branch between her legs. Amid her screams, he whispered in her ear. 'The more you struggle the more painful it is.' She relaxed a little and closed her eyes to the world as the wood slowly entered her vagina.

When he felt some resistance the chaplain turned to the crowd to show his work. He found the face he was looking for and perceived a nod. Turning back to Pulcelina, he breathed heavily in her face. 'You made the wrong enemies my dear.' Then using all his strength in both hands, he grasped the branch and gave it a mighty push.

The primeval scream sent spittle over his face. Still he pushed, grunting with the exertion until she fainted and he fell away from her, his chest heaving for air.

Another soldier arrived having run from the palace. He stood in front of the Chaplain Cranston, and then gazed in at the sight of the naked woman, looking in amazement at the phallic appendage between her trembling, bloodstained legs.

The chaplain admonished him. 'What is it soldier? This is God's work not a whorehouse show.'

In a quiet voice, the soldier relayed his news. 'The money has been taken back. Nothing has been paid.'

Cranston walked to soldiers holding the children. 'Let the children return to their families. He led them by the hand, some only toddlers who followed him blinded by the false smile, back into the house. The relief of the children's voices being returned was mixed with the cries of mercy from their elders.

The chaplain ordered his men to light the torches. 'Satan and his demons reside here. Let us burn Satan from this house and if any are innocent then God will look after his own!'

Jacob was annoyed at the jibes from the children in the courtyard. When they started to throw stones at him, he walked out of the main gates and asked for directions to the house of Pulcelina. Looking up at the slope, he could make out a crowd of people gathered at the junction near the top of the road.

The sound of women screaming made him hurry and soon he was barging his way to the front, upsetting some who were in his way. 'Let the Rabbi through,' someone cried out and those at the front let him through, appreciating the addition of more ingredients into the well of violence.

It only took a moment to absorb the horror of the scene before him. They were about to set fire to the house and he was in no doubt that Ephraim and Baruch were inside and about to be burnt to death. The rage welled up inside at the sight of the naked woman chained to the door and he burst through the front row, heading for the instigator. Arms outstretched he nearly bowled the chaplain over. 'How dare you perform this abomination in the name of God,' he lamented. 'Shame on you...shame on you all!' He jabbed his finger into the chest of the chaplain. Two soldiers grabbed the old man and thinking he had escaped shoved him towards the door. He collided with Pulcelina and the crowd laughed at the sight of the old Jew holding on to the naked woman.

Inside the house, it was so dark he could not make out the faces of those tied up against the pillars. Some of those lying on the floor rose to their knees pleading to free them. Sensing their own mortal danger, the children crowded around him crying.

Suddenly the house was filled with smoke and a gasp went up from the crowd outside as the tinder dry roof burst into flames. Jacob felt his lungs fill with smoke and he leant against one of the central pillars. Burning debris fell from the ceiling and instantly enveloped his cloak in flames. The pain up his arms and back shocked him and he let out an involuntary scream.

Those on the floor scrambled away from him and gathered their children closer. As the flames licked around his torso, Jacob believed he was finished and prayed silently for the souls of the frightened children huddled with their distraught mothers. His beard began to burn and tears of pain ran down his cheeks.

With his eyes closed, he never saw Ephraim and Baruch risk their lives by rushing into the house. They dragged him outside by his arms, throwing soil and dirt over the old rabbi until the flames were extinguished. The crowd edged closer trying to see the burns he had suffered.

Word circulated fast. Apparently, the Jew was an important Rabbi of Troyes and highly respected in the court of Champagne. In obvious pain, he was carried to a well and his burns soaked from a bucket of water.

Attention soon changed to the main event and the men in the crowd began to dare themselves to run forward and touch the private parts of the woman while she was unconscious. So far, the flames had avoided her and then someone threw a pail of water over her face. The crowd cheered as she opened her eyes and glared in terror at the smoke and flames. The sight of the naked Jewish witch struggling to avoid the flames catered for the hunger.

Now screams were coming from inside the house as the burning roof started to collapse. Two men staggered outside and appeared relatively unharmed. The crowd booed, until the soldiers pushed them back inside with spears. Flames began to burn through the ropes holding them together and more men tried to escape, only to be jeered again by the crowd. The soldiers pushed the escapees back inside to the sound of cheers.

The crowd fell deadly silent as a toddler stumbled through the door; her skin blistering from the heat inside. Crying and helpless, she fell to her knees then stood up again. They gasped in surprise as her mother stepped outside and grabbed her baby, taking her back inside to be with her family. The reward for such blind bravery was a ripple of applause from those who appreciated such a revolting spectacle.

As Baruch dabbed Jacobs's burns with a wet cloth, the screams from inside the house reached a crescendo and were accompanied by the stench of burning flesh. Some began to turn away; their places quickly taken by those eager to see the sickly show of entertainment.

Ephraim witnessed the morality of men crumble everywhere he looked. He closed his eyes and covered his ears, sobbing and praying that the ground would swallow him up. The interior was now an inferno and the screams subsided as the flames subsided. All were dead except for Pulcelina still chained to the door.

The flames suddenly grew stronger above her head. A cheer could be heard as some men dared to squeeze her breasts and pull on the stick protruding between her legs. One even wagered to pee over her thighs and buttocks before running back into the cheering throng of boisterous faces to collect his coins. The pee quickly turned to steam but the woman's eyes were fixed on an anonymous face in the crowd.

The crowd fell silent again as the flames performed a deadly dance over her body, slowly turning the blistered skin from red to black. Chaplain Cranston turned to face the crowd and he raised his sword as if to offer a merciful end. Amidst the calls for compassion from those watching, he waited for a signal from an anonymous source. But no gesture of mercy was forthcoming.

Lowering his sword, he rammed it into the soil. He had seen enough and pushed his way passed the crowd to return to the palace.

Under a sheet of flame, the woman curled up like a baby and the large wooden lintel above her head brought an unwitting end to the day's atrocity, by crushing her skull in a blaze of flames and sparks.

The driver of the cart shouted for the crowd to make way and as he drove away, Baruch could see the mysterious woman at the driver's side. The wind caught her cowl and for a fleeting moment, her face was revealed.

'There goes the countess,' one passer-by remarked.

The thought that Theobald's wife had perpetrated all the horror he had witnessed that day, made Baruch nauseous. But of course, the count's chaplain could not have instigated the slaughter without some form of consent from the palace. While he pondered, he became aware that Jacob was whimpering in pain from his burns and they had to find a physician as soon as possible.

No Jewish doctors had survived the massacre, and no Christian doctor would treat Jacob for fear of reprisal from the count. In an empty synagogue, his blackened and blistered body was placed on a mattress. From time to time, he spoke, as his skin began to putrefy in a sea of pus. In his delirium, it was difficult to separate what was sane from the insane. For hours, he would repeat the name of Miriam and utter words that seemed to end in a nightmare of death and guilt. Perhaps he was reconciling his life from long ago, thought Baruch.

Jacob knew he was close to death, but there was always one subject he returned to. Late one night after sucking on a herbal root to dull the pain, he spoke quite lucidly. 'Find Maimonides,' he told Baruch. 'Together you can use your talent to prevent more massacres...and who knows, one day you could find the means to expose the truth of Lydda.'

'Do you mean Lydda in the Holy Land?'

'I have often told you of Earl Warenne and the knight called Peverel...these were brave men who ran into a burning building to save me from crucifixion. Not unlike your own selfless act of bravery.'

Baruch nodded. The old man often recalled the day he was assaulted by the mob in Ramerupt and how the two knights had saved him from a terrible death.

'What I never told you is that Peverel died in Lydda...looking for a relic of Christ. I have no doubt Peverel's father also died for the same cause, and they would not have been the only ones. Who knows how many more suffered and died. I heard that Count Hughes himself died at Lydda...all on the words uttered by my Grandfather Rashi.'

Baruch thought he knew all the extensive works of the famed Rabbi Rashi. Then Jacob started rambling again and it was difficult to find sense in any of his words.

'I was five years old when I witnessed the demon that killed my Grandfather. Rashi was burnt to death as they tried to burn me. The same evil was present in the eyes of everyone who watched today...those poor women and children...how could they stand by...' His words drifted as he closed his eyes and grimaced in pain. 'The demon was misinformed,' Jacob uttered.

'What do you mean misinformed,' Baruch asked, pressing a bowl of water between Jacobs lips.

'Rashi was mis-quoted or mis-translated, I don't know which. Everyone was mis-led into looking for the Christhead. There never was the head of Christ at Lydda. My father told me of the exact translation. The Gospel of Nicodemus was quite clear…he called it the shame…'

Baruch was confused by the incoherent flow of words. 'I do not understand. What do you mean? What was the shame? Was it a sign or an omen?'

Despite his pain, Jacob forced a smile. 'Peverel told me that Abbot Bernard of Clairvaux demanded the crypt destroyed with all its contents. The abbot understood the dangers to the Christian faith…if the relic was suddenly discovered…'

Baruch still looked baffled.

'Listen with the ears of a gentile not a Jew. Those who heard the story were wrong to believe 'the shame' referred to the Romans killing Christ. According to the Christian doctrine, it was essential that Christ was publicly crucified and his resurrection witnessed. But if parts of His body were found, the resurrection would have to be denounced as fakery, existing only for self-interest. From every pope to every priest…exposed for propagating a lie for a thousand years. The Christian church would die in disgrace.' His voice tailed away with the effort of talking. 'Promise me you will find Maimonides…look for the cross under the crypt at Lydda…'

Jacob fell into unconsciousness and he never uttered another word.

For the next three days, every hour seemed an eternity. When Jacob finally died, Ephraim gave thanks to God and exhausted to the bone, he went to lie down.

Baruch had fared a little better and his first thought was to leave the tiny Jewish house and fill his lungs with fresh air. He left a note to Ephraim and after checking that no one saw him leave the house, he scurried up an alleyway.

The path led to the ruins of Pulcelina's house and he watched for a while as two peasant workmen cleared out the debris. Every time they came across the charred remains of a corpse amongst the ash and rubble, a squabble would break out over the gold rings and jewellery they found.

He was shocked to see Cranston the chaplain walking from the burnt out shell towards his horse. Under his arm he opened a satchel and placed inside a silver necklace handed to him by one of his cohorts. Baruch saw him ride towards the bridge into the city and sped after him, not knowing why he was chasing the chaplain. Perhaps he would just challenge him. Perhaps he would kill him.

People were making their way to and from the market and the bridge was amass with people. Midway, the chaplain's horse ground to a halt and Baruch was able to catch him up. As he reached out to grab the horse's reins the skittish mare was startled by the sudden movement and its front legs reared up and the back legs kicked out.

'Get away you fool,' the chaplain yelled, lifting his riding crop and hitting Baruch on the shoulder.

The pain incited the rage buried deep with Baruch. 'You are a murderer of women and children. Get down and face me...'

The horse became even more frightened at the raised voices and cramped conditions. Panic stricken, the back legs and rump pummelled the bridge wall. Holding the crop in one hand and trying to retrieve the reins with the other, Cranston was unprepared and he fell from the saddle, landing heavily on top of the wall. Winded by the fall, he breathed in deeply, trying to catch his breath.

Pandemonium broke out as people tried to get out of the way and again the mare kicked out, hitting the chaplain in the belly. He lost his balance and grasping at thin air, he fell head over heels into the mud at the rivers edge.

Gasps of shock filled the air and people quickly gathered to shout for help. Some ran down the riverbank and tried to traverse the mud. A rope was lowered from the bridge but failed to reach the struggling chaplain. Those on the bank tried to form a chain but could not reach, and all the while the chaplain was sinking into the stinking effluent. His screams for help stirred men into more attempts to reach him but by now his fate was secured.

Overlooking the far end of the bridge, Baruch mingled with the crowd and watched as the chaplain's head slipped under the slime, leaving only bubbles to mark the spot. Questions began to reverberate around the shocked crowd; some openly saying they had seen a Jew attack the chaplain's horse. Imaginary fingers were pointing in his direction and he hid under his hood, evading the suspicious looks of those around him. Making his way back to the house, he woke up Ephraim.

'I have to leave,' he explained to the young clerk. 'You must stay and see that Jacob is given a proper burial. Is that clear?'

Ephraim nodded solemnly. 'Where are you going?' he asked.

Changing his cloak, Baruch opened the door and looked left and right. 'It is better you do not know. Good luck.'

Peering down the street Baruch looked for signs of the mob. He felt he was a hunted man and events had now conspired to make his next decision easy. Glancing over his shoulder he pulled the hood around his head before closing the door behind him. His mind made up, he knew exactly where his destiny lay.

Chapter 16

Winchester
England

Few of King Henry's advisors understood his decision to abandon the delicate negotiations in Ireland and return temporally to see Bishop Henry on his death bed. The king reminded his council that although the bishop was no friend of the crown, he was the brother of the late King Stephen and a descendant of King William, the great conqueror.

The truth of the matter was a little different. The imminent demise of the bishop provided a fortunate excuse to meet with Marshal Bryce. Some seven months had passed since he had dispatched the marshal on a clandestine mission to the north and before leaving Ireland, he sent a messenger to ensure Bryce was at Winchester to meet him. Written messages were never fully secure so he needed a first hand account of how the pursuit of the four fugitives into Scotland had progressed.

King Henry rode into the Bishops Palace at Winchester and was pleased to see the distinctive black stallion belonging to Marshal Bryce tethered at the stables.

Walking into the lobby a servant pressed a cup of wine onto his hand while another took his cloak. Feeling obliged to see Bishop Henry first, he marched impatiently into the private apartments, scattering servants and monks before him.

One look at the bishop told him he did not have long to live. He was painfully thin and his face had a deathly pallor. The king comforted him for a while, even though the bishop never recognised who was sitting alongside.

After paying his respects, King Henry left the chamber and walked back to the lobby for some fresh air and he gazed into the afternoon light to absorb the warm glow of the summer sun.

At the sound of footsteps approaching, he turned to see Marshal Bryce who gave a short bow. 'My liege, it is always good to see you, though I am surprised to see you at the Bishop's Palace.'

The king continued to stare into the light. 'During the civil war he often held the power of the crown in the absence of his brother. He is seventy years old and save only a few, he is the last of his generation.'

'And soon the last of that generation will join him.'

The king scowled at Bryce. 'Watch your tongue and don't talk in riddles. What do you mean?'

'Earl Bigod lays ill in York with a mortal fever. They say he will not rise again from his bed.'

The king looked into the fading sunlight as it passed behind a cloud, and for a moment the pale shadow of guilt hung over him before he turned on Bryce. 'Was it not your idea to entice him up to Scotland. To keep him out of the way while I was in Ireland, you said.'

Bryce countered. 'You always said the man was born a rebel and that you could never trust him to behave with honour…'

The king interrupted. 'My God, the man must be in his middle seventies. What harm can he do other than spit at you and throw his walking stick!'

'Yes its unnatural,' Bryce agreed. 'The man must have a pact with the devil to live so long.'

The king ignored the casual insult at Bigod. Then he remembered it was only a few months ago while planning the Ireland campaign, that it was *he* who feared Bigod could lead a rebellion in his absence. He sighed heavily. 'So tell me what happened.'

'Following our advice, the fugitives took off to the north. I left

Hugh Bigod and his son following a cold trail across half of Scotland.'

'Why did you leave him?'

'I was unwell. Besides he had his son Roger, and William Albini for company.'

The king looked closely at Bryce's face. 'And what of the fugitives?'

'They nestle in d'Morville's castle in Knaresborough awaiting your deliberation,' Bryce replied smugly. 'And you were right to fear the threat of rebellion. The Earl of Leicester has apparently taken a sympathetic sourjon to visit Count Philip of Flanders and King Louis in France. Your son Henry is also in France and spends an inordinate amount of time in the presence of Louis. It could only lead to trouble ahead.'

King Henry closed his eyes and swore into his cup. What ever had he done to attract such ill feeling amongst his son and his peers? First, his wife had deceived him and could no longer be trusted. Under her influence his sons seemed intent on biting the hand that feeds them. Where will it all lead, he wondered?

Just then, a novice physician entered the room and coughed discreetly. 'Sire, the Bishop of Winchester is ailing fast and has been given the last rites.'

Drawing on a long gulp of wine, he thumped the empty cup on the table. He drew closely up to Bryce. 'I want a first hand report on Earl Bigod's state of health...and confirmation of his death before I return to Ireland.'

The weather north of the border was wet and miserable but thankfully not too cold. The search party had been weaving across Scotland and the north of England for most of the spring and early summer, all to no avail. The information they were receiving from the local agents led to nothing but dead ends and it began to dawn on Hugh that they were on a fool's errand. Someone, somewhere, had planned the whole charade and he hated being made a fool of.

While in Berwick he declared his intention to abandon the search for the four fugitives. 'I have a chill coming on,' Hugh complained truthfully, 'and my throat is red raw. I am going back to Framlingham.'

William Albini accused him of disobeying the king's orders while Roger remained silent. Hugh believed his son agreed with him but was not prepared to say as much.

After a prolonged argument, William and Roger decided to continue their search for another three weeks along the English side of the border while Hugh was determined to return south, accompanied by Bonham and three knights.

By the time he reached York, Hugh was feeling much worse. He had developed a raging fever and his men sought out the abbey where he could receive some treatment. With such an illustrious patient as the Earl of Norfolk, the best physicians were called upon and for three days his life hung in the balance.

Monks were implored to give extra prayers and as if upon command, his fever peaked. Father Abbot sat on the bed next to the earl and watched as Hugh sipped at a bowl of broth. 'The lord has shone a light on you these last few days. Your revival is nothing short of miraculous. How do you feel?'

'Much better, apart from this cough,' Hugh replied. 'I am sorry but I must confess that I do not believe in God.'

Wiping a bead of sweat from Hugh's forehead, the abbot smiled. 'Oh but God believes in you, and he has heard your confession. I think He has saved you for another purpose. This was not your time to die.'

Without the strength to argue, Hugh lay his head down and closed his eyes to rest a little more.

A few days later Hugh found he was healthy enough to rise from his mattress and after a further week of convalescence, Hugh handed the abbot a few silver coins in genuine gratitude for the medical treatment and stated he was ready to leave.

Bonham was still concerned for his health but Hugh insisted he was well enough to ride. Besides, he said he felt the need to return to Framlingham without delay.

'Do you think there is a problem at the castle?' Bonham enquired.

Hugh said while stroking his wiry stubble. 'I don't know what it is, but I think that Marshal Bryce may have led me astray deliberately. He wanted me out of the way for some reason and I intend to find out why. Believe me, if someone has taken me for a fool, they will have to
pay.'

Bonham nodded, without fully understanding. All the knights had been away too long and were simply happy to be returning to Framlingham.

It was a long journey fraught with bad storms and impassable roads. When they reached sight of Framlingham, an ominous air of false tranquillity hung over the castle. Hugh and the knights approached from the north and could see the drawbridge was down with no guards at the gate to challenge them. The castle walls appeared to be manned by a few faint-hearted townsfolk with spears.

Hugh dismounted and was filled with dread as he immediately began to fear for the safety of his wife and child. Signalling Bonham to go on ahead, he looked around the empty stables. The grooms were nowhere to be seen and except for a few old nags, all the horses were gone with no sign of any fresh oats or hay. No horses had been stabled at the castle in weeks.

Bonham came running back outside. The news was not going to

be good.

Gently patting the shoulder of his steed, Hugh felt his legs suddenly weaken and he had little stomach for the horror that lay within the walls of his castle.

'My lord, your son is safe.' Bonham gasped, catching his breath. 'Only your household staff remain. The entire garrison left having been mis-informed of your death in York.'

Behind Bonham, a line of people shuffled across the bailey. There were cooks and serving girls, maids and woodsmen.

Bonham smiled broadly. 'They did not believe me. They are coming out to see you for themselves.'

Then out of their midst ran a little boy. Hugh bent down as his son ran into his arms. They hugged and cried until the earl could no longer crouch so low without hurting. Standing upright, the maid held out her hand and collected the boy into her arms. Daring to speak, 'He is fine my Lordship...he just misses his mum and dad.'

'Thank you my girl. Your loyalty shall be rewarded.' Hugh spoke so they could all hear. 'You shall all be rewarded for holding your ground against such adversity. Now where is my wife.'

Hugh noticed another figure appear from the main entrance and recognised Marcus. Slowly he walked towards Hugh, unsure of himself. 'My lord, it is a miracle to see you alive. But I have to tell you, that upon the news of your so-called death, Earl Wills of Albini has been overseeing your castle, though he currently resides in Arundel and has yet to make an appearance.'

'Wills Albini is in charge! The fuck he is!' Hugh cried loud enough, so that everyone could hear. 'Walk with me Marcus and tell me everything that happened here. Leave nothing out.'

The two of them walked slowly while the kitchen staff happily went ahead to prepare dinner. The delight at seeing the earl alive was tempered by the air of gloom that pervaded every nook and cranny of the castle, when they realised the earl was still to hear of the fate of

Lady Gundred.

The story that unfolded from the lips of Marcus made the hairs on his neck stand up. His recollection of events from the raid, nine months ago was detailed and unequivocal.

'Word spread fast that for some reason you were returning unexpectedly. But the lookouts were mistaken and they opened the gates to the raiders. They said they saw your colours flying...but I don't believe they were that clever. They numbered over thirty,' Marcus explained. 'The guards who stood unprepared did not stand a chance. The raiding party wore hoods over their faces to hide their identity. About fifteen men at arms were killed but all the knights were captured and held in the storeroom downstairs.'

'For fuck's sake...where is my wife?' Hugh repeated still wondering why Gundred had not made an appearance.

Marcus looked at the ground. 'She has been taken, my lord.'

Hugh steadied himself against the wall. His head was filled with dread thinking of his wife being held by uncivilised outlaws.

Marcus continued. 'Celia, the young girl who took care of young Hugh was found dead at the foot of the south wall. She had jumped and taken her own life rather than face her attackers. Hers was the only innocent death. But I am sure your wife will be returned after an appropriate ransom has been paid.'

'So you think it was a kidnapping...a civilised kidnap and ransom?' Hugh urged.

'I don't know...'

'But you said they were anonymous...wore hoods...that is the mark of outlaws and murderers.'

'They were not murderers, my lord. Your son was unharmed.'

'But have they made contact?' Hugh yelled, wanting to shake the information out of Marcus.

Hugh stared breathlessly into Marcus's face and the trembling in his legs returned. He looked behind for a bench to sit upon.

Marcus helped the earl. 'Let me ask for some food and wine to be brought. You are exhausted, my lord.'

Hugh nodded and took off his boots. His life had collapsed all around him and his head was dizzy with fear. Suddenly he felt very old and tired. 'Bring it to my chamber. I want to rest for a while.'

Chapter 17

Framlingham Castle
Suffolk

Messengers were sent by Hugh all over England, and to the king pleading for information regarding the disappearance of his wife. The news of the earl's wife going missing was greeted with little sympathy, and in many quarters with amusement. To those who heard the plea, it was hardly a surprise that the old embittered earl had suddenly found his wife had deserted him.

The lethargy that beset Hugh was unrelenting. For weeks he refused to rise from his bed, save for a call of nature, and those around him feared he would withdraw from his life to make his peace with God.

Meanwhile Marcus kept a vigil over the earl, seeing he was fed and watered. He would advise him of the lack of responses from his many letters, causing him to feel even more helpless and sorrowful.

Bonham would encourage him to take an occasional walk and lift his spirits by telling him how hundreds of people were actively involved and would not be long before his wife was found.

Breaking through a frosty puddle, he walked with the earl one day along the ramparts of Framlingham Castle. They sat in the glow of a winter's sun that hardly bothered to breach the horizon and they chatted amiably stamping their feet to keep the cold at bay. Bonham picked his moment to breach an awkward subject. 'My lord, there is something that has been riling me for many weeks now and I feel it is my duty to...'

'Oh come on, stop your dithering. What is it? Got one of your fair maidens pregnant?' Hugh smiled for the first time in an age.

Bonham smiled back. 'No my lord...but not for the want of trying.' His expression and voice changed to take a more serious tone. 'It's about Marcus.' Bonham looked at his feet finding it difficult to find the right words. 'When we returned he gave the impression that the raid and kidnap were but an inconvenience and that everything was getting back to normal...almost making light of the calamitous events. But listening to the staff in private, they tell a different story.'

Hugh was intrigued. 'What do you mean?'

'They say that someone opened the gates to let in the raiders. All the men were locked in the storerooms while most of the women ran off into the village...apart from some unlucky ones that were badly assaulted. No one remembers seeing Marcus. He told the knights he had been knocked out and left unconscious near the chapel. But at least two women told me they had seen him later that night...riding through the gates with a saddlebag so heavy, he needed a barrow to lift it inside.'

'Well, I am sure there is a reasonable explanation,' Hugh said, trying to think of one.

Bonham looked around but they were alone. 'Yes, I agree. That is until I went to Marcus's apartment this morning to borrow this fine fur cloak I am wearing. I also used the garderobe and noticed in the torchlight a large stone in the floor was loose and had been moved. Curiosity got the better of me and I moved the stone aside just a finger width. Inside was a horde of gold coins. I called for Marcus but a servant told me he has gone away for a few days. He could not say where.'

Hugh stood up and paced the rampart his mind awash with conjecture. 'Have you replaced the stone exactly where you found it?'

'Yes...yes,' Bonham stammered.

'Good. Now we can leave and he will none the wiser.' Hugh stood upright once more, his eyes brighter.

'Leave where my lord? Are you sure you feel well enough?' Bonham was surprised at the sudden transformation.

'To find my wife of course. Prepare the horses and tell the grooms we are going to London to see the king.'

'But I told you yesterday my lord; the king is in Normandie.'

'Then to anyone who asks, I will appear to be a confused old man on a wasted journey. Or I could just be laying a false trail for any one who asks.'

Bonham walked down the rampart steps towards the stables and called to Michael, his squire. He tried to keep up with the earls thinking but sometimes it was like living inside a riddle.

The journey to the coast was a swift one and a few days later, the winds and the tide from Portsmouth were favourable enough for Hugh and Bonham to reach the Cherbourg peninsular.

They were heading to the Cathedral at Avranches where a covert meeting was taking place between the papal legate and King Henry. Apparently the purpose was to decide the fate of the assassins of Becket and the penance to be given to the king for his part in the murder.

'Of course, the king vehemently denies any wrong doing,' Bonham said. 'Those knights took it upon themselves to carry out the murder.'

Hugh had given the matter some thought. 'I don't think the king knew himself what he really wanted. He hated the man he loved,' Hugh replied enigmatically.

Bonham looked astonished. 'So you think they were in love?'

Hugh reconsidered his words. 'Perhaps not love...not in any physical sense. But they were so obsessed with each other, they rode themselves to the point of madness. Like the worst kind of marriage.'

Hugh missed the awkward expression that passed between

Bonham and the two squires. Sometimes he feared for the sanity of the earl.

Arriving at Avranches cathedral they noticed the sizeable audience beginning to disperse. Bitter disappointment seemed to rankle amongst the congregation who were expecting more contrition from the king. 'Bloody waste of time,' said one peasant.

'Didn't even bare his chest,' another muttered.

With barely a pause, Hugh boldly entered the cathedral and made slow progress through the throng of bishops, nobles and courtiers. He spotted the king on a dais, surrounded by his inner entourage. Upon seeing Hugh approach, the circle fell deathly silent.

'Well, is it the Earl of Norfolk I see, or an apparition,' sounded the king, trying to make light of his sudden appearance. 'So the accounts of your death were somewhat embellished.' Barely a chuckle was heard.

Hugh gave a respectful nod of the head and at the same time spotted his prey keeping out of sight behind a pillar. 'My lord king, I apologise for interrupting your ceremony but I must question your marshal regarding a raid upon Framlingham Castle in which my wife was kidnapped.'

Marshal Bryce stepped forward onto the dais. 'My liege, I have nothing to hide from Earl Bigod. Please my lord, ask your questions.'

Hugh was thrown by Bryce's gall. He did not expect a voluntary confrontation. But things had gone too far now to back down. 'I charge you with attacking my castle, my servants and kidnapping my wife.'

Bryce perceived in Hugh the momentary flash of weakness and stood tall, bristling with indignation.

But it was the king that spoke. 'These are very serious allegations. Where is your evidence for these charges, Earl Bigod?'

Now Hugh was completely unnerved by the king's direct intervention. 'I shall find the evidence and present it to you my lord king.' He started to sway a little as a bead of sweat ran down his cheek.

'Perhaps you still suffer with a fever.' The king looked to Bonham. 'Please take the earl home where he can recuperate in comfort.'

Hugh opened his mouth to accuse Bryce again but Bonham steered him back the way they came.

Calls of 'shame on you...you were better off dead...' crossed the nave and the walk to the door was the longest he could ever remember.

Gasping in the fresh air, Hugh was stunned at the stupidity of his actions. 'My God, what the fuck happened in there?' he asked Bonham rhetorically. He sat on the steps among the throng of people and horses and waited for the grooms to appear.

Suddenly Hugh was startled by the sight of six horses being led across the square towards the busy market that had just sprung up. He tugged Bonham by the arm 'Quickly, come with me.'

Bonham was frightened for the safety of the earl. 'My lord, what have you seen?'

Hugh had wild staring eyes as he pointed at the horses. 'That mare; the hazel one with brown legs. I recognise her.'

Bonham peered at the horse but said nothing.

'Don't you remember it, you fool. She was due to foal six months ago. I had that mare for near on three years.'

The recognition hit Bonham. 'Yes I remember now. My God, she must have been stolen in the raid.'

Bonham no longer believed they were on a fool's errand and was angry with himself for thinking so. He should have had more faith in the earl from the start.

The horse sale was about to start as Hugh and Bonham entered the stables unchallenged. They rounded on the squire and pushed him to the rear where they were unseen. The poor man wondered what on earth he was doing being held by two well groomed nobles; one probably a knight and the other an old man with thin wiry hair.

'My lords, please have mercy. I have a wife and children...'

Hugh looked closely at the man, then slapped him hard. 'Shut up you prick. We all have wives and children. Now what is your name, young squire.'

'My name is Terrowin, my lord...'

Hugh unsheathed a dagger from his belt and placed the blade under the squire's chin. 'We can do this the easy way Terrowin, or the hard way.'

'Please my lord...'

Without flinching, Hugh ran the blade down his cheek. After a pause, the blood ran down his face and dripped onto his chemise.

'Where did you procure that fine hazel mare you have brought here to sell?' Hugh asked.

Terrowin gulped in air looking around for any sign of help.

Bonham pinned the man against a railing, as Hugh held the dagger over his eye. 'Think carefully Terrowin. If your next words do not answer my question, I shall have your left eye out. Is that clear?'

Fearing for his sight, Terrowin decided to bare all. 'I was given the mare as a reward by the king's marshal. She will fetch a good price.'

Hugh kept the blade resting on the cheek. 'Were you with the marshal when he raided Framlingham Castle?'

Terrowin did not dare risk a pause. 'Yes, my lord. I am squire to the marshal. If it pleases my lord to put down the knife, I will tell you truthfully everything you want to know.'

Slowly, the blade was taken from the face of the squire and returned to its sheath.

Terrowin began to breath normally. He was about to ask the identity of the two men but then thought better of it. 'You are not from Framlingham, are you my lord?'

Hugh suddenly realised Terrowin had no idea who they were. 'No. But you are misinformed. Marshall Bryce promised the horse to me. But you say the horse was stolen from Bigod'

Bonham listened intently, impressed by the agility of the earl's thinking.

Terrowin nodded. 'Yes but only after meeting Waleran the Earl of Warwick Castle and another man who I took to be his steward. I don't usually listen in to such conversations but I remember the Earl of Warwick had trouble claiming his proper inheritance due to an impostor.

Then his steward spoke about the Earl Bigod of Norfolk who also claimed to have an impostor in Normandie, only this one apparently was no impostor. He actually was the Earls elder brother and more than that, he was still alive in the Holy Land.'

Bonham felt uncomfortable with what Terrowin was saying. 'My lord, do you think this is relevant…'

Hugh had a glazed expression. 'It's all right. When was this meeting.'

'Not long after Archbishop Becket was murdered. I remember the marshal saying that the king could not trust Earl Bigod, and wanted him out of the way. Then they talked about his wife, Gundred, who was the elder sister of the Earl of Warwick. Waleran hated her for marrying Earl Bigod. He called her a traitor and a few other things besides.'

'Go on,' Hugh whispered, his jaw and fists equally clenched.

'Earl Waleran said he would pay a fortune to wreak his revenge on his sister Gundred. So, they concocted a plan. I remember it because I helped Earl Waleran with a chest of gold from his strong room. The chest carried Waleran's coat of arms and Bryce told me to pick up two small boxes from a baggage cart outside. I carried them indoors. They were plain, without a lid but I remember his initials scratched on the bottom, S B. He says only his mother knew his first name. Earl Waleran filled them to the brim with gold then had them taken back to his strong room. Bryce said he would lead Bigod to the north, 'chasing shadows' was the term he used. Meanwhile he returned to Framlingham Castle where the steward said he would ensure the gates were open. He kidnapped Gundred and brought her back to Warwick and Earl Waleran handed over the gold.'

Hugh and Bonham looked at each other as they bathed in the dawning light of such incredible revelations. 'Do you think the steward could have been Bigod's steward?' he asked quietly.

'I don't know. It just seemed like he was Earl Waleran's man.'

'I see,' Hugh nodded, remembering where Marcus had originally served. A deathly silence fell about them.

Terrowin was suddenly afraid he would be killed if he stopped talking. 'Earl Waleran was very religious...just like his father. He founded a priory...that was where he took Gundred to be looked after by the Cistercian nuns.'

'So where the fuck is she?' The dagger came out in a flash and Hugh thrust it again, up against his cheek.

'At the priory...she was taken to Pinley Priory, near Worcester. Please my lord, have mercy.'

'Do you know who I am now?' Hugh asked menacingly.

Terrowin whimpered. 'I think I have made the biggest mistake of my life. Everyone said you were dead Lord Earl.'

'Then you know of the madness that burns inside me. If word of this conversation reaches anyone, I shall have out both your eyes. Do you hear me Terrowin.'

He nodded furiously.

'And pray we find my wife is unharmed.'

Terrowin nodded again. 'I am sorry my lord for everything. I never your wife any harm but I must tell you about Pinley Priory...'

'Shut up and let me think.' The earl backed off. 'You will show us the way to the priory then ride with us back to Framlingham.'

Bonham was almost as surprised as Terrowin. He opened his mouth to speak. 'Is that wise…'

'I am always in need of another squire,' Hugh said looking at Terrowin. Especially one who owes me his life, but remember this. I need you to bear witness when the time comes. Is that clear.'

Terrowin looked at the dagger in the Earl's hand and nodded furiously. 'I swear you my allegiance my lord.'

Bonham simply shook his head in despair.

Chapter 18

Pinley Priory
Warwickshire

Although Pinley Priory and nunnery was a large religious house, it took a whole day to find it nestled away in the heavily wooded countryside.

As they arrived at the gates, the the inappropriate sound of laughter carried across the courtyard. Two men approached on horseback and Bonham rode forward to ask their business at the priory. They grunted an obscene reply before riding off.

Hugh immediately pushed his horse through the open gate. 'No time for pleasantries,' he told Bonham nodding to the substantial dwelling to his right. 'Brandish your swords and enter that house. Find out who is in charge.'

Terrowin sidled nervously up to Hugh. 'My lord…I must warn you, this place has a reputation…'

Bonham kicked open the door and nuns scattered in all directions.   A few moments passed then he signalled to Hugh to follow him inside. One of the sisters was stood unmoving alongside the Mother Superior seated at her table.

'Go now, Sister Meslier,' the Mother said calmly.

The sister looked at Hugh and then slowly left the room, closing the door behind her.

'This is the Mother Superior. I have asked if your wife is here,' Bonham confirmed.

Hugh stood in front of the Mother, so close she could feel his breath on her face. 'Her name is Gundred and I want to see her…now.'

The Mother bravely held his stare and stood back a pace as if something had passed between them. She knew any defence or excuse would be pointless. 'I take you now. She is in our infirmary.'

Hugh winced at the guttural accent. He told Terrowin to return to the horses and he followed the Mother Superior. Glancing across the cloisters, Hugh detected two more scruffy looking men being ushered towards the gate by two nuns. The more he observed the more he became unsettled.

They entered a large dormitory lit by a single lamp and Hugh stared at the row of filthy mattresses that lined the walls. Twenty poor souls lay strapped and helpless in their own filth. Some stared at the shadows that danced on the ceiling, moaning at unseen ghosts. Some were beyond making any sound at all. If any of them had a soul, it had long given up hope of reaching heaven.

'All of them are sinners,' the Mother Superior said grimly. 'God has no place for them...we take sins onto our shoulders. They are ill in head.'

Hugh's feet froze to the floor as a wave of nausea threatened his stomach. 'What did you say?' Hugh murmured, trying not to breath in the all-pervading stench.

The Mother pointed to her temple. 'You understand...they are ill in head.'

'There my lord...there is your wife.' Bonham was pointing to a scraggy haired, middle aged woman comprised of skin and bone with little more than a thin shawl to cover her modesty and keep the chill air at bay.

Before Hugh could utter a word or move a muscle, the Mother called to a novice.

'When she brought here...she had much poppy juice. Last month it finished. Now she eat nothing...head is full of demons from hell. They said her husband wanted her kept here. Now you want her back?'

185

The Mother ordered the novice to take off the straps and bring the woman into the light coming from the cloisters. Hugh was shaking inside, still unsure if the poor excuse for a human being, truly was Gundred. Unsteady on her feet, she stumbled over another woman lying on the floor. 'Careful…she fight,' the Mother warned.

Hugh stepped forward and held Gundred in his arms; gently lifting her head back so he could make sure. Looking into her eyes, he saw there was no mistake.

'You give donation now,' the Mother urged. 'To pay for baby, yes.'

Hugh looked confused. 'A baby…?' he repeated.

'Yes…a baby. Do you want to see?'

Still in a state of shock, Hugh nodded slowly. They walked into the large adjoining cell that was a little cleaner than the one before, stunned at the sight of three cribs all carrying babies of various ages. A nun was breast-feeding and covered herself up when she saw the men appear at the door.

Hugh was in a daze 'But this place…it is a nursery?'

'We cater for the sins of all men,' the Mother Superior replied coldly. She admonished the frightened nun and led Hugh to the third crib, pointing to the baby wriggling under a tiny lambs wool blanket. 'Now she is three weeks old. She will grow up to be a good sister…full of God's love.'

Hugh glanced at the diminutive face of the baby girl and knew immediately he was not the father. Quietly, he told Bonham to take Gundred outside to Terrowin and ready the horses while he took care of a gift for the priory.

Still in a daze, he followed the Mother back to the women's side of the infirmary, noticing she walked with a twisted limp. Inside a small reception room the sunlight flooded in through an open door and windows. The Mother smiled broadly in anticipation.

'How did you get that limp?' he asked.

'Long time ago…as a child. It is no matter…please.'

In the daylight, her face stiffened, no longer smiling. Her head lifted and she gave a piercing stare. Lifting her trembling hand, she pointed at Hugh. 'I know you…you are 'bad brother.''

Hugh recognised her instantly as the child-witch from the Lyons-la-Foret.

'And I know you…you are the witch that gave me the potion for the first King Henry. What devil made you a Mother Superior.''

You killed my Aunty Annie…'

'I should have killed both of you…' Hugh yelled. 'How many lives have you destroyed here…in the name of God?'

'They are unwanted…we care for them.'

'You run a whorehouse, you fucking bitch!'

'No fucking…men give them what they want.'

In a rage, Hugh pulled a dagger from his belt.

Steeling herself the Mother Superior boldly picked up her walking stick and took a step forward. 'You cannot touch me.' she hissed. 'They will hunt you down…'

In a flash, Hugh grabbed her by the hair and pulled her head down, and smashed his knee into her face. The Mother crumpled to the ground and moaned; blood running profusely from her nose.

The door burst open and Bonham rushed in to restrain Hugh. 'My lord, what have you done?'

Hugh shrugged him off. 'She fell against the table.'

'I think we should go now.'

The Mother uttered curses as she crawled onto her knees.

Hugh stood his ground. 'Tell me…why did you call me 'bad brother?''

With eyes blazing with hate, the Mother Superior rose to her feet like a wounded beast. She pulled out the broken front teeth that had pierced her lips. 'When I was a small girl 'good brother,' he save me. She spat a mouthful of congealed blood aimed at Hugh' face. 'My brother hacked everyone to pieces. I curse you…!'

Hugh wiped his face and slammed the door behind him, ignoring the ranting of a madwoman.

'Listen to my curse Hugh Bigod! I curse you...!'

The nuns rushed into her room to find the Mother Superior sobbing into her apron, delirious with rage and grief. Every time they touched her, she screamed incoherently. They tried to carry her to the infirmary but she fought the nuns, shrieking wildly with arms flailing and blood running freely down her face and throat.

Sister Meslier looked on dispassionately ordering the nuns to bring cords to restrain the Mother. 'The demons are strangling her soul. Take her to the infirmary.'

The nuns carried the Mother kicking and screaming from the room. Sister Meslier removed a bag from a draw and muttered a prayer. 'Oh Lord, with these implements I pray the soul of Mother Amelda will be cleansed and the demons flushed from her body.'

The screams carried as far as the gatehouse but Hugh did not look back. After wrapping a warm cloak around Gundred, he used the straps left around her wrist to secure her arms around his waist. Departing through the gate with his long lost wife, he left behind her newborn baby and the memories of a wretched year in Hades.

After riding a mile, Hugh became more concerned. One look told him she was barely conscious and needed urgent attention from a physician.'

Terrowin said he could help. 'I know of an abbey about an hour from here, founded by the king. I know because I visited with the court not long after it was finished. They have a good physician there.'

'What is it called?' urged Hugh.

'Stoneleigh Abbey, on the road to Kenilworth castle.'

'My lord, can we trust this...vagabond?' Ever since Terrowin's sudden change of allegiance, Bonham had been uneasy with receiving his unbridled assistance.

Terrowin looked at Bonham and spoke quietly. 'Not only can you trust me, but I will prove to you my allegiance...in more ways than you can see.' The solemn expression made Bonham blink and for a moment, he was lost for words.

Hugh was busy comforting Gundred. 'You will dearly regret any betrayal. Lead us to Stoneleigh Abbey.'

They spoke very little on the road to the abbey and as they approached the walls, Terrowin said he would gallop on ahead, to ensure the physician monk was awake and ready to see Gundred. Bonham told Hugh to ride with him.

The abbot worked efficiently as he guided Hugh to the infirmary with the minimum of fuss. Thanks to Terrowin, the monk was briefed as to her condition and true to his word, he was competent and experienced with medical matters.

After a preliminary examination, he ushered the men from the room so he could examine her 'private parts' to ensure there was no long-term damage to her womb. Reluctantly, Hugh left the cell and a short while later the monk asked him back. 'She is grossly malnourished,' he said 'but this can be rectified with good food and plenty of rest. We can treat her for the mild fever and the lice. Her mood swings were associated with her dependence on the effects of poppy juice but I suspect this has virtually worn off now.' The monk lowered his voice. 'I must inform you that she has received a great deal of internal damage and is lucky to be alive. There appears to be no pus, so with a few weeks of convalescence and tender care, she should improve. The rest will be in God's hand.'

The relief was evident on Hugh's face. 'He turned to the abbot. I know your loyalties lie elsewhere and you owe me no favour. But I shall be staying here with my wife and nothing will be gained by anyone finding out. Can I rely upon your utmost discretion?'

189

The abbot smiled for the first time. Though he had no liking for the reputation of the Norfolk Earl, he did speak the truth. 'As you say my lord, nothing would be gained by indiscretion and I shall personally ensure the continuing services of the physician... no matter the cost.'

Hugh understood the terminology. He nodded to Bonham who took a small bag of coins from his tunic. 'Rest assured, there will be more next week but needless to say, if our peace here is disturbed I shall take it back...with interest.'

Chapter 19

Stoneleigh Abbey
Kenilworth

The following weeks were the most restless Hugh could remember. While they wiled away the hours and the days, he would lie next to his wife and hold her hand, dreaming with his eyes wide open of the raw vengeance that was to come.

Gradually, she came back from the dead. In the first week, he daubed the sweat from her fevered face and she would occasionally smile. But nothing could stop the horrors of the mind that resurfaced during the night. Sometimes, she would open her mouth to speak, even though the words were difficult to hear.

By the second week, she was capable of conversation and the first time her wits joined up with her words she let out a pitiful cry. 'Where is my baby?'

Hugh comforted her in his arms and broke the news that her baby had died at birth. 'Think no more of it my love. I was told the baby did not suffer and went straight to heaven.'

Gundred cried till dawn, and then awoke to cry some more.

By the third week, she was well enough to walk around the abbey gardens and pray alone in the church. She talked of missing her son Roger and of returning to Framlingham Castle to see him.

Hugh was happy to oblige with any wish she had.

But first he unveiled his plans for the destruction of those who were responsible for her horrifying ordeal. 'Warwick castle is not far away and Earl Waleran will pay for his cruelty…'

'You will leave my brother Waleran out of this,' Gundred interrupted sternly.

Hugh looked at her aghast.

'Oh Hugh, be careful where you look for guilt. I know what Waleran did was wrong but I forgive him. The guilt was mine for leaving him and our mother in time of need. And as for my poor father, well you are as guilty as anyone.'

Hugh was reminded of his involvement with the scheme to take Warwick Castle from the earl at the end of the civil war and he readily admitted that his actions probably did contribute to his death. He looked out of the window at the blue sky and thought it better to agree with Gundred…for now.

'And what about Bryce?' he asked, still with his back to her. 'What of his guilt?'

'My forgiveness has its limitations. As far as I am concerned, you can slice him up slowly into tiny pieces. But don't forget his captain. Tobin was his name. He killed Celia you know…threw her like a rag doll from the ramparts. He tortured her insides for hours…knives, hot pokers…' Shoulders heaving, Gundred looked down with tears in her eyes. 'I know because he made me watch everything he did.' Suddenly she burst out screaming as the realisation hit her. 'My God, he made me do those things to her…it was me…it was me!'

Her screams pierced the air and her fists started flailing the air. Hugh called for help and the physician monk ran into the room. He went to a cabinet and poured a liquid into a cup. 'It is a mild sedative to calm her,' he yelled above the high-pitched shrieks. 'Please help hold her steady.'

An hour later, Hugh was still holding her in his arms until the sobbing died down and she fell asleep. His heart was pounding and his stomach was churning so much he thought he would be sick. They would need another week in the tranquil surroundings of the abbey before Gundred was well enough to leave.

And yet all the tiredness; all the fatigue of the past few years had evaporated. It had been replaced by a single desire that now burnt itself into his soul, and it led in only in one direction.

But first, they would return to Framlingham so he could reclaim his castle and his lands and there would be no more talk of his premature death. There would be plenty of opportunities ahead for his actual demise, but not just yet.

Ever since that fateful night in Bayeux, when Earl Bigod's words had deliberately worked the king into a state of uncontrollable rage, Marcus considered the Earl had gone too far. Later, when Le Breton burst into the castle to confess his part in the murder of Becket, he saw fear written large on Earl Bigod's face and considered that it was too dangerous to be caught alongside him. He needed to escape his company for a while.

By the next morning, Marcus had excused himself of his duties, saying he would be away for a few days. He rode to Warwick Castle, where he had spent most of his life in the employ of the Earl and his children, Gundred and Waleran. The new earl greeted him kindly and insisted he stayed a while so he could hear news from Framlingham Castle. He recalled the next few days were to change his life.

The next day they were joined by Marshal Bryce who was recruiting a number of knights for a mission to capture the murderers of Archbishop Becket. As was the Kings right, Bryce asked to take six knights but Waleran could only agree to three. He told Bryce he could not take any more as he was engaged in fighting an impostor who was claiming his inheritance. His grief stricken family was left hanging by his sister Gundred deserting them by running off with Earl Hugh Bigod; the man responsible for his father's untimely death.

Marcus then delighted in telling Waleran of Earl Bigod's deception with his own brother William, now an old man living in the Holy Land.

Waleran was staggered by the coincidence and the revelation stirred his resentment even more. 'I would pay a fortune to see Bigod dead! And as for my fucking sister...,' Waleran said sourly through a haze of strong wine.

Then Bryce came up with the plan that would satisfy Waleran's lust for revenge and make both of them rich. They discussed the scheme with Waleran then went to help the squire Terrowin carry two boxes from the stables. Dreams of wealth and riches filled Marcus's head.

Framlingham Castle was empty of power and Marcus strolled nonchalantly though the Earl's apartment. His dreams of wealth had become a reality and now he needed to leave his life of perpetual servitude behind. He had agreed with Earl Wills of Arundel to stay on at the castle as Castellan but time was passing and he had a lot of money to spend.

Picking over some of the clothes in the chamber, he would live better than this. Only the finest cloth would do, and a young buxom wife he could spoil. Poor Earl Bigod had disappeared, some swore he was already dead. Even if he was alive, he was unable to command a herd of sheep, never mind an army.

Chuckling inside, he dreamt again of his new life as a rich merchant with his own wool business in Flanders. With his newfound wealth he could make his dreams come true.

Just then, he heard someone shout from the ramparts below. Horsemen were approaching the castle. Peering out of the window, he could see it was Earl Bigod. 'Shit...why do you still live?' he muttered to himself. Still he would greet him cordially.

He moved to another window for a better view. What he saw shook him to the bone, and he staggered back in disbelief until he was sat on the earl's bed, still shaking his head. Of all the people he had expected to see, he could never have believed he would ever see Gundred again.

What to do…what to do.

His head swirled in a thick soup of indecision, trying to remember if she would even be aware of his involvement in her kidnapping. Perhaps Waleran had betrayed him…what to do. He only had moments to think. He needed some assurance; something he could hold against the earl, to bargain with if necessary as a last resort. Then it came to him. Instinctively he took his knife from its sheath and called out. 'Little Hugh, where are you?'

A thin voice came from the room next door and the maid brought the boy in. Marcus took young Hugh by the hand. 'Come on. Lets go and greet your mother and father.'

Gundred was nearing full recovery, though around her eyes were the tell tale signs of torment and deprivation and she readily admitted to being too skinny, even though her appetite had returned. But most importantly, her mind was repaired and although her manner was self-contained, she remained bright and cheerful when around people.

Upon arriving back at Framlingham Castle, Hugh looked for Marcus but he was nowhere to be seen. Dismounting at the stables, servants began to mill around and some of Gundred's closest maids broke down in tears. Bonham pulled Hugh's arm and nodded towards the main doors.

Hugh had deliberately kept from Gundred his suspicions regarding Marcus's betrayal, as he did not want her to fall into another spiral of anguish. But he could never have envisioned the nightmare that was unfurling before his eyes. Marcus stood by the main door, holding young Hugh by the hand.

Hugh smiled at his son and slowly walked forward. Just as

Gundred began running towards her son, Hugh grabbed her by the arm. 'Don't alarm the boy, my love.'

Still clutching young Hugh, Marcus gave the impression of genuine delight, and said he always believed Gundred would return one day. Hugh gently pushed his wife to one side, while not taking his eyes off Marcus.

The steward had difficulty delivering his words. 'My lord, it is a miracle that you and your wife have returned. God be praised.' Marcus had a pale, beleaguered look in his eyes. Tears were running down his cheeks.

Hugh kept his voice steady. 'Thank you for taking care of my son, Marcus.' Just a few paces away, he knelt down and beamed with delight at young Hugh. 'You can let go of him now. Can't you see he wants to come to me?'

'You know I can't do that,' Marcus whispered, unable to stop his tears. The sun glinted off the dagger blade held at the side of his son's neck. 'I have to leave now. Please, I need to get my horse.'

Gundred was walking away but began to sidle behind Marcus.

Hugh was still on his knees and thought his heart would burst. He had to distract Marcus…keep him talking. 'Put my son down and we can talk. I know about you and Bryce. You can keep the money just put my…'

There was a sudden movement as Gundred rushed at Marcus from behind, with her arm raised high. Marcus saw her, but too late. The boy pulled away from his grasp and ran to his father.

Marcus let out a gasp and his eyes bulged. Gundred's arm flashed again and again, until Marcus slid in an untidy heap to the ground. Blood was staining his shirt from the wounds in his back. Gundred knelt down and continued to thump her tiny dagger into his neck.

Hiding his son's face from the horror of Marcus's bloody slaughter, he beckoned Bonham to take the youngster. Hugh went to his wife and took her arm. 'He is dead, my love. He cannot hurt us now.'

'No one holds a knife to my son.' Then she burst into tears, the strain of her ordeal adding to her already tortured soul.

Hugh took the knife from her hand and held her tight. The traitor lay quivering in his dying throes.

In the space of a few weeks he had nearly lost his entire family. Never again would he give a servant his absolute trust. Biting his lip, he was not sad to see Marcus die. But he could have used him as a witness, to help bring down the real culprit.

Word soon spread that the Earl of Norfolk was alive and well and he was heartened when all his old cohorts and knights drifted back to Framlingham, happy to swear their allegiance to him once again. Soon the castle was brimming with knights and men-at-arms as well as a full contingent of servants, and grooms.

Despite her showing goods signs of recovery, Hugh was aware that his wife still needed his love and care but the revenge he sought was far stronger.

Gundred seemed less concerned than usual when he said they were to cross the English Sea and embark on a journey of one hundred and fifty miles to Chinon on the River Loire. 'We will take a month to get there at least,' Hugh informed her, 'but it will be worth the effort, to be present at the king's table for the Christemasse celebrations.'

As preparations went ahead for the journey, it was reported that the pope had excommunicated the murderers of Thomas Becket. He also demanded they take the cross to the Holy Land to fight the Saracen infidel.

Not much of a punishment, thought Hugh. And how ironic; for the laxness of the church in punishing its own had started the feud between the king and Becket, all those years ago . Now his murderers were to be spared the justice of an execution.

He could hardly believe that by the time they reached Chinon, it would be two years since the murder of Archbishop Becket.

Chapter 20

Chinon Castle
Loire Valley

The Christemasse court held at Chinon castle was one of the finest royal events of the year. All of the king's extended family, all the phalanx of lords, friends and wastrels, gathered for one of the most anticipated celebrations in the entire kingdom.

Hung from the ceiling of the grand hall were banners and streamers of all colours while the best musicians played from a gallery high above the revellers. On the floor were jugglers and magicians, troubadours and dancers, all creating a whirling spectacle of sight and sound.

Chefs had been brought in specially from the west and the south to provide the most exciting mixture of tastes anyone had known. The courses were endless and the banquet was set to last into the middle of the night.

In a grand gesture of reconciliation, Queen Eleanor had agreed to reside at Chinon for the celebrations, adding to the joyful mood of the occasion.

The only sore that grated with the king was the omission of his eldest son, Henry the young king. An hour earlier, he had received a discrete message from William Marshall, his son's appointed military mentor, that Henry would not be attending as he was holding his own Christemasse court in Rouen.

Determined not to let his son's absence spoil the celebration, the king engaged his wife in light hearted banter, clapping at all the entertainment and cheering every course of food that arrived.

As the sun began to set, the eastern fire-eaters in their exotic clothing, lit up the hall with their daring manoeuvres, and everyone agreed it was the best festivity they had ever attended.

On the king's left sat Marshal Bryce and for some unknown reason he sprang to his feet and looked intently from the raised dais towards the back of the hall.

The king followed his stare but his line of sight was obscured. The singers and dancers halted their performance and parted to let through the new guests that had arrived. An ominous hush befell the entire grand hall as all eyes gazed silently at the two figures stood in the centre of the floor.

Bryce's voice boomed out. 'My eye's must be deceiving me. Allow me, my liege to have these two uninvited miscreant's thrown out.'

The king had not yet seen who had entered the hall and in utter frustration, he stood up and threw his cup of wine over a troubadour who was stood in front of him. 'Oh, its you Earl Bigod.' The king sat back down. 'Are you to provide us with some more entertainment?' A thin veil of laughter echoed around the hall.

Hugh and Bonham bowed respectfully. Then Hugh looked the king in the eyes and spoke confidently. 'On the last occasion we met, my lord king, you invited me to present evidence to back up my accusations regarding a raid carried out by Marshall Bryce on my castle and my wife.'

Bryce laughed out loud. 'I am amazed he can even remember back that far. Perhaps he is here to provide entertainment after all.' There was little reaction from the audience. Everyone watched the king for his witty riposte. As always, his expression remained unscrupulous and they were surprised by his reply. 'That is correct as I recall. So what evidence do you wish to give the court.'

'I have a witness to call my lord king. My good wife, Gundred.' Hugh waved his arm and as the hall filled with fervent whispers, Gundred walked from the rear of the hall to stand next to Hugh.

'She pointed to Marshal Bryce and spoke loud and clear. 'I swear by almighty God, that man is guilty of rape, torture, kidnap and murder. May the Almighty strike me dead if I lie.'

Such a powerful oath hit a potent note with the audience and many gasped in anticipation. Even the king remained speechless.

But Bryce did not conceal his disdain at the accusation. 'I do not doubt the self belief in your wife's oath. But she is very wrong to allege that I was responsible. What possible motive could I have.'

The king was about to speak when two servants brought forward a heavy box that was hidden under a cloth and placed it at Gundred's feet.

Hugh stepped aside so everyone could see the box and addressed the king. 'Marshal Bryce brought two boxes to be filled with gold by his sponsor. This is one of them.' Hugh nodded and the servants tipped the box over and spilled the coins over the floor. The sight of the gold glinting off the torchlight sent a wave of near hysteria around those gathered. Two nobles stepped forward out of instinct before remembering where they were.

Marshal Bryce stood firm, his fists glued to his hips, appealing to the crowd. 'So what…some fool lent him a box of gold, just so he could pull a trick. It is not mine.'

Hugh took two steps closer to dais and looked Bryce in the eye.. 'Then why is your name carved into the base.'

Bryce opened his mouth but nothing came out. The inane grin on his face slipped and Hugh was not the only one to see the bead of sweat trickle down his nose. He turned to the king. 'My liege, anyone could have scratched my initials on the box. Don't you see how insane this is?'

Suddenly Bonham spoke up. 'He didn't say your initials. The earl said your name was carved.'

Bryce looked up in panic, his mouth opening and shutting making incoherent noises. The faces of those around him could not look his way. Out of the corner of his eye Hugh noticed the marshal's captain sidle towards the door, but Bonham had already seen him and signalled to Terrowin to intercept.

Then the king stood and everyone followed. 'Earl Bigod, please tell me what initials are inscribed.'

'SB, my lord king.'

To the utter shock of everyone, the king picked up his platter and hit Marshal Bryce across the face, the physical shock rippling around the grand hall. 'How dare you slander Earl Bigod and his good wife. How dare you make a fool of your king! You will pay for this dearly Silcot Bryce. Take him out of my sight!'

Any number of firm hands grabbed hold of Bryce and pulled him through the side door, still shouting and proclaiming his innocence as they took him across the courtyard to the Tour du Moulin.

The king addressed Hugh again. 'You say he has another box like that one.'

Hugh nodded in confirmation and the king ordered that the marshal's apartment should be searched. He then beckoned Hugh into a side chamber. 'As a king it is always difficult to apologise. Do you know who his sponsor was?'

'I do not my lord king.'

'Oh well, I shall see that you receive one of the boxes of gold. That is only fair recompense, I think.' The king took his wine and looked across the hall, ready to finish the sour matter.

Hugh stood up straight, his face glowering with contempt. 'I don't accept your apology. And I don't accept your gold. The hand of the Devil has tainted it, but you won't mind keeping it for yourself.' He lowered his voice to a whisper. 'I know you ordered Becket's assassins to hide in Scotland. I know you told Bryce to lead me astray in the north to 'keep me occupied'. Well I nearly died up there while my wife was hanging onto life by a thread.' With his tirade over, Hugh turned his back on the king and walked back to Gundred.

Well-wishers who had not been privy to the exchange of words had surrounded Gundred and he barged his way through, saying they had to go.

'What have you done now?' she gasped, as he led her to the main doors of the grand hall.

'I just told the king to fuck off.'

They reached the courtyard where Bonham and Terrowin had apprehended Captain Tobin.

'Good, you got him,' Hugh said nervously looking around.

Bonham nodded to his left. 'Well actually it was William Marshall who tackled him. He didn't stand a chance.'

Out of the shadows loomed one of the most famous knights of the realm and mentor to the young king Henry. He had a glint in his eye. 'You know the king will probably release Bryce within a few days. If you want, we can get the bastard from the tower. What do you say?'

'It sounds mad to me,' Hugh said. 'Though I shall happily stay here with Gundred and Captain Tobin while you try.'

Bonham ran alongside William Marshall to the tower with swords drawn and Gundred rounded on her husband. 'How could you turn on the king like that? He might have reprieved you and given you the gold.'

'He would never of done either, and deep down you know it,' Hugh replied adamantly.

Captain Tobin took his opportunity to speak for his life. 'I was only following orders from Bryce, my Lord. You have to believe me.'

Before Hugh could respond, Gundred took a step towards him. 'Think yourself lucky you still have a dick between your legs.'

'You didn't complain when I was fucking your arse you bitch! You loved it...'

Before he could utter another word, Hugh kicked him between his legs with such force his testicles ruptured.

'He won't be saying anything more tonight,' Hugh said.

Gundred stared at Tobin with a malevolent expression and held up his head while she whispered in his ear. 'That is nothing to what I have in mind.'

Hugh was relieved to see William Marshall, Bonham and Terrowin reappear. Trussed up behind them was Bryce with a gag wrapped around his mouth. No one commented on Tobin writhing in agony on the ground.

Immediately, William Marshall took charge. 'Now the only way we can get away with this is to walk calmly to the stables. Remain confident and keep your heads held up. The guards are not brave enough to stop us, besides most of them are the worse for drink. If we are split up for any reason then meet at the tavern in the centre of Saumur, a few miles from here.

They did as they were told. They thought they had succeeded but two of the king's knights gave chase and Hugh and Bonham were separated from the others. But it was Christemasse and the knights had no inclination to be chasing shadows, risking life and limb around the Loire countryside. They gave up the pursuit and an hour later Hugh and Bonham rejoined the others at the tavern in Saumur. Wrapped up against the cold, they found Terrowin and William already asleep. Hugh could not see Gundred or the prisoners. He shook Terrowin awake. 'Where is Gundred?'

Terrowin sat up. 'Probably watching over Bryce and Tobin in the workshop next door. Don't worry, we trussed them up with wire.'

'Come with me,' Hugh said with a grim expression.

They followed the path that led into the small outbuilding. From a small window they could see a faint light. Terrowin swore he did not leave one lit.

Bonham went in first with his sword drawn and all Hugh could see was the expression of shock cross his face. Terrowin went in after him and turned as white as a ghost. Hugh ignored the look on his face.

Gundred was sat on a wooden bench shivering in the cold, holding a large blacksmiths hammer in her hand. Her breath turned to mist as her chest heaved from her exertions. Bloodstains covered her clothing and the next sight made him wish he had stayed at his wife's side.

Both Bryce and Tobin were still trussed up, but facing each other nose to nose on top of a workshop bench. They were both naked from the waist down. Hugh took his lamp and approached the table, taking a while to understand what terror had taken place.

Gundred had placed them deliberately with their rears sticking out. Then she had forcibly hammered various wooden and metal implements into their rectums. Both were bleeding profusely and judging by the sharp objects smashed into his bowels, Bryce was certainly dead. To his utter disbelief, Tobin was still alive.

Looking aghast, Hugh turned silently to the others, not knowing what to do. He looked again at Gundred.

'Don't you dare help him,' she ordered calmly. 'For my sake and that of Celia, let him die like the animal he is.'

They watched in abject horror, unable to look away from the image before them. The rusty metal spike sticking out of Tobin was quivering as his breathing became more erratic.

Hugh knelt next to Gundred. 'My love, can't you see, this is not right.'

Bonham unsheathed his sword, knowing exactly what to do next. But before he could raise his blade, Gundred pushed Tobin backwards onto the spike until it disappeared and burst out through his intestines. She took a step back, satisfied that her work was complete. 'They tortured me for days...I wanted to die so much. Now you can kill him.'

The sword ran true across his throat and his body quivered for a moment then relaxed. Behind them, the door suddenly swung open and William Marshall stood and stared at the scene in disbelief. 'We had better make a move before anyone wakes up. Henry the Young King is holding court in Rouen and we can be there the day after tomorrow.'

No one uttered a sound that night as they rode across the Loire valley, save Gundred who hummed her favourite Christemasse song.

Chapter 21

Cairo
Egypt

Grim faces surrounded Saladin as the council meeting was adjourned for the second time that morning. He beckoned his father to sit next to him on the carpet while his advisors and other family members talked amongst themselves.

Now into his seventies, the years had treated Ayyub kindly. He looked concerned as Saladin grimaced in pain. 'You look terrible. What ails you my son,' he asked. 'You cannot keep suspending the meeting, so let me postpone it for another day, until you are better.'

Saladin nodded and amid a noisy outbreak of disappointment, the delegates were hastily dismissed. Two servants helped him rise onto a cushioned trestle and as he stretched out, the pain in his stomach began to recede.

Ayyub gave him a bowl of sweet mint tea. 'We don't need a gathering of ten advisors to make the decision anyway. It is obvious that you cannot cede Egypt to Nuradin. If you do, then everything you and my brother worked for would have been for nothing.'

Saladin knew Ayyub was still hurting from a recent visit to his brother's grave. They were very close and both of them had shown loyalty to Nuradin.

Saladin frowned. 'I respect you too much to disagree, but it is easy for you to openly express your loyalty to Nuradin then say the opposite to me. If I am to defy Nuradin and keep Egypt for myself, I do not have the luxury of lying. I have to be prepared for him to carry out his threat.'

Ayyub dismissed his concern with a slight wave of his hand. 'For all his bluster, Nuradin will never invade Egypt. Besides after the earthquake he has his hands full rebuilding his palaces and castles. Even most of your council agree with me on that point.'

Deep down Saladin knew that Nuradin would not be swayed by earthquake damage but any disruption no matter how big or small may work in his favour. 'Is it true that the Cathedral of St Peter in Antioch collapsed on top of Patriarch Athanasius, killing the entire congregation?'

'Yes, it was Allah's will,' Ayyub confirmed.

A physician arrived and began massaging Saladin's lower stomach. 'Take care you cretin!' he yelled, as the probing fingers seemed to do more harm than good.

'Why don't you let that other physician try and help. His methods come highly recommended.'

'You mean the Samaritan Jew. Why should I have his grimy fingers anywhere near me? The man should be in prison anyway.'

'Why? Just because he bargained an arrangement to save hundreds of his people when the Christian murderers entered the town of Bilbeis,' Ayyub countered. 'And before you disagree, he says he belongs to a sect that long ago converted to Islam…though he is not a Muslim.'

'Then what is he?'

Ayyub was exasperated. 'Why not let him explain while he offers you a diagnosis, your stubbornness.'

If he were not in so much discomfort, Saladin would have laughed at the tease. He dismissed his physician. 'All right, you win. Bring in the stranger, but search him thoroughly first.'

A bustle of activity broke out down the corridor and Saladin wrapped himself in a silk gown. A well-dressed man about the same age as Saladin was brought before him. Despite hearing good reports, it was the first time Ayyub had met Maimonides and was surprised at his genuine warm greeting. Smiling broadly, the Jewish physician looked to Saladin.

'You may grin like a monkey but tell me why I should not throw you in prison,' Saladin warned as his face curled in pain. Groaning out loud, he lay on his side with his legs drawn up.

Ignoring the petty bullying, Maimonides took an instrument from his leather bag. 'What colour and consistency are your stools?'

'What!' Saladin cried.

Standing over him, Maimonides placed his hearing device over the swollen bowels. 'I am going to feel and listen to your innards. Please lay on your back and keep still.' The examination was quick. Putting away his device, he repeated his question.

With his face turned away, Saladin replied. 'I have not done my ablutions today.'

Taking a jug of water, Maimonides mixed a potion with ingredients from his bag. Holding the cup, he smiled at Saladin. 'You soon will. Drink this purgative, my lord sultan. You must clear out your insides now.'

Saladin looked affronted by the request. 'How do I know if you are any good?'

'I have spent six months studying and working at the Hospital of Nuradin in Damascus. You must know of it.'

Saladin was alarmed. 'Of course I do…so you are a servant of Nuradin.'

'Yes…a servant but believe me, I am no friend of Nuradin…'

'Just do as he says, Saladin. I will vouch for him,' Ayyub interrupted impatiently.

Glaring at his father, he took the small bowl from the smiling physician and drank the mixture in one.

'You need to go to your toilet and stay there. You will vomit and your bowels will expunge for the next six to eight hours.'

A movement begin deep inside and Saladin swore under his breath. A wave of nausea swept though his stomach and he gathered his gown beckoning two servants to help him as he swiftly left the council chamber.

Now they were alone, Maimonides turned to Ayyub. 'You are very kind, my lord and your words of support have saved the life of your son.'

Ayyub's concern turned to shock. 'So, you think he was poisoned?' he whispered.

'I could smell almonds on his breath.' The physician lowered his head. 'It is a sign I know. Before word of this escapes, I will visit the kitchens to look for the culprit.'

'I shall arrange an escort...'

'No, I don't want to raise any alarm.'

Maimonides hurried out of the council chamber and across the gilded hall. He followed his nose down a staircase before entering the kitchen. The physician he had seen earlier was talking with one of the cooks.

'What do want in here?' The physician was surprised at seeing the new arrival.

Maimonides had to think quickly. 'I am a newly appointed servant to the sultan and he wants serving with his favourite figs to ease his stomach pain.'

'A servant, eh. I thought you were a prisoner of the sultan.'

'Allah be praised. The lord sultan is very forgiving.'

The cook took a bowl of figs from the store and handed them over.

Maimonides looked into the bowl and sniffed. 'And a selection of fruit, if you please.'

He noticed the physician give a slight nod to the cook and a bowl of cut fruit was placed in his other hand. Maimonides smiled and thanked them before returning swiftly to the chamber.

A flurry of activity burst forth from the garrison. The cook and the physician were immediately arrested along with others suspects from within the household staff.

Throughout the day and night, Maimonides checked on Saladin's progress and the next day he was well enough to join them in the private chamber adjacent to his boudoir. Luxurious cushions filled the floor and Maimonides was sat cross-legged next to Ayyub, filling a kettle with tea as Saladin entered the room.

Ayyub hugged his son, and thanked Allah for his safe return from illness.

Maimonides stood up, and gave a respectful bow.

Taking a cushion next to his father, Saladin gestured to the door. 'You may leave us now, physician.'

'I don't think you will be so dismissive when you hear that he saved your life,' Ayyub said.

He went on to describe the extraordinary events that led to the discovery of the plot to have Saladin assassinated. 'The suspects are under interrogation as we speak.'

Trying not to look impressed Saladin forced a frown across his face. There was something about Maimonides that made him feel uncomfortable...as if he knew too much.

His father continued to eulogise. 'Listen to what he has to say, for he is no ordinary physician. As well as being a Rabbi, he is a gifted astrologer, philosopher and scientist and translates the works of the Ptolemy and Aristotle...'

Saladin put up his hand. 'They say you are the saviour of the Jews of Bilbeis. To me it sounds as if you sit astride the heavens, choosing your God like choosing a pair of slippers.'

Maimonides was quick to answer. 'My lord, you exaggerate my importance. And when you compare us mere mortals with the heavenly sphere, do we not occupy a lowly position? In case of doubt I do believe in the Almighty, but not because He resides high in the heavens but with respect to absolute existence, greatness and power.'

'You sound like a philosopher and an arrogant one at that. So tell me how I should view the future,' Saladin asked.

Maimonides paused and gave an unerring smile. 'In order to understand everything you must first study logic, then all the branches of mathematics, then physics and metaphysics…'

Saladin huffed. 'I suggest you stick to astrology and give me a reading, you prick.'

Unruffled by the tense atmosphere brought about by Saladin's intimidation, Maimonides ignored the request and poured a fresh cup of sweet chai then handed it to the sultan. 'This special mixture of leaves has been handed down through my cousin's family for many generations. I find it very relaxing.'

'You must have some,' Ayyub nodded. 'It is as sweet as heaven.'

Looking to his father, Saladin kept his peace and sipped the cup before finishing the tea in one gulp. The exotic taste lingered on his palette and he instinctively licked his lips.

Maimonides poured another cup and passed it to Ayyub. 'Your father exaggerates my skills…a little. But his litany omitted my considerable gift of story telling. I think you will find it more entertaining than a reading.'

Ayyub settled back into his cushions while Saladin remained cross-legged, still trying to come to terms with the stranger who had suddenly entered his life. He decided he would listen for a while before having the Jew thrown out.

'Cast your mind back to when the Sky God's dwelt in a timeless world, where ten thousand years was but a fleeting moment. To a time when they spread their seed amongst the mortals and their offspring became deified as Earth Gods. Little is known of their existence except for the stories that were passed down for generations. Today we worship the memory of Ra, Osiris, Marduk, Gilgamesh and Baal. But when you mix your seed with mortals, you take on all the worst attributes of men. The lust for power left all

212

moral authority barren. Men have always had a stark choice. Truth, modesty and good government, or deceit, greed and war; the concept we would recognise today as the choice between good and evil.'

Wide-eyed with wonder, Ayyub listened with admiration to the beautiful oratory.

'Much of this I have heard before,' Saladin grumbled.

'I am sure you have,' Maimonides replied knowingly. 'The kings and Pharaohs that followed tried to emulate the God's by building great temples and pyramids that they hoped would transport them safely through the underworld all the way to the heavens. And it is not just the Egyptians, for I have travelled to many lands and seen with my own eyes the great stone monoliths that fill the ancient landscape with circles and lines. They were built by civilisations that have come and gone, but all of them were dedicated to the ever-changing movement of the sun, moon and the stars. They inspired the study of astrological formations that enabled the mortal descendants to predict certain events.'

Saladin gathered his silk gown around his torso. 'What events?'

Maimonides hesitated, trying to read Saladin's face. 'I am sorry, I thought perhaps the Sultan has heard all this before?'

Saladin's face reddened as he stared back.

Ayyub was insistent. 'No…please, let us hear more of your tale.'

Sitting cross-legged, with his hands placed on his lap, Maimonides continued. 'Only the most skilled astrologers can define the actual alignment of the cosmos, such as an eclipse of the sun. But imagine if you like, the ability to predict every thousand years when the door between earth and the stars opens up. Those descendants of the Gods who are receptive to the signs, are burdened with breath-taking abilities.'

'What do you mean, 'burdened'? Surely all power is good,' Ayyub suggested.

'Without the wisdom of their forefathers, the Earth Gods simply proved themselves incapable of controlling the power they possessed. The burden became a curse. One single catastrophe was centred on Baalbek and laid waste to all of Syria. You have heard of the Earth God Gilgamesh, a demi god, who wrote of a time when the Sky Gods returned. They were so offended by the sight and sound of humans constantly mating, that they caused a gigantic wave to destroy mankind. The story was stolen much later by the Hebrews and referenced in the scriptures as Noah's flood. No one knows the true extent of the power of Gilgamesh, only that he was so feared by his people that the River Euphrates was diverted over his grave to seal him in Gehenna forever.

'What is Gehenna?' Ayyub asked.

Sipping his tea, Maimonides cleared his throat 'It goes by the names Hades or purgatory but is best recognised as the underworld.'

Staring at him stiffly, Saladin felt his insides churning. 'You mentioned the God Baal.'

'Baal was a particularly interesting and powerful God and with the urging of the Goddess Astarte, they inflicted unparalleled cruelty upon mortal men. He propagated numberless offspring, who were impelled to imitate their depravities, denying the people the good that could come from the power they possessed. That is until the schism occurred.' Again, Maimonides paused, wondering how much he should impart.

Ayyub was spellbound. 'The schism? Please go on.'

Maimonides remained calm and sipped his chai. 'The time of King Solomon, descendants of Baal continued to adhere themselves to the forces of ignorance and evil, while others members of the family saw the potential for enlightenment. A rift occurred between those who wanted a positive use of the power for the benefit of all, to create rather than destroy. Hiram Abiff, the architect of Solomon's Temple was one such guardian, but those that opposed his wondrous vision of a world had him murdered. Fortunately, the generations of good

214

men that followed were inspired by his selfless act to follow his example. Today they are known as the Sabians.'

Ayyub was stunned. 'My word, you tell a fine tale, my friend. How did you ever come to think of such unworldly things?'

Maimonides looked again at Saladin before continuing. 'I am one of the Harranian Sabians.'

The name sparked a distant memory and Saladin jumped to his feet just as one of his councillors entered the room. He bowed before speaking. 'Sultan, the physician has given way under interrogation. We have found a bag of gold buried in the orchard. He says it is a part payment from an Egyptian officer, to have you assassinated.'

'Does he know any more?' Saladin asked.

'No my lord.'

'Then have him opened up and hung from the...'

'If I may say something a moment,' Maimonides interjected, ignoring the fierce glare from Saladin. 'Why not have the physician meet the officer on the premise that you are dead. Once discovered and questioned, he will no doubt lead you to the true paymaster.'

'That is a clever idea.' Ayyub clapped Maimonides on the back. 'I told you he was a genius.'

Saladin hesitated, then nodded and gave fresh orders to have the physician followed and his contact captured.

For much of the next day, Saladin remained in his apartments while arrangements for the deception were carried out. During his imaginary 'death', Ayyub and Maimonides agreed to keep him company.

Saladin's initial irritation with Maimonides had been replaced by curiosity. He knew of the Sabians as highly respected intellectuals, being at the forefront of Arab scientific advancement for hundred of years and although their history was shrouded in mystery, he was taught as a youth of the origin of the name.

Five hundred years ago they came as immigrants from ancient Persia and settled in the town of Hurran, where they would meet to share their learning and beliefs with other like-minded students. The locals recognised them as benevolent if rather eccentric scholars. But with the onset of Islamic rule, they were told to adhere to one of the accepted religions as recognised by the Koran.

Fearful of being castigated, they studied the Koran and found mention of an unknown race called the Sabians. Not even the most learned of Islam knew where the name came from, so they collectively took the name and agreed to acknowledge an obscure Greek God also approved by Islam.

Maimonides went on to explain. 'The choice of the name Sabian was purely incidental but it gave us the protection of Islam.' He took a deep breath as if unsure of his next words. 'Like I said, our primary purpose is to identify those descendants of Baal who pose a threat to the world, and do our best to encourage those of wise temperament and sound values. Fortunately, most of them are unaware of their legacy and live their lives in blissful yet evil ignorance. But history has shown that some inherit any number of powers and are sought out by priests and shaman, with the intention of rediscovering the inherent power of the Gods.'

Saladin clench his fists and stood gazing out of a window.

This Sabian Jew knows too much. Was he a danger or not?

The voice of Maimonides continued. 'My studies have revealed that one thousand years has passed since the death of the last descendant. Like many that have gone before, he had a pathological desire to wipe out Jerusalem and much of Judea. There are numerous descriptions of how he succeeded.'

The name fell from the lips of Saladin. 'The Emperor Hadrian.'

Maimonides took an uneasy breath. 'You are probably correct my lord, though there is evidence that his daughter was a shaman and

216

held the real power. You know your history well...perhaps you are already aware that you were born exactly one thousand years after the death of Hadrian. To the day.'

In the taut silence that filled the room, Ayyub suddenly laughed out loudly and clapped his hands. 'Fascinating! What a storyteller. Is any of this true?'

Looking at Saladin squarely in the face, Maimonides took a sip of tea. 'All of it is true...except for one thing. Saladin cannot be a true descendant of Baal.'

Saladin's expression changed to one of surprise. 'And why do you say that?'

'Is it not obvious? Because your father Ayyub is not a descendant of Baal.'

Stunned into silence, Saladin made a sudden movement that knocked over his drink. Cursing under his breath he failed to hide the bead of sweat that slipped from his brow.

The atmosphere had fallen flat and the silence was filled by a loud yawn from Ayyub. 'Most amusing...what fine story telling. However it is not good enough to keep me awake any longer.' He stretched his legs and left the room for his bed.

Now they were alone, Saladin sought some answers. 'You know so much about me, so it is only fair you tell me more of your life as a Harranian Sabian.'

Maimonides noted Saladin's discomfort. 'The Sabians scoured the world for books to add to the great libraries of the Islamic world. One of our earliest and greatest exponents was Thabit ibn Qurra. His study of the celestial heavens propose the world to be round and not flat.' Ignoring the look of disbelief, Maimonides continued. 'His personal collection of writings and books were guarded in the library of Toledo in Al-Andalusia, for some three hundred years. Then inexplicably, the entire collection was stolen by a motley band of knights posing as scholarly monks. They were the very same knights who first resided in the great mosque in Jerusalem.'

This was another revelation that unsettled Saladin. 'The Knights Templars,' he said flatly. Somehow, it came as no surprise that the hated Knights had entered the story.

'Many scholars, including myself believed that Thabit ibn Qurra had collected the secrets of the sacred geometry as written by Hiram Abiff from the ruins of the Solomon's Temple. I know many in Islam would malign the theory as blasphemy, but consider this. Only a few short years after stealing those secret books, the west was filled with mighty cathedrals that reached high into the sky. I have seen them with my own eyes and is not mere coincidence.'

'You appear to be well travelled,' Saladin conceded.

But Maimonides had not finished. 'And speaking of coincidence, you have not questioned my inference regarding your birth exactly one thousand years after Emperor Hadrian.'

Saladin flushed but gave nothing away. 'What do you expect me to say?'

For the first time, the smile disappeared from the face of Maimonides. 'Some sixty years ago, the Sabians of Hurran received a letter from Kemah ibn Qurra, a direct descendant of Thabit. The letter gave dire warnings of a stranger from the west called Lugermann who apparently had an undeniable resemblance to an engraving of the Pharaoh Shishak. Lugermann was killed but years later his son was kidnapped and had his mind contaminated by the infamous shaman Tammuz. In honour of the mighty destroyer, the boy was renamed Shishak. In the letter, Kemah claimed that Shishak would take his vengeance upon the world and wreak untold destruction. Unfortunately, a clerk ignored the letter, mistaking it for the paranoid ramblings of an old man but years later, a wise scholar recognised the name 'ibn Qurra' and asked me to investigate the story. I went to the house of Kemah in Acre and discovered the remnants of his scrolls that confirmed his obsession with the descendants of Baal.'

Pausing for breath, Maimonides took a sip of water. 'My search revealed yet another interesting coincidence. In Damascus a young, charismatic Faranji known as Shishak was often seen in the presence of your mother Amalek. Nine months before you were born.'

The next morning Saladin was woken by a nervous servant. 'Sultan, the officer has been arrested. I was to wake you with the news.'

Wiping the sleep from his eyes, Saladin pulled away from his wife leaving her covered by the silk sheets. He walked to the washbasin and splashed water over his face. 'Go on.'

The servant spoke slowly and deliberately, his nerves jangling. 'The officer has been arrested and he has given the name of your failed assassin. It was Lord Muzawi.'

Saladin spun round on his heels, his silk gown flowing around his legs. He slapped the servant hard and he tumbled to the floor. 'Who told you to say that?'

The servant crawled onto his knees and sobbing with fear, he pointed behind Saladin. 'He told me!'

Stepping into the bedroom, Maimonides apologised to the servant as he scuttled away. Turning to Saladin, he could see the fury was still blazing across his face. 'We need to talk, my lord sultan. I suggest your wife and servants are dismissed.'

Without taking his eyes from the physician, Saladin gestured to the two maids who were stood expectantly at the door. They helped dress his wife and then left the chamber.

Now they were alone, Maimonides turned to face Saladin to apologise for his dramatic behaviour, only to be greeted with a solid punch to the jaw that sent him reeling across the floor. Saladin stood over him in a blind fury. 'No one ever speaks to me like that, you arrogant bastard! Now get out of here before I have you thrown into the deepest dungeon!'

Sat on his rear, Maimonides felt his jaw and wiped a trickle of blood from his lip. 'Muzawi will kill you unless we stop him…'

'Muzawi is dead! I have seen his skeleton. You were taken in by a lie. Now, stop interfering in my life and get out of here.'

Maimonides was still moving his jaw, checking if it was broken. 'Believe me, Muzawi is now more powerful than you can imagine. The spy was called Edom and his stubbornness cost him his testes. He had no reason to lie. He said that Muzawi has been to Tanis and he now carries a single sphere in a coffer made for two.'

Saladin froze by the door, aghast at the words. 'No one should know all this? You know too much for a mere mortal…'

'Whatever ability flows through my body I just choose to use it for good, not evil. I trust we are of like minds.'

If the comment was meant to be a question then Saladin chose to ignore it.

Maimonides stood up and swilled water around his mouth before spitting it out. 'I am sorry…I deserved your anger. But I must know your true motives in this enigma that surrounds you.'

Saladin checked the door and sat down to pour himself some fresh water. 'I don't know if I can trust you…I don't even know you.'

Maimonides said nothing. He rubbed his chin and waited.

A beacon of understanding slowly dawned on Saladin. Everything began to make sense and now he felt the need to release the burden of truth. 'After I left Muzawi in the catacombs of Alexandria, my spirit drained from my body, even though I had conquered an entire country. I knew it was all over when the mace became too unwieldy and cumbersome. It became a burden, no longer able to recharge my soul. Then one day the mace vanished and I have never seen it since. The power of the Gods had passed me by. And all I did was blame it on the death of Muzawi.'

'And Shishak?'

Saladin nodded. 'You must never tell Ayyub that Shishak was my true father,' he ordered.

Relieved of the weight of his disclosure, Saladin now felt unsure of himself. 'So now you know the truth, what is to happen next?'

Maimonides took a deep breath. 'You should look closely at the world and see yourself as a scale with an equal balance of good and evil. When you do one good deed, the scale is tipped to the good and the world is saved. When you commit one evil deed the scale is tipped to the bad and the world is destroyed.'

Maimonides stood in front of Saladin and looked into his eyes. 'Muzawi has turned his back on you and I believe he has taken your place as his own. The first sphere will be his inspiration, but as an instrument of power he will need to find the second one, and then the two sceptres.'

'The second sphere is in Lydda,' Saladin admitted. 'Arius buried it under a crypt that eventually held his own coffin. The one believed to be the crypt of St George.'

'That is strange,' Maimonides said to himself. He looked to the ceiling as if deep in thought. 'The Count of Flanders, from the first Army of God, had his men to take the remains of St George back to the west.'

'The Christians are thieves...'

'That is not what I mean. All of them, all holy men, became ill and died on the way back to Flanders.

Saladin frowned deep in thought. 'The curse. Muzawi said that when he read of the horrific death of Arius he recognised the symptoms. I did not understand the connection but he often spoke of a terrible curse, known only to him.'

Maimonides nodded. 'If Muzawi unleashes the power they hold, then this land will be destroyed and will return to an age of darkness.'

Saladin shivered as if a cold draft had eaten into his bones. 'Walk with me to the palace mosque.'

Both of them were deep in thought as they walked across the sunlit gardens.

Maimonides broke the silence. 'Of course, it had to be Lydda.'

Saladin looked baffled. 'What do you mean?'

'It is written long ago…the gates of Lydda are to be the site of the next apocalypse. The place where Christ and the Anti-Christ battle for the fate of the world. The End of Days.'

Saladin was dismissive. 'Again you dwell on myth and legend…'

Maimonides looked up to the sky. 'If men only believe in myth and legend then they can never be taught the truth. The 'time of promises' is happening and soon the next alignment will soon be upon us. Events will be put in motion that cannot be stopped and the Lord of devastation will reign once more.'

Saladin kept on walking. 'I have known all this for some time. One day I will lead an army into Jerusalem. But first, I must take Gaza. It is the key that will open the door into the Christian held territory.'

'And Gaza is controlled by the Knights Templars.'

Saladin gave a wry smile. 'Why have only one objective when you can complete two.' Covering his head he entered the mosque, leaving Maimonides to dwell on his words.

As a first major incursion into Palestine, he thought the plan was too premature and too ambitious to succeed, and in time, he would say as much. But he doubted that Saladin would listen.

Chapter 22

Jerusalem

Princess Sybilla lay as still as a leaf on the bed, reciting the book she had once read as a child. It was a story of endless love and aching hearts that no self-respecting fourteen year-old girl should ever have read. But the book had come from the courts of Champagne and the tale had swallowed up her imagination, leaving her blushed and clammy in the mornings.

Then she was told of her Prince Stephen who was on his way from the courts of Burgundy. That he wore shining armour and was a chivalrous knight both brave and kind with the wisdom of Solomon. There was no doubt in her mind, he would sweep her off her feet and carry her away on a cloud of romantic poems that would echo with his love for her. He was someone who would cuddle her, laugh at her whimsical stories and run joyously through the fields of corn and maize. To begin with, she would be coy. Then after a year or two she would succumb to his desires, whatever they may be.

Shaking herself from her daydream, Sybilla felt the man lying next to her stir. She trembled on the soft chiffon bed covers and tried to edge her way across the sheets until she no longer felt his body next to hers. The soreness between her legs stung so much it made her sob. This was the sixth night she had laid with the man from Burgundy and by now she had learnt to cry silently, for she must not make a sound lest he should wake and hurt her again.

She hated him with all her heart. As he snored next to her, she could smell his western stench. In six days, he had never washed; never changed his clothes. She clawed at the sheets again, crawling away from him, slower than a snail.

He was supposed to be her prince from the courts of Champagne. But her dreams lay shattered by the stinking monster that threw her into bed, tearing at her clothes until she was naked; tearing at her body until she lay battered and bruised. Crying was a waste of time for no one would come.

Where was her knight now, his shield held high and proud, ready to sweep her off her feet.

Now he woke, the clammy hands pawing her innocent body like an animal. Trying to hold her legs together, she whimpered then cried, frightened of what was to come. Instinctively she pulled away, only to fall in an untidy heap on the rush matting. Something inside her told her to run and she made for the door. Any moment she expected the horrible hands to grab her and pull her back, but they never came. The door was already open and she ran down the corridor as fast as her feet would take her.

Stephen sat up and swung his legs over the side of the bed, not attempting to run after her. Biding his time, he waited and played with himself, safe in the knowledge that some servant would bring the snivelling little sod back to his bed.

He was suddenly startled to see a young boy climb onto the bed behind him. He recognised Prince Baldwin. 'My God, you are the leper prince. Stay away from me.' He pushed himself away but the boy followed.

Prince Baldwin began to unfurl the bandage from around his hand. 'I need to tell you something important,' he said sounding older than his years.

Stephen watched transfixed, as finger by finger the boy's ghastly hand was revealed. 'Don't you dare come any closer or else…' He raised his cuff to strike.

Baldwin stopped moving 'It isn't me you need to be afraid of. They haven't told you why they want you married so quickly, have they?'

'Told me what exactly?' Stephen asked nervously.

'That Sybilla has leprosy just like me.' Baldwin squeezed a clump of pus and flesh from around his knuckles and held it in front of Stephen's face.

William Bigod woke from his dream with a cry. Sweat was running down his cheeks and as he wiped his face, a servant entered his room, a look of consternation on his face.

'Fear not Gerash, I am still alive. It was just another dream.'

Gerash brought William his walking stick and helped the old man from his mattress. 'I still think you should see a physician about a sleeping draught. That is the third time this week you have cried out in your sleep.'

William shook his head dismissively. 'I don't think the dreams are as simple as that…I think they are an omen. Time and again, the same image is emblazoned in my mind.'

'Well you know what I suggested,' Gerash said, knowing full well his advice would be ignored.

'Yes I know, but surely understanding the enigma is better than destroying it.'

Gerash resigned himself to say no more on the subject.

Instead, he reminded William of the business of the day. 'You remember we are expecting the commandant to collect the three mares today.'

'Of course I remember, I am not yet an imbecile.' William would never admit that his memory was now beginning to falter with each day that passed.

As he took his bread and oatmeal on the terrace he watched as three of his best mares were brought from the enclosure and paraded in front of him. As always, he would inspect the gait and tendons of each horse that went to the Knights Templars, ensuring that the best quality would maintain the top price.

Looking down the track to his left, he noticed the arrival of his friend Jacques de Exemes, the Knights Templar and garrison commander of Ramleh. His magnificent stallion was named Mica and William recalled the sale as the only time he had agreed a concession, though they had been close friends for more than ten years. With each elegant stride, the red and white insignia that covered the chain mail on the head and flanks wafted in the wind, a perfect match for the red cross emblazoned across the white tabard of Jacques.

As the massive beast was tethered, William went to greet them both, the stallion nuzzling against him affectionately. 'Mica, it is good to be remembered but you are a mighty warhorse and should put aside your friendship. Come and sit Jacques; it has been too long.'

Sipping limejuice, Jacques was concerned that William appeared pale and tired, and told him so.

William sighed. 'I am blest with good health. Just remember I am fast approaching my eightieth year, with the miracle of God's blessing. But if truth be told, I am fatigued with such dreams that would badly affect any man younger than me.'

Jacques still marvelled at William's ability to hold a conversation; his inflection almost had an endearing quality. 'So tell me what ails you about your dreams and God willing I can help.'

Mulling over his drink, William conceded that it would do no harm to share his fear of the night. 'Strange as it may sound, it starts with a vision of an old stone column. The image of a man adorns the circumference, like an apparition. The man is frightened, unable to hide the fear in his eyes. Under the face appears a bloodstained hand. A knight attacks the column but his blade enters the apparition as though it were mist. The knight then falls to his knees and is instantly converted to follow the command of Christ.'

Jacques waited for the rest of the dream. 'Is that it? You are losing sleep, over a simple dream like that?'

William suddenly felt foolish. Jacques was right; it was just a simple and silly reoccurring dream. Feeling embarrassed he decided to keep one vital ingredient of the dream to himself. The column is identical to one he had seen before. 'Well I told you it was strange, not life threatening,' William said defensively. 'Now let us discuss the horses. I have an idea regarding Mica. I want to take him back to breed with my mare Adelice, before she gets too old. The bloodstock of each horse is the best anyone has ever produced. Just imagine the quality of the beast that would be sired.'

Jacques had to agree. 'Such a horse would be unique.'

That evening they passed the time talking of all matters, some trivial, some not.

Jacques said he had some good news to impart. 'It involves Lydda. I have spoken to the Grand Master and agreed that a small garrison should be built by the square: just six or eight Knights to patrol the villages where there have been Egyptian incursions.'

William was surprised. 'You think it is necessary.'

'They are a nuisance that will only get worse unless we react with force,' Jacques replied.

'Then I had better burnish my sword,' William chuckled.

Jacques was pleased to see that William had perked up and told him of the recent revelations from the royal court in Jerusalem. 'You remember when we last met, I told you of the sad story that blighted King Amalric's only son.'

William nodded, recalling the tragic fate that had befallen Prince Baldwin. At only nine years of age, while playing 'dare or do' with his friends, it was discovered he had contracted leprosy. But the shock that ran through the royal court were soon replaced by pragmatism.

'Granted it seems dispassionate, but a decision was made to find another heir to the throne to marry Sybilla, the daughter of Amalric. They agreed that the aristocracy of the west should be called upon to fulfil that honour.' Jacques took another sip of wine. 'You will never believe who was chosen. None other than the younger brother of Count Theobald of Blois and Henri of Champagne. You must have heard of him; Count Stephen of Sancerre.'

William looked blank, then pulled his memories into place. 'Yes of course, Stephen of Sancerre was named after his grandfather, the one who deserted the first Army of God. I was just nine or ten years old, but every boy remembers the shame he must have felt. Then upon his return to die a martyr's death. Do you know he was killed in a tower within a mile or so from Ramleh?

Jacques shook his head and laughed. 'Your memory as a ten year old is better than my recollection of last week. But listen; I haven't finished. A few days ago Stephen of Sancerre arrived in Jerusalem, eager to meet Sybilla his bride to be. The age difference horrified the court but no one dare speak out. Stephen was an overweight, forty year old letch and poor Sybilla a sylph-like fourteen.' Jacques found it hard not to laugh out loud. 'I swear, she was half his height and stood next to him he could not even see her. Anyway he had his way with her for six days; then unbeknown to anyone, he fled with his entourage back to Jaffa and caught a boat to Constantinople...' Jacques could barely finish the story for laughing, '...only to be shipwrecked off the Turkish coast...and robbed of every coin and piece of clothing.'

William slapped the table hard, joining in and barely able to control his laughter. 'My God, it is so good to have these times together. I cannot remember the last time I laughed.'

The good humour continued and it was some time before either of them could keep a straight face.

Chapter 23

Norwich
England

It was a busy and important day for Norwich cathedral. Not only was it bustling with hundreds of visiting pilgrims for Easter, it was also the official reopening of the cathedral after the fire of three years ago, when much of the roof was destroyed.

The crowds that filled the market in front of the cathedral gates ignored the old man and his servant as they crossed the square. Like many of the pilgrims, they jostled their way towards the mighty edifice built over the main doors. With hooded cloaks covering their faces, they could have been taken for any merchant and his servant. None would have seen the anonymous pair and thought they were the Earl of Norfolk and his trusted knight.

A young tyke, the worse for too much ale barged into Hugh and made him lose his footing on the uneven paving. As the drunken whelp scowled and swore at Hugh, his knight instinctively went to his sword.

'No, don't!' Hugh directed with a wave of his arm. 'We can't risk showing ourselves.'

Swearing under his breath, Bonham walked on ignoring the jeers of the young ruffian. Crossing the square, they were soon at the gates of the cathedral.

Hugh paused a moment as he felt the emotion swell inside.

For weeks his need for vengeance had steamed like a boiling pot but Gundred was right to call for calm before the storm.

At her suggestion he went to pay his respects to his mother's grave and his fathers resting place. The small pilgrimage to Norwich

Cathedral and Thetford Priory would give him chance to reflect on her wishes. He discovered she was right.

Now as he walked into the bosom of the church, all the pain, all the suffering came flooding back, and vivid flashes of his father filled his head. He was eleven when his was killed. Bishop Losinga dragged his father away on a litter from Thetford Priory to Norwich Cathedral. All the while his inconsolable mother begged him to stop.

The bitter tears had dried, but the hate had lingered for the last sixty-six years, burning a hole in his heart, dissolving all goodness. Never would he understand why any God would be so pitiless to let his father die at the hands of a bishop.

Trudging behind the feet of the congregation, down the side aisle, he came to the spot in the floor marked by an inlaid stone where his father was buried. Pilgrims tried to push him out of the way as Hugh tried in vain to stop them from trampling over Roger Bigod's worn-out memorial stone. No one gave his father any respect.

Many of the pilgrims were drawn to a small chapel to the north of the altar and Hugh could hear a monk speaking to those around him. Worming his way forward, a shrill voice echoed off the walls.

'…and it was twenty years ago that our own Brother Thomas had visions of the Holy Bishop Losinga, the founder of this cathedral. In those visions, the bishop ordered the body of young Saint William be brought from the monk's cemetery, to the cathedral. Our youngest saint, one of God's own children, mortified on the cross as was our lord Jesus Christ by the actions of those void of faith …whereupon miracles and visions spring forth from his tomb.'

Hugh appeared startled by the words and turned to Bonham. 'That was the tanner boy…the one that was crucified.' His face began to redden with suppressed anger. 'They dare to honour that boy over one so great as my own father.' Hugh had no tears left to shed. Just an abiding abhorrence for the hypocrisy of the religious order he saw all around him.

Bonham sensed Hugh was upset and led him back towards the chancel where it was less crowded. On the chancel steps, Hugh stopped in his tracks, staring at the floor only a few paces away. On the most prominent placement in the whole cathedral, a large black inscribed tombstone was centred in the floor. Pilgrims knelt and prayed at its side, reverently placing coins and offerings upon the words of dedication.

Bonham was curious at Hugh's reaction. 'Who is buried there? It must be someone important.'

A large globule of spit shot from Hugh's mouth, landing on the face of the tombstone. Faces turned round in disbelief as Bonham pulled Hugh through the crowds, up the nave and out of the main doors.

'For God's sake Hugh, why…'

'That was the resting place of Bishop Herbert Losinga. I owed him that just for fucking up my life. Still, I pretty much fucked up his.' Hugh grinned inanely, not giving a care for the commotion he had caused as people began looking around, unsure of what had happened.

'So much for keeping a low profile,' Bonham muttered looking around for the two squires. 'We need to find the horses and get out of here quickly, before we start a riot.'

Hugh gave a devilish smirk. 'Wouldn't be the first time.'

Against his better judgement, Bonham agreed to ride on to Thetford, to pay respects to Hugh's mother Adelice. He pleaded with Hugh not to cause a scene like he had just witnessed in the cathedral. He reminded him that they were on the Warenne estates and they would have loyalty to the king. Hugh grunted then scoffed at having to maintain his feeble disguise as a merchant.

To his surprise, he found the family manor had completely gone.

All the stonework down to the foundations had been robbed out and reused to extend the priory on the other side of the river.

Crossing the river to the priory, he was able to walk the corridors of the old church without restriction. The monks simply nodded or ignored him, assuming he was just a rich merchant, making a discrete donation.

He stopped in front of the alabaster relief of the Virgin Mary in a niche on the wall of the quire and remembered how it had always been a favourite of his mother's. The prior walked from the nave and stopped next to Hugh. 'I see you admiring the Virgin Mary. We had it moved into this niche only six months ago.' The prior gave Hugh a sideways glance. 'I always thought that another one on the opposite side would be make a lovely pair.'

'Yes I am sure they would,' Hugh smiled benevolently. 'I shall have my clerk see to a donation.'

The prior perked up and gave a discreet bow. 'If you are here for the dedication, then it is not until the morrow but we can offer accommodation…'

'Oh, what dedication is it?' Hugh asked.

'Haven't you heard. News has reached us that the pope has sanctified the great martyr. He will be known throughout all lands as Saint Thomas of Canterbury.'

Hugh bit his tongue. 'Of course I had heard, but I came to pay my respects to a relative.

They walked outside to the cemetery, asking the prior to be alone while they prayed. They found his mother's gravestone; cracked and uncared, indistinguishable from the undergrowth with her name and the date of death barely visible.

Hugh uttered a mixture of undying love and recurring threats that baffled Bonham. He ended his diatribe with a menacing promise. 'The bastards will pay for this.'

'What bastards do you mean exactly,' Bonham asked soberly.

Hugh stared at the headstone. 'They know who they are. Vengeance will be mine saith the lord and in the months to come, they will taste the vengeance of Earl Bigod.'

Patting the headstone, he walked back through the long grass to the stables, Bonham following behind, mystified by the day's experience.

Confusion was written over the face of the prior as he waved off the merchant and his servant. He counted the few coins left to him by the visiting strangers, hardly enough to pay for a pot of paint.

The old priory cellarer ambled up next to him and waved his cane. 'Good riddance,' he cried after them, his voice hoarse with age. 'So what did old Bigod want here anyway?'

The prior glanced at the cellarer and gave a condescending chortle. 'Earl Bigod you say. No, I am afraid he was just a cloth merchant from Norwich.'

The cellarer shook his head. 'If he was a merchant, then why come all this way to stand and pray in front of the grave of Earl Bigod's mother?'

The prior's face narrowed as he watched the two horsemen ride through the gate. 'If he was the old Earl then he must be very aged. Perhaps he is facing death himself and wanted some comfort.'

The old cellarer had lost friends in the civil war and harboured only bitterness. 'No good has ever come from that man. If he faces death then the devil take his soul, for God would surely spit it out.'

Framlingham Castle had never played host to so many earls and knights and the household staff was rushed off its feet. Three months of planning had become six, as the complexity of the rebellion reached the point where the pieces were beginning to fall into place. The rebellion would simultaneously take over England while King Henry was ensconced in Normandie, surrounded on all sides.

There were doubters in England who preferred to wait but Hugh was sure that if King Henry lost Normandie, all the undecided English barons would join forces with Harry the young king. Hugh had deliberately used the young kings nickname after his courtiers and stewards had begun to use 'Harry' to distinguish him from his father, and the name had stuck.

Young Harry had already induced some barons with unbelievable offers of large tracts of land, some with entire counties. All Hugh had asked in return for his support was the city of Norwich. Not only had the young king promised Norwich but the honour of Eye as well.

But just as Hugh expected, nerves were rubbing raw as some around the hall counselled caution. Rumours were rampant that the King's Justicar, Richard de Lucy already had the city of Leicester under siege. Sat at the head of the table, Hugh held his tongue. He had seen it all before.

Amidst the quarrelling voices he chose his moment to stand up, and out of respect for their host, the assembled earls, lords and knights calmed down so he could be heard.

'My brave friends, it sounds as if this rebellion has stalled before a sword has been drawn. All I hear are words. Words are the weapons of cowards who blanch at the sight of a sharpened blade!' The strength of his voice surprised them and some held their heads in shame at the verbal assault. 'I know many of you have estates in Normandie. And as I speak, our young Harry, just eighteen and crowned a king, is bravely bearing arms, to fight the armies of his own father. Such is the gravity of injustice that Count Matthew of Boulogne and his brother, Count Philip of Flanders fight alongside him, assailing King Henry's strongholds from the east. King Louis of France is about to move against the town of Verneuil and in the west the Count of Meulan and our own Earl of Leicester are fighting in Brittany. I hear this day that King Henry's own Chamberlain of Normandie, with a force of a two hundred and fifty knights has joined our just cause to see the 'old' King ousted. Even his own cousin, the Bishop of Worcester, has openly suggested that the rebellion is supported by the murdered Saint Thomas, as a punishment for the king's arrogance and egotism!'

A cheer rose from the assembly and they banged the table appreciatively.

'And where is King Henry, I hear you ask. He shies away in Rouen, with only his guilt for company, surrounded by our righteous allies. Now my friends, it is only a matter time before the fight comes these shores so prepare yourselves. Return to your strongholds and assemble your best knights who simply want to fight…for justice.'

'When do we do battle!' came a shout above the clamour of voices.

'When the King of the Scots crosses the border, that will be the time for us all to rise in unison. Just remember, the old King Henry threatens our lands and our livelihoods. He wishes to strangle the power we hold and have us whimper at his feet like puppies. Well I for one will not cower to Henry! I say King Harry holds the crown and England belongs to him!'

A deafening cry of defiance echoed around the hall and Hugh nodded to his servants to bring in the food and ale.

Gundred wandered through the crowd to congratulate her husband for his rousing speech but she struggled to articulate the words. It had been a trying year since her rescue and the horrors she had suffered had changed her life forever. All her maids, servants and friends were distraught at the frequent hysterical fits and long periods of depression that she now endured. A ghostly, haunted expression was fixed upon her face as she stared into faraway lands; somewhere the nightmares could never reach her.

As for Hugh, he had more than enough hatred to spare, to avenge his loving wife.

Chapter 22

Verneuil
Normandie

On the approach to Louis's camp, young King Harry looked across the gentle slope towards Verneuil. The rampart around the lower burgh had been breached and the few streets of peasant houses and outbuildings were but smouldering ruins. But above the lower streets, a fortified wall adjacent to the castle wall protected the major part of the town. Although the walls had suffered some damage, it appeared the siege was far from over.

Before entering the French king's tent, he threw water onto his face and entered unannounced. Sat at the end of a large trestle table, Louis held court with half a dozen councillors, and was taken aback by the young king's dishevelled appearance.

Realising too late the need for etiquette, Harry gave a slight bow.

Louis forced a smile and opened his arms in greeting. 'My lord king, please take a seat.'

Harry gulped down a cup of wine from the table. 'I have bad tidings, my lord. The Count of Boulogne has taken an injury from an arrow and both he and his brother Philip have left the field to return to Flanders.'

There was no reaction from those around the table.

Slowly, the Earl of Leicester rose from his bench. 'We know Harry, a messenger arrived but an hour ago.'

The young king was surprised to see the Earl of Leicester.' I thought you were in Brittany, my lord.'

Leicester sat back down and looked away, uncomfortable at the question. 'Our defences were not ready and the king ...I mean your father took us all by surprise. Suddenly he was upon us and we had no supplies to withstand a long siege…it was best to retreat intact.'

'But my father is supposed to be in Rouen…'

Louis interrupted. 'There is no cause for concern. It is only a temporary setback. I have it on good authority that the Count of Flanders will rejoin the field, once his brother recovers from his wound. You look hot and bothered; I shall have a bath prepared.' Louis called a servant then carried on talking to his council of war.

Harry left the tent feeling as though he had been dismissed. His squire helped him take off his mail and behind the tent he spied a beautiful maid who smiled as she filled a metal bath with steaming hot water. He needed no further encouragement and swirled the hot water around his body.

Later that evening, Harry joined Louis and his council in time for dinner. Three more mangonels were due to arrive at dawn and would ensure the towns surrender. Just to make sure, a fresh squadron of four hundred mercenary archers and men-at-arms would provide covering fire, most of them arriving under the command of the Earl of Leicester.

As the food was being served a messenger arrived and a steward read the letter. His face dropped and Louis beckoned him over to read the letter himself. There were few words and he turned the parchment over to read the name of the recipient. 'I think this message is marked for the attention of the Earl of Leicester.' The steward handed over the scroll.

Louis waited for a reaction and it came loud and vociferous.

The earl thumped the table, scattering a platter of fish sideways. 'Jesus fucking Christ! Richard de Lucy has taken the city of Leicester. My seat of power and my earldom…!'

In a furious state, he barged past the steward. 'That bastard de Lucy hates me. I just know he will have burnt the city to the ground. I spent thousands on new walls, on a cathedral…all of it gone…'

'The letter says nothing of the sort,' Louis argued. 'It is more likely they surrendered peacefully.'

Leicester did not listen. The rage had reached boiling point and he stormed out the tent.

The meeting finished on a sombre note and made for an early night as they all dwelt on the sobering news. Some felt sorry for the earl, whereas most deemed his misfortune as simple bad luck. De Lucy was a good strategist and viciously loyal to King Henry. Someone was bound to feel his wrath and it just happened to be the Earl of Leicester.

While some stayed awake to plan escalating the assault on the defences of Verneuil, Louis and his entourage retired for an early awakening. Everyone assumed that Leicester had returned to his tent to find solace in drink. Instead, he found consolation in his wife.

She had ridden with the messenger and was expecting her husband to come back to his tent, and she anticipated his foul mood.

Like a good wife, Petronella rose to greet him and hugged him tightly. He tried talking but she gently shushed him saying 'I know, I know…'

The litheness of her body wrapped around his, clinging at first, then rubbing intimately, softly touching then grabbing forcefully till he gave a yelp of pleasure. The night was hot and his tunic was easily discarded along with his britches and underwear. The passion was short-lived but afterwards he felt relaxed for the first time in an age.

Both were naked and excited to be in each other's company. They talked about revenge and how his enemies would pay.

'I want those dogs out of my city,' Petronella hissed, 'or I shall hang every one of them from the walls.'

Earl Robert nodded in agreement. 'We cannot go running from country to country; city to city. The first job in hand is Verneuil.'

Petronella spoke quietly. 'I have information that Louis does not yet know. King Henry is already in Conches, only fifteen miles away.

Leicester sat up, alarmed at the news. 'We must tell…'

Petronella wrapped her hand around his mouth. 'If you let this out then half the army would be gone before dawn and the war is over.'

She wrapped her legs around him. 'What if we keep this war going a while longer. Fuck Verneuil and its French peasants. We will make them bleed and steal their gold.'

The earl recognised the flash of malevolence cross the face of his wife. 'What do you have in mind?' he squeezed her buttocks.

'I want you to find Louis's most trusted herald and give him an urgent order.' Then she told him her plan.

In the glow of a half moon and with his banner of truce fluttering next to the king's colours, the herald rode to the town gates, flanked by the Earl of Leicester, his wife and a squire. They stopped at the gate and as was customary four horsemen rode out to meet them.

The herald nodded to the mangonels as they rumbled into position. 'You can see with your own eyes the forces now reined against you. As the sun rises, King Louis of France will destroy your town…or will enter the burgh in peace to discuss the terms of your surrender. He demands you offer five hostages of note…and yourself.'

The men spoke for a few moments amongst themselves then one rode back into the town to round up the other hostages. The noble burgher answered. 'Tell King Louis we accept his offer to discuss terms. The gates shall be opened at sunrise and you agree that the mangonels will stay inert.'

The earl nodded and the squire led the hostages at speed through the deserted outer burgh, back to the camp. Flanked by the earl and his wife, the herald commented on how well the truce had gone. 'The town must be starving by now. Those mangonels have won the day.'

As they passed under the deep shadows of a derelict barn, the unmistakable sound of a sword being drawn made him spin in his saddle, but it was too late. The thrust of the long blade through his back exited out of his heart.

As dawn was about to break, the mangonels were silhouetted menacingly against the horizon. Earl Robert of Leicester burst into Louis's tent and told his steward to wake him immediately with the good news that the arrival of the mangonels had made the town offer surrender.

Upon hearing the news, Louis called his dresser and within half an hour, he walked from his tent to the congratulations of his council. Beaming his brightest smile, he gave the order for his herald to be dispatched to agree terms of surrender.

The Earl of Leicester stepped forward. 'My lord king, I took the liberty of sending the royal herald an hour ago. We have six noble hostages but as yet the herald has not returned.' The sun broke through the clouds and Louis stepped forward to survey the landscape. The mercenaries were gathered within an arrow flight of the walls. 'I am sure my herald will want to report to me, not you. You can order your routiers to stand down and I will lead the negotiation party into the town. I think a religious theme to my entry would be wise. I want to be flanked by my bishops and cannons, carrying the cross before them.'

The procession slowly made its ceremonious way across the wasteland of the outer burgh and Louis was annoyed that the routiers were still embedded in the ruins. Approaching the defensive walls, the gate opened and a reception made up of town burghers, priests and knights, came out of the gates and lined the entrance and the drawbridge across the inner fosse.

Suddenly the captain of the guard drew up in front of the king, stopping the procession. He spoke with some urgency to King Louis's steward, then pointed to his right with a look of horror on his face. All eyes followed his, toward a ruined barn. Everyone now saw the body of the herald hanging by the kings banner from a roof beam. His eyes had been taken out and his lower entrails sagged between his legs.

The Earl of Leicester shouted above the cries of despair. 'They have lied my lord. It is a trap. You must return quickly to your camp!' The urgency in his voice sparked an immediate response. The king's bodyguards swung the king's horse about, quickly followed in chaotic order by his ecclesiastical escort. The havoc immediately put the mercenaries on alert and word spread like wildfire that a trap had been sprung. Without waiting for orders, the mercenaries burst into action.

The reception party looked at each other with baffled expressions at the sudden onset of mayhem in front of them. Inexplicably, the king's party appeared to have panicked and out of the dust, the swell of routiers arose from the ruins as one and swarmed towards the gate. Bewilderment turned to abject fear. They were too late to act and were felled by a volley of arrows from close range.

The guards manning the gates were caught up in the confusion and the army of cut-throats and murderers entered the town without any opposition.

Still in a state of shock, Louis arrived back at the camp and he turned to observe the pandemonium at the town gates. 'What in the name of God happened? What happened to my herald...did they fire upon us?'

No one offered an explanation. They were all transfixed by the sight of hundreds of enraged mercenaries tearing down the last vestiges of defence the town had to offer.

All who stood witness would be scarred for life. All of the women were lining the streets and holding up the children, in the hope of food being distributed. Instead, they were hacked to pieces where they stood or dragged off to be raped and murdered.

King Louis opened and closed his mouth like a stranded fish, dumbfounded and pale with shock. It was the first time young King Harry had witnessed the slaughter of innocents and the fact he retched uncontrollably, summed up the feelings of those watching.

Church leaders fell to their knees to pray, and good men got angry, demanding to know what had gone wrong with the surrender. No decent noble wanted to be openly associated with such butchery.

The Bishop of Sens turned to plead with Earl Robert. 'Most of the routiers are of your employ. Can you not order them to stop this…this evil carnage?'

The earl gazed into the town, engrossed by the terrifying spectacle. The plea from the bishop gave him the ideal opportunity to take charge of the sacking and benefit a little himself. 'I will do what I can your grace. I shall muster a dozen of my best knights and with God's help restore some order in the town.'

From a distant church tower, the bell for midday was heard, but in the smoke-filled sky's above Verneuil, it was difficult to tell night from day. Earl Robert was sat at a table in one of the finer merchant houses, searching through boxes of jewellery; discarding all but the best pieces.

The family of the house were perched on a bench in the corner of the room, watching silently as the fruits of their livelihoods were being picked over by human carrion. The father aged about sixty, held onto his wife while the two grown up sons sat next to their respective wives. Three children aged between five and ten sat terrified at their feet.

Petronella wore her chain mail as well as any man and swung her massive sword about her head. Unfortunately, she could not hold her drink and lurched precariously against the table.

'Put the fucking sword down before you hurt yourself,' snarled her husband. He passed her some jewellery. 'Here put these rings on.'

Only two of them fit her fingers. Swearing loudly, she slammed the blade into the table. She tried to prise it out the blade but it held firm. Out of the corner of her eye, she saw one of the men run across the floor towards the door. Grunting with the effort, the sword came free and she took staggered forward, slamming the sword into the back of the man. As he tumbled to the ground, she noticed the five year old in front of him. He cried out. 'Pee pee Dada…want a pee pee…'

Suddenly the mother leapt to her feet and as she pulled her child back. Petronella struck her across the collar bone, detaching most of her shoulder and arm. The rest of the family stood up aghast and moved forward as one.

The earl only had time to cry out once. 'Stop! Petronella…stop…!'

Amid a torrent of screams for mercy, the oversized blade hung in the air and hovered awaiting the impulse to oblige with mass murder.

Her torso heaving with the rush of adrenalin, Petronella slowly lowered the sword and the earl took it from her hand. Gently he said her name and she turned to meet his stare. Splashed with blood, her face was unrecognisable and her long hair and yellow tabard was dripping red puddles on the floor.

The earl's voice was hoarse with shock. 'Oh God, what have you done?'

Petronella wiped her face on her sleeve. 'Did you want them to recognise us? They were Jews anyway.'

Earl Robert tore his eyes away from the children as they tried in vain to revive the corpses of their parents. He snapped shut the chest of booty he had accumulated that morning. 'Let's get out of here now before King Henry arrives. If he finds us responsible for the slaughter of Verneuil he will show no mercy.'

At the door of the house, the streets appeared quieter than before. The incessant screams had quietened as many of the routiers drank in the shade, having sated all their desires and discovered new ones along the way.

The squires rode in from the end of the street with the horses. 'My lord, thank God we have found you. The army is leaving in haste. King Henry has heard of the massacre and will be upon us any time now.'

Earl Robert helped his drunken wife onto her mare and leapt onto his own before speeding off towards the east gate. The stench of burning flesh hung heavily on the air and more smoke was whipped up by the north wind. The town was slowly burning to death.

He checked that Petronella was safely tethered to her mare. The swift exit had made her vomit copiously, but it proved to be for the better. They sped through the empty French camp, ignoring the few hundred laggard's picking their way through the wasteland.

When he enquired if she could keep a lively pace, the air turned blue, even embarrassing her squire. 'Which route are we taking?' she asked.

'We shall ride to Boulogne and meet up with the Counts of Boulogne and Flanders. We can try to convince them to join us,' her husband replied, more in hope than truth.

'Join us where exactly.'

'In the invasion of England of course. We have enough money to buy an army of mercenaries. After we have retaken Leicester then we draw a line across all England, from the Wash to Carlisle. With the Scots covering our rear, we will march into England. Louis and Harry will keep King Henry busy in Normandy. Even he cannot be in two countries at once.'

Never before had Petronella felt more lustful towards her husband. His sense of purpose, his strength in command and his unlimited ambition made him irresistible. She promised herself, that whenever and wherever they next stopped, she would throw herself on him and not take no for an answer.

Chapter 23

Verneuil
Normandie

Since witnessing the aftermath of the massacre of the innocents at Verneuil, Roger Bigod had been greatly out of sorts and become quite withdrawn. King Henry knew Roger was at odds with his father. He was now twenty-three and had grown into a likeable and upright character, quite unlike Earl Hugh.

The king spoke to him in his tent. 'News of the death of Count Matthew of Boulogne has reached Wilhelm Mandeville. He wants to pay his respects to Matthew and share his grief with Count Philip. He was brought up in the court of Flanders, so I am obliged to agree, providing he has an escort. I would have sent William Albini but he was last seen alongside his father Earl Wills, chasing the tail end of Louis's army. So I have decided you should go with Wilhelm. It's about time you were given more responsibility duties, young man. All the better to get away from the stink of mass graves.'

Roger suspected the duty had much to do with proving his loyalty. On the journey north, he spoke only when necessary, appearing to be wrapped up in his own thoughts. Then out of the blue, he surprised Wilhelm with a question. 'How was it with you when you found out your father was a monster?'

The question took a time to register. 'As you know, I was sent to live with Philip and Matthew in Flanders. I truly have no memory of my father, so all my feelings were based on stories, not reality. It's the same with my little stepbrother, Joab. We have never met, though I hope to do so one day. During the civil war, he stayed with my father so who knows what horrors he witnessed. Many years passed before

I learnt the truth of my father's evil reputation, and like any father he is someone I would have hated and loved in equal measure.'

'You mean you could forgive him for all his atrocities...'

'I never said I could forgive. But no man can honestly say he has no love for his father, no matter what his crimes were.'

Such were the extraordinary divisions of this conflict that Wilhelm had to remind himself that he was on the opposing side to Matthew and Philip. They had been like brothers to him during the long years of the civil war. 'We conceived some outrageous escapes. Aged about sixteen, we rescued our 'uncle' Picot from the dungeons, though we were not actually related, and secretly shipped him across to Walton Castle, into the hands of his companion. Your father no less. They were great friends.'

'I have heard the name but at the time, I was only a babe in arms,' Roger said dismissively.

At King Henry's insistence, they had a sizeable escort of knights and caused quite a stir on the slow climb to Boulogne castle. The good intentions of the party were hastily accepted and Count Philip himself rode out of the gates to give Wilhelm his warmest greetings. While the escort were left to camp outside the gate, Count Philip took his two guests inside the city walls to the stables.

Wilhelm grinned as he introduced Roger Bigod to Philip.

'My good God, so you are the son who has rebelled against his own father, the greatest rebel of all time. Generations of kings have failed to quell your father. Tell me, how is his health...he must be aged...'

'Seventy seven,' Roger answered blandly. He felt no pride at his father's extraordinary longevity. In fact, he felt nothing but contempt, and often thought the devil must have a hand in his endurance.

'My God, he is that old.' Philip gazed into the distance.

247

'Are you thinking like I was, of our jaunt across the sea with 'uncle' Picot,' Wilhelm surmised.

'Christ, we were but young boys then, but you guessed right my friend.' As they stood alongside the horses, Philip turned to Roger and saw he was feeling excluded from their recollections. 'You must not feel too badly about your father. After Picot was murdered, I believe your father exacted his revenge under extreme danger and without a care for his own safety.'

Roger was unimpressed. 'His prerequisite in life is revenge. He has never contributed anything good of which I am aware. No doubt, he will die a man hated by many and missed by few.'

It would serve little purpose to argue, thought Philip. 'Such a shame you feel that way. One of the worst feelings I have ever known is to lose someone close, and to have more regrets than happy memories. I hope the same never happens to you.'

Roger mulled over Philip's words and the thought crossed his mind that perhaps he was too obsessed with his father's misgivings.

Count Philip put his around Wilhelm's shoulder and spoke to Roger. 'While I show Wilhelm my brother's burial place and memorial, could you please wait here. My men are nervous enough with having your oversized escort camped outside the walls. We will return in an hour or two and in the meantime the servants will bring some food and drink from the kitchens.' With those few words, they set off along the city wall, talking avidly.

While he waited for his refreshments to arrive, Roger helped his squire brush down and feed his horse. The afternoon sun had penetrated the roof of the stables and Roger laid back and dozed in the heat of the day.

He was startled by the sound of horses stood a few paces away. With the sun behind them, he squinted to see who the riders might be.

A loud, strident voice boomed out of the dazzling light. 'My God, is that young Roger Bigod! What the fuck are you doing here. Don't tell me you have changed sides and now fight with your father, instead of against him!'

Roger moved to one side and shielded his eyes. Now he was able to recognise the Earl of Leicester. 'I am here at the behest of the king to escort Wilhelm Mandeville in paying his respects to Matthew of Boulogne.'

Leicester grinned. 'And of which king do you speak? Did you not know there is a newly anointed one?'

Roger knew he should be nervous but instead he felt a growing repugnance for the earl. Trussed up across the haunches of his mount lay a stag; blood weeping from its mouth and nose. By now his wife had pulled up her horse alongside to hear the exchange.

'I am on the side of justice and righteousness,' Roger responded bravely.

'You don't look wise enough for such long words,' Petronella sneered, 'and you should be ashamed of yourself, fighting against your own father…'

'How dare you speak of shame and wisdom in the same breath. I have seen the carnage you wrought at Verneuil. The bodies of hundreds of women and children, scattered like offal in a slaughterhouse.'

The earl snorted at the rebuff, but Petronella suddenly dismounted and confronted Roger. 'You know nothing of war. How your father conceived such an untrustworthy brat, I shall never know…'

Fighting back the tears of hate, all Roger could see was a red mist, smeared with the bloody remains of women and children. He lunged forward and struck Petronella off guard. She tumbled backwards onto her bottom.

Enraged at the assault on his wife, the earl leapt from his horse and facing Roger, he pulled his sword, waving it in front of his face. 'For that, I shall tie you to my horse and you drag you all the way to England.'

Without a sword, Roger resorted to pulling a dagger from his belt. As the earl stepped forward, Roger gathered himself low, capable of making a strike. The earl paused, suddenly aware of the awesome consequences of the confrontation.

Sensing her husbands reluctance, Petronella dusted herself down and drew her sword. 'Let me have the bastard…'

'Put down your weapons, all of you!' shouted Count Philip. He immediately placed himself with his back to Roger, facing the earl and his wife. 'You shall not draw swords here while my brother lies newly buried. I want you all out of here now!' As he spoke, men-at-arms began to appear from all directions.

Leicester and Petronella reluctantly remounted, but the earl was determined to have the last word. 'You mourn like a washerwoman mourns her husband. We don't need you anyway. Money speaks louder than words of loyalty. I have afforded thousands of Flemish mercenaries that are gathering along the coast for the crossing. In a few days my army will join up with the Scots and others, and England will be ours for taking.'

'Your money is stained with the blood of women and children. You are damned for eternity…' Roger retaliated.

Count Philip shouted Roger down. 'That is enough! The earl will be gone soon enough.' His men-at-arms armed with spears were nervously stood around the earl's horses. He ordered his captain to stand down and Wilhelm took Roger aside, leading him to the rear of the stables.

When Earl Leicester had assembled all his men and provisions, his entourage slowly withdrew. The earl then cut loose the stag's carcass, dragging it behind his horse's hooves.

Roger absorbed the significance of the act, grateful it was not his body bumping across the drawbridge.

Count Philip had waited till the earl was out of the castle before scolding the young noble. 'I am getting sick of spoilt brats like you and Harry, hardly weaned from playing with toy swords, unaware of the subtleties of warfare and diplomacy. I just wish you would grow up and leave the fighting to proper men of substance. Now I strongly suggest you take your leave.'

Wilhelm apologised on behalf of Roger. 'I am sorry Philip for all this…and you should know that I too am devastated by the loss of Matthew. He was like a younger brother to me.'

'Thank you for coming Wilhelm, but you appreciate it is too difficult to accommodate you being here. You know I had nothing to do with Verneuil, but the atmosphere is too temperamental and one spark could set off another mêlée…'

'I understand,' Wilhelm nodded and Roger Bigod belatedly offered his apologies and condolences. They mounted up and left the Count to continue his vigil over his brother's demise.

Once in open country, Roger apologised to Wilhelm and explained how the confrontation had occurred.

'Forget it,' he replied magnanimously. 'You were right to accuse Earl Robert and his wife, and no doubt they will be damned. Did you know at the peace conference at Gisors the earl lost his temper and drew his sword on King Henry? Believe me, he has burnt all his bridges behind him.'

Roger was relieved to hear the words of support.

Wilhelm continued. 'More importantly, your outrage inspired the earl to loosen his tongue a little too indiscreetly. Now we know that he intends to invade England with an army of Flemish mercenaries and common routiers. Most likely comprised of wool merchants than a trained army. And where he lands in England, will determine who he is expecting to support him.'

'You mean my father, for instance.'

'I swear, I don't know about your father. But I doubt if the Earl of Leicester is aware of all the latest news from England. I heard just before we left Verneuil, that after taking the surrender of the city of Leicester, Richard de Lucy and Humphrey de Bohun rode north and beat back an incursion by the Scots King. The earl will be disappointed when he finds no support from that quarter.'

Chapter 24

Rouen
Normandie

Many nobles feared King Henry had spread himself too thinly trying to protect his empire from his rebellious son Harry, ably encouraged by his brothers Richard and Geoffrey.

Few understood, how these over ambitious teenage boys could be the cause of so much chaos across the realm. In Normandie, all of King Henry's good fortune on the battlefield had been nullified by the unwillingness of his sons to agree to his terms. They demanded the king should forgive their mother, but Henry had made it clear that Queen Eleanor would not be a factor in any part of the settlement.

Just as guilty as anyone was King Louis, who like a warlock of old fables, continually stirred the cauldron of discontent, just enough to keep the rebellion on the boil, adding the ingredients of good men and bad men at will.

But more than any of them, King Henry reserved his wrath for the Earl of Leicester. At the so-called peace conference, the earl was so blinded by his anger, he committed the worst blunder of all, by drawing his sword at the King. Even his supporter's recoiled in horror.

The king's council waited patiently for their final orders knowing that he was in the next room making the decisions that would affect the lives of all of them in the days and weeks to come. His confident stride into the hall belied the doubts he had put aside, and like all good leaders, his sheer force of presence made everyone stand up and pay attention.

He spoke quietly at first, almost conversationally. 'My loyal lords, nay my loyal friends. You may or may not be aware of the latest information so I shall ensure you know as much as I know, for I abhor the chatter of rumours. Unless of course they are favourable ones.' A nervous laugh passed around the gathering. 'The Earl of Leicester has one hundred knights under his command and has recruited some six thousand Flemish routiers and are gathering as we speak north of Wissant. My informants tell me that the Count of Flanders is still in purdah and neither he nor my son will be taking part in the invasion.' Henry hated being interrupted, but the buzz from the floor made it difficult to be heard. He took an empty pewter jug and banged it on the table until all was quiet. The tenor of his voice began to increase. 'Yes, I use the word invasion to describe an uninvited force with the sole purpose to pillage, rape and the seize power over my country. My country will not be subjected to a tyrant such as Earl Leicester. My country will not be violated like a whore, and the good citizens of my country will not be butchered like those at Verneuil!'

A rousing cheer rose up from the assembly.

Henry's voice rose to the rafters. 'My country is governed by one man. And that is me. The defence of the realm is my sacred duty, empowered in me by God for which I was anointed. Under my kingship and with God's help, my country will become our country, to share in its peace and prosperity. Are you with me?'

The cheers and clatter of appreciation reached a crescendo and continued unabated out of the grand hall of Rouen palace, into the bailey and then the faint echoes were heard in the streets outside.

Henry received all his plaudits modestly then sought out his favoured few to withdraw into his chamber to complete his final instructions. He looked at the beaming faces around him. Even old Wills Albini, the Earl of Arundel suddenly looked a decade younger than his seventy years as he spoke excitedly to his son William. Stood with William was Roger Bigod, not unlike his own son Harry and perhaps a better son at that. He made a mental note to speak with him personally before he left.

Catching the eye of Wilhelm Mandeville, Henry nodded and they were quickly brought to order and seated around the table.

'My lords, I have gathered you here to discuss our strategy and to advise you of secret information that just come to light. Its source is "Machabbe" and is therefore remains exclusively within this room.'

A hiss of excitement was fermented by the fabled name of Henry's top spy in Normandie. Many suspected he had been invented by Henry to keep everyone paranoid, and that he never actually existed. Others swore he was a Jew who passed anonymously as a money lender throughout the courts and armies of both friend or foe.

'He has intercepted a message from Hugh Bigod intended for the eyes of Earl Robert of Leicester. He intends to meet the Earl of Leicester at Orford with seventy knights and a thousand men at arms. They aim to take the castle.'

Their faces fell silent, some looking at Roger without thinking.

The king continued. 'In addition to that message, "Machabbe" has brilliantly intercepted a reply from the Earl of Leicester, saying 'besieging Orford would be wasting his time.' He intends to land at Walton Castle.'

All eyes looked blankly at the king, Earls Wills asked the obvious question. 'Then which is it to be. Orford or Walton?'

Henry's eyes narrowed. 'Machabbe has suggested that the reply could have been planted deliberately. I for one do not think it was planted. Leicester is not that clever.'

A few grinned and raised a light chuckle.

'Secondly, I don't think Leicester would enter into a long siege of Orford Castle knowing that I could have him surrounded on the peninsular within a week. No, Orford is Bigod's idea. It's presence has been a thorn in his side for years.'

Again, a few faces automatically looked to Roger but he kept his peace. The fact he was sat at the king's table was surety enough.

The king lifted his head, a sure sign he had made his decision. 'Yesterday I received conformation that Richard de Lucy and Humphrey de Bohun have cut short their harrying of the Scots in Northumberland and are at present heading to Suffolk with all haste.' The king turned to Earl Wills. 'With luck, Leicester's army of miscreants are still assembling around Boulogne. I want you and your son William to proceed to Honfleur with a hundred knights and two hundred of the best men-at-arms. A small fleet is standing-by. Then I want you to disembark at Orford.'

They all looked at the king as if he had made a mistake. 'Surely you mean Walton,' Earl Wills corrected.

Taking a sip of wine, the king lowered his gaze for a moment. 'At Orford Castle there are four knights being held under arrest, in secret for obvious reasons. They were due to be shipped over to Flanders this week but are still in Orford as events took precedence. They are Reginald FitzUrse, Hugh de Morville, William de Tracy and Richard le Breton.'

A gasp of disbelief passed around the table. 'Was this by design or…what?' Earl Wills asked.

'Simple bad luck,' the king admitted. 'The murderers of Archbishop Becket were due to kneel before the Pope in Rome and proceed as pilgrims to the Holy Land. You must get to Orford and seize them before Leicester or Bigod releases them and get them on a boat back to Rouen as soon as possible. Then rendezvous with de Lucy and do battle with Earl Leicester. Under no circumstances should you engage Leicester without joining with de Lucy's army.'

'What about Hugh Bigod?' Earl Wills asked.

The king gave a dismissive shrug. 'It would be better if he did not join up with Leicester but engage him only if the odds are in your favour.'

Wilhelm intervened. 'Leicester has been recruiting scum from all over Flanders. His so-called army of mercenaries are large in number but are untrained and little more than merchants and wastrels.'

'Wilhelm is correct in his assessment,' the king acknowledged. 'But we cannot accept any risk of defeat at this early stage of the campaign.'

Nothing more could be said to bolster the mood. Earl Wills and his son left to organise and assemble the knights while the king asked Roger Bigod to join him for a moment in his private chamber.

King Henry sat back in his chair, looking tired and drawn. 'I am giving my authority for you to join Earl Wills. I am told that you have been handling yourself well these few weeks. I thought it was time we spoke, as all this cannot be easy for you.'

Roger took the cup of wine handed to him by the king and wondered what his question meant. 'Do you mean my father?'

The king smiled at the tall young man, so unlike his father in every way. He offered Roger a seat opposite. 'I was told a few years ago by an old retainer that you bore a passing resemblance to your uncle William Bigod. Apparently he died quite young, on the White Ship disaster...apparently.'

Suddenly Roger had no idea what to say. Was it just polite conversation or a verbal trap? He took another sip of wine and simply nodded. 'Yes...apparently.'

Whatever his thinking, the king did not pursue the statement. 'I find your relationship with your father interesting. You do not see eye to eye, indeed you are willing to fight against him, I am told. Do you see any resemblance to my own circumstances?'

Now his train of thought was clearer. 'I believe my father is morally wrong and yes, I am willing to fight for my belief. But only you know the morals of you own sons and whether your differences are worthy of shedding blood.'

The king was skilled in giving nothing away with his expression.

'You answer very diplomatically, but heed my warning. The real question is what you would do when holding a sword to your father's face. Prepare yourself now for the answer, and not when the moment of indecision is upon you.'

Roger stared blankly into space and accidentally spilt his red wine over the white tablecloth.

'Leave it for a servant to clear. Go now and join Earl Wills and his son William of Albini. And I pray that God will help you with your answer…more than he ever helped me.'

After a long hot summer, the burgeoning fields of East Angles had been harvested long ago. The leaves were starting to wilt and curl on the trees, but the people were comforted by the thought of a winter without hunger or famine. Of course, some men knew better than most, and they quailed at the thought of the inevitable war to come that could rival that of Armageddon itself.

Hugh Bigod did not believe in Armageddon but he did believe that in war, the strongest side would prevail. If the country was to split into factions and tear itself apart, then so be it. As long as he was one of those left standing.

When he had heard that Richard de Lucy had stopped the Scots in their tracks, he made light of his disappointment in front of his men, for he knew that any rumours hinting of a defeat could adversely affect the moral of the rebel forces.

To add to his woes the army of knights and men-at-arms that had assembled under his banner were causing havoc in the castle and around the town. For two weeks now, Framlingham had become a vicious playground, as boredom began to manifest itself into abuse and violence, making life a misery for his household and the townsfolk.

Everything now depended on Earl Robert of Leicester who by all accounts was due to embark with an army of mercenaries near Boulogne. News from Flanders was thin and he was still awaiting replies from any number of messages he had sent, telling the earl to land at Orford Castle and rendezvous there with his army.

Amidst the constant noise from every floor in the castle, there was no room for privacy. Hugh paced back and forth in his bedchamber, mollifying his wife Gundred who refused to leave the room. Sat on her bed, she would jump at the sound of every shout, clatter or raucous laugh.

She begged him to put a stop to it. 'I want it peaceful and quiet; like it used to be, she sobbed. 'And I want to see Roger. He is due to be married soon to Anna?'

In her state of forgetfulness, Gundred often put recent events out of her mind whilst remembering others. Though he had heard rumours that his son was soon to marry the daughter of a lord, this was the first time he had heard her name and he had no idea who she was. He dismissed the thought, knowing they would never be invited and besides any wedding would certainly be postponed while the rebellion was afoot.

Later that night Hugh walked along the ramparts, racked by a myriad of emotions. By the time he walked to the knights billet hall, the servants had retired and he climbed the steps to look for Bonham. Upon approaching the knights' chamber, he called out and as a door opened, Bonham appeared in front of him.

Hugh gave his orders to assemble his army at dawn. 'We shall leave a garrison here of just twenty knights with fifty men-at-arms. The rest of us shall go to Orford and await the arrival of the Earl of Leicester. I don't like splitting my forces but it cannot be helped. Tis only ten miles to Orford...'

Bonham looked surprised. 'My lord, we will need every able bodied man…'

'I will not leave Framlingham castle undefended,' Hugh retorted firmly.

Bonham immediately understood, Hugh's trepidation at leaving his vulnerable wife without any knights.

Turning back down the stairs, Hugh yawned. 'And pass on my orders to Terrowin. He's probably shagging some wench in the stables.'

By early morning, they had gathered weapons, armour and provisions, and settled into ranks for the ten-mile march to the coast. When Hugh informed Gundred the army was leaving, the relief on her face was palpable.

Comforting his wife, Hugh promised he would be back as soon as Orford castle had surrendered or been destroyed. She said she understood and asked how long before he would return. He dare not tell her it may be months before he saw her again, but then doubted in her present state of mind if she even understand where Orford was.

She smiled back at him and touched his lips tenderly. 'Just remember you can be back here in a hour if you try.'

Hugh kissed her on the lips and for a moment, it seemed as if the past had never happened. Perhaps, as life returned to normal at the castle, he hoped her temperament would continue to improve.

At Orford Castle, Reginald FitzUrse, Hugh de Morville, William de Tracy and Richard le Breton watched as the Constable Bartholomew de Glanville was dragged in front of the dungeon doors. He had been badly beaten and both his eyes were blinded. A middle-aged, hooded stranger dressed in black surcoat and britches held him up by the neck and calmly slit his throat before discarding the body to one side. He unlocked the cell door and told them to join the rebellion.

'Who the fuck are you?' de Morville asked.

'A friend,' came the simple answer.

Running outside they breathed in the fresh air and took in the scene of cruel debauchery. The castle lay naked, devoid of defenders.

Twenty or so mercenaries were engaged in violent rape with the household servants. Mothers fared the worse as they were murdered within sight of their children who were screaming as men took their turn at ravishment and brutish violence.

The four knights watched from the top of the courtyard steps, frozen to the spot with a heady mixture of horror and excitement.

The stranger walked past and prised one of the young girls from the arms of a mercenary and pulled the girl into the dormitory. After weeks of incarceration, three of the knights needed no further encouragement and ran down the steps to join in the orgy of violence.

Richard le Breton stood aloof from them all. Although he realised since the murder of Becket, his soul was a lost cause, he stood his ground, refusing to join the dammed monsters. Feeling hungry, he walked further along the courtyard wall into the rooms above the dormitory, hoping to find some food.

Looking around, he heard a muffled scream come from the floor below. Through a gap in the floor he saw the back of the hooded stranger, crouched over the naked young girl laying on her stomach and crying for her mother. She was gagged and now he slowly pulled back his hood and turned to look up at le Breton.

He stared for a few moments then pulled a dagger from his belt. The lamplight flickered as his attention turned back to the girl, burying the blade between the girl's legs. To quell the screams and flailing limbs, he smashed his fist into her head. The lamp went out.

Le Breton ran back outside and wretched on an empty stomach. The evil of the mercenaries knew no bounds but once they had slaked their lust for flesh, the blood of the innocent had to be shed.

A pit in the centre of the courtyard was uncovered and various limbs and body parts were thrown in. One naked woman ran from the horrors around her and deliberately jumped into the pit seeking some kind of sanctuary, incensing her capturer. He heaved a barrel of oil over to the pit and tipped it inside. In a drunken stupor he threw a burning torch after the barrel.

This enlivened everyone else to follow his example. Moments later the pit was full of screaming victims as more oil was brought from the cellars. Le Breton had seen enough of Hades and crawled back to the cell, fearing for his own life. And his own soul.

Earl Wills Albini of Arundel ensured the king's colours were held aloft on a large dune and watched his force assemble on the beachhead and make their way across the marsh paths. His destrier stamped his hooves impatiently and his squire worked hard to settle him down. 'He thinks were going into battle, my lord,' he said apologetically.

William rode up next to his father and nodded at the towering curtain walls of the castle only a mile distant. 'Sir, I have sent scouts on ahead and to the south towards Walton, just to warn us of being outflanked. It seems a little strange that no one from the castle has been out to greet us. They can see our banners.'

On the beachhead, Roger Bigod was organising the boatmen telling them to drag the ships higher up the banks.

The earl smiled at Roger giving orders. 'You and the Bigod lad have been good friends for some time. I am sorry to have doubted your judgement. You know it is because of his father....'

'You don't ever need to excuse anything to me.' William was so proud of his aged father and decided to tell him so. 'To me you are a leader as great as any king that has ever ruled this land. And the worst injustice of all is that your achievements will never be recognised by those you have made great.'

A smile flickered over his face. 'Just remember, sometimes honour is more important than blood. Roger Bigod appears to have learnt that lesson well.'

The knights had all gathered and their mounts were chomping at their bits. Everyone was impatient to leave the beachhead that lay open to the biting wind off the sea. The earl ordered them to move on.

Approaching the Orford castle, William held up his hand, pausing to inspect the walls. 'There are no lookouts. Something is wrong.'

Earl Wills agreed and sensed the same bad feeling. 'Where are our scouts?'

Before anyone answered, they all saw the smoke rising from the inner bailey on the far side of the tall majestic keep.

'Well we can't sit here all day. Advance; ranks of five abreast and be ready for anything,' the earl ordered.

No sooner had they gone a hundred paces around the ramparts, when the scouts came into view, riding at speed. The earl waited for the report from his captain, ever watchful for signs of danger.

'My lord, the garrison is dead... ' He stopped to gather his breath. 'They killed the Constable Bartholomew de Glanville, and five knights…then threw the rest into a burning pit, the maids and servants as well…' he paused again…'while they were still alive.'

'Who committed this atrocity?' the earl demanded.

'They are saying it was mercenaries; but my lord, to the north under cover of a coppice of trees, I have seen the banners of Earl Bigod with an army of knights and men-at-arms.'

Earl Wills hissed under his breath, his face the colour of thunder. 'Bigod…that murdering bastard.'

'We also have a prisoner, my lord, none other than Richard le Breton. He was in the cells when we found him and now he demands to be heard.'

Earl Wills could only hear his blood pumping in anger. 'Get him shipped off to Normandie.' He turned to Roger with undisguised disdain. 'You can see to that, can't you?'

Roger's face paled at the hint of anger aimed at him. 'Yes, my lord.'

Earl Wills gave the order to his expectant knights. 'We will advance and charge only on my command. I want Earl Bigod alive, to be held to account for his evil deed.'

His mind in a quandary, Roger rode the short distance to where le Breton was being held. A long beard covered his face and what little skin was showing appeared badly bruised. His hair was long and caked in blood but despite his unkempt appearance, he still held his head high. 'Who might you be?' he asked as Roger approached.

'I am Roger Bigod and you are a murdering bastard...'

'The son of the father...well I never.' Le Breton wiped the thick mush of blood from his mouth. 'Your men were a little enthusiastic when tying me up. Oh, but Leicester was so clever. He bribed Bartholomew de Glanville to open the gate at middle night. He sent a force of just thirty of his murderous cut-throats...they entered the garrison and killed most of the men as they slept. When we were let out from our cells, I was pleased to have my freedom. But then I saw what they did to the household maids. I would rather stay in chains than join their company.'

'Whose company exactly,' Roger asked intently.

'FitzUrse, de Morville and de Tracy. But a hooded stranger led them on, someone I had never seen before. Under his call, they became like ...animals. No worse than that ... I suppose I was lucky to find my way back to the dungeon. I don't scare easily but I locked the door to my own cell.'

'What did they do?'

Le Breton looked down in shame. 'They raped the women and children. Then they had everyone thrown alive into a fire pit. Fifty of them, maybe more. They tipped in a barrel of oil...then another.'

'Was my father part of this...?'

'He would never dine with these devils. Your father has been waiting to the north for two days now.'

Roger had heard enough. He jumped onto his horse and galloped after the vanguard of knights as they neared the lines of his father's ranks.

Chapter 25

Orford Castle
Suffolk

For two days, the cold winds and drizzle soaked Hugh's army as they waited in the fields, on a small coppice to the north of Orford. At least his tent kept him dry but a succession of captains bemoaned the poor conditions of the men-at-arms curled up in hedgerows and haystacks.

His indecision was beginning to wear him down, when suddenly news came from his lookouts. They reported that a commotion had broken out in the grounds of Orford Castle and he ran outside to look. For half an hour or so, the gate remained open then was closed as people began running about inside. Then all was quiet. 'Shall we attack my lord,' one of his knights asked, desperate for a fight.

'Don't be stupid,' Bonham replied caustically on Hugh's behalf. 'We are not here to besiege the strongest castle in all England.'

The knight thought the castle looked virtually unmanned, but kept his peace.

They were all baffled to see a large plume of smoke rise from inside the bailey to be swept away in the wind.

Hugh gave his instructions. 'We will wait another hour then move back to Framlingham.' Then his instinct for being wary took over. 'Reinforce the lines behind the stakes and tell the men to stay alert.'

Bonham made sure his orders were completed just as he heard the shouts come from the front ranks. 'Knights advancing...knights advancing!'

'Stand your ground!' Bonham shouted. 'They won't get through if you stand your ground!'

Bonham recognised the colours as Hugh stepped from his tent and stood alongside. 'They are the colours of Earl Wills of Arundel, my lord. He has a few more knights than us but we have five times the men-at arms. We shall prevail as long as we stand firm.'

Hugh relinquished his battle command to Bonham. 'Go and give the order, Bonham.'

Stepping up behind the ranks of men, Bonham raised his voice to quell their fear. 'Remember lads to stand firm. They are coming uphill and will not be expecting our little surprise.'

The warhorses were within a hundred paces and he gave the command. 'Archers now!' A volley of arrows struck the first ranks of knights. Some fell and some slowed but the line did not waver.

'Spearmen now!' came the second order.

The archers slipped back to reveal a line of spearmen standing boldly behind a line of pointed staves firmly planted in the ground.

Just then a lone horseman came galloping from the right and rode across the field between the first and second ranks of charging knights. The first rank wavered in front of the staves and spearmen; some with their vision obscured impaled themselves while others were unseated. The second rank froze in its tracks and gradually withdrew out of range of the archers.

A cheer rose across the field of men, sweeping away the misery of a few hours ago. Some foolhardy spearmen ran from the ranks, endeavouring to capture some of the unseated knights but without the combat skill, they perished with a single thrust before the knights remounted and withdrew. The more experienced infantrymen sought out those that were injured and struck their spears into the weak spots under the arms or groin, and robbed them rather than attempt capture.

Bonham raised his sword high to raise a cheer but noticed that Hugh was standing quiet and still. 'Are you all right my lord?'

Hugh nodded. 'We should withdraw now back to Framlingham

before they outflank us from behind. We were lucky today but they will not make the same mistake tomorrow.'

'What do you mean, my lord. We stopped them in their tracks.'

For a moment, Hugh looked irritated. 'That horseman who galloped into the second rank, where the Earl and his son rode.'

'Yes, a wounded horse perhaps…'

'No, not a wounded nor a panicked horse. He deliberately rode at speed right up to the earl and stopped him. Moments later, the advance ceased and they withdrew.'

Bonham was perplexed. In the heat of the moment, he had failed to see the horseman. 'What do you think was said?'

'I do not know. But the next time I see my son I shall ask him.'

Earl Wills was on the point of fury. 'If you have cost us a battle just to save your father's skin I shall have you hanged for treason…'

'Father! Just listen to Roger for one moment!' William yelled.

The earl had never been shouted down before and was shocked into silence by his son's behaviour.

Stepping forward, Roger Bigod explained all that he had been told by Richard le Breton. He finished by saying, 'So you see, my father had nothing to do with the killings at Orford.'

Earl Wills was not impressed. 'All this, on the word of the murderer of the archbishop…'

'But why would he lie?' Roger pleaded.

'I don't know. Perhaps he is in league with your father!'

Silence fell between them as a scout appeared and caught the attention of William then passed on his message.

'My lord, this scout has returned from the south. Listen to his words yourself.' William stepped aside and the nervous youth was thrust centre stage.

'My lord earl, we have ridden to the estuary seven or eight miles away and looked across the water to Walton. We counted over eighty ships on the beach but more were coming...the mist was bad you see...'

'Must be the main force of Leicester's mercenaries,' William interrupted.

The scout could see they were hanging on his every word. 'They were on the move. Thousands of them...too many to count. But the estuary is wide all the way inland...we followed a bit but we had to stop and hide.'

He caught his breath before continuing. 'There were a bunch of about twenty or thirty men that had come from the direction of Orford Castle. They looked bloodied, like they had been in a fight. Anyway, they split up, some rowing back across the estuary but a smaller party left on horseback on the St Edmundsbury road.'

The old earl sat down and hung his head. Everything the scout had said backed up the story by Roger. He had been too quick to jump to the wrong conclusion and accuse Hugh Bigod. Some of the knights quietly thanked Roger, for his brave intervention had possibly saved many of them from riding onto the staves.

William praised his scouts, handed over a small bag coins then asked all six of them to gather around him. 'Now it is imperative we join up with de Lucy and de Bohun. Your next task is to find out where and when we can rendezvous. Split yourselves into two teams of three, and cover the ground between St Edmundsbury and Cambridge until you find them. No doubt, they will have scouts doing the same. In the meantime, we will shadow the Earl of Leicester and his mercenaries and rendezvous with de Lucy as soon as you find him. Travel light and fast. God's speed.'

The scouts left with renewed vigour and fresh horses as well as few coins for extra incentive.

William had remained quiet throughout the evening and into the next morning, when without warning he asked to see his father Earl Wills and Roger. 'I have been thinking, trying to anticipate what the rebels will do next, when I had a sudden thought. What if Earl Robert intends to retake the city of Leicester?'

The earl thought for a moment. 'You could be right. It depends on which way he turns at Ipswich. Turning to the north means he will join up with Earl Bigod at Framlingham. If he breaks out to the west, he will sack St Edmundsbury and on to the city of Leicester...'

'No, no, you are missing my point,' William interrupted. 'On the way to St Edmundsbury is Haughley Castle.'

Earl Wills and Roger both looked at each other. 'Shit...fucking shit!' Roger swore forcibly. 'Both Anna and Matilda are there...'

'And they have probably have six thousand sex starved murdering Fleming mercenaries heading their way,' William cried looking around for his squire. They both paled at the thought.

'Wait!' Earl Wills roared. 'I cannot weaken my army splitting it in two, so you must do this yourselves. And you cannot take the direct route to Haughley without being captured by Leicester's men. In all likelihood, they will take some time ravaging Ipswich before moving on. Your only chance is too overtake them on the north side.'

'But that would take us across my fathers terrain.' Roger queried.

'I know. But is that not a better alternative.'

'Damn and fuck it!' William swore. 'The scouts have taken the fastest steeds.'

Roger was making for the line tethering the ranks of horses. 'No matter, through hells fire we are going to save Anna and Matilda.'

Bonham did not question why Hugh had slowed the pace on the way back to Framlingham, for he knew that Hugh was averse to his army filling his castle and marauding his estates.

News from his scouts had so far come to nought, so he was relieved to see one arrive from the south, even if he did wear the colours of the Earl of Leicester. 'My lord Bigod, I carry a verbal message from the Earl. Here is his seal.' He showed a blank parchment with the unmistakable seal in red wax. 'The countryside is crawling with the kings troops so nothing dare be writ down in case of capture.' He caught his breath and took a drink before continuing. 'Leicester landed at Walton and he currently takes stock in Ipswich. He wishes you to make your way to St Edmundsbury and join him there. Apparently de Lucy and de Bohun approach from the north and he wants to engage in battle as soon as possible.'

'You know Earl Wills of Arundel is shadowing the progress of Leicester,' Hugh reminded him.

The messenger obviously knew. 'The Earl of Leicester gives little credence to the army of the Earl of Arundel. They number only three hundred. Leicester's wife has landed further north and presumably will also make her way to St Edmundsbury. Then we will number a hundred and sixty knights and ten thousand Fleming mercenaries, all converging on St Edmundsbury.'

Hugh smiled broadly. 'Even de Lucy will turn tail when faced with that number. After the victory, we will draw a line across the country from the Wash to the Mersey.'

The messenger cocked his head to one side and lowered his voice. 'The earl has a problem with trust, though I hasten to add, not with yourself. But he is concerned of your son's loyalty to Earl Wills and his son.'

The verbal blow hurt Hugh deeply and looked around to see who had heard. 'Tell Leicester we shall meet him sooner than he thinks. Now go on your way in case someone should steal your precious parchment of wax.' Hugh made it clear he wanted no further discussion.

The messenger smiled at the mild rebuke, handed the water skin to Hugh, and then turned to ride back to Ipswich.

Hugh swilled out his mouth and spat out the water. He turned to Bonham. 'Leicester must take me for a fool if he thinks I am going to St Edmundsbury to take on de Lucy while he rakes in the spoils across all Suffolk.'

Bonham concurred. 'Then let us ride to Ipswich and join him.'

'Ipswich will already be a wasteland. No, we will get ahead of him.'

While Bonham rubbed his beard deep in thought, Terrowin stepped forward. 'My lord Bigod, Haughley Castle lies on the road to St Edmundsbury some twenty miles from Ipswich. Ralph le Broc holds it for the king. With God's speed we should reach the castle well before the Earl of Leicester.'

Bonham sounded excited by the prospect of pillaging and fortune hunting. 'That is perfect my lord. No doubt there will be rich pickings to be had throughout his estates.' The other knights overheard Bonham and a number joined in with the call to head for Haughley.

Hugh nodded his agreement and the knights rounded up their squires. It was particularly pleasing that he had been seen to regain the initiative, though he had been looking forward to seeing Gundred sooner than expected. But this is what he was good at. All his adult life had been a matter of keeping the upper hand against his opponents and one step ahead of his allies.

All the uncertainty of the last few days was lifted and he joked with his knights as they craned forward to listen to the news they had been waiting for. The captains called together the men-at-arms and the sound of bravado and bawdy laughter carried around the whole of Hugh's army. At last, they were heading west, to fight, to pillage, and to walk away with enough to eat and drink till the next opportunity for fortune came knocking.

The twenty knights that remained at Framlingham Castle were mostly young and inexperienced, and unhappy at missing the opportunity to fight and steal the chattels of the defeated. How else could your reputation and status be enhanced unless you supplemented your finances by taking from others? How would your liege lord or the king ever be in a position to grant estates and personal favours unless he knew of your achievements?

To be garrisoned in a castle was the most boring stance and soon all the talk was of those knights lucky enough to be called into battle with Earl Bigod.

But before the garrison could settle down, a lookout from the coast reported that Flemish reinforcements had landed at Orford and was approaching Framlingham.

From the battlements, they watched the approach of the mercenaries with trepidation. Hugh's army had stripped most of the land bare and Framlingham had not yet replenished its stock of grain and meat. What little they had was barely enough for the garrison.

The commander decided to take an escort of six knights to ride out to the mercenaries with the hope of diverting them away from Framlingham to join the army at Haughley. To his utter amazement, a woman clad in chain mail came forward to greet him. On either side, rode an escort of ten knights and horse archers.

She was used to the surprise on the faces of such men who met her for the first time and they were often rendered speechless by her manly appearance. 'I am Petronella, the wife of the Earl of Leicester. If you stop gawking at me long enough, perhaps you could tell me why Earl Bigod is not here to greet me.'

The commander struggled to recover his poise. 'Earl Bigod has departed...to meet your husband...of course.'

'Then why did the bloody fool want us to land at Orford?' she replied loudly, her voice dripping with arrogance.

'The original plan was to take Orford Castle...'

273

'My husband took the fucking castle days ago, you moron!' She shook her head while the commander was too flustered to reply.

He had never heard a noble lady curse before.

'Enough of this, we are going into Framlingham Castle. My men are hungry, but don't worry. They will behave themselves.' Without looking back, she rode off with her knights and a line of mercenary captains rode close behind.

High up in her chamber, Gundred saw the approaching horses and called to Mary her nanny. She quickly appeared, her face fraught with anguish, as she too had seen the horsemen looming over the horizon. Holding her hand was young Hugh.

Gundred spoke calmly and gently. 'You know the secret compartment. Go there now and make sure you have fresh water and some food. Never open the door to anyone but me or my husband.' She knelt down to kiss her son on the lips. 'Go quickly. Please be a good boy and stay quiet for mummy. Pray God there will be time for tears later.' Mary led the boy away and Gundred sat on her bed, unsure if she had the strength or the will to stand up.

Looking down she saw her hands were shaking. The nightmare was about to begin all over, but if she had her way, it would not end the same as before. Under her pillow, she reached for a dagger and hid it under her linen tunic, within quick and easy reach. Now she waited in her chamber, humming quietly to herself.

Voices shouted from within the walls and in no time the hall below echoed to the sound of running and screaming. Heavy footsteps slowed outside her door and she stood up to face who ever was about to enter. The enormous figure burst into view and stood staring at her, his sword waving in front, as he surveyed the room. He shouted something in a Flemish accent that prevented anyone else from entering then he slammed the door shut behind him. Again he spoke, and again she could not understand his words, but his expression left her in no doubt as to his intentions.

'I am Gundred Bigod, the wife of Earl Bigod of Norfolk.' She had spoken loud and clear, pronouncing her words slowly and with authority. The mercenary just smiled and as he took a step forward, she reached inside her tunic.

In the blink of an eye, he had pushed her back onto the mattress and was on top of her. With his left hand, he held her by the throat, while his right hand busied with his britches. Slowly his face expression changed to one of disbelief then he grimaced in pain. Still staring at Gundred he rose to his feet and loped off to the left, unable to stem the flow of blood between his fingers.

Her heart was beating so fast and she could hardly catch her breath. The white skin of her knuckles contrasted with the bright red trickle of blood that dripped from the upright dagger.

The mercenary swayed a little but did not move his feet. Rooted to the spot with his eyes wide open and clutching his stomach he let out a gasp of pain. Gundred flew to the door and immediately ran into two other mercenaries. They were surprised to see her and pushed her back into the room, where they saw their captain standing white faced and fearful, not daring to remove his bloody fingers from his wound. He uttered just two words to his comrades before falling to his knees. 'Kill her.'

The two men drew their swords, giving Gundred a look of sheer contempt.

She backed away not wanting to meet death head on. Another person entered the room, dressed differently to the stinking thugs that were about to slay her.

Pulling the band around her head, Petronella let her hair fall around her shoulders and shouted an order in Flemish.

The two mercenaries did not give way. They nodded to their captain who lay dying in a pool of blood, answering that the woman deserved to die.

Petronella nodded and drew her sword as she took a step forward. Her long blade flashed, taking of the arm of the nearest mercenary just below the elbow. It fell to the floor with a dull thud. The second mercenary watched as Petronella's bodyguards moved alongside her and he instantly lowered his sword in submission.

'Don't tell me he left you here all alone?' Petronella said to Gundred. 'Your Earl is a cretin of the highest order. And these cretins have disobeyed my orders.'

She walked over to the mercenary who seemed concerned for his friend without an arm. 'I told you there should be no violence.' The man nodded but before he could take a single stride, she had thrust her sword into his throat and out of the back of his head. Withdrawing the blade, he crumpled like a rag doll next to his dead captain. 'I am so sorry, Gundred, I hope he did not touch you...'

Gundred screamed in terror. Her chamber now resembled a slaughterhouse and began to sway up and down to the sound of a monotonous buzzing.

The woman's face was in front of hers, shouting grizzled words and profanities. She tried to escape out of the door but the mercenary with the dismembered arm was pulled outside into the corridor and someone slit his throat and stabbed him in the chest, his blood spraying against the doors and walls. As the a dark cloak of night fell around her, the woman continued to shout but Gundred could only hear the buzzing sound in her head. She closed her eyes and prayed that the darkness would last forever.

Chapter 26

Haughley Castle
Suffolk

Having learnt that a relatively small band of men could exploit the craft of deception, the small band of knights proceeded with a plan to gain entry to Haughley Castle. Once inside they would seize the castle for themselves and strip it of everything of value before moving on to St Edmundsbury, always keeping one step ahead of King Henry's army and the mercenaries of Earl Robert.

Even in the mix of grey light and drizzle, the guards on the tower above the castle entrance recognised the king's colours being held aloft. In such uncertain times, it was always better to check with the captain of the guard before allowing entry to the castle so he asked the knights to wait. The captain ran across the bailey, looked down at the knights, and called to them to identify themselves.

'We are the vanguard from the army of the Earl of Arundel. He comes this way to fight the Earl of Leicester and commands that you allow shelter for the night.'

Earl Wills of Arundel had visited the castle before and had never sent an advance party to demand anything. Something was amiss. The captain peered out over the wall, unable to recognise any of the riders under their hooded mantles. Caught up with indecision, he had to think quickly. 'Is that the Earl's son William that I see?' he asked.

There was a long pause before the answer came. 'Yes. My father is due any moment. You cannot keep him waiting.'

The captain shouted above the sound of the rain. 'My lord William Albini, what is the name of your good wife?'

Again a pause. The captain nervously signalled to the guards to have spears ready. He called out to them. 'I am coming down.' The captain planned to rouse everyone by ring the alarm bell by the gate. Running down the wall steps two at a time, the captain slipped on the wet stone and fell to the bottom, letting out an agonising scream as he realised his leg was broken. Gazing into his face was Lord Ralph le Broc.

Suddenly, the drawbridge lowered and clanged heavily to the ground.'Please my lord, do not let them in,' he muttered unable to raise his voice due to the pain. But the horsemen were already advancing slowly across the drawbridge towards the outer gate and the portcullis and the bar were slowly being raised.

From a distant window, a tiny voice called out but the words were lost in the falling rain.

Le Broc shook his head, disappointed at the action of the captain. 'What were you doing, questioning Lord Albini, as if he were a commoner?' Le Broc called for the guards to carry the captain back to the keep.

Two of his men lifted the captain onto a litter taking little account of his leg. The sound of metal on stone screeched as the portcullis was raised.

With his last gasp, the captain cried out. 'It's not William! Close…the gate…'

Le Broc looked vacantly at the unconscious captain then towards the horsemen. Before the points of the portcullis were fully raised, they dipped heads and entered the bailey riding past le Broc and the guard. No one knew what to do. More horses entered and began to circle the small bailey. The rain was falling heavily and visibility was negligible. Torches were sodden and the only light came from the nearby guest house and stable.

Walking from horse to horse, Le Broc slipped and slithered in the mud, trying to find William Albini. The lead horseman gave a signal and the knights drew swords before anyone could react. The first to fall was lord Ralph le Broc with a single thrust through the neck. The two knights stood next to him did not have time to raise a blade until they to were cut down where they stood. In desperation, one guard threw his spear injuring a horse then ran away. The knight rode him down and hacked the defenceless man to the ground, dismembering his right arm. The guards carrying the captain dropped the litter and the knight encouraged his destrier to trample him to death.

Two other men-at-arms ran to the castle keep. In the doorway they passed two more knights who asked what was happening as they peered out into the murky night. Neither of them had yet picked up a sword.

Determined to keep the initiative, the lead horseman ordered everyone to dismount and follow him inside the keep. As the knights entered the keep, hardly anyone had time to react. Most of the garrison were cut down still putting on gambeson's and shouting for their squires.

From the window of the solar, above the dark maelstrom of men running and shouting, Anna had seen and heard the exchange between the captain and the knights outside the wall. She had established quicker than anyone that the knights were not William Albini and his men. Her shouts were ignored and she looked on horrified, as her father ordered the gates to be opened, only to be cut down without mercy.

Anna ran as fast as she could into Matilda's bedchamber, explaining what was happening. Matilda looked disbelieving at first but when Anna said her father had been killed, one look at Anna's face told her it was true.

'I know how we can escape. We must take your son to the cellars quickly before they get inside. There is a trapdoor to a tunnel that leads to the village.'

Without hesitation, Matilda lifted William, her eight-year-old son from his bed and followed Anna downstairs. As they swung down the staircase, her doubts over Anna's warning vanished as she heard the sound of fighting and screaming coming from outside. The kitchen and scullery girls passed them on the steps in a panic not even pausing to wonder why the three of them were going downstairs.

Anna ran across the kitchen floor and opened a larder filled with empty shelves. On the floor was a thick piece of matting and she lifted it to one side to reveal the handle to a trapdoor. Matilda took a torch from a wall sconce while Anna opened the door. Taking care not to slip on the damp steps, Matilda led the way. By now, William had woken sufficiently to walk, though with his eyes half open he seemed more asleep than awake as he balanced precariously to the foot of the steps.

Holding up the torch, Matilda looked back up at Anna who was frozen to the spot, her head on one side, listening. She could hear her mother crying out.

'Quickly, go now before they come,' she whispered. 'I will get mother and follow you.'

Before Matilda could say anything, Anna had closed the trapdoor. Replacing the matting and closing the pantry door, she ran back up the stairs. Then just as she turned the corner, a massive hand reached out and grabbed her.

'Look what I just caught. What a beauty,' FitzUrse scowled lustily.' He nodded to de Morville. 'Better look downstairs for any more like her.'

As de Morville edged past Anna, he felt her large breasts. 'She's not a virgin you cretin. I'll bet she's been fucked more times than you have. Still, I'll have her after you. I'm not bothering with the old hag. De Tracey can have her…he likes them well worn.' They both laughed out loud.

Anna screamed at the sight of her mother lying on her tummy across the oak table where they had finished their dinner that night. As the knight was raping her from behind, she looked up with terror in her eyes and saw Anna, and contemplated the horror to come. 'Please God no…please God no…' she kept pleading. But the night belonged only to the demons from hell.

FitzUrse pushed Anna onto the same table and ripped open her tunic and skirts. Although she let out a scream as he entered her, she promised not to let her mother see the pain etched on her face, and turned away. Thankfully, the knight finished quickly and withdrew once he was spent.

But before she could draw breath, the knight de Morville was smothering her with his face, probing deep inside her mouth with his tongue while fingering her roughly before pushing his prick inside. He started his thrusting then pulled out. 'I told you she was a whore. Its slack I tell you, slack!' Turning her onto her stomach, he entered her other orifice and she screamed out with the pain. He smiled and grunted with pleasure. 'Hell bells…that's better.'

De Tracy brought some jugs of wine up from the cellar and the macabre drunken dance began as the mother and daughter were passed between the three knights until they lay spent and exhausted, swilling wine in a drunken daze.

An hour passed by and every time Anna tried to move from the table one of the knights grunted and pushed her back down. She prayed that in time they would fall asleep and she could escape.

The door opened ever so quietly and another knight came in from out of the rain. He stood in the shadows, his hood over his head, the drips falling to the stone floor. Watching those around him, he absorbed his surroundings, his eyes finally coming to rest on Anna. Walking slowly around the table, he ran his hand deftly over the white flesh on the inside of her thigh, smudging the blood that had run down her leg.

'Get you paws off her, she's mine!' FitzUrse bawled, trying to focus on the intruder.

The mysterious knight said nothing, as he surveyed the other knights asleep in a stupor on the floor.

FitzUrse held up a lamp. 'Who the hell are you...pull back your hood.' A moment passed before he recognised the knight. 'Oh its you,' he said, steadying himself against the table.

'Take another drink and sit down,' the stranger whispered. It was not an order but FitzUrse did not argue. He took a gulp of wine and in a drunken haze, promptly fell onto his rear, spilling the cup.

Turning to the door, the knight placed a bar across its width and took off his wet cloak. Again, he took in the scene about him. Stretched across the table were two terrified women probably mother and daughter. Anna trembled as he ran his hands over her full naked beasts. Tearing a strip of cloth from her blouse, he stuffed it into her mouth. He took his time abusing her body, sometimes sitting back to think of his next obscene action, stroking his manhood into action.

The hours passed by and in time he had spilled his seed in every orifice. As she lay moaning, her body gripped in pain, her mother reached out to hold her hand.

Touched by the scene, Joab turned his attention to the mother. Moving around the table, he lifted her skirts and turned her onto her stomach. From his cloak, he took a short riding crop and proceeded to hit her across the pale skin of her rounded buttocks.

The crop fell again and again and Anna's mother squeezed her Anna's hand so hard it hurt, until she squeezed no more. The knight threw the bloody crop on the trestle then proceeded to thrust his groin into her bloody buttocks.

When he finished with her mother, he picked up the whip again and flicked it from palm to palm, occasionally slapping it across Anna's back. 'Please my lord, I will do anything you want, but don't hurt me.'

Joab said nothing. He started humming and yawning as if he was bored. When he thought he heard a noise coming from the floor above, he ran swiftly up the stairs and looked around but could see no one up there. Then a horrified face appeared at a window and the shutter was slammed.

Joab returned downstairs and poured himself some wine taking care not to stir FitzUrse from his drunken slumber. Sensing that time was running short, he stretched his arms and flexed the riding stick. With an air of nonchalance, he turned Anna over onto her back and ignoring her young, pleading eyes, he rained a tumult of blows on her breasts and face. Excited by his exertions, he then penetrated her, spilling his seed deep inside her bloodied womb. Thankful for small mercies, Anna felt nothing as her body drifted in and out of consciousness.

Another two hours passed by. In a daze of Anna stirred into consciousness and immediately began to fret. Her eyes refused to open. Then she sensed a little daylight breaking through the shutters. A wave of numbness afflicted her body and she feared that the beating had damaged her beyond repair. Her broken nose made breathing difficult and she spat out the rag from her mouth. Trying to call for help, she could only raise a hoarse whimper.

Outside there was a commotion, as shouts came from all quarters of the castle. She heard someone say a large troop was coming over the horizon and if it was Earl Robert approaching, they were as good as dead.

FitzUrse stirred before the others and quickly gathered his wits. Kicking de Morville, he gave a curt order. 'Make sure the bags are strapped tight to the horses. We don't want a trail of coins.' He spitefully kicked Anna's mother on the leg. 'You must have lived like bloody paupers!' he shouted into her face.

De Morville looked across at Anna and grimaced. 'Who the fuck did that to her face? What a fucking mess.'

FitzUrse wiped his ashen face. 'Joab was here last night.'

'Fuck me,' de Morville replied. 'Has he gone?'

FitzUrse nodded solemnly.

'She didn't stand a chance against that fucking maniac.' He looked at her for a moment, remembering what a beauty she was, but there was no time for sympathy.

The other knights put on their chain mail. De Morville picked up Anna and carried her outside while FitzUrse and de Tracy carried her mother. They were laid side-by-side on the wet earth, without even a cloth to cover their nakedness.

Anna yelped out in pain as de Morville laid her down. He was surprised the girl was still alive. 'What's your name,' he asked guiltily.

Through her broken jaw and cheeks, she tried to answer. 'Anna, and my mother Gwen.' She prayed her mother was still alive and reached out to comfort her. Anna recoiled as she heard a gasp of air escape from her mother. Her hands tried to stop the flow of blood from her throat.

'Sorry, but we can't have no witnesses, can we,' de Tracey said placing his bloody knife in his belt.

FitzUrse was in a hurry. He walked over to Gwen and kicked her in the face and neck. 'Die you fucker…die!' Then he looked down at Anna and scowled.

'Please sir, I'm pregnant…'

'So what?' FitzUrse kicked her hard in the ribs and then stamped on her belly. Checking her inert body, he grunted and steadied himself to kick her again.

'Leave her…that's enough!' de Morville yelled, pulling FitzUrse away. 'They will be here any moment. We go now!'

They mounted up and were galloping across the drawbridge and across the fields.

Moments later the next horsemen entered the castle gates.

The smell of death was familiar to any experienced soldier or knight but the sight of women brutalised and left to rot in the open was the worst sight most men would endure.

Bonham had seen it all before but the horror at Haughley Castle was particularly bad. From the entire household, his men had found just two servants who had kept themselves alive by hiding in the bailey cesspit for more than twelve hours.

Hugh Bigod rode gently into the bailey and dismounted, trying to take in the carnage that lay around him. The women were laid randomly around the bailey; dumped for the animals to finish off and disguise evidence of the violence they had suffered. His men were gaping at the naked bodies and he ordered them into the castle to look for more survivors.

Bonham brought him the witnesses and he asked them what they had seen.

Nervously the two servants stood in their shirts, covered in stinking excreta from their hiding place in the cesspit. 'They were just a few knights and squires…less than ten in all. Pretended to be the Earl of Arundel's men and one said he was William Albini, but I knew he weren't. It was Lord Ralph who let them through…in good faith. We saw him cut down…and his knights, then we ran.'

The other servant repeated the story. 'His Lordship thought it was Lord Albini but I never truly heard their real names…I don't know who they were.'

From about thirty paces away, Bonham called out. 'Lord Bigod, this girl is still alive!'

Hugh came over and recoiled at the bloody broken face and limbs.

Bonham's grimace told the true story. 'It's a miscarriage my lord, as well as being violated.'

Through the mists of her pain, Anna had heard the name. 'Lord Bigod, I am so sorry…'

'Who did this,' Hugh asked, kneeling next to the girl.

'They were demons of the night…'

Hugh ordered Bonham to find a physician in the village.

'You must forgive Roger…you must…' Her incoherent words trailed away.

Hugh recoiled at his son's name.

One of the servants came to stand beside him. He was distraught to see the girl in such a state. 'Its Lady Anna…his Lordship's young daughter. Oh pray God almighty, what have they done to you my beauty?'

Next to Anna, he nodded to the older woman with her throat slit. 'And that was Lord Broc's wife.'

Although this kind of extreme violence against women affected Hugh, it was not unusual, particularly in times of war and rebellion. But he sensed this something different. His hands shook as he lifted the poor girls head. 'You know my son, Roger Bigod?'

The answer was costing the girl dearly as her life force began to ebb. He knelt closer and put his ear to her mouth, not daring to hear the truth.

Blood filled her mouth but she strived to be heard. 'Getting…married…'

Bonham ran back into the bailey and shouted across to Hugh. 'My lord, Lady Petronella is approaching with a large escort.'

'Never mind that, just get a physician, now!'

Hugh seemed to crumble from the inside and Bonham saw the tears on his ageing cheeks. 'My lord, are you all right?'

'Why? Is it wrong to cry for an innocent such as this?'

The clatter of hooves on the drawbridge drowned out his thoughts, as Lady Petronella entered the bailey,gazing at the bodies taken to the mass grave outside the walls. 'You have made short work of this place!' She rode closer to Hugh, grimacing at the naked body of the young girl in his arms. 'Perhaps your libido gets stronger with age. By God's breath Bigod, you certainly had your way with that one didn't you. What's the matter? Isn't your Gundred up to the job anymore? Old age is a blessing and a curse is it not?' she mocked.

Incensed by Petronella's jibes, Hugh turned on his heels and would have leapt up at Petronella had his legs not began to buckle. 'That girl was betrothed to my son.'

A flash of shame passed fleetingly over Petronella's face before she quickly regained her superior air. 'Is that the same son who fights against you and me? The same one who fights for the false king? You need to make sure whose side your family supports before more mistakes are made. And by that I mean you should not have left your wife defenceless.'

Hugh turned red with anger. 'What do you mean? What have you done, you witch?'

Taking no regard of his ranting, she turned to issue a few orders to her steward and marshal, then turned back to Hugh. 'We will take what provisions there are. My husband will pass this way shortly and his army will be none too pleased to see the castle ransacked and burning. We will rendezvous with you tomorrow at St Edmundsbury, then we proceed to Leicester, and retake the city.' She took great pleasure in inflicting the last comment. 'In the meantime you may wish to visit your wife. When I left her she was rocking back and forth with a dagger in her hand. Oh...how I deplore weakness.'

Swinging her horse around, Hugh shouted after her. 'If you have hurt Gundred...I shall kill you.' She ignored his threat and rode off.

The girl was dead and Hugh sobbed his heart out. Gently he covered her corpse with a blanket given by the servant. His anguish was bitter and his torment swelled his heart. A hundred thoughts entered his head but only one was bright and good. Of a day when the girl and his son would have presented him with a grandchild.

Bonham was worried for the state of Hugh's mind and body. As he helped him to his feet, he reminded Hugh they must leave before the Earl of Leicester arrived.

Flames erupted from the great hall, swamping the bailey in thick smoke. Hugh wiped his tears, smearing her innocent blood over his face. 'I don't give a fuck for that thug Leicester. I need to return to Framlingham now.'

Chapter 27

Haughley Castle
Suffolk

In their desperation to reach Haughley, Roger and William rode at speed but kept vigilant, as they had to avoid the marauding armies of both rebel earls. Mercenaries came cheap because they expected to reap a harvest of money, property and women for themselves. But they were often uncontrollable and totally lacking in discipline. Most were accomplished rapists, murderers, and empty of basic moral values. For that reason alone, all contact had to be avoided.

The erratic route to overtake the Earl of Leicester's army put an extra ten miles on their journey but having seen the thousands of mercenaries camped in and around Ipswich they were confident that they would reach Haughley before them.

As night fell they decided to wait in the shelter of a wood-man's hut before proceeding further. The rain drummed a relentless beat on the inadequate roof of twigs and branches and the earth floor was puddled with running water.

They sat for three hours under a leaking roof before William stood up, angry at the weather and himself. 'We must be mad. You realise we have nothing but our own swords. No squires, no food. There is no way I can sleep.'

Roger agreed and stood up to stretch his cold aching limbs. 'Fuck it! It's not that far now. I say we ride the horses to the edge of the woods then move on foot the last mile. Its more direct and we won't be spotted in this weather. Even on foot, it can only be another hour before dawn is due to break.'

They felt happier with themselves by keeping on the move. Across a field was a line of poplars and William pointed them out to Roger. 'I think those trees line the road to the castle. We can tie the horses here, out of sight.'

Roger agreed and they kept up a steady pace, following the line of a drainage ditch. Before long the castle came into view. The drawbridge was down and in the grey light everything seemed quiet. Never taking their eyes off the castle, every pace closer gave them more confidence that Haughley castle was still in safe hands.

Roger stopped first and before William asked the question, he too could hear the unmistakable sound of approaching horses. They dipped into the ditch and waited with bated breath to see who was racing down the track towards the castle.

About twenty horses rattled by and turned across the drawbridge. As they gathered inside the bailey, Roger looked to William. 'Did you see…it was Petronella no less, dressed in her chain mail.'

Men were milling about the drawbridge and William shushed Roger quiet. 'Shit in hell,' he proclaimed. 'What in God's name do we do now?'

They could hear raised voices as someone shouted in anger but they could not make out the words.

They sat shivering in the cold drizzle. 'I can't hear any screams. Surely that is a good sign,' Roger whispered.

William gave a slight nod and chewed nervously on a dry piece of bread someone had thrown into the ditch. 'Surely to God, they must have all escaped through the trap door.'

Roger had felt enormous relief when William told him of the secret trapdoor. Like William, he saw every reason why at least all the women had escaped. 'Perhaps we should go to the mill in the village and meet them there.'

The thought had crossed William's mind but reasoned they would probably be seen. 'Later,' he whispered. 'Just try and listen.'

The only two voices they heard were Petronella's and the same angry voice they had heard before.

'It sounded like he was threatening her,' William said. 'Did you hear?'

Roger turned onto his back, his face ashen white, his heart pounding. 'Yes I heard. And I think I recognised who spoke.'

The horses proceeded to leave the bailey and in the centre rode Petronella. William watched her leave and then turned to Roger. 'Well, who was it you heard in there?'

'Don't you know? It was my father,' he said angrily.

William frowned. 'Well, do we wait or do we give our selves up to your father?'

Roger was about to answer when a burst of flames erupted from the keep. Movement came from the inside bailey and they crouched low as the colours of the Earl of Norfolk flashed in front of them. 'The bastard has burnt the castle,' Roger spat.

William was more pragmatic. In warfare, the destruction and pillaging of your enemy's castle was normal practice. 'I heard the king only a few days ago describe the two Earls as "the damned leading the damned," or something like that.'

Roger only had one thing on his mind. 'Its quiet in there now. We must see inside before I go mad.'

William agreed. They had waited long enough. 'All right, lets go…but quietly.'

Slowly they rounded the drawbridge and peeked through the gate. The stables were empty and only a few people were milling about. No one seemed bothered to put out the fire raging through the castle. Some were weeping over the dead while others were digging muddy graves.

The fact they entered on foot meant few heads even bothered to turn. The smoke changed direction and Roger recognised one woman but when he called, she ran away.

'It's me Roger!' he called after her, but she disappeared amongst the bailey buildings. A number of despairing faces now looked anxiously at the two young noblemen. The dead were being carried onto a cart for burial outside the bailey. So many of them were young serving girls. Now the fear crept into their hearts. Why didn't they escape down the hatch with Matilda and Anna, like the family had planned long ago?

A wailing cry sounded from a large lady that Roger recognised as Lady Broc's maid. She waddled towards Roger her arms held aloft. 'They are dead…they are all dead...' Her sobbing sent paroxysms of fear through them both. William ran forward and grabbed the maid by the arms. 'Who is dead…show me!'

Her hands shook violently as she pointed to three bodies that had been sensitively draped over the bodies.

Roger and William ran over and looking to give each other strength, they pulled the blanket back to reveal the first two bodies. Though they felt aggrieved by the sight of Lord Broc and his wife, neither of them showed any change in expression.

William gave a final tug on the curtain and they both held their breath as the third body was revealed. Putting his head in his hands, William did not have to witness the grief shown by Roger. Taking a deep breath, he looked to the sky for consolation, and selfishly prayed that Matilda and their son had been spared such inhuman butchery.

Roger's face was wrought as his heart fell into the abyss. His mouth opened but words had failed him. He rejected William's arm around his shoulder and pulled away to crawl on his hands and knees next to his sweetheart. Unable to touch her damaged face, he kissed her lightly on the forehead and took off his tabard to cover the rips in her clothing where her white skin shone.

With his head lowered, he sobbed into his chest. 'They hurt her so bad she miscarried…my baby boy…'

Unfortunately, William had heard stories of similar atrocities at the time of the first civil war. Clearly, the lack of good kingship drives men to beat on the devil's door, begging to be let into the gates of hell. Looking towards the cart being filled with bodies, he shuddered at the thought of looking for his wife and boy.

The sobbing stopped and Roger's ashen face was screwed up by painful grief. 'Whoever did this was not human. No man can destroy with such impunity.'

William rose from his knees to speak. 'Roger, please understand, I must leave you to grieve while I look for Matilda and my son.'

Roger nodded without listening as he fussed over, Anna wiping away smears of blood and mud.

Suddenly a cry was heard coming from the drawbridge. William spun round at the sound of his name and through a swirl of smoke; he saw his wife with arms outstretched and his son running towards him.

His elation was suddenly tempered by the shock of them seeing Anna lying exposed on the ground. Grabbing both of them, they all hugged with joy and relief while he gently steered them away from the bodies.

But Matilda had seen Roger kneeling in the dirt and guessed immediately that something was perilously wrong. William could not hold onto her as she wrenched from his grip and ran to be at Roger's side. Each stride towards him brought Matilda closer to a nightmare that she feared ever since she had emerged with her son from the tunnel exit at the mill. Not knowing the fate of Anna, and Lord and Lady Broc, brought her running back to the castle as soon as it was safe to do so.

Glancing down at the three of them, she screamed with so much anguish that everyone turned her way, for only a glance was necessary to fill her sleep with nightmares for years to come. Through the tears, she sobbed. 'Anna saved us. She showed us the way then ran back to save her mother. How can God let this happen...she gave her life to save us.' Sinking to her knees, she put an arm around Roger, gritting her teeth so tight her jaw hurt and together they wept.

Two hours later, all those vanquished had been buried and grief and heartache soon proved to be a poor substitute for all the wrongdoing. People from surrounding hamlets and villages turned up to pay their respects to the family of Lord Broc for they had grown to appreciate the great character of the man so rare amongst his peers.

Respect turned to anger and the roads that led to St Edmundsbury quickly filled with peasants and surfs, many carrying the first weapon to come to hand. It was time to simply fight for their land, their lives and what was right. Vengeance was to be had, and on a scale never felt before.

Bonham had been patient enough and could not wait any longer. He opened the door into Hugh's chamber. 'My lord, you must come now. Your knights await and the battle will soon be afoot.'

Seated on his bed, Hugh had his arms wrapped around Gundred, rocking her back and forth. She had aged twenty years in as many months and a wave of sadness swept over the knight. For two days, Hugh had comforted her, humming with her, promising never to let her down again, even though he knew he must.

Bonham tried not to be distracted. 'My lord, Earl Wills of Arundel and his son met up with de Lucy yesterday afternoon at St Edmundsbury and are now assembling to do battle with Earl Robert of Leicester to the north of the town.'

Hugh did not leave Gundred's side but continued to stroke her hair. 'Is my son with William Albini?' he asked.

Bonham nodded to confirm. He had hoped to avoid any mention of Roger due to the irrational effect it had on Hugh.

'So it's only fifty miles away. Have all the mercenaries and half the knights leave now. We will follow within the hour.'

'Only half, my lord?' Bonham queried.

'You heard.'

Bonham frowned and paused as if to speak, then left the chamber without further comment. On another day, he would have argued the seven hundred Flemish mercenaries were not a valid fighting force. Most were simple adventurers, eager to pillage but of little use in a fight. He had seen some of Leicester's army of ten thousand Flemings and they too were not up to an acceptable standard.

On another day, Bonham would have argued that to have only thirty or so knights in the vanguard would fail to instil any bravado into the mercenaries. But his Lordship had been so distraught since the events at Haughley, it was best not to argue.

Hugh had never felt so low. Gundred had been in a fragile state but whatever had happened when Petronella had entered the castle, had taken her over the edge of sanity, into a world of abject depression. She had suffered a nervous disorder of a kind that could not be breached.

When had her hair turned grey, he wondered. Great clumps of her once beautiful locks were scattered over the floor where she had been curling it around her fingers and pulling it out. Open scabs too often picked were dotted on her face and neck, and her once voluptuous figure was skinny and malnourished as she refused any food. Taking only an sip of goat's milk, it was barely enough to keep a mouse alive.

Her stained mattress smelt of urine and her nightdress was wet, causing a rash around her thighs that looked angry with open sores. No one was left to look after her needs, for in his absence all the maids had left Framlingham Castle and gone into hiding, fearing the return of the thugs and the rapists.

In the midst of such despair, he could not avail himself of the truth about Roger and Anna for it would be the end of her. Of that, he had no doubt. But before he left he would ensure that the village priest would take care of her welfare. No point in thinking too far ahead. Everything else would depend on the outcome of the battle.

Chapter 28

Battle of Fornham
Suffolk

By the time Hugh Bigod reached the impending conflict, the Framlingham knights had already joined up with Leicester's forces on the high ground. As Hugh approached the opposing armies, he kept to the north, avoiding the mercenaries. Riding past the church of St Genevieve, he watched the royal army on the east side of the River Lark, then stopped to assess the state of play.

Incredibly, the main force of Leicester's knights had just forded the river and were now trying to assemble in battle order on the west bank. They appeared in some disarray and the reason soon became apparent. The massive army of Fleming mercenaries were also attempting to join the knights but the recent rains had swollen the gentle stream into a torrent, effectively cutting them off. Now they struggled knee deep in the water meadow.

On the west side of the river, about a mile away, three hundred of the king's knights assembled and were advancing in orderly ranks, led by the aged Justicar Richard de Lucy. Alarmed at seeing the sudden and unexpected arrival of de Lucy, the rebel knights felt exposed without the protection of the mercenaries and galloped to and fro, some trying to get back across the river.

Hugh appeared quite relaxed and seemed more interested in the banners of the opposing army. 'I recognise that of de Lucy's next to the king's colours, but what is the third banner?'

Bonham knew from one of his sources. 'They are carrying the banner of St Edmund the martyr.'

'Very clever, to have a saint on your side,' Hugh said sarcastically.

Much to Bonham's dismay, Earl Hugh was still troubled by a malaise and seemed bereft of a willingness to fight. Perhaps the old warhorse had finally accepted he was too old to lead his men. Perhaps concerns for his family had clouded his judgement yet again. Bonham had told him he considered it a grave mistake to leave so many of his knights to stand guard at Framlingham Castle.

The few dozen knights he had brought with him could see the first ranks of de Lucy's knights were gathering to charge. They itched to hear Hugh give the order so they to could ford the river and join the impending battle. Terrowin rode through the ranks of knights and reported to the earl. 'My lord, your left flank is eager for battle and Leicester's knights have crossed the river a mile to the south.'

Bonham noticed his face was a picture of pure excitement. 'My lord, Terrowin will stay with you if you allow me take command of the charge.'

A flash of disappointment crossed the face of Terrowin.

Hugh sat high in his saddle and spoke quietly. 'Look at the battle array of de Lucy compared with Leicester's. Do you honestly think we will win?'

Bonham spoke with an air of gallantry. 'My lord, do you think by now it really matters?'

The thin smirk on Hugh's face was one of resignation as he watched for de Lucy to commit himself to the charge. All around him, his troop could barely restrain themselves as the kings' knights moved forward and slowly gathered momentum.

Hugh looked down at the mass of Flemish mercenaries milling through the trees around the riverbank and spoke to Bonham. 'You must keep a goodly distance from Leicester's mercenaries. They are supposed to be on our side but you cannot trust them with common sense.'

Perched high in his saddle, Bonham looked for the best place to cross the river. One area south of Fornham bridge seemed devoid of mercenaries. His men cried out and he saw de Lucy's knights were galloping at full charge. There was little time for a speech. 'Onward men, let us join our friends and while we fight and spill our blood, let us make sure that de Lucy never forgets the sharp edge of our swords.' With a rousing cheer, they surged after Bonham with lances raised.

'God be with you, Sire!' Terrowin shouted, wishing he were alongside the knights.

As they approached the river, it quickly became apparent why the mercenaries were avoiding the crossing point. The trees had disguised the marsh and the ground proved too muddy for the horses. Looking to his left, Bonham was dismayed to see the marsh extending as far as he could see. He turned to warn the other knights, but they had already seen the boggy ground and swerved to the right through the trees, bringing them towards the army of mercenaries still attempting to cross the fast flowing river.

Thinking a troop of the king's knights was outflanking them, a flash of panic swept through the Flemish mercenaries. With the fear of being surrounded, they fell upon the small band of 'friendly' knights, attacking their warhorses and pulling them out of the saddle. There was no thought of ransom as the fear of death outweighed any thoughts of money. Some knights instinctively fought back, but only made matters worse for them all. Many were killed as they lay on the ground, screaming that they were not the enemy, unable to make their mad assailants comprehend their last words.

Above the crash and noise of battle, Hugh dipped his head in disbelief at the disaster and Terrowin gasped in shock as the knights were cut down like defenceless dogs.

Some of the mercenaries looked their way and Terrowin shouted at Hugh that they should withdraw. He led Hugh and the squires back towards the church, just as the fighting was beginning to spread across both banks of the river. In an instant, the remaining force of Leicester's knights suddenly crumbled and fled, leaving the mercenaries to fend for themselves.

Terrowin recognised that defeat was imminent and sought to protect the Earl of Norfolk at all costs. 'I shall lay down my life for you my lord, while you escape.'

'Don't be stupid,' Hugh replied harshly and looked ahead. 'We will get back to the church and wait for de Lucy to agree terms.' He tapped the bulging saddlebag laid over his pommel. 'I always carry my terms into battle, just for such an eventuality.'

Petronella felt someone tugging at the rings on her fingers. Her eyes were still blurred and through the pounding pain in her head, she tried to make sense of her surroundings. Slowly her conciousness returned. She could not move her legs and one glance told her they were covered in thick, slimy mud. She had no idea how she got there but she sensed the trickle of blood running down her cheek.

Her right hand grasped the familiar hilt of her sword as the long haired mercenary now gleefully inspected the ring in his hand. It proved to be a big mistake. There was no time to react as her sword cut through the air, slicing into his skull.

Turning onto her stomach she dragged herself out of the quagmire and crawled to the edge of the marsh before regaining her feet. Mercenaries swarmed around the boggy ground, trying to avoid the royalist knights. To her right she saw a group of peasants assembling with staves and spears. Through a gap in the trees, she glimpsed the church and ran as fast as her legs could carry her towards the sanctuary on the horizon.

Never had Roger Bigod felt so exhilarated before. He was in the front rank of knights that charged into Leicester's knights and his first clash upended one knight onto the ground. There was little time to think, as the scene around him quickly descended into hand-to-hand combat.

Then at a critical moment, he spotted a row of knights near St Genevieve church. It was difficult to see the banners clearly, but he thought he recognised the family colours. He asked his squire whose eyesight was hawk-like and he agreed with Roger. 'Bigod colours, my lord.'

His father, the eternal rebel and murderer of his betrothed, had deemed to leave his snake pit and make an appearance at the battle that would decide the fate of the nation.

In no time at all, the rebel knights were scattering or surrendering. Many lay murdered by their own mercenaries. Looking round for William Albini, his squire informed him that he had joined the Earl of Arundel, intent on chasing down the Earl of Leicester and his inner circle of rebels. Quickly gathering his squires, he rode out to the north and found a relatively quiet place to cross the river below Fornham bridge. They kept clear of the mercenaries; his outriders smiting anyone stupid enough to challenge them.

Enveloped in a mist of anger, he rode towards the Church of St Genevieve. Judging by the way they stood, it was obvious the men guarding the entrance were more than simple squires. Roger was in no mood to barter and signalled his men to dismount and draw swords.

As they eyed each other's strengths and weaknesses, a priest suddenly rushed out from the church door. Pushing his way in between the two parties, they dipped their blades; his fierce expression and throaty roar belittling the dozen protagonists. 'There will be no swords in my house of God, this day. If you wish to spill blood, then seek your enemies in the fields below, not on this sanctified ground!'

Roger was tall, and despite feeling small in stature alongside the well-built middle-aged priest, he retorted loudly. 'I believe my father, the Earl of Norfolk is inside and I wish to see him now.'

'Then put down your sword and enter in peace.' He turned to the others. 'Your men will stay outside and any man who enters will have my club to answer to.' From beneath his cassock the priest drew a massive wooden club that looked as if it had cracked a few skulls in its time.

Through a crack in the door, Roger could see his father's back to him as he stood in front of the small chancel. Without another word, he struck the earth vertically with his sword and as it wafted hypnotically back and forth, he strode through the door.

Hugh turned round and although he was surprised to see his son, he did not show it. He smiled and opened his arms a little to show the absence of his sword. 'I suppose that fire-breathing dragon told you to leave your sword outside as well.'

Roger said nothing as he slowly walked down the aisle, staring at his father while noting those stood alert in the wings. He could hardly believe how old and worn his father looked. Strands of hair grew untidily around his bald patch and his face was had been drained of life by years of inner torment. Torn by his desire to kill his father, he stepped forward and pushed him hard. The old man fell onto his back and Roger lay astride him, holding a dagger to his throat. 'You killed my wife to be, and now I will kill you.' His father was barely conscious and Roger paused, recalling the words of the king, warning that he must be prepared before this moment arrived. As his dagger hovered, he looked up to seek guidance from the cross of Christ. Instead, he saw a mailed figure striding towards him wielding a large sword.

Leaping to his feet, he could not evade the blow that crashed into his side. Protected by a thick layer of mail and gambeson, his flesh was not cut but he felt at least one rib crack.

'Stop moaning you poor boy, I could have had your head if I wanted.' Petronella took off her helmet, letting her hair fall onto her shoulders. 'But now you are mine to ransom, as I please.'

Sitting at his father's feet, holding his side, Roger put on a brave face. 'I should die before you receive the pleasure of my ransom.'

She ignored his bravado but kept her sword wavering over both men. A wicked smile curled her lips. 'So your bride to be was that poor soul at Haughley that your father raped and murdered? How fucking outrageous.'

Hugh lurched towards her trying to grab her sword but she slashed out across his left hand, gouging a deep cut between his thumb and forefinger. Blood ran freely from the wound but he did not flinch. He turned to meet Roger's eyes. 'Her depraved renegades did the deed. No sane man could cause such malevolence. I swear I found her dying and listened to her last words.'

Looking down at Hugh, Petronella shook her head. 'You are no bloody use to anyone. Look at you wallowing in shame in front of your own son, waiting for someone to take you home to your not so pretty wife. By the way, how is Gundred? Is she still talking to the fairies?'

'No thanks to your men...'

Petronella came closer and leant over Hugh. 'I'll have you know, the men who assaulted your wife disobeyed my orders and paid the price...'

From the floor, Hugh suddenly swung his arm in an arc, reaching under her chain mail skirt, stabbing Petronella in the thigh with Roger's dagger and the blade went deep into the flesh before hitting bone. A look of horror crossed her face as she realised Hugh had lurched forward deliberately, to reach the dagger on the floor. Dropping her sword, she screamed in agony trying to pull the blade from her leg.

Roger scrambled to his feet and grabbed her sword, just as a flurry of men ran into the church, fearing the worst. They stared in disbelief at seeing Petronella bleeding from her leg.

The priest again intervened demanding calm and the dropping of weapons but this time Roger held on to his sword. Gasping in pain, he turned to his men. 'If either of these devils make a move, you have my permission to kill them.' Without a backward glance, Roger turned around and his squire helped him to the door.

Terrowin ran to help the earl to his feet. Hugh shouted emphatically after his son. 'I swear to you, of all the deeds I have done, I did not kill anyone at Haughley.'

Once outside the church, Roger mounted up. His squire was concerned for his injury and he agreed to return to St Edmundsbury to have a physician bandage his ribcage. They met de Lucy and de Bohun and told them that Petronella and Earl Bigod were under guard in the church. 'Then its all over,' de Lucy reported gleefully. 'William Albini and his father have captured the Earl of Leicester. His wife will be delighted to join him in chains.'

De Bohun excitedly added to the news. 'We also captured FitzUrse, de Morville, and de Tracy. They escaped Orford castle but managed to murdered the entire household at Orford including all the women and children. Even so, the king must still appease the wishes of the pope and have them transported to Rome for punishment.'

Roger could not share in the exhilaration. 'Then my father should join them, for all such murderers should rot in purgatory,' he panted holding his side.

De Lucy noticed his injury was making him short of breath. 'Make sure they take good care of you in the town young man, for I am sure the king will want to see a smile on your face when he eventually returns to these shores. Oh, and take a wide berth down below. The peasants are busy taking out a merciless vengeance on the mercenaries.'

Forcing a smile that turned into a grimace, Roger bid them farewell and slowly descended the slope. His squire stopped and pointed to the marsh on the left. 'By all that is holy, have you ever seen such a bloodbath. I swear the river has turned red.'

The villages from miles around had emptied of all men and able-bodied women and encircled the Flemish mercenaries, backing them into the marshes. Trapped by the river they had nowhere to run. One after another, they were dragged from the bog to be butchered by the peasants armed with pitchforks, scythes and spears. Some preferred their chances in the river but found the enterprising peasants had formed a human chain and pulled them from the water.

Thousands of discarded bodies were piling up along the riverbank to be systematically robbed by the women and children, laughing raucously while engaged in the bloody chore of stripping them. Those unlucky to be still alive had their eyes gouged or speared for fun by the children.

The squire was shocked. 'No doubt they will kill them all. The peasant knows nothing of honour in death.'

Roger spurred his horse on. 'They were mercenaries of the worst kind. They should have known the risks,' he commented glibly, offering little sympathy for the thousands dying like cornered animals.

Chapter 29

St Genevieve Church
Fornham

Inside the Church, the priest was wrapping a bandage around Hugh's hand. He winced in pain, then out of the corner of his eye he glimpsed de Lucy walking down the nave. He sighed, then stood up to face his accusers with all the bravado he could muster. 'I have played no part in this battle. Leicester used my influence but I never gave my full support. I swear my knights are still at Framlingham Castle but you are welcome to confirm the fact if you do not take the word of an Earl.'

De Lucy was not impressed. 'And what of the men you had under your command at the start of the battle. We are not blind, you old fool,' he said scornfully.

Hugh picked up a large saddlebag from the front row of benches. 'Maybe this will make you see things differently.'

De Lucy reluctantly looked inside the bag and saw the mass of coins. Before he could say anything, de Bohun grabbed the bag and put it over his shoulder. 'I say that in the heat of battle, we saw only you with your squires. You were found to be willing to give your oath not be party to any more rebellion or unrest against the king.'

Forced into agreeing, de Lucy nodded. Get back to Framlingham and await final word from the King Henry,' his voice full of contempt.

Hugh held up his bandaged hand. 'I shall see to my wound first and as for…'

Hugh was about to say more but Terrowin interrupted him, thanking the Justicar for his goodwill and quickly led Hugh outside the church. With a backward glance, Terrowin saw them counting out the silver marks between them.

Ever since the mercenaries had entered Ipswich, the abbot and brother's of St Edmundsbury Abbey had fasted and prayed for a speedy and decisive outcome to the conflict. Still emblazoned on the minds of the older monks, was the devastation of the countryside during the civil war between King Stephen and Empress Matilda. It had raged for tens of years and committed entire populations to years of violence and famine. Untold damage had been wrought to the abbey and the surrounding towns and villages, many of which would never recover from the after effects.

Abbot Alexander believed the prayers had worked as the movement of men virtually seemed oblivious to the town and abbey. The abbot had rarely left the front of the altar of the church and turned when he heard footsteps coming down the nave.

Brother Wend, the infirmarer, was walking speedily down the nave. He blurted out the news. 'The rebellion is over. King Henry had prevailed over the ambitions of his wayward sons and the rebel earls.'

The abbot stood up and rubbed his aching knees. 'Thank you Brother Wend. Our fast and prayers have answered our call. Now we must prepare the infirmary for there will be those who seek attention for their wounds.'

'The infirmary is ready with all our supplies of clean water, bandages and herbs and potions, though we only have a small vial of poppy juice,' Brother Wend confirmed. 'Extra mattresses have been made and spread around the dormitory for those with minor wounds, but I don't know if we will need them.'

'I thought there were many thousands…'

'We have received a message from the Justicar not to treat any

Flemish mercenaries.' Brother Shanks looked down at his feet.

'I see.' The abbot turned to the altar and bowed respectfully. 'At least our prayers will be heard for all the departed souls this day.'

The abbot went to inspect the infirmary and already some men-at-arms and knights occupied a number of beds. 'Make sure you identify any nobles so they receive priority attention,' he said quietly.

Brother Wend nodded to one of the larger occupied beds. 'That is Roger, the son of the Earl of Norfolk, though he fights for the king. He has a broken rib, maybe two.'

As he walked over to the bed, Abbot Alexander reflected on the complexities of the Bigod family over the years. Roger was bandaged tightly around his torso and lay against a straw pillow, taking a drink of watered wine.

'My lord Bigod, I pray we are treating you well. How is your injury.'

'Much better for being bound, though it is difficult to breath properly,' Roger replied.

'After your drink I shall have you escorted to more appropriate quarters for the night, before you decide on your plans for the morrow.'

Roger thanked him and finished the rest of his wine before a novice monk led him and his squire to the guest house.

'Now, I shall make sure the refectory has plenty of food for the next few days,' the abbot said, thinking he would indulge himself with a hot rabbit stew before it was all gone.

Barely a mouthful had passed his lips before Brother Wend came rushing through the door. Abbot Alexander had never seen him look so perplexed and asked him to remain calm and explain what calamity had vexed him.

Brother Wend was much younger than him, about thirty, and although he was strong in spirit, he was lacking in good health. He wheezed a while trying to gather his breath before imparting his shocking news. 'Father Abbot, the Earl of Norfolk has just entered the courtyard…and wants treatment for his injured hand…what shall we do?'

The abbot faltered over his plate, a trail of gravy running down his chin. He had to act quickly. 'Take the earl to the infirmary and tell the brothers not to impart anything of his son. I shall treat him myself.'

With his hand wrapped in the heavy cloth, Hugh stumbled from his stallion. Terrowin glanced at the fresh flow of blood and wondered if the earl might collapse. They had the immediate attention of two monks who tried to help but Hugh waved them away. 'I can walk by myself, thank you,' he said petulantly. Feeling increasingly dizzy, he nearly fell onto the bed.

Entering the cell, the abbot smiled at the earl while ordering hot water and fresh dressing to be brought. 'My lord, it is an honour. I wish the circumstances were different. Now, take some wine while I take off this cloth and see what needs to be done.'

Carefully washing off the dirt on his right hand with warm water, the abbot revealed the deep cut between the thumb and forefinger that bubbled bright red blood. 'You will be unable to wield a sword again. For that we should be truly thankful.'

Hugh snatched his hand away. 'It would be unwise of you to make a jest of this,' he snarled.

'I was thinking of the poor Christian soul receiving the blow, my lord. Now, the cut has severed your flesh to the bone. I can sow the wound with cat-gut and pray that the flesh heals, at least enough for you to ride a horse.'

'I don't need your prayers,' Hugh said sullenly. 'I want to be out of here by tonight.'

'If your hand blackens and your blood turns to poison, you will be in need a priest, my lord. But that shall be in God's hand.'

Hugh winced as the abbot rubbed some powder into the cut, then proceeded to sow the wound.

In the guest house, Roger Bigod sat exhausted on his mattress. Sleep was beckoning when his squire entered the room. 'My lord, in the next room is the steward to Ralph le Broc. He has told me of the murders he witnessed at Haughley Castle.'

Roger winced in pain as he stood up. 'I know him well enough. He is a good man. Ask him to come here now and impart the truth.'

Steward Talbot Menzies was already at the door and walked over to Roger to shake his hand. The old man had been a servant at Haughley for decades and they recognised each other from the times they had met at the castle. Settling down with a cup of wine, Talbot recalled the day the knights raided the castle. He spoke quietly, as if reliving a nightmare. 'I was in the keep and looked out of a window to see his Lordship open the gates to let in the knights.' A flush of shame crossed Talbot's face. 'When they slew him without mercy, I thought if I rushed outside, they would kill me for sure. So I hid under a mattress.' A tear ran down his face.

'Go on,' Roger asked filling the stewards cup with wine.

'So help me God, I could hear every sound from the room below. All through the night, the rain battered the shutters, but nought could disguise the sounds of hell as the mother and child were torn asunder.' The tears rolled down Talbot's cheeks. 'Much later, when everything seemed quiet, I found the courage to step down the staircase. God could not save me from what I saw. Pray never say I was a coward for the devil and his demons were rampant that night.' The steward's skin turned a pale grey and he took several gulps of wine.

'Tell me, who were these devils?' Roger demanded, staring into his sobbing eyes.

'Lying in their own vomit, I saw FitzUrse and de Tracey. No

doubt, de Morville was with them as well.'

Roger banged the table with his fist. 'My God, I knew as much!'

'My lord, they were but minor demons; for the devil himself walked into the hall that night.

'What?'

'He carried no badge, no colour or insignia. He was the silent one. Striding around the room, looking calm and sober, his nonchalance, his very demeanour filled me with terror for I could not meet his eyes for fear of being overpowered. He had with him instruments of torture and he laboured over his work till the dawn banished him back to hell.' Even allowing for exaggeration, the ashen face of the steward and his faltering voice made the statement even more terrifying.

'Give me a description.'

Talbot thought hard. 'He was not young; probably forty, dressed in black tunic and britches. He had dark hair and a round, almost childlike face.'

Roger turned to his squire who was stood rooted to the spot during the entire story. 'We are going to need all the help we can get to find this devil. Send out a messenger to ask William Albini to come here. He will know what to do.'

Outside the door, the squire issued a few orders then came back into the chamber. 'My lord, I thought I saw one of your father's knights outside your chamber but he has gone now. Shall I follow him?'

'Leave him. We have more pressing matters.'

'My lord, if I may be so bold. You realise that your father is innocent of the charges you have made against him.'

If truth be told, Roger had known all along that his father could not have murdered Anna and Lady Broc. But knowing he was innocent did nothing to stop him feeling bitter and vindictive. The man was guilty of a hundred sins and one day soon, he would have to answer to God. 'So if I happen upon him, I shall apologise,' he sneered scornfully.

Abbot Alexander cleared his throat and Roger was surprised to see him stood at the side of his bed. 'You are a brave man, my lord,' said the abbot. 'The lord blest us mere mortals with many abilities and many choices. Do you know which is the simplest act in which we all fail, because it requires the most courage? Forgiveness. Only the bravest souls ever accomplish such an act. I shall see to it that a novice keeps you company through the night, though of course he will disturb you as he attends Nocturnes and Lauds. But please feel free to join him in his prayers and psalms.'

'Nothing shall please me more than to join you in prayer,' Roger agreed.

The abbot smiled and left the chamber. Once outside, he scurried across the forecourt, pulling up his hood to keep off the persistent drizzle. Arriving back at the infirmary, he went over to the Earl of Norfolk and inspected his hand and wrist for discolouration. 'My lord earl, I know you are not a man of God but I beseech you this night to join the monks for Nocturnes and Lauds. I pray that the presence of the lord can only benefit everyone this night.'

'Too right I am not a man of God. And you can be certain that the almighty would have a fit if I ever attended a service of forgiveness.'

'My lord, you must settle down for the night. I will stay at your side to look for any discolouration.'

Coming from the stables, Terrowin entered the cell. 'I think the abbot is right. You need as much rest as possible.'

Hugh did not want to admit it, but he felt exhausted and was not comfortable in the presence of the monks of St Edmundsbury. He looked at his hand. 'I am sure you cannot wait to cut it off,' he said mordantly.

The abbot did not blanch. 'I can assure my lord; I am experienced in all form of surgery, especially burns.' The abbot looked into the earl's eyes. 'Do you remember the siege of Ipswich Castle, some twenty years ago?'

'Of course I do,' Hugh replied. 'What the fuck has that…'

'As a young monk and physician, my most pressing patient was King Stephen's son, Eustace.'

Hugh fell silent. Along with most of the population, he had heard how the young prince had died the most horrible death, though only a few knew of his order to unleash the boiling oil that killed him.

'Do you still say there is no room for forgiveness, this night?' the abbot said knowingly.

'Speak your mind, abbot. I have seen you running around your corridors like a man full of secrets.'

'My lord, it is no secret that before his death, a man should do his utmost to seek absolution for his sins.'

Just then, Terrowin looked to the door and let out a cry. 'Oh, thank God…!'

Bonham walked into the infirmary.

Hugh shouted to him in delight, relived at seeing his best knight again. 'My God, I thought you were dead for sure…'

'My lord, I have been looking for you in the guest house. In your stead, I find your son planning to round up everyone suspected of killing his bride to be. If you are well enough we should leave straight away.'

Hugh quickly pulled on his boots and left the abbot stammering in his wake with only a look of acrimony to remember him by.

Chapter 30

Lydda
Palestine

William Bigod washed his hands in the bowl at the side of his bed. For the first time he had slept in his new abode adjoining the church of St George in Lydda, and opening the only shutter he was blest by the morning sun as it radiated on his face.

Gerash and his son Abdul had virtually been running the farm anyway, so he was happy to let him look after the stock and carry on the business of breeding and selling. Over the last few months, the number of incursions by Egyptian raiders had increased and he no longer felt secure at his horse farm.

One such onslaught by the Egyptians had led to a battle with a detachment of Templars, outside Gaza though the knights held the town as their own. Their courage and bravery in the face of a much larger force had forced the Egyptians to retreat to the Nile.

But it was the name of the Egyptian General that had really affected him. His name was Saladin and a stab of fear instantly hit his heart when he heard the name for the first time in so many years. He closed his eyes to recall the young boy who had become a young man, under the tutelage of his evil mentor, Muzawi.

At the siege of Ascalon, they had murdered Geoffrey Bisol, the last of the founding knights and many other Templars. The rise of Saladin could only mean bad news for everyone.

William always had an inkling that one day he would find himself looking after the crypt and the secrets it held. But a recent incident involving the Bishop of Ramleh sealed his future as its guardian.

Out of curiosity, the bishop had wanted to inspect the crypt and even though William had advised against the entry due to the lethal gasses, the bishop waited for William's absence then had his entourage lift the slabs around the altar.

One at a time they nervously descended the steps and discovered the entrance to the hidden chamber. The pungent smell gathered strength and before they could react, an explosion occurred, killing one of the bishop's cannons. Quickly sealing up the entrance, the bishop was then grateful to accept William as the custodian and subsequently only appeared at Lydda when he had to.

William had continued to suffer with his recurring dreams. Now he sought comfort from his room, adjoining the church and overlooking the new Templar garrison across the square. Usually he could observe the Templars as they came in a line to pray inside the church, but for the last eight weeks, the stables had been empty except for his pride and joy.

His one concession in moving from the farm was to bring his mighty stallion Perseus, aptly named after a Greek hero and slayer of monsters. Now they would both live under the protective wing of the Templars. Nearly two years old, the specimen already towered above the other horses in the stable. Sired from Jacques' old stallion Mica, and his own favourite mare Adelice, the young stallion was the pinnacle of breeding excellence and with a temperament to suit. Jacques was the only one who could ride him, spending all his time training him to be fearless in battle. Despite his insistence that the warhorse was ready for battle, William refused saying he was still too young and needed more time to develop good muscle form and strength.

The square had been relatively quiet since the Templars had departed on a mission to escort a secret delegation who had visited King Amalric in Jerusalem. The small garrison looked empty but for a squire who was dutifully brushing down Perseus outside the stables.

Opening his door, William picked up his walking stick and strode into the east aisle of the church about ten paces from the chancel. He was about to cross the nave towards the kitchen on the west side, when he heard a noise coming from the choir and he froze at the sight of two men attempting to raise the marble slabs around the altar. Instinctively William shouted, and they looked up. Then two more strangers appeared from the east aisle, with swords unsheathed.

William's sudden appearance had obviously surprised the men in their act of thievery but now the two men opposite walked menacingly towards him. One was dressed in a black cloak and a shoufa scarf wrapped around his face and the bald one wore a white garment resembling a monk's habit.

For a moment, his world slowed down and was filled with a vision from long ago, almost identical to the one he now faced. Nearly fifty years had passed since he had witnessed the death of Count Hughes of Champagne, crucified on the marble altar of Christ, just a few paces away.

The bald headed intruder chilled William to the bone. So intense was the wall of hatred, he almost fainted in the presence of pure malevolence.

Hopelessly outnumbered and defenceless, William nimbly backed into his room and pushed a cupboard and a table against the door. He spun round and shouted through the window, attracting the attention of the squire, who called to a sergeant standing nearby. With swords drawn, they ran across the square and into the main doors of the church.

Shaking with anticipation, William listened intently. Suddenly the other side of the door echoed to the sound shouting and the clang of swords until the air broke with a scream to signal a blade entering flesh. The silence that followed, seemed to last an eternity. Then a voice called from the aisle on the other side of the door. 'Master William, it is Sergeant de Cresse. Are you all right?'

Pulling back the furniture, William opened the door and was relieved to see the squire and the sergeant standing over the wounded stranger. Blood was seeping through his fingers from a stab to his side though it did not appear fatal.

'By God's breath, they gave me one hell of a fright. I am not as young as I used to be,' William admitted, his heart still racing.

The sergeant dragged the thief onto his feet and marched him outside. 'The other bastards got away. But we will see what confession this one has to offer.'

The day passed slowly as William became absorbed in writing his journal. For a long time William had believed the story of the Knights Templars to be an important one, and whether it was because of his speech impediment, he had always felt more comfortable writing down his personal experiences than talking about them.

Darkness fell and still he had not heard from the sergeant. Trying to sleep, his mind kept returning to the strange man in white and the unearthly sense of dread that shook his soul.

Four hours after sunset, Jacques appeared in the church. His men recited psalms at Matins, as he came to sit with William in his room. 'I have seen the prisoner and he still refuses to give any answers. Sergeant de Cresse is under orders to use any means to extract information. It's strange though; he does not look like a common thief. There is a persuasion about him…'

Not wanting to dwell on the fate of the captive, William asked Jacques how his extended mission had gone.

The Templar looked forlornly at his feet and sighed. 'I seem to remember you are well versed in the ways and means of the

Assassins.'

Many of the Templars believed the stories about William, though he still refused to acknowledge his involvement alongside the early Assassins, and denied he was implicated in the death of the great Lord Zengi. A flicker of a smile passed over his face and he waited for Jacques to continue.

'Well a delegation from the mountains has been in negotiations with King Amalric and they have agreed to form a truce. In fact, the Assassins have stated they want to Christianise their sect. Can you imagine how much that would upset Nuradin. Christ, they must hate the man. Still, a truce would be of benefit to us. All they asked in return was to withdraw a tribute paid to the Templars of Tortosa. We escorted the delegation as far as Tripoli before we turned back. The next day the envoys were attacked and killed by a Templar named Walter de Mesnil. He swore he had permission from the Grand Master, Odo of St Amand, to ambush the Assassins. Despite protestations from Odo, the king rode with a force of fifty knights to Sidon and captured Walter, hauled him back to Tyre and threw him into prison. Can you believe, Amalric is so angry at the arrogance of Odo, he has written to the pope asking the Templars to be disarmed and disbanded.' Jacques shook his head in dismay. 'Things were bad enough between Amalric and the Order but now this…unholy mess.'

William had never seen his friend look so dejected.

'Odo went too far this time, just to protect a small tithe from a few mountain villages. I have to agree with Amalric,' Jacques said in a hushed voice.

As they contemplated the political fallout, Sergeant de Cresse knocked and entered the room, looking a little unsure of himself. 'My lord, the thief has killed himself.'

'What! How…'

'He grabbed a knife from my belt and slit his own throat before I had a chance to stop him.' Knowing it to be a poor excuse, the sergeant held his head low.

Dismayed at the sergeant's ineptitude, Jacques shook his head. 'Join your brothers at Matins. I shall deal with you in the morning.'

Before walking back through the door, the sergeant hesitated. 'He cried out a name as he drew the blade across his throat. 'I think the name was Muzawi.'

Jacques looked open mouthed at William.

Turning away, William suddenly realised the truth. Only hours earlier in the church, he had detected the hate on Muzawi's face. He was after something and his instinct told him his true target was the secret chamber below the crypt.

He closed his eyes to envisage the sadist that had once shattered his life. All those years ago, the monster Muzawi had killed his wife and family, hanging them from the rafters of his barn. At the time, he believed it was in retaliation for his part in the assassination of Zengi.

There seemed little doubt that his life had revolved around the chamber at the foot of the scree slope. An endless stream of adventurers had sought the secrets held within its poisonous walls: secrets he had sworn to protect.

His sense of foreboding overwhelmed his aged bones and the urge to escape from this latest revelation overpowered him. He tried to walk but without his stick, the movement proved too much of a strain and he fainted before he reached the latch.

After the abortive attempt to enter the crypt at Lydda, Muzawi returned to Cairo to revise his plans. Taking the first sphere from its coffer, he allowed himself a moment to stroke the perfect roundness, hoping for some divine intervention. A throbbing sensation made his hands tingle and he restored the sphere to the safety of its container.

Had he been so blinded in his effort to retrieve the second sphere that he had lost sight of his limitations? Surrounding himself with slavish but incompetent men had been a mistake and despite his unique skills; he now realised he could not walk unchallenged into a Christian church like a common thief. If only he had the gold to secure his own army. But Saladin had kept it all to himself.

The installation of a new garrison in the square ruled out any direct attack on the church but it also dawned on him that other factors were gathering to conspire against him. How could he have been so blind as to miss the old Templar now living in the church precincts? And what unnatural powers did he have? He was the assassin who had killed the once mighty Zengi, though he recalled that rumours had implicated his young son in the murder. Saladin was right: he should have killed the boy and his father when he had the chance. He would not repeat the mistake by underestimating his enemy, no matter how aged he appeared.

But first he had a nagging problem to solve. He missed Edom. The man had succeeded in stealing the mace from under Saladin's nose. Proof enough of a worthy aide. Edom was to important to be left rotting in a Cairo dungeon. It was time to rescue him.

The guard prodded Edom with his stick a second time and still he failed to move. After weeks of inflicting torture to his body, it was hardly surprising he could barely move. Now all the guard had to do was keep the prisoner alive so they could hang him up in the market place and butcher him to death. Prodding him again, he heard a voice calling him quietly and the guard turned round to see the tall, bald official looking down at him.

'I am an officer of the court and the prisoner is to come with me. Is that clear?'

The guard was startled by the sudden appearance of the officer. 'Yes, with you.' he replied flatly.

The man gave another order. 'Take him by the steps through the rear door by the store room and out onto the street. Put him on the cart.'

Ignoring the passing comments from the other guards, he did as he was told and once outside he squinted in the bright light of day. In front of him were two horses and he shook his head as if to clear his wits. 'Where are you taking…?'

'Don't be impertinent, you stupid man. Help me lift him onto the rear of the cart.'

Once Edom was laid flat on a mattress, the bald man gently pushed the guard back inside the doorway and in the deep shadows; he pulled a thin dagger from his belt and effortlessly pushed the blade under the ribcage and into the heart. The guard looked wide-eyed as Muzawi covered his mouth to stifle his cry of pain. Muzawi let him slither to the ground then mounted the horse-drawn cart. With a glance at Edom, they rode down the centre of the busy street.

An hour later, they arrived at Muzawi's house in the Cairo suburbs. Though still in pain, Edom was quite lucid and once they were safely inside, Muzawi made him comfortable while a servant collected some water and food.

That night, Muzawi let Edom rest, then early next morning he woke him from his broken slumber. He dismissed the servant and took a bowl of rice and vegetables to Edom's bedside.

'So, did you see Saladin?' Muzawi asked.

Slowly, Edom shook his head. He was nervous at the close attention given by his master. 'No, I did not see Saladin.' Edom hesitated before continuing. 'My flesh was weak and I let you down, my lord.'

Muzawi understood and smiled weakly as he helped Edom with his food. 'Nature dictates that all men are fragile. It is the way of things. You have nothing to fear for there is little shame in being a eunuch. What did you tell them.'

'I told them your name and how we took the first sphere from

Tanis. I am sorry, my lord.'

Ignoring Edom's concerns, Muzawi paced the chamber, deep in thought. 'What else can you tell me?'

Edom thought for a moment. 'The guard told me the interrogator was a Hurran Sabian. The Sabian ordered restraint from the torturer, but my flesh was weak…'

Muzawi crouched closely next to Edom. 'Tell me about the Sabian,' he insisted.

'His questions were clever. He made me reveal things without realising…and the guard said that he was highly respected by Saladin…'

'And what was his name?'

Edom licked his lips and became more nervous as the questions intensified. 'Maimonides.'

Lifting his head towards the ceiling, Muzawi let out a deep breath and nodded in recognition of the name. 'The forces that emanate from the heavens are strong indeed but unfortunately I am not the only one who is able to read the signs. Maimonides is the most dangerous, with the insight and intelligence to match my own.'

Deep in thought, he gave Edom a cup of water then proceeded to pace the room. 'He will have envisaged my plan and will now be advising Saladin to take the second sphere from Lydda before I can reach it. You have done better than you thought. Your failed attempt to assassinate Saladin could not have worked out any better. Now Saladin fears me, and his only solution is to raise an army and take the second sphere for himself. But he will fail to see me walking in his shadow. I will take the second sphere from under his nose.'

Edom understood little of what Muzawi meant but plucked up enough courage to ask the question that burnt in his heart. 'So why are the two spheres so important. Do they have magic powers?'

Muzawi held his gaze with cold, piercing eyes. 'There is no magic. The Gods have entrusted me with powers the like of which have not been seen for thousands of years.'

Edom believed in the power of Muzawi. Even though he was helpless, he did not fear his master's wrath.

'Are you a God?' he asked naively.

'I am an instrument of the Gods. The 'time of promises' approaches fast. Those that have gone before me have failed...even Saladin. I will receive the ancient powers and use them...'

'Use them to destroy Jerusalem?' Edom interrupted fearlessly.

'Yes ...and I shall rebuild a city fit for the return of the Gods.'

As if recovering his thoughts, Muzawi closed his eyes for a moment. 'Take heed, my vengeance runs deeper than one mere city.' Edom shivered at the cold, lifeless words that followed.

'When Moses led his tribe across the desert he was ordered by God to attack the tribes of the Amalekites and the Midianites. They slaughtered all the men and women, saving only the virgins for themselves. My ancient ancestors were Midianite and it is time to return to the land of my blood...to Petra. Only there will the alignment be written in the sky and the Gods will demand that a sacrifice must be made. On the same altar as tainted by Moses.'

Edom shuddered as Muzawi tensed his body and lowered his voice to a malevolent hiss. 'Judea will bleed like never before and the entire world shall shake at what is to come. And on the day the Gods return they will be gratified and invite me to join their ranks.'

Turning his head, Muzawi could hear the Voice calling. He exhaled then walked purposefully to the middle of the room. Moving a table to one side, he knelt down and briefly glanced at Edom before lifting a wooden board from the floor. Reaching into the hole beneath, he lifted the heavy mace effortlessly from its hiding place. With a graceful ease, he swung the weapon into the air and the mace crashed onto the table, smashing it into a hundred pieces.

'Now it starts.'

Chapter 31

Cairo
Egypt

Saladin welcomed reports that King Amalric was engaged in retribution against the pirates that had kidnapped Stephen of Sancerre. But his good fortune changed when Nuradin took the opportunity to summon Saladin to infiltrate the Christian territories along the River Jordan and lead a surprise attack on one of the God's mightiest castles.

Kerak.

Relations between Nuradin and Saladin had never been so bad and they both knew that the summons would test the value of trust they held in each other.

His failed attempt to take Gaza from the Knights Templars, depleted Saladin's confidence and he hesitated in replying to the summons.

However, his father Ayyub was keen to offer advice. 'You should do as Nuradin asks. Kerak Castle would be a magnificent prize and worthy of a sizeable reward from the Sultan.'

Ayyub made everything sound so simple but Saladin knew there was nothing simple about scaling one of the mightiest castles ever built. And then to hand it over to Nuradin who would use it to curtail his ambitions outside of Egypt. He dare not say as much, but he preferred to have the Christians as a buffer against Nuradin.

Nuradin continued to urge Saladin to do his bidding and despite his misgivings, Saladin reluctantly took his army into the Christian territories south of the Sea of Salt and and across the Kerak plain until they arrived at the castle. The siege weapons began to batter the walls.

The army of Nuradin swept down from Damascus to meet him, when a messenger arrived at Saladin's tent.

Out of respect, the messenger dipped his head. 'My lord Sultan, I have ridden from Cairo; sent by your physician Maimonides, to tell you to return. Your father is ill and unlikely to recover.'

Saladin looked to his advisors.

'Nuradin is but one day's march to the north,' one of his captains confirmed.

Saladin looked back at the messenger before announcing his decision. 'It is an omen. Lift the siege now: we ride back to Cairo.'

The return to Cairo was a miserable affair. Saladin was lost in his own dark thoughts, gazing into an unsure and bleak future. Not long ago, he had been so sure of his destiny but since the death of his Uncle Shirkuh, his prospects seemed to be falling apart and now he was about to lose Ayyub, the only father he had known.

Even the royal family of Egypt had sensed his weakness and were in collusion with the Franks to overthrow him and reinstate the Caliphate to power. But above all, his greatest loss was that of his talisman, Muzawi. Now it seemed his one time shaman had risen from the dead and was inexplicably intent on killing him.

Maimonides met Saladin on the steps of the palace and quickly briefed him on his father's health. 'His advanced years count against him. That and his lack of will to live.'

'What condition ails him?'

'He fell from his horse and broke his thigh. The break refused to heal and has become poisoned. I could remove his leg…'

'No! Let him die with some dignity,' Saladin ordered.

One look at Ayyub told Saladin all he needed to know. As he held his hand, Ayyub opened his eyes and smiled. 'My son, I am so proud of you. Nuradin will be so pleased you took Kerak. One day you will be a great leader of men…wise and just. Have more children for one day they too will grow to be great men. Don't be swayed by the others…listen to Maimonides…' The effort of talking proved too much and Ayyub closed his eyes for the last time.

Maimonides spoke quietly. 'For six days he has lived through unimaginable pain, just to tell you how proud he was of you.'

Saladin closed his eyes and asked everyone to leave, saying he wished to be alone with his father. Within an hour, his breathing had become shallow and he leant over to whisper into Ayyub's ear. 'My father, I promise I shall make you proud. Take the flight of steps to heaven and sit by the side of Allah.'

That night they took Ayyub's body for burial and an advisor took Saladin to one side. 'My lord Sultan, I bring news from Nuradin. In a state of utter fury, he has retreated to Damascus, fighting off the franks at every turn. He has sworn to attack Egypt and wipe you and your family from the face of the earth.'

Saladin sighed. 'Then pray we can make a good account of ourselves, before we meet our maker.'

The advisor looked horrified. 'My lord Sultan, is that all you can say? Surely, you must agree terms…'

'What do you want me to say…?' Saladin barked.

Surprised by his outburst, everyone in the room turned to face him. This was it, thought Saladin. This is where he would have to admit defeat and agree to let Nuradin take Egypt while accepting his own fate with dignity. He held his head high as his council looked on expectantly.

Suddenly Maimonides entered the room, trying to catch his breath. 'My lord Sultan, a rider has just entered the gates with news from Damascus. Nuradin…is dead.'

Not a sound could be heard from the chamber. Everyone held their breath, fearing any movement would change the words they had just heard. Then the young messenger entered the chamber. Maimonides encouraged him to speak. 'Speak up boy.'

'My lords, Nuradin has been struck down with the quinsy. The pus accumulated so fast in his throat, he could not draw breath and he suffocated.'

The physical shock of the news lifted and all eyes turned to Saladin. He spoke with genuine respect. 'He was a great man; one of the greatest Sultan's ever to have lived, and I shall not have a word said against him.'

Everyone nodded solemnly in agreement and Saladin whispered into the ear of Maimonides. 'But Allah himself must have heard the threats he made against me and forced his own words back down his throat.' He looked up at his advisors. 'Call the council to the chamber!'

Knowing the importance of good intelligence, Saladin immediately sent out a number of agents to spy on the courts of Jerusalem and Damascus. His fears were realised when after two months his best agent returned from the court of the new Prince regent of Damascus. 'My lord Sultan, one of his first acts was to invite King Amalric to Damascus to discuss terms for the overthrow of Egypt. They agreed that Saladin must die and they would split the riches of Cairo between them.'

Saladin had predicted such a move and showed no surprise. 'Is that it? Go back to Damascus and...'

'My lord, there is more,' the agent interrupted. 'King Amalric became ill in Damascus; unable to rise from his toilet. I followed his delegation back to Jerusalem where he was so ill he collapsed. My spies tell me his bowels are constantly vacating. What the Franks call dysentery.'

Saladin turned to face the wall and muttered to himself. Needing some time to think, he dismissed the agent and asked a servant to call for Maimonides.

'My lord Sultan, he is due back from Fustat this evening. You recall he is meeting a Jewish Rabbi who has travelled from the city of Troyes, in the Frankish provinces.'

Saladin remembered, just as the sound of cheering crowds came from the gates of the palace. Before he could think, the agent had re-entered the room, his face beaming. 'My lord Sultan, listen to the people. King Amalric is dead.' Right on cue, all the doors opened as his council stepped into the parlour. Everyone was speaking at the same time, trying to take in the latest turn of events.

Two of Saladin's councillors interrupted his thinking. 'My lord Sultan, we must send envoys immediately to Damascus, Aleppo, and all the Syrian cities.'

'You must ride to Damascus and claim all that is yours...' urged the other.

Saladin calmly nodded his approval. 'Yes, I must leave for Damascus but first I have to protect Egypt.' He beckoned over his captain of security to his side and issued a lengthy list of names.

The captain left in a hurry, collecting a troop of guards as he went. They ran down the corridor with swords drawn.

Shouts were coming from the palace grounds but Saladin did not raise his head. Instead, he sat crossed-legged on a plateau of satin pillows against the wall, stroking his short beard.

Maimonides entered the room, and took some time to find Saladin. He sat down on a cushion next to him. 'I rushed back as soon as I heard. All your enemies are leaderless and I don't know how, but the whole of Islam is yours for the taking.'

Saladin still looked ahead, his face stony. 'Someone has blessed me with good fortune.'

'Forgive me, but you seem underwhelmed by these momentous events,' Maimonides observed. 'Am I right in thinking you find your change of fortune difficult to believe?'

'What do you mean?' Saladin asked, even though he knew his physician to be correct.

'King Amalric was only thirty-eight; surrounded by the best Greek and Muslim physicians and quite capable of fighting off his dysentery. The same applies to Nuradin and his sore throat. I had never met a more healthy man in my life. Just perhaps...there are other forces at work.'

'You think they were all assassinated.' Saladin stated flatly.

'Rumours are always heard when someone dies unexpectedly,' Maimonides said, not daring to admit to his true thoughts just yet.

But Saladin's mind had already run away with the idea. 'The old man of the mountains agreed an alliance with Amalric. Are his Assassins behind the killings?'

Reluctant to agree outright, Maimonides shook his head and sighed. 'Truly, I don't know. Another alternative would be...'

'And what of my father? Saladin interrupted. 'Did the Assassins kill him as well?'

'No, that was an accident,' Maimonides conceded. 'But as for the others... I believe Muzawi may have been instrumental.'

Saladin stared at Maimonides. 'Have you lost your mind?' he hissed.

Someone clapped to signify the council meeting was ready to start and all eyes again turned to Saladin. His chief advisor approached There are two absences my lord Sultan. I have sent messengers out...'

'That will not be necessary. Tell everyone we shall meet in the gardens in one hour. The light is much better there.'

Saladin dismissed his chief advisor. He then frowned at Maimonides. 'I was not expecting you back so soon. You may prefer to see how your Rabbi friend is settling in, rather than witness what happens next.' Unable to hide the flash of guilt on his face, he turned away to talk with the captain of his Mameluke bodyguard leaving

Maimonides with a shiver of anticipation that chilled his bones.

An hour later, sixteen of his council followed Saladin onto the large veranda that overlooked the gardens: all of them wondering what to expect. A bright sun lit up the beautiful flowerbeds and exotic trees but the sight that greeted them made them gasp in disbelief. Amongst the beauty of the gardens stood two man-sized crosses each mounted with a body screaming silently into tightly drawn restraints around their mouths. Blood was dripping from the wounds in their hands and feet.

Saladin confronted his audience. 'These are just the first. Please remember this sight, for this is what happens to agents and supporters of my enemies.' Two more crosses were pushed upright and everyone gasped in horror as they recognised the agonised faces of the two missing councillors.

Saladin walked across the grass towards his bloody victims. 'Crucifixion is too good for those who are willing to betray me.'

From the veranda, Maimonides called out. 'My lord Sultan, please think through your actions. Why are you doing this?'

Saladin chose to ignore the interruption and his council looked at Maimonides in disdain as they separated themselves from the source of the ill-advised outburst.

Picking up a large hammer, he looked up at the two crucified councillors and struck their legs one after the other. The crack of broken bones echoed around the gardens and was met by gasps of horror from his audience. Both councillors sank onto their broken limbs, gasping for breath.

Panting from his brief exertion, Saladin strode back to the veranda and the council parted to let him through. Some had been violently sick, while others whose loyalty was beyond doubt, nodded their heads, agreeable to the punishment meted out.

Maimonides was now stood apart from the others, and shook his head in dismay at what he had witnessed. 'I thought you had control over your cruelty and mindless slaughter. I am ashamed that…'

Saladin grabbed Maimonides by the throat, his eyes ablaze with fury. 'You can say whatever you want about the passage of the moon and the stars and you can advise how to heal my wounds and catch assassins in the kitchens. But you never interfere in my politics. I had no choice but to rid myself of known enemies that lie in my midst. The others will remember this. Now I can safely depart for Damascus, knowing Egypt will still be here when I return.' His anger subsided and he released the physician from his grip.

Rabbi Baruch had attracted his fair share of racial antagonism as he started his journey across Spain and the Great Sea to Egypt. But he reasoned that the added hostility went some way to harden the three years of bitterness that had filled his heart. The death of Rabbi Jacob and the burning of the Jews of Blois were memories that could not be erased. Instead they drove his efforts into fulfilling the promise he made to the old Rabbi.

Finding Maimonides had become an obsession, but as his journey progressed, his task had become easier. They said, *'the most gifted of men,'* *'the wisest and most intelligent,'* were just some of the qualities ascribed to the renowned scholar born in Spain who had travelled over much of the world. Wherever he went Maimonides had made an indelible impact on peoples lives. Baruch supposed that had he been a Christian, then Maimonides would no doubt have been a saint.

Riding through the Muslim states, Baruch no longer described himself as a lowly clerk but as a Rabbi from the famous Yeshiva of Troyes and a descendant of Rabbi Rashi. Although untrue, the description elevated his status among both Jewish and Muslim communities alike, making his journey through Egypt run relatively trouble-free.

When he eventually met Maimonides at Fustat in the suburbs of Cairo, he was delighted to see he was about the same age as him, looking no more than forty. On the way to the palace of Sultan Saladin the streets were alive with the news that King Amalric of Jerusalem had died. Baruch had little knowledge of eastern politics and he was captivated as Maimonides explained the complex power bases of Egypt, Syria and the Holy Land.

'You will find the palaces of Egypt much more civilised than the rat-infested Christian fortresses.'

Unfortunately, as they walked up the steps of Saladin's palace, it became obvious that something was wrong. Even Maimonides was unnerved by the sight of the palace bodyguards running back and forth, seemingly arresting people and dragging them towards the gardens at the rear.

When they saw two man-size crosses being carried in the footsteps of those arrested, Maimonides quickly paled. 'I fear the Sultan has reverted to type. I will take you to your chamber and I suggest you wait there for me until things calm down.'

Baruch obeyed but could hear shouting coming from the terrace adjacent to his room. Curious to see what was happening, he lent over the terrace balustrade so he could see the gardens. The sound of hammering caught his ears and some distance away he could see the two crosses laid side by side. The sight of two men being crucified sent a shiver of cold fear through his bones and he wondered into what nightmare he had stumbled. He had seen enough blood and sacrifice in Blois to last him a lifetime.

Orange trees obscured his line of sight but he guessed there were more than two crucifixions taking place. Engrossed by the spectacle he caught a glimpse of Saladin pick something up and strike out at the first two victims. The sickly sound reached his ears and he quickly closed the door to the terrace. Baruch climbed into his bed, and extinguished the lamp, ignoring the fruit placed invitingly in silver bowls, wondering what horrors awaited him the next morning.

An hour passed in fitful sleep when someone trying his door disturbed him. Assuming the worst, he drew his knife from under his pillow and listened to the door opening and the footsteps approach. He was relieved to see the face of Maimonides lit by the lamp he was carrying.

Sitting at the foot of the bed, Maimonides noticed the open door to the terrace overlooking the gardens. 'I don't know what to say. I must apologise for what has happened but Saladin had to exercise his new-found power by eliminating any possible opposition and make a lasting impression on his supporters and enemies alike.'

Baruch shook his head. 'But I saw him break the legs of those wretched men…'

'Perhaps he wanted to quicken their demise. Without support they would die quicker,' Maimonides offered.

Baruch shook his head. 'I was hoping we would have time to talk but your work here seems so wrapped around the Sultan…'

'Believe me your arrival in Egypt has unwittingly heralded an enormous opportunity to Saladin that he must now grasp with both hands. I was also looking forward to hearing the works of Rabbi Jacob and your proposals to help the Jewish communities. Testing times lay ahead. Please join me so we can discuss our common interests further. Tomorrow we ride to Damascus.'

Chapter 32

Framlingham Castle
Suffolk

Gundred's eyes were no longer vacant. They opened wide with a flash of fear, as she heard the arrival of horsemen in the courtyard below. At first, Hugh ignored the sound of the horses, then changed his mind when he saw Gundred's reaction.

The last time a knight walked into her chamber she had screamed herself hoarse.

Hugh thought it best to leave the chamber and greet whoever had arrived. Gone were the days when servants would rush into his presence to tell him the comings and goings, but since many of his staff had left his employ, the castle seemed strangely void and lifeless.

As he stood by the main door to the grand hall, and peered towards the stables, he hoped it was Bonham; for an age had passed since they had last met. In the weeks after the rebellion, Bonham had been temporarily seconded by Justicar de Lucy and according to a message he had received a week ago, he was expected to arrive at Framlingham any day.

A rare smile broke over Hugh's face as he recognised the familiar banner that fluttered by the stable. Terrowin ran to greet Bonham enthusiastically and took his palfrey, covering her sweating flanks with a blanket before wiping her down.

Bonham was genuinely pleased to see the old earl standing outside his grand hall. It always surprised him how well Earl Bigod appeared given his advancing years. Only one other baron came to mind that was nearing the same age as Hugh and that was the Earl of

Arundel, an old adversary of the earl. Like many feuds that had stood the test of time, he wondered if the protagonists could even remember why they were at odds, for no one he knew could begin to offer an explanation.

Over his long life, Earl Bigod had attracted many enemies but none so unfortunate as his son, Roger. The loss of his future bride Anna had filled the young man's heart with revulsion and Hugh had become a casualty of his all-encompassing malevolence.

Bonham wiped the grime from his face and approached Hugh. 'My lord, I beg of you a cup of wine... my mouth is as dry as sand.' He stretched his back and Hugh ordered wine and food.

Once sated, Bonham quickly recovered from his fatigue and was keen to impart his story. 'As instructed by the king, I joined the escort of the prisoner Richard le Breton, from Orford Castle to London. On such a long journey we naturally talked and he was keen to tell me of the massacre at Orford Castle. They were led by a charismatic figure, quietly spoken but merciless in his actions. De Morville, de Tracy and FitzUrse actually followed his lead in the slaughter that followed. Le Breton says when he witnessed the household being thrown into the fire pit, he wanted no further part in the killing and went back to the cells until the castle was reprieved.'

Hugh stood up to face the window. The air chilled and the hairs on the back of his neck stood up.

Bonham continued. 'Le Breton told me his identity. It is Joab Mandeville, the bastard son of Earl Geoffrey de Mandeville.'

Hugh showed no surprise as he bathed in the thin sunlight coming from the window. 'I thought so. Thirty years ago, I was witness to his depravity...perhaps then an unwitting party to it. But Joab was the devil's child and now he wears his father's crown with relish.'

Hugh turned to face Bonham, his face riddled with guilt. 'And I know what you are going to say next. That he killed Anna, Roger's wife to be.'

Astonished at Hugh's insight, Bonham nodded solemnly.

Hugh closed his eyes. 'Mandeville must die. Where is he now?'

'My lord, he was rounded up with FitzUrse, de Morville, de Tracy and le Breton. The pope has excommunicated them and they now face deportment to face the Pope and the retribution of God Himself.'

Hugh threw a cup of wine against the wall. 'That is no fucking retribution! That fucking moron in a white cloak holding a prayer book will pat him on the head, and forgive him his sins!'

Bonham was devastated at Hugh's reaction. 'My lord, I am sorry, I did not realise...'

'Where is the king now,' Hugh snapped angrily.

'He is due to land at Southampton any day now and then he goes to Canterbury.'

'Why Canterbury?'

'I don't know...I am told the king has been in a strange, melancholic mood of late.'

Hugh paced back and forth, mulling over his anger. 'Then we have only one course of action. We must appeal to the king direct.'

Recognising Hugh's impatience Bonham knew it was time to act quickly. 'I shall gather the knights and ready them for a dawn departure.'

'There are only five knights present...the rest are scattered across East Angles,' Hugh admitted. 'We will take two knights with Terrowin of course. Let him decide how many more squires we need. Leave the men-at-arms here; they will only slow us down.'

Bonham nodded and made his way to the knight's quarters, speculating on the loyalty of the knights and servants who had lost confidence in the old Earl and deserted him.

Despite having succeeded in quelling the rebellion, some bishops still openly questioned King Henry's ability to govern, calling his reign calamitous. He proclaimed himself a righteousness king, but it was said the blood of the martyr Thomas had indelibly stained his reputation, some inferring that God would continue to punish him, until he repented. Worst of all, they said a king without God on his side would ultimately be a beaten king.

Near on every day, news of even more miracles were announced from the steps of Canterbury Cathedral, each one feeling like a slap across his royal face, keeping him from his sleep, tossing and turning throughout the night.

Waiting by the harbour in Barfleur for the stormy weather to abate, Henry could take no more. He ordered the boat to be readied. On board were his wife Eleanor, and Earl Robert of Leicester and his wife Petronella. They had all been arrested and held at Falaise Castle in Normandie until the king was ready to return to England.

Henry turned to the Bishop of London. 'All of us shall throw ourselves at the mercy of God. Under a storm at sea, what better way to truly test his anger.'

'Do not take the Lord's name in vain, my lord king,' the bishop admonished. But as the boats were loaded, Henry's mood remained defiant.

As the waves tossed the ships about as if they were twigs, Henry steeled himself for the worst. His only comforting thought was if he died, then they would all enter Hades together, though not wanting to tempt the lord, he swore upon the cross that if he were to survive the crossing, he would serve more than just a token penance. For his part in the death of Thomas Becket, it would be a hard and righteous penance.

Arriving at Southampton, the king dutifully told his entire party to bend their knees and pray and relieved to be alive the entire company and household knelt on the quayside. .

Before setting forth along the old Roman road to Canterbury, the king met Roger Bigod and William Albini who had been waiting at the harbour. The first question on Henry's lips was to the health of William's aged father, the Earl of Arundel.

William replied proudly. 'My lord king, my father has taken to his estate in Wymondham though I am pleased to report that little ails him other than old age and aching limbs.' Not wanting to trouble the king, William deliberately omitted to say his father was virtually paralysed from the waist down and was being attended to by the monks from the abbey.

The king smiled lightly then turned to Roger. 'I shall not ask for the health of your father, lest he bites my head off.' A knowing ripple of laughter rang around the courtiers and Roger obliged with a wry grin.

The king took Roger to one side. 'Queen Eleanor will be separated and taken to Sarum, but I want you to take the Earl of Leicester and his wife to the London Tower, where they shall await my pleasure. I understand that Petronella was instrumental in your bride's death.'

Roger hesitated. 'Not exactly…it is more complicated than that...'

'By the breath of God, she nearly killed you at Fornham St Genevieve. If it wasn't for your father…'

'The sins of my father…' Roger interrupted, then he saw the king frown and he bit his tongue .

'Your father is guilty of many sins, but he did not kill your bride. You should apologise to him for intimating as much. Heaven knows, it may calm him and take some of the bite from his angry jowls.'

Roger hung his head submissively.

The Bishop of London caught the king's eye and he looked up to see the lateness of the hour. 'So, talking of sin; if Petronella should befall some unfortunate…accident it would only be seen as Gods punishment. You understand?'

Roger nodded and then as the king rode away with his company in tow, he reflected on his words and wondered what on earth they meant.

William Albini rode up and pointed to the prisoners that had been loaded onto a cart. 'We need to go now if we want to reach London by tomorrow and I have no wish to make this journey any longer than necessary.'

The small troop moved depressingly slow. Every mile they rode, Petronella harangued Roger mercilessly and they only managed to reach a copse outside of Winchester before they stopped for the night.

Roger checked the chains of the Earl of Leicester, his face looking pale and sanguine in the moonlight. A tarpaulin was stretched over the cart, keeping the damp air from settling on the king's wife. Queen Eleanor briefly smiled at Roger, and as she pulled her blanket up to her chin, he appreciated how her natural radiance and beauty had captured the hearts of two kings. How strange now that both of them despised her so much.

Everyone else was asleep, except for Petronella. Her soft voice carried from under the tree where he had left her chained. 'Come and tuck me in, my boy soldier. I will suck your prick for you and send you to sleep. Is that what she used to do for you...your little Anna? Or did she prefer sucking off your daddy...'

Roger leapt to his feet and struck Petronella across the face. She spat out a bloody froth and her face cracked into a wicked smile as she whispered. 'That's my boy...my strong, brave boy. Just loosen these chains and I will let you fuck me.'

Roger knelt in front of her and undid her mantle and her leathers. Ripping at her outer tunic, then her underclothes, he exposed her breasts.

'That's it, do your worst...suck my tits and loosen my arms so I can give you everything you want...'

His breathing became heavy and he felt himself being sucked in by her alluring voice. 'Just shut up you fucking witch,' he scowled, staring at her nakedness.

The smell of excrement assaulted his senses and to his left he saw a small pile made by Petronella. He punched her in the stomach, then took a handful and shoved it into her face. Pinning her to the ground he reached out and took handfuls of earth to fill her mouth until she gagged for air. After hours of verbal torment, the stifled silence was a relief.

The months of pent up vengeance rose suddenly and violently within him and when he pulled his dagger from his belt, he wondered what he would do next. The power he held in his hands ran through his veins and swelled his heart till he thought it would burst.

For once, Petronella looked frightened. Her face puffed out in panic and unable to scream, she shook her head violently from side to side.

The motion was no different to skinning a rabbit. A white mist clouded his vision and a comforting humming sound filled his ears as his blade worked in a jagged fashion, with only minimal tearing. By the time he had finished, Petronella had passed out.

For a moment, he contemplated doing worse, but the thought quickly disappeared from whence it came. She was no longer that inviting. The results of his effort were thrown into a bush and the ever-present feral dogs rushed to claim the offering. He stole a clean sheet of cotton from Queen Eleanor's maid then proceeded to bind her chest to try and stop the bleeding and when he finished, he sat back to look at his handiwork. Then he felt the wave of guilt come crashing down upon his head. Walking back to his mattress, he felt smothered as if his soul was being engulfed and he curled up tightly and sobbed.

Just before dawn, a high-pitched scream ripped through the air, waking them all. William and the squires leapt for their swords in fear of being under attack.

Turning over, Roger pulled up his blanket over his face against the morning chill, terrified that he could have committed such an atrocity and afraid of the inevitable consequences.

Chapter 33

Lympne
Kent

The news that the king was still stationed at Lympne, fifteen miles from Canterbury, had done little to quell Hugh's anger. Rallying his men, he pushed on quickly to the south, hoping to reach the king before nightfall. Hearing the king was at the church on top of the ridge, Hugh rode on until the king's bodyguard stopped him at the gate and refused him entry. Hugh insisted on the urgency of the matter in hand and eventually the Bishop of London allowed him to enter the church alone.

Peering down the nave, Hugh could see the king was appearing to take advice from a number of clergy, but as soon as they saw him, they stopped talking. Dressed in the white gown of a monk, the king alighted from his bevy of advisors and gestured to Hugh to sit down.

'Earl Hugh, to what do I owe this unexpected pleasure?'

Hugh went straight to the point. 'I want you to stop the deportation of that bastard Mandeville and the four assassins to Rome. They are all guilty of grave and murderous crimes, but Joab is pure evil...'

'Hugh, I cannot defy the pope's wishes. They sailed from Dover yesterday and that is the end of the matter.'

Hugh looked disappointed and a brief silence separated the men.

Then the king spoke. 'Hugh, in all this time, I have never punished you, even against a mountain of advise to the contrary. I always believed that deep down you were worthy of loyalty to me, your king.'

Hugh clenched his fists. 'You have set free the murderers of my son's wife to be...is that not punishment? Roger is turned against me and you have kept Norwich from me when it is rightfully mine...'

The king was distracted for a moment when he saw a messenger enter the church and report to the bishop. 'There is no one more than me who wants you to make amends with your son. I told him as much yesterday.'

Hugh looked blankly at the king. 'Yesterday?'

'Your son wants to apologise for blaming you for the death of his bride to be. He would say as much himself, but he is escorting the Earl of Leicester and his wife to the tower.'

'Is he with William Albini?' Hugh asked, failing to notice the king becoming more impatient.

'This is why you interrupt my church council...to interrogate me over your petty feuding. After all your demands, all your betrayal and rebellion, you have the nerve to stand here and question me!'

Hugh knew he was risking the king's wrath but he could not help himself. 'All I ever wanted was Norwich!'

'You cannot have Norwich! While I live and breathe, you will never have Norwich. There, is that clear enough!'

Some of the council moved closer, ready to pull Earl Bigod away if he raised a hand against the king.

Hugh saw the movement and turned on his heels before he suffered the indignity of being ejected from the church.

The Bishop of London sidled next to the king. 'I pray he will not discover that the King of Scotland has invaded Northumberland and your son young Henry waits with the Count of Flanders to cross into England with an army of Flemings. You know it will only encourage him to rebel again.'

Now Henry turned his anger against the bishop. 'For the sake of God, Bigod has no knights to speak of, his wife has lost her mind and his son hates his guts. The man is seventy-eight years old; so tell me...how many more rebellions does he have in him?'

The bishop sighed. 'God's purpose is a mystery to us all, my lord king but I must tell you, we have more news from the north and it is not good. The Scots have the devil between their teeth and are intent on shaming all humanity. There are stories of babies being cut from the womb and carried on spears as well as monstrous perversions and slaughter amongst the women and children. Priests are made to watch the nuns being raped before being slain on the altar of Christ.'

The king shivered and steadied himself against the pews. 'Tell me we have gathered an army to combat such evil.'

'As we speak good soldiers gather at Prudhoe under the banners of de Glanville, Uumfraville, de Vesci, de Tilly, and Balliol.'

'Gilbert, your words lack lustre. De Glanville is good but the rest are not battle hardened. Everything will count on the Scots being defeated. Then again, even if we do prevail against the Scots, my son the young king will attack Normandie with Count Philip while I am in England.' The king shook his head in despair. The idea of an endless cycle of battles on both sides of the sea suddenly depressed him.

Bishop Gilbert grasped his shoulder. 'My lord, keep your head high in front of your council. And fear not, for after tomorrow we will have God and Becket on our side. I have spoken to the abbot and the monks of Canterbury. Everything is ready for the morning, as you requested.'

A thin smile appeared on Henry's face. 'Thank you Gilbert, now let us all pray for the poor wretches of Northumberland.'

Turning to face the altar, the king recognised William Albini suddenly appear at the door and present himself to a steward. He walked hastily towards him.

What new calamity is this, thought Henry. William was supposed to be in London by now.

William paused to draw his breath. 'My lord king, I have to tell you Roger Bigod has confessed to a terrible crime.'

The day after seeing the king at Lympne, Hugh arrived in London and discovered his son Roger was staying at a hostelry in Cheapside. Bonham went on ahead and was able to confirm his son was prepared to meet Hugh in an adjoining private room.

Sat alone by the window, Roger's gaunt face stared back at his father.

Hugh paused in the doorway and immediately he saw the apprehension in his son's eyes. 'Fear not, I come unarmed Roger.'

Roger placed his sword on the windowsill while Hugh turned to Bonham and told him they did not want to be disturbed. Hugh waited until Bonham was outside and watched him walk with Terrowin and the horses to the stables.

'What ails you? Do you have a fever?' Hugh asked tentatively.

Roger poured both of them some wine from a large jug. It was early morning and Hugh guessed that more than a few cups had already been consumed.

Saying nothing, Roger glanced again out of the window.

'Are you waiting for someone?' Hugh enquired.

Roger shook his head. 'Did you see the king at Canterbury?'

'I saw him at Lympne. Gave him a piece of my mind as well.'

Roger frowned, as if his next words were difficult to impart. 'I think I owe you an apology. I was told...wrongly...that you were responsible for Anna's death.'

Hugh's face reddened. 'I know.'

'I was escorting Petronella...to London...' Roger looked down at his feet, ashamed at his own confession. 'I cut off one of her breasts and fed it to the dogs.'

Hugh spluttered into his wine cup and stared at his son in disbelief. 'Is she still alive?'

Gazing at the floor, Roger kept his head down. 'The king told me she needed punishing…I just lost my senses I guess. I can't really explain…'

Instinctively, Hugh reached out to his son then pulled his arm back before making contact. 'If the king gave the order then so be it. She got what was coming to her.' Hugh shifted on his seat. 'But it is all the more shame that the real culprits have escaped punishment.'

Roger lifted his head. 'You mean Becket's assassins.'

'That's right. But do you know it was Joab Mandeville who led them on.'

Thumping the table, Roger leapt to his feet. 'My God, so he is the mysterious one we have been searching for.'

Hugh continued. 'Mindless butchers all of them. Hanging would be too good for them. There are witnesses to the atrocities they committed, all of them good men. But instead of punishing the murderers, our wise King Henry has sent them to Rome to be dealt with by the pope.'

Roger paced the floor. 'They killed Becket, murdered the household of women and children at Orford Castle, as well as butchering Anna and her parents. They don't deserve to live.' Becoming more agitated, he pushed his fingers through his hair. 'I must go after them and you can help me. Get me to Count Philip of Flanders and I will convince him…'

Suddenly the door clattered open and in rushed the king's men-at-arms. Roger's hand went for his sword, then realised it was still on the windowsill. As they pushed him roughly against the wall and bound his hands, there was no point in struggling.

Hugh stood in front of the captain. 'Stop this now! On what charge do you take my son?'

The captain was taken aback by the presence of the infamous Earl of Norfolk. 'My lord, on the orders of the king, I am arresting Roger Bigod for attempted murder against a prisoner of the Crown. He is to be held at Westminster under house arrest.'

Grateful it was not the tower, Hugh looked at his son. 'Don't worry, I shall personally oversee your release.'

Roger was less than confident. 'Father, I beg only one act on my behalf.' As he was pushed through the door, he shouted out. 'You kill Joab Mandeville!'

Hugh followed his son out of the hostelry to see he was not mistreated and watched as he was placed on horseback.

As he rode out of sight, Bonham approached and apologised. 'My lord, I was too far away to warn you...'

'Bring the horses from the stables,' Hugh ordered. 'We ride at once to Canterbury.'

The crowds around the cathedral square were so packed that Hugh wondered if they were waiting for the king to give a speech. He had been told the king was at the Cathedral and his squires made room for him to reach the front of the crowd but the row of guards prevented him from going further. The press of pilgrims and peasants on all sides made it difficult to move and Hugh decided to stay put.

Terrowin did his best to keep the pilgrims at a distance from the earl but a yelp of excitement broke out on the south side of the square and Hugh strained forward to see what was happening.

Just then, a man pulled at his arm and introduced himself. 'Earl Bigod, my name is Lord Ralf de Lahay. Please, we must talk.'

Hugh was about to call out to Bonham for assistance.

'I come with the express wishes of Count Philip of Flanders,' the lord explained.

Hugh looked closer and could see he was dressed in fine clothes and glancing over his shoulder, he could see Bonham talking avidly to the lord's aide. 'This is a peculiar place to meet Lord Ralf. What can I do for you.'

'Given the close proximity of our common foe, it is best we meet away from the prying eyes of the court. I came to Kent to drum up support for the young King Harry. He waits with the count on the coast for good weather to cross with an army into East Angles.'

A murmur of anticipation ran around the crowd as everyone pushed forward as some monks came into view and Terrowin tensed to keep the pilgrims from pushing against the earl.

'What sort of support do you want from me?' Hugh asked as he peered into the square. Amongst the jabbering pilgrims, he missed the heavily accented words of Lord de Lahay. When the king appeared a shock wave rippled through the eager pilgrims. Walking in the simple white gown of a pilgrim, his bare feet were bloodied with sores and his back was laced with the bloody stripes of scourging. Escorting the king were three monks who took it in turns to strike his back with their ceremonial flails.

'They say he's walked three miles like that,' one pilgrim pronounced, dutifully impressed by what he witnessed. Like many of the crowd, he crossed himself and chanted his prayers.

Hugh was stunned, unable to grasp the outlandish display of pathetic penitence. 'What the fuck is going on?'

Lord Ralf muttered in his ear. 'It is disgraceful that a king seems fit to humiliate and mutilate himself, just to plead for the forgiveness of a dead priest. The man is not a king; he believes himself to be a martyr to a long lost cause, perhaps even a saint.'

'You mean he does all this because of Becket, three years after his death!' Hugh cried in disbelief.

The king hobbled through the door of the cathedral followed by a bevy of bishops, monks and priests, chanting incantations and psalms. The crowd that lined the streets could not contain their excitement and enthusiasm.

Lord Ralf had to shout above the cheers. '…thirty knights and three hundred men at arms and the same number of Fleming mercenaries, have already landed!'

Confused by his accent and all that had happened, Hugh looked again at the lord. 'What has all this got to do with me?'

The crowd brushed past Hugh, making for the cathedral steps. Hugh wished he had understood what had been said. 'What…what is going on? Speak clearly…'

Pushing his way through to Hugh, Bonham shouted in his ear. 'My lord, the Scots king is ravaging the north of England, and a Flemish army led by the young King Harry and the Count of Flanders await at Gravelines. My lord, it is an invasion.'

'But Lord Ralf said they had already landed,' Hugh pointed out. They both looked at the smiling lord.

The lord spoke slowly. 'They have landed at Orford and they look for your support. As we speak, they march to Framlingham. My informants tell me you were here this day and I praise God for the good fortune…I found you.'

Hugh blanched at his words then felt his anger rise. 'An army is heading for my castle and you smile in my face. When will this stop!'

Before Hugh could waste any time getting angry, Bonham led him towards the horses.

At first sight, the scene at the castle was not as bad as they had expected. Most of the Fleming mercenaries and the knights were still arriving and were encamped in the fields around the castle. The summer sun bathed the village in light and on the surface; everything appeared peaceful with people going about their normal business. With closer inspection, Hugh noticed the local tradesmen were busy selling to the troops and plying their wears and there was even an orderly queue for the blacksmith.

Lord Ralf de Lahay had followed close behind and as they crossed the drawbridge and entered the inner bailey, a cheer rose from the knights assembled inside. About thirty were billeted inside the walls and they waved their banners and flags in unison at the Earl of Norfolk's arrival.

Lord de Lahay brought his palfrey alongside Hugh. 'You see Earl Bigod. I said you have no reason to fear my men...that they were well fed and well behaved.'

Since the moment they had met, Hugh had loathed Lord Ralf, and his constant reassurances did nothing to appease him. He dismounted and left Bonham to walk the horses to the stables with Terrowin. Walking past the chapel, he was pleased to see it untouched, with all the precious glass windows and carved door still intact. The kitchens were filled with staff, cheerfully preparing venison and game birds, and the knights quartered in the garrison house seemed in good humour. The grand hall door was open and he steeled himself for what he might find inside. Adjusting to the darkness, there were three knights sat around the table, enjoying a jug of wine. As he entered the room, they stood up and bowed.

The frown never left his face but his anger was beginning to abate, for he knew all along that the true test would be the state of his wife. About to enter her chamber he paused and knocked gently so as not to startle her. Gundred's maid, Ulrika opened the door and as he looked to the bed, he could see his wife was not awake.

Ulrika stood in front of Hugh and curtsied as she spoke quietly. 'My lord, I prayed for your swift return. Her lady-ship is well and is sleeping. The physician gave her a potion and she has slept peacefully since the soldiers came. But she was in a dreadful state when she heard the horses arrive with all the shouting and swearing. But on my oath, not one man has entered her apartments.'

Keeping his peace, Hugh walked to the bedside and saw for himself the terrible cost written on Gundred's face. Her eyes were circled with dark rings that looked even more pronounced against her thin lips and pale complexion. Under her pillow, he noticed a glint of metal and he picked up the knife that was hidden there, and tucked it into his belt.

'Sire, I beg you to open your heart and see the truth. Her lady-ship does not belong in the world of men. A few days ago, she was well enough to leave her bed. Then came the soldiers. I swear it is only her mind that is affected but after the last time…she cannot be blamed for feeling threatened.'

'Yes I know,' Hugh said flatly, walking to the door. 'Let me know when she wakes up.'

Bonham was waiting in the doorway, restless and impatient. 'Lord de Lahay is waiting downstairs. Food and drink is on the way.'

'Good, now let us hear what he has to say for himself.'

Hugh poured himself some wine and sat at the head of the table next to his guest and another six high-ranking knights were eagerly waiting for the food to arrive. 'My lord Ralf, I am pleased to say I appreciate the good conduct of your men. But I must ask that you take your leave at the earliest…'

'My lord, forgive me for interrupting but you do not seem to understand. All this has been agreed between you, the count and the young king. Tomorrow we are to ride into Norwich and you will be pronounced the lord of the city.'

Only Hugh heard the low, desolate moaning come from the floor above and the others at the table talked amongst themselves. Ulrika hurried down the stairs and discretely whispered in Hugh's ear.

Hugh turned to address Lord Ralf and the assembled knights. 'My lords, there has been a slight change of plan. We leave for Norwich this very night.'

Chapter 34

Norwich
Norfolk

Along the road from Ipswich to Norwich, Hugh rode at the head of thirty knights, three hundred men-at-arms and three hundred Fleming mercenaries. At his side were Lord de Lahay and his senior knight Bonham. Having left Framlingham well before dawn, they were all tired except for Hugh. The tribulations with Gundred still preyed on his mind as he stared blankly towards the horizon.

When Gundred had woken, her plaintive wailing had sent Ulrika running down the stairs to tell the earl that his wife was threatening to jump from the solar window unless the soldiers left. The visage that faced him no longer even looked like his wife. In her stead was a sick and demented woman who he barely recognised, whose soul had been tormented and torn beyond repair.

As he left Framlingham, he knew there was only one course of action he could take and he would have to rely on Ulrika to see to the arrangements while he was gone. At least the knights and the soldiers had left her in peace.

His explanation to Ralf de Lahay and his men sounded quite appropriate. They would leave for Norwich as soon as possible so as the city would be surprised at his arrival and have little time to mount a defence.

Once the city came into view, he began to remember his early days. Since he had been Constable and Governor of Norwich nearly sixty years ago, he had dreamt of this moment. Surely, there was no question the city would greet him with open arms as a saviour from an oppressive regime.

On the roadside, Hugh called a halt to the march and dismounted so he could stretch his legs and take some bread and honey from a stall. The shopkeeper and his son were scared stiff as their stock quickly dwindled to nothing. The earl introduced himself and asked the man to ride into Norwich to announce his imminent arrival, saying his son was capable of looking after his stall. Nervous of disappointing the earl, the man leapt onto his old horse too eagerly, hitting his face on the gravel road. To the sound of raucous laughter from the knights, he galloped off down the road. Bonham left a generous pile of coins for the boy and Earl Bigod mounted up to proudly lead his men on the last few miles to the south gate of Norwich.

The shopkeeper galloped through the gates, shouting at people as they went about their normal business to get out of the way. His words gave a dire warning, that an army led by Earl Bigod was fast approaching. The awful state of his bloodied face told its own story and the streets quickly emptied. He made straight for the Merchants Hall near the market place where he knew the wool master would be opening his warehouse. In less than half an hour, some fifty merchants had assembled in the hall. Led by three town burghers, all of them demanded to know what the shopkeeper had to say.

Everything had suddenly become serious and the truth suffered as his story took on a grievous turn. 'The earl himself stole all my goods for his men and threw me to the ground.'

'Where is your son?' shouted one of his friends. 'Did they take him?'

'I don't know where my son is. I hope he is looking after my stall.'

'We should be asking the whereabouts of the Castellan?' an anonymous voice shouted

'He will be sleeping with his wenches…we cannot rely on him?' answered another.

The meeting descended into a shambles and one town burgher

waved his arms in the air, calling for calm. 'We do not know that the earl means any harm. We are all aware he has always believed in his right to govern Norwich.'

'But what if you are wrong?' the same voice replied. 'What if he has come to sack and pillage...'

Just then, an excitable youngster ran into the hall. 'The soldiers are coming...the soldiers are coming...'

Since the days when his father had been the Sheriff of Norwich, each king had conspired against him to ensure he was denied what was rightfully his. 'Even the Empress Matilda broke her promise,' he muttered out loud.

'Pardon, my lord,' Bonham replied. 'I did not hear.'

Hugh gave a wry grin. 'Nothing. I was just reminiscing.'

Bonham took the opportunity to speak his mind. 'I hope it was a wise decision to warn the city of your arrival.'

'Warn them. You make it sound as if I intend to use force. No, this will be a homecoming. You know my father was the sheriff of Norwich and the first King Henry gave me the governorship of the city when I was but twenty.'

Bonham had heard of the reputation of the earl's father. 'Your father was one of the great barons of this land. I have seen his memorial gravestone in the great cathedral.'

Hugh went red in the face. 'Well...you are wrong,' he stammered. 'He should have been buried at the Priory in Thetford. It was the bishop you see...I was but a boy, but they stole his body on a litter...'

Bonham had heard the story before. Suddenly the earl appeared upset and incoherent, hardly able to get out his words. 'My lord, are you all right?'

The earl was obviously aggrieved by the memories that had been stirred from deep within. 'Don't you see. That is where it all started, with the death of my father. The bishop was an evil man who was intent on destroying my mother and me.'

Bonham spoke calmly. 'But surely the bishop was only trying to maximise the universal appeal of your father. He must have been well loved by the people to have a special place in Norwich Cathedral.'

'No, you don't understand. He humiliated my mother…'

'My lord, we are at the gates,' Bonham interrupted. 'You do not look well…are you sure you want to proceed?'

In the bright morning sun, Hugh was sweating profusely, his heart pounding furiously and under his mail hauberk he could hardly breathe. The wide-open gates of Norwich beckoned, and once inside his men slowed to a halt behind him.

Bonham was concerned for the earl's state of mind. 'I shall take a dozen men-at-arms and go on ahead, my lord. You should rest here a while till I return.'

Terrowin rode up alongside the earl and they both watched Bonham ride sedately down the main street with a small troop, towards the castle. Barring a few drunks, the streets of Norwich were empty of people. Not a soul was there to greet him; even the whores and beggars had stolen away.

As Bonham led the small troop through the market square, the crowds emerged from the side-streets suddenly emboldened by such a small force. The single knight led his men right up a small street that led to the enormous façade of the castle.

The town burghers and aldermen spilled out onto the market place to see for themselves, surprised that some troops were already inside the city gates. 'But they number only a dozen or so,' the burgher observed.

From across the drawbridge emerged the castellan. Somehow, he had managed to muster twenty men from the garrison and now confronted the knight. Large crowds of onlookers had gathered in the market square and were now pressed against the rear of the troop, preventing them from retreating.

The castellan had obviously dressed in a hurry and wore no chain mail or helmet and his horse bore no saddle. 'My name is Milton Revel, appointed by the king as castellan of this castle. Why are you here and what do you want?'

As a gesture of goodwill, Bonham took off his helmet. Nervously he glanced to his left and right, annoyed at himself for being so casually trapped in the tiny street. Compared to the castellan, his voice sounded thin. 'Earl Bigod declares Norwich as his God-given right,' the knight claimed.

From all around voices of discontent stirred. 'We don't want that prick here!' shouted one man.

'The man is a murdering bastard,' another cried.

Suddenly a large stone landed with a thud between the two horses and shattered amongst the hooves. Another followed, this time hitting Bonham on the head and he fell heavily to the ground. Immediately the men-at-arms surrounded Bonham, keeping the throng of citizens from trampling over the knight. Despite calls for calm from the castellan and the town burgers, the shouting intensified and a rain of stones followed.

One of the trapped soldiers panicked and stabbed blindly with his spear, with the inevitable consequence that a casualty fell to the ground. A cry of murder incensed the mob even more and the violence quickly escalated. Ordinary citizens grabbed whatever weapons were to hand and openly attacked the troop.

When Hugh arrived with his knights, the entire incident had escalated into a violent fracas. The sudden appearance of the knights led to an immediate panic amongst the citizens and many in the square turned to run away. Just two or three were so maddened they turned their staves and clubs onto the knights.

'Where is Bonham?' Hugh cried out. He caught the eye of the castellan who spun his horse around to head back to the castle but now he too found it difficult to move as the throng of citizens filled the street behind him.

One of the men-at-arms pushed his way through to the earl. 'My lord, I saw him fall from his horse. I fear he dead.'

Terrowin overheard the words and let out a piercing denial. 'No! They will not have him!' Pulling his sword from its scabbard, he pushed his horse forward, hacking at the skulls of those in his way.

Hugh watched frozen in his saddle as Terrowin cleaved a path into the midst of the fighting. Confused and frightened at the sight of his world crumbling about him, he ordered Ralf de Lahay to restore order. The lord simply let loose his men.

They came running down the slope yelling a war cry that chilled everyone who heard. Hugh tried to direct them into the street where Terrowin was outnumbered and now fighting for his life, but they made little headway. If he was to save the lives of Bonham and Terrowin, there was only one more course of action. Reluctantly, he ordered his knights into the fray.

The senseless carnage that followed depressed Hugh even further. As he was responsible for the slaughter, he knew he could not turn away for fear of losing the respect of his knights. Within half an hour, the street was lined with more than two hundred dead bodies and Hugh called for the knights to form up alongside. The foolish and the brave lay bleeding with the old and the young.

A priest and a handful of monks appeared from behind the row of houses. They had come from the cathedral at the outbreak of violence and now felt brave enough to give succour to the injured and the dying.

Hugh edged his horse forward as his captain stepped over the bodies to report.

'My lord, both Bonham and Terrowin lie amidst the fallen.' His head fell to his chest and Hugh noticed him wipe away a tear.

Hugh dismounted to see for himself and the captain pointed them out. Both bodies were in badly hacked and unrecognisable. The bile rose in his throat and he could hardly speak through the grief. 'Why did Terrowin lay into the crowd like a man possessed...why...'

The captain could not hold back the truth. 'My lord, did you not perceive what they held for each other. It was well known; they were more than knight and squire.'

Hugh was confused at first then a wave of nausea hit his stomach. Shouting came from behind as a large bearded man ran across the square. He was wielding a short axe and on a state of utter rage shouted that his son had been killed. He pushed aside two knights with ease but they slowed him down enough for him to loose his footing. A blow from a third knight hit his spine and crippled the giant; but not before he threw the axe with all his might. Spinning through the air, Hugh watched in horror as the blade struck his horse in the neck. The spray of blood that squirted into the air told its own story and before he could dismount, the beautiful stallion had fallen to its knees.

Ralf de Lahay rode into view and dismounted next to Hugh. 'So sorry my lord earl. That was a great destrier but there are many more that can take his place.'

Hugh did not bother to look up. He stroked the horse's head in it's final death throes. Spattered in blood, Hugh wiped his face with the back of his hand.

Intent on lifting the earl, Ralf gave a quick smile. 'My Flemings have captured many hostages for ransom and we now hold the castle. Norwich is yours, my lord.'

The veil of grief and sadness was replaced by utter desolation of spirit. Hugh stood up and looked at the castle then coughed as a swirl of thick smoke clawed at the back of his throat. The smell of burning even overpowered the raw stench of spilt blood.

The captain shouted from the square. 'The Flemings are putting the city to the torch. What shall we do my lord?'

Hugh stared at Ralf de Lahay and his voice hissed with malevolence. 'Let it burn. Every fucking house…every fucking street. Let it burn.'

Brooding over the devastating loss of Bonham and Terrowin, Hugh spent two days inside a large house in Norwich, simply saying he was in need of rest. There he grappled with the disaster of Norwich and his emotions as he tried in vain to understand the relationship of his two most trusted soldiers.

At the sight of Norwich burning, all his Framlingham knights drifted away, knowing at last that the ultimate prize had finally been laid to rest by the greedy hands of Flemish mercenaries. The foreigners filled the castle and a good night's sleep became a luxury that evaded Hugh.

Then without warning, on the third morning of his occupation, everything fell silent. He drifted downstairs and was met by the sight of Ralf de Lahay taking council from his senior knights.

Ralf stood up. 'My lord earl, you join us at an important time. We have just received word from the Count of Flanders.'

Hugh was astute enough to read the drawn expression on his face. 'Judging by your miserable visage, I assume it is bad news.'

Ralf gave an apologetic look. 'I do not blame you for being upset. None of this is your fault,'

Hugh kept his anger in check. 'So, what has happened?'

The Scots king has been captured along with all his generals, and the young king and the count have abandoned the invasion of England. They lost over a thousand men to a storm at sea, however they have successfully led the rest of their army into Normandie.'

Hugh sat down and took a swig from a cup of wine. 'If you say it quickly, it does not sound so bad, does it.'

Ralf looked bewildered at the sarcastic remark.

Hugh poured himself another cup. 'You are a fool, my lord Ralf. They never had any real intention of landing in England. While the king was in England, they were always going to attack Normandie.' Hugh finished the cup and poured another. 'But do not worry yourself, I was stupid enough to believe that Norwich was mine.'

'What do you advise, my lord earl.'

Hugh mulled over his cup and noticed that the smile had long gone from Ralf's face. 'Well I suggest you dig your ditches deep and your ramparts high, for the king will come at you like a lion who has not fed for a week.'

Ralf translated for his knights and they broke into fervent discussion.

'Of course I can help you out of this crisis.' The assembly fell silent again as the earl spoke. 'No doubt, you have made a fortune from your plunder and ransom. I will need that fortune to pay off the king and save your fucking miserable lives. I shall be leaving for Framlingham before middle day so I shall give you some time to discuss…my terms. Shall we say one hour.'

As they frantically argued, Hugh climbed the staircase from the great hall, up to the battlements. Clearing his head, he looked over the smouldering devastation around the city and the orderly lines of bodies awaiting burial, dutifully guarded by the monks. Two children cried, probably brother and sister as they held onto the hand of their dead mother. He should have wept at the sight of the homeless children and burnt out homes, but his body had been drained of all emotions. He wandered to the other side of the castle and noticed two of his squires were still in attendance in the stables.

Hugh decided the hour was up. He wanted desperately to leave the city once and for all. The health of his wife was praying on his mind and she was the one good thing ever to come from his long and sorrowful life. His duty to his family must come before his own foolish ambitions.

Entering the hall, it appeared the Flemings had made their decision. They carried four sacks of coins to the stables and he placed two over his mare while the squires took one each to the other horses. Hugh knew they had taken more than that but he was in no mood to argue.

Twenty Flemish horsemen escorted Hugh through the south gate but turned back after only two miles. A long journey back to Framlingham beckoned and the thought of carrying four thousand marks made Hugh all the more nervous.

Chapter 35

Canterbury
Kent

After serving his long penance at the tomb of Thomas Becket, King Henry was struck with a bout of lethargy and self-loathing. Feeling sorry for himself, he prepared to leave Canterbury and lick his wounds.

Then early the next morning, his chamber door opened to the calling of Bishop Gilbert, saying that a miracle had taken place. Gilbert could barely keep the excitement to himself as he told the king what had happened. 'The hand of God was directed by the sainted martyr and has snuffed out the rebellion with a single stroke.'

It was more than just a triumph. The rebellion was crushed and the king truly believed that he had finally made his peace with Becket. Never had Henry felt such elation and he quickly made plans to head north with his army and accept the surrender of his errant rebel lords.

First he took the surrender of Huntingdon, then entered Earl Bigod's territory, where he was informed that Hugh was willing to cede to his demands.

No one knew where Hugh was hiding but the king wasted no time finding out. 'We will simply take all his castles,' he announced to his council. 'The time has come to be taught his lesson.'

From Ipswich, the king rode east around the estuary for Walton castle and found no resistance from the small garrison of fifty men-at-arms. His marshal asked the king what should be done with the castle.

'Get Bigod's men to tear the bloody walls down,' he ordered. 'I can spare only a few to keep an eye on them, so threaten them with prison if they disobey my direct orders.'

The next day the king headed north to Framlingham, where he now assumed the earl had taken up residence to await his arrival. When it was discovered that Hugh had abandoned his stronghold, the king was at first surprised and began to show his irritation.

As with Walton, he proceeded to have the curtain walls pulled down by the sitting garrison then proceeded to instruct his council. 'My lords I am not going to play games with Earl Bigod. I want word spread that he shall be severely punished if I do not receive his surrender forthwith.'

No one argued with the king, for Earl Bigod had never had any supporters at court. Besides, since leaving Canterbury the king was held in such esteem no one dare even question his motives. Never had he become so unassailable.

'Perhaps the earl has fled abroad, my liege,' one royal steward ventured.

The king mulled over the thought. 'You mean to my son?'

'Or the Count of Flanders,' the steward offered, not wanting the king to dwell again on the misconduct of his crowned son, Harry.

'Yes, they are known to have a history, as well as a mutual admiration,' the king agreed.

Richard de Lucy rose stiffly from his chair and everyone sat up to pay attention to the ageing Justicar. 'We should not be deflected from the course on which you have now embarked, my liege. Destroying the earl's castles is the best defence. No rebel in his right mind will ever stand against you again. I suggest we proceed to Bungay then deal with Ralf de Lahay and his Flemings in Norwich.'

De Lucy sat down and the king thanked him for his undying loyalty as the council banged the table in appreciation at his wise and powerful words.

Before the king reached Bungay castle, it was confirmed that Earl

Bigod was in residence and willing to give his surrender. Many pondered why he would rather hide inside a castle much smaller than Framlingham, but the talk amongst the council now was the punishment he would receive.

To the north of Bungay Castle, King Henry lined up his army in an impressive formation and waited for his herald to return.

'My liege, the earl is slippery as an eel, you would be wise to insist on an unconditional surrender,' de Lucy advised as the herald approached. 'And don't let him know you have destroyed his castles.'

The herald bowed. 'My lord king, the earl asks that you approach the walls so that he can plead his case in person, and he swears on the life of his youngest son that it is a genuine plea.'

'I told you so,' de Lucy mused.

'How old is his youngest son?' the king asked, ignoring de Lucy's remark.

'He looked about eleven, sire.'

'Very well, let us get this over with.' The king rode forward, and the herald took his banner aloft, signifying to all at the castle that the king himself was approaching. A ripple of concern ran around his generals but before they could react, the king was waiting on the drawbridge staring up at the castle walls.

As Hugh was telling his son to wait in the keep while he negotiated with the king, his captain reported that he was already on the drawbridge. Hugh tugged his son's ear and smiled. 'You see, even the king of England waits for Earl Bigod.' He turned around and climbed the steps up to the top of the wall overlooking the drawbridge. 'Is everything ready,' Hugh asked his captain.

'All four bags are at your feet, my lord,' he replied.

Leaning over the wall, Hugh could see the king sat on his mighty black stallion. It reminded him for a moment of the beautiful destrier he had lost at Norwich. 'My lord king, I am indebted for your forbearance and I humbly await your demands.'

'My demands are quite simple. You and your men lay down your arms and surrender this castle forthwith.'

Hugh paused. 'I agree to your demands, my liege.'

The king held his tongue and tried not to show his surprise.

'No doubt you have already destroyed my other castles. That means I have nowhere to live, so where am I supposed to look after my sick wife and bring up my son?'

'You should have thought of that before you rebelled again. My generals were much too lenient and I don't intend to make the same mistake again.'

'I was led astray by your own son, making false promises to an old soldier like me. I pray my son Hugh never treats me like shit,' Hugh said, trying to find any weakness in the king's thick skin.'

For a moment, the king blanched then quickly recovered his composure. 'If you have no abode in this country then so much the better.'

'Then I shall live abroad,' Hugh retorted, noting he had achieved his first concession.

'Very well,' agreed the king reluctantly. The same thought kept entering his head. What had he to fear from a seventy-eight year old?

'I shall come down now. Will you agree not to harm or punish my wife and children.'

'Of course, that goes without saying. Come on now, I am waiting.'

At last thought Hugh, the king was growing impatient. 'I have a present for you to ensure their safety and safe passage home for the Flemings.' Hugh started to lower a sack of marks over the wall.

'I don't know about that…what is in the sack?' the king asked.

The sack dangled over the drawbridge. 'One thousand marks if you agree to my simple request of safe passage.'

The king looked to his herald and was unable to hide his shock. The offer of such a vast sum of money was a total surprise. The sack was lowered to the ground and the herald confirmed the approximate value was correct. 'Shall I take the money, my liege,' the herald asked.

'Take it straight back to the Justicar,' the king ordered as he slowly turned his horse around.

'We are coming out now!' Earl Bigod proclaimed for all to hear. The gates opened, and the Earl of Norfolk rode out alongside his son, followed by his captain, four sergeants and seven squires. They rode casually up to the front ranks of the king's army, numbering some four hundred knights and two thousand infantry.

Everyone stared in disbelief. 'Where are the rest of your men?' demanded de Lucy.

'What you see is what you get, my lord Justicar. I have disbanded my entire army. As for my wife, as of two days ago she was admitted to the nunnery across the way. God bless her sad soul.'

The king sidled up alongside Hugh. 'I notice your sergeants carry three more bags.'

'This is my donation to the nunnery, to ensure my wife is well cared for. I am sure you would not deny Christ and his blessed servants have a cut of the cake.'

The king was speechless, knowing he could have demanded more for the earl's release. He rode off without another word.

Hugh smiled at de Lucy. 'I suggest that I shall ride with you to Norwich to peacefully secure the release and safe passage of Lord Ralf Lahay and his Fleming contingent,'

The Justicar spun round to face the herald. 'Surely we did not agree to give safe passage to the Flemings?'

The herald gave blank look then nodded. 'The earl is correct...that is to say...'

Hugh was far from finished. 'You will also find the king agreed not to harm or punish any of my family. You understand that does include my son, Roger.'

De Lucy was outraged. 'What! After what he did to the earl of Leicester's wife, I think not...'

'The king accepted the money thereby agreeing to the terms, my lord,' the herald interrupted.

'You think you are so clever, you traitorous bastard,' de Lucy scowled. 'But you have nowhere to live and I will see to it you are hounded out of the country.'

Suddenly a cry was heard from the left flank about fifty paces away and chaos broke out amongst the Templars who were providing a bodyguard for the king.

Hugh followed de Lucy to look at the cause of the outcry. Apparently while the king was loading the bag of marks onto the horse of Tostes de St Omer, it kicked out hitting him severely on the leg. Surrounded by his knights the king was crying in pain as they pulled down his britches to see if his leg was broken.

With a broad grin on his face, Hugh returned to his men, secretly delighted that the king had received what was owing to him. 'Maybe there is a God after all,' he muttered to himself.

The smile soon disappeared from Hugh's face when a dozen of the kings' sappers set about dismantling the walls and keep of his castle. As he left the field for Norwich, he forced a glance across the road towards the nunnery, and the reality of his plight began to darken his mood.

'Are we leaving Mama behind?' his son asked.

'I told you she is unwell and needs some time to get better.' Hugh felt for his son's anguish, then told himself his son would have to bear such sadness and disappointment with stoic determination, just as he had done for the whole of his life.

Chapter 36

Damascus
Syria

For more than a week, Saladin waited at his father's house in Damascus, leaving his army of seven hundred horsemen in the orchards to the south. The people had greeted him enthusiastically and the city elders were impressed when he undertook his solemn pilgrimage to pray at his old family home.

Eventually a messenger arrived to formally invite him to the Citadel, where he received homage from the elders and councillors. The installation looked likely to take all day so Maimonides and Baruch found a quiet corner on a terrace that caught the morning breeze.

Baruch was still nervous of his surroundings though he appreciated his friend was trying to make him feel more comfortable. It was the first chance they had to talk at any length.

'So tell me about your master, Rabbi Jacob ben Meir. News of his death in Blois shocked the Jews all across the east as well as the slaughter of the innocent families he was trying to protect.'

Baruch closed his eyes as he recalled the painful memory. 'I was there. I dragged him from the flames and nursed him for weeks before he finally succumbed.'

'He must have been a great man,' Maimonides nodded slowly.

Baruch paused as he searched for the right words. 'On his deathbed, Jacob entrusted me with two tasks and I have sworn to uphold my promise. One was to discuss with you ways of protecting the Jews from persecution. The problem has been bad for many years across many provinces. And I know you are famous for protecting the Jews of Fustat during the fire that burnt half the city to the ground.'

Maimonides ignored the compliment. 'Since the fire I have given instructions to many Jewish communities to organise a central fund that can be used to buy their freedom if such a monstrous act occurred again.'

'Together, we could write a universal format that all Rabbi's could follow,' Baruch said optimistically as he wrote some notes in his journal.

'You said there were two tasks you had to fulfil.'

Baruch immediately looked serious again. 'At the age of five, Jacob witnessed the death of his grandfather Rashi, the greatest Rabbi of all. One of his first memories was of a giant demon that smiled as his grandfather's chamber was filled with the flames from hell.'

Maimonides calculated the years. 'That must have been some seventy years ago.'

'In the anti-Jewish riots at his home in Ramerupt, Jacob was nearly burnt to death. He owed his life to a Christian knight who died in a small town near Jerusalem.' Baruch sighed and squirmed in his chair, uncomfortable at having to explain the story. 'Rashi was one of the most skilled translators of his time but this one particular translation was like a curse that led to the deaths of everyone who read the words.'

'Please, go on,' Maimonides urged.

'There is a secret held in the church crypt at Lydda. Once it is revealed…the consequences are too great for the world. I don't know if I dare say anymore…'

Maimonides was stunned. He could not believe that the story of the sphere had somehow fallen into the hands of the Rabbi's of the western provinces. 'You don't have to say anymore. Saladin and I know all about the…ancient secret in the crypt. As soon as Saladin has gathered his army, we will take Lydda to prevent it from falling into the wrong hands. Then he will besiege Jerusalem. But tell me, how do you know about the secret of the chamber under the crypt?'

Now that he understood Saladin's plans, Baruch was in two minds as to what to say.

The awkward silence was shattered by a shout from the other end of the terrace and they both turned to see Saladin's vizier calling for them to return to the stables immediately.

They hurried across the courtyard, wondering what had happened. Saladin was already mounted on his black stallion. His face was red with anger and he leant over to speak with Maimonides. 'The fools have let General Gumushtugin take the regency. While we waited at my fathers house, he paid off the Governor and his cronies then rode off to Aleppo, assembling his army along the way.'

'Where are we going?' Maimonides asked breathlessly.

'To Aleppo of course. We will commence the siege while the rest of my army comes from Egypt.'

The siege was not going well and Saladin was becoming impatient. Every day, Gumushtugin sallied from the fortress to disrupt his supply lines and attack his siege engines. On the third night, Saladin wearily took to his tent, only to be disturbed by shouting coming from his guards. Listening to the sounds of clashing swords, it was apparent they were under attack.

By the time his Mameluke bodyguards had surrounded him it was all over. The captain of the guard appeared holding a lamp and a bloody sword to report that thirteen assassins had penetrated the camp but all of them had been killed.

Saladin was outraged. 'I knew it! The bastards will not stop until they have killed me. Tell the men to assemble at dawn. We are heading into the al-Nusayri mountains and we will attack the villages and strongholds of Rashid ad-Din Sinan, until he surrenders.'

Maimonides had been drawn to the commotion and took Saladin to one side. 'My lord, I do not believe these were the assassins of Rashid. They attack with stealth, in ones or twos, not thirteen at a time.'

Saladin dismissed his opinion. 'If they are not the old man's assassins then whose are they?'

A cry for help from one of the tents echoed through the camp and they all ran towards the sound with swords drawn.

'That is Baruch!' Maimonides yelled as he pushed in front of the guards and ran to his friends tent. Pulling the flap aside, he saw a servant trembling over Baruch's bed, mopping up the blood seeping through the sheets.

'Bring hot water and strips of clean linen,' Maimonides ordered as he pulled back the sheets to inspect the knife wound. The blood was deep crimson and he suspected the blade had pierced the lungs. He pressed down hard to stop the bleeding but it still seeped through his fingers. Feeling for a pulse, he was relieved to feel it was still quite strong.

Saladin entered the tent and looked pale in the weak lamplight. 'This was to be my tent. Your friend came here by mistake. That could have been me.'

The servant returned with bandages and hot water and Maimonides asked for more lamps so he could stitch the wound. Slowly the tent emptied and the physician threaded the catgut into his needle. Pulling against the skin Baruch squirmed as the needle did its work, then he fell unconscious.

Throughout the night, he monitored the bubbling sound coming from Baruch's chest. The sound of the army setting off at dawn did not deflect Maimonides from his charge. At middle morning, Baruch woke up and Maimonides gave him a draft of white poppy juice to help quell the pain. Only time would tell now whether his friend lived or not. If the cut became infected, and his blood poisoned then it was likely he would die.

He charged his assistant with looking after Baruch while he searched out the bodies of the assassins. They had been piled up unceremoniously at the edge of the camp and a group of gossiping gravediggers sat nearby. As soon as they saw Maimonides, they picked up their shovels and started digging enthusiastically. He ignored them, but studied the tangled bodies of the assassins. None of them wore face-masks and at least six of them were clothed in a uniform under their cloaks. Some wore helmets with the same markings.

One of the diggers was bold enough to speak out. 'They are not assassins sent by the old man. They are soldiers dressed up to look like assassins.'

'How do you know that?' Maimonides asked, coming to the same conclusion.

'Cos I've seen the real thing. Rashid ad-Din Sinan is his name but they call him the old man of the mountains. His men are called hashasshins because they fill the lungs with demon smoke that makes them near invincible. Or so they think.'

Maimonides threw the man a coin in appreciation of his candour. 'You had better keep your supposition to yourself.'

The men pulled the bodies along the ground towards the pit they were digging and Maimonides noticed the arrowheads sticking out of the backs of nearly all of them. One thing he had learnt about Rashid's assassins is that they never turned away from a fight. They would rather die as martyrs than show cowardice in the face of their enemy. So how was it he wondered, that most of the soldiers had been brought down as they ran away?

A call from his tent distracted his thinking. He hurried back to Baruch, who was sat up in bed talking quite lucidly to the servant even though his face was pale and his voice sounded congested and breathless. 'I don't have much time. Before Rabbi Jacob died, he made me promise to use the Gospel of Nicodemus wisely. I understand now what he meant…why he knew it was so important and I charge you, as a good Jew, to keep that promise on my behalf. 'The shame' is a powerful tool that can be used to elicit much obligation from the Christians. They will do anything to have such a relic. We Jews must make them pay with guarantees that cannot be overturned. With your wisdom, the secret of the cross can buy back the Promised Land. The Christians will oblige rather than see the relic exposed for what it is. For the sake of the Jewish race, you must succeed. Inside the secret chamber…you must take down the crossbeam and…' Blood started bubbling from the corner of his mouth and then he coughed a bright red mouthful across his sheets.

Maimonides knew his friend was dying and the slow realisation of his words began to dawn on him.

Baruch had another coughing fit and spat out more blood onto the bed. 'My friend, listen to my words. From the beginning to the end, I give you the true story.

Maimonides listened to every painful word that racked the dying body of his friend. He did not sedate him for fear of letting him sleep. All Maimonides could do was watch Baruch tell his tale as he battled against the fever, shaking uncontrollably throughout his barely coherent story. In the end, he just prayed that Baruch had found some comfort in his last hours.

Saladin's forces ran amok through some minor settlements within the territory governed by Rashid ad-Din Sinan, the old man of the mountains. But there was little they could do to penetrate the impregnable hill top fortresses that dominated the al-Nusayri mountain range.

One morning in the hours before dawn, he lay awake in his tent. Turning over in his bed, the hours passed slowly as he began to question the wisdom of spending months, if not years, flailing around trying to take cities and fortresses without any coherent plan. He sat up, determined that it was time to rethink his strategy.

Someone entered his tent and he turned to see who it might be. There was no light, and although he felt the compunction to cry out, he could not utter a sound. He heard a grunt and the unmistakable sound of a dying breath, only five paces from his bed. A diffuse moonlit sky barely penetrated the tarpaulin but he could make out the figure of a man holding a knife across the throat of another. Then slowly the dead one sank to the ground. The man put the knife away and sat at the foot of his bed. Not only was Saladin unable to speak he found he could not move any of his limbs. He even wondered if he was still asleep and everything around him was only a dream.

The old man had a grimy face and long hair and his simple clothing was typical of the traditional mountain villagers. His voice was high pitched with a heavy accent that sounded almost comical if the circumstances were not so terrifying. 'These men who attack you…it is pathetic and an insult to believe they work for me. I have no argument with you, Saladin, but I want you stop these incursions against my people now. Those that say I tarnish you with the same brush as Nuradin are liars. Behold the truth. Gumushtugin approached me to do his dirty work and order your death, but I refused, for he is a man of little virtue or consequence. You, on the other hand, I find interesting, though you are easily fooled. While your anger blinds you to the truth, Gumushtugin bides his time strengthening his army in Aleppo.' The old man stood up. 'I shall leave you to revise your plans but let me say this. I hope for your sake we do not become enemies.' Like a ghostly shadow of the night, Rashid ad-Din Sinan slid towards the open tent flap.

Still Saladin was unable to move or speak.

The old man turned around to speak. There is one more thing, so as there is no confusion. Neither Gumushtugin nor I were responsible for the death of Amalric or Nuradin. I give you this warning free of charge. Another party seeks the same as you. I consider him a dangerous man whose powers far exceed my own. And by all accounts he knows you very well.'

In the blink of an eye he disappeared and Saladin felt his arms and legs tingling. He crawled from his bed and stumbled outside the tent. All the guards were scattered about the tents, some sat in a daze others simply asleep.

He wanted to see where the old man of the mountains had gone but the astonishing sight that lit up the sky took his breath away. A blaze of crimson and orange lights coalesced and danced along the horizon. Never before had he seen such a display of night-lights. For a moment, he stood transfixed, as if the swish of a curtain had stirred up a river of blood across the sky.

His wonderment was quickly replaced with trepidation and he gave the order to leave the mountains and return to the camp outside Aleppo. The captain of his Mameluke guard had no recollection of seeing any intruders that night, though he still appeared to be confused and bewildered. He remained baffled right up the moment his head was sliced from his body by Saladin's executioner. No one was happier than Saladin to be leaving the strange mountains, steeped in fear and menace around every corner.

Arriving back at camp the next day, Saladin made straight for the tent where he had left Maimonides and noticed immediately that Baruch was no longer there. Respectfully, he dipped his head and muttered a prayer before ordering the servants to leave.

Maimonides told him how Baruch had died a horrible, demeaning death and of the terrible pain he had endured.

Saladin listened in silence throughout and when he had finished the look on his face turned sour. 'That could have been me. I was the target, not your friend.' He proceeded to tell Maimonides of the campaign, and his strange paralysing encounter with the old man of the mountains. 'You were right about Gumushtugin being behind the assassinations,' Saladin acknowledged. 'But the old man warned me someone else was behind the deaths of Nuradin and Amalric.'

'And now there is another victim,' Maimonides replied flatly. 'I heard today that Miles de Plancey, the acting Governor of Jerusalem was assassinated just a week ago in Acre. The Christians are rudderless. But don't you see, it is as if someone is making your rise to power too easy.'

Saladin remembered the dire warning given by the old man about the anonymous assassin. He was about to tell Maimonides but bit his tongue and clenched his fist. 'So we should press our advantage and raise an army. Yes…after I take my revenge against Gumushtugin, only then will it be safe to proceed…'

'Oh for the sake of all our souls, just make your peace with Rashid ad-Din Sinan,' Maimonides retorted sharply. 'Stop this madness of running after your enemies and use your head for a change. If you pay the old man enough gold, he will gladly have Gumushtugin assassinated. That fat pig of Aleppo has made a fool of both of you!'

Saladin was surprised by the outburst but put it down to Maimonides still suffering the bereavement of his friend and walked from the tent without another word. He would let him grieve alone.

Maimonides could have told Saladin that he was knew who was responsible for the assassinations of Nuradin, Amalric and now de Plancey. But he was irritated by Saladin's lack of direction and did not want to irritate him again with talk of the assassin. Anyway, he suspected that Saladin knew deep down it was Muzawi.

Now another dilemma prayed on his mind. Should he tell Saladin the story of the Shame of Nicodemus and more importantly if he did tell him, could he trust Saladin to do what was right?

There was no reason to disbelieve the words of a dying man and if

Baruch was proved right and if the story was true, then the fate of all Jews in the Holy Land was at stake. And would Saladin give a single moment to consider the fate of the Jews?

Maimonides sighed as he went from the tent and looked up at the stars. Nothing he said or did could change the course of events to come. The night before, he had seen the aurora light up the night sky and knew it to be the final harbinger, giving bloody notice of the battle to come.

He wondered what the Sky Gods thought. Then again, he doubted they cared or were even interested. But of one thing he was certain. The prophetic words of the great Thabit ibn Qurra were destined to come true. The battle between good and evil would take place at the gates of Lydda and the confrontation would seal the fate of the world, once and for all.

Chapter 37

Hedingham Castle
Suffolk

Hugh remembered the night he was told that Canterbury Cathedral had burnt down.

It was the same night he witnessed a display of night-lights that blazed across the sky. Like shimmering curtains of crimson and orange, that emptied the streets of all but the brave. Many saw the display as an omen of bad tidings, while others determined it was a sure sign that God had left his mark on Canterbury.

The king had told everyone that his victory over his rebellious sons and the French King was due to his penance in front of Becket.

Now, only a month later, Hugh grinned, reflecting on God's ability to punish anyone who had become too proud and arrogant to believe a simple prayer and a few lashes were sufficient to excuse the murder of His archbishop.

His attention turned back to his wife and he accepted that little more could be done. The money he had bestowed with the Bungay Prioress was more than sufficient for the continuing care of his wife and although she reassured him that Gundred would fully recover from her malaise, Hugh privately doubted her damaged mind would ever be normal again.

Young Hugh had been entrusted to the de Vere family at Hedingham castle and he waited until his thirteenth birthday before visiting and spending some time with his son.

Despite a life striven by violence and war, young Hugh had grown up strong, learned and well adjusted. The de Vere family had remained reliable friends and undertook to bring him up to be a fine lord and earl.

While walking along the ramparts one evening, Hugh asked the Earl de Vere if he could speak in private. The earl dismissed the attending servant and squire and they sat down to watch the moon rise through the silver-lined clouds.

Hugh stared into the bright orb, his voice quiet and easily lost in the breeze. 'For many years your father was a good friend of mine. I thank you for your generosity and goodwill in looking after my interests while I am abroad. But I have one further favour to ask.'

Earl de Vere nodded. 'Please go on.'

Hugh paused, finding the words difficult. 'Near Worcester is Pinley Priory. There is a girl now aged five or six. She is the daughter of my wife Gundred, though not a child of mine. I tell you this because…I don't think my wife wants to remember. But someone has to know the truth. No one should live a life in ignorance of their parenthood. Perhaps, when the girl is old enough, you can tell her who her mother was.'

Hugh wanted to say more but the Earl de Vere placed his hand on Hugh's shoulder and poured them both some wine. He solemnly raised his goblet. 'Consider it my honour to protect her from ill-will and to carry out your wishes.'

'Thank you,' Hugh said, feeling relieved of the burden of responsibility.

'And what does the future hold for you?' de Vere asked.

'I shall live out my days under the protection of Count Philip of Flanders. He has Gravensteen castle in Ghent…but of course I shall visit Hedingham again.'

Both earl's knew that would be unlikely.

Hugh knew with his passing, the future of the earldom would take more than just fine words and good intentions. Inevitably, there would strife between young Hugh and Roger, as they fought over his legacy, for all it was worth.

Since the day of Roger's arrest in London, he had not seen his son, although it was well rumoured that the king had agreed to show leniency and to keep him under house arrest at his pleasure. There was little to be gained from seeing him again and nothing he could add to the last time they met.

Now as he approached his eightieth year, Hugh had decided it was time to make amends for his past, before departing to Flanders. There was an ancient warrior to settle his account with. News had reached him that the health of Earl Wills of Arundel was failing fast.

His arrival at the gates of Wymondham Abbey caused quite a stir amongst the monks.

Hugh muttered to Humphrey his young squire.' Bloody hell, don't they know the rebellion is over.' Hugh ordered him to ride on ahead to quell their fears and announce his presence. The eighteen-year-old had been in his service for just two years, but had proved capable of looking after his stallion and mare. His other charge was James, a middle aged and competent servant who had served the household well.

Although on the surface they both showed loyalty to Hugh, he doubted they would stay with him if given a better opportunity.

The third rider to accompany him remained quiet in his saddle. Hugh asked him if he had ever met Earl Wills before and he shook his head.

Hugh had grown to hate all religious houses and as he entered the stable of Wymondham Abbey, he saw nothing different to all the other houses of the holy.

The unnatural austerity clawed at him from every stone. How anyone found soulful sanctuary inside such cold, grey walls was beyond him.

Appearing from a side door, the abbot seemed flustered and gave a forced smile as he formally greeted the Earl of Norfolk. As his squire and servant weaved their way to the refectory, the abbot looked towards Hugh's mystery guest but there was no inclination to introduce him.

Leading them through the infirmary, the abbot confirmed that Earl Wills had agreed to see Hugh, and led them into a private chamber adjoining the infirmary. The light from a single window barely lit the interior and the abbot lit two candles for the benefit of the guests.

Hugh was disturbed by the sickly appearance of Wills. Sat up in his bed, the broad chest had disappeared and the hollow features on his pock marked face showed little of his former command and presence.

The attentive abbot brought some hot wine from the refectory and said they should call if they required anything further, before leaving the three of them alone.

'You look well,' Hugh lied, pulling up the only chair in the room alongside the bed. 'Have they said what ails you?'

Wills stared wide-eyed at Hugh, and spoke with a surprisingly strong voice. 'Old age and aching joints, mostly. My legs are useless, unable to walk for weeks now. Then I see how much weight you have lost and how healthy you look, and I wonder if there is a God.'

Hugh ignored the cynicism. 'I may be blest with rude health, but my prospects are non-existent.'

'As are mine, believe it or not.' Wills said, studying Hugh's guest. 'Aren't you going to introduce me?'

'I am sorry; this is Simon de Moorslede and he is the aide-de-camp to Count Philip of Flanders. He has come to England on the orders of Count Philip, to escort me to Flanders.

'And why would he do that?' Wills asked, refusing to return the smile from the aide. He considered most men from Flanders as enemies of the king.

'The count became aware of my personal predicament and invited me to stay at Gravensteen in Ghent for as long as I wanted. I intend to live out my years in Flanders instead of ending my days in misery, cowing down to King Henry. My son Hugh will remain at Hedingham for the time being and will be able to visit his mother.'

Simon stepped forward to speak. 'The count has respected Earl Bigod for many years and he is very grateful for his intervention and his kindness. He is particularly grateful for overseeing the release of the Flemings from Norwich Castle after the rebellion.'

The depiction of Hugh as a kindly character drew a sceptical smile from Wills. 'Well I am sure you and the count have much in common. At least I have the good abbot to care for my needs and the Lord God to forgive my sins. Do you intend to fill your remaining time with more acts of kindness in order to earn redemption from your sins?'

Hugh gave an embarrassed smile. 'I suppose not.' He asked Simon to join the others in the refectory so he could be alone with Wills.

In the awkward silence, they looked at each other, self consciously sipping their wine.

Wills shifted his weight and grimaced. 'Have you seen Norwich lately. Its still a bloody mess but unlike you it will recover from its tribulations.'

The mention of Norwich immediately rankled with Hugh. 'Norwich was always denied me. My father was once Sheriff and all I wanted was to follow…'

'Norwich was denied you by Theobald, King Stephen's brother,' Wills interrupted.

Hugh looked baffled. 'But why…what possible reason…'

Wills smiled at the irony. 'Oh Hugh, there is so much of which you are blissfully unaware. Theobald let Stephen be king on the condition that you would not receive any benefit from Norwich. The reason, I am told, is because your brother William persuaded his beloved uncle, Count Hugues of Champagne to go to the Holy Land searching for relics. Hugues died within a few weeks and Theobald blamed the Bigod name with a vengeance. He would not concede any Bigod acquiring any benefit under Stephen.'

Hugh stood up and walked to the window, his fists clenched as he tried to absorb the consequences of his guilty past.

Wills guffawed. 'Always quick to show anger, even when it is a result of your own doing.'

Against his instincts, Hugh bit his tongue. The tension eased as the abbot passed the door and asked if he could bring some more wine. Hugh nodded his approval.

'The abbot is a good man,' Wills remarked. 'I shall find some solace here in what time I have left.'

A cold stillness dropped like a stone between them. Hugh thought it was time to clear the air and redirected the conversation. 'I thought your abbot reminded me of Stephen, Prior of Thetford, when we were children, without a care in the world.'

'I cannot remember a time when I never had a care in the world,' Wills said gruffly.

Hugh took a gulp of wine and wiped the corner of his mouth. 'Do you remember when Bishop Herbert and Abbot Bund interrogated us over the relics brought by our Uncle Ilger. How the bishop beat me and sodomised me over the altar, and you watched from the scaffolding...and neither you nor William did anything to stop them...'

'Wait...wait a moment. Why do you wait a lifetime to bring that up...unless it has prayed on your mind all that time? Heaven preserve us, you really are sick in the head.'

Hugh leapt to his feet in indignation. 'You say I am sick! What of those bastards that sodomised me! Christ, I was only eleven and you saw them... you saw what they did!' Hugh tried to hide the tears of shame that formed in his eyes.

Wills stared at Hugh and spoke quietly. 'Sit down you stupid bastard and I will tell you what I saw,' he said defiantly. To aid his memory he closed his eyes. 'I remember the bishop dragging you from the classroom into the church. Your brother stayed in the classroom, silently praying like me that we would not have to answer to the bishop's cane. Abbot Bund told us to remain seated. But I panicked and crept into the church to hide. I climbed up to the scaffolding that ran the length of the new church aisle. From on high I looked down at the bishop as he held you by the wrists while Abbot Bund was caning you. But then the bishop returned to the classroom.'

'No...no that's not right...' Hugh stammered, his eyes blinking.

Wills ignored Hugh, his face fraught in concentration. 'Then the bishop left and Father Adam entered the church through a different door. He told Bund to go to the classroom door and stop anyone from entering the nave. Bund did as he was told. It was the priest who drugged and sodomised you...not Bishop Herbert or Abbot Bund, though I dare say they could have prevented it. And as for William, he never knew what was happening. He never left the classroom.'

Hugh became agitated. 'Yes he did...I saw him with Abbot Bund in the confessional, sucking his cock...William grinned at me...'

Alarmed at the claim, Wills sat up grimacing with the pain. 'No you stupid sod. Bund saw you being sodomised and pulled Father Adam away from you and into the confessional. He sat down and pushed him onto his knees and ordered him to pray for forgiveness.'

Hugh looked aghast. 'But it was William...'

Wills shook his head and repeated. 'No...William stayed in the classroom. He assumed you had just received a few strokes of the cane and was just as scared as the rest of us.' Wills could see the pain written on Hugh's face and he lay back against his pillows, breathing heavily from his exertions. He closed his eyes. 'Surely you remember, Father Adam and your brother were the same stature. They were both dressed in quire smocks, for quire practice. You stupid bugger…you mistook the priest for your brother.'

A flood of guilt engulfed Hugh and his life-long memories that had twisted and haunted him all his life, were smashed to pieces upon the cold, hard stone of reality. 'He…he kept plying me with poppy juice...my sight was blurred but I was sure it was William…and I saw you in the scaffolding and you did nothing…'

'For Christ's sake Hugh, I was about seven years old and had no way of telling perversion from punishment. All I remember was being scared out of my wits. If I had been caught up there...'

Hugh hoped the earth would swallow him up. 'All this time I blamed William because I thought he laughed at me while enjoying his perversions. Then afterwards, he seemed to spend all his time thereafter with the monks…'

'Yes and it was all to do with estate business. By then your imagination was so twisted by what happened, you were blind to the truth. And for all those years of drunkenness, I looked after you…like a big brother,' Wills recalled. 'We all suffered in silence but all we wanted was to forget what had happened. Yes, I am sure Father Adam and the abbot had perverse leanings to each other but why would your brother know anything?'

Hugh visibly sagged in his chair and his bitterness fell away. 'I hated both of you so much. You were my best friend and he stole you away from me.'

Wills scowled. 'Is that why you kept him imprisoned in Normandie after he survived the White Ship disaster? Because you hated him for befriending me.'

Wanting to hide from the world, Hugh held his head in his hands.

Wills became visibly angry. 'You took his title and his earldom, because you hated him. They cut out his tongue because you hated him. You lost the respect of your son, because you hated him.'

Hugh stood up and turned away from his accuser, reeling from the waves of nausea in the pit of his stomach. His secret world of acrimony and lies that had pervaded his entire life was laid bare on the altar of despair.

Again, the silence fell between them. Only the singing of psalms echoed in the distance.

Eventually Hugh found the courage to speak. 'How did you find out?' Hugh whispered, staring at the wall.

'Years ago, the Grand Master of the English Knights Templar came back from the Holy Land and told me the story of your brother. William is still honoured by the Order as a hero who fought alongside Hugo de Payen and the founding Knights.'

Tears stung his eyes as Hugh stared at the wall wistfully, trying to recall the years that had passed him by. 'There was a night at the Abbey of St Bertin, in St Omer that I shall never forget…some fifty years ago. The night William Cliton died and Thierry took his place as the Count of Flanders. The de Payen knight was sat on Cliton's deathbed. By God's breath, no wonder he questioned Stephen so intensely.'

Wills shook his head in dismay. 'You were lucky he did not run you through with his sword.'

Again, they sat in silence as old wounds were uncovered and past trials stirred their thoughts.

'When did my brother die?' Hugh asked sadly.

'Who said he was dead.'

Hugh's face lit up. 'You mean to tell me he still lives…'

'And there it is…at last. Do I see the truth reveal itself just as the veil of lies is finally lifted? So Lord Bigod, have you by chance, now found your path to redemption? In order to lift your excommunication, you must seek absolution for your sins in the Holy Land. You must relinquish your earthly chattels and seek out your brother William, the true Earl of Norfolk, and plead for his forgiveness…before it is too late. The salvation of your soul is at stake.'

Hugh huffed. 'You think I am going to the Holy Land at my age...I do not think so...'

'You must. Your entire life has been a lie and it is the only way you can redeem your soul. You have been stripped of your castles and your Earldom is null and void. There is nothing left for you in this country or with those Fleming bastards.'

Simon appeared at the door, embarrassed at the cursing. 'Earl Bigod, the hour is against us if we wish make Dover by tomorrow. It is time we left for the coast.'

A frown appeared on Wills face. 'One day that shell of yours will break open and a human being will be revealed. Before you go, I must ask that human being a favour. Just one favour, in return for all the pain you have inflicted upon others.'

Hugh nodded his head shamefully.

'In her final years, my wife Queen Alice took an exceptional artefact...a vase or jar from the Holy Land, inscribed with ancient writing. She loved the piece and I believe she kept it near her until her death. I would like to honour her memory by having the vessel with me...as my final days approach.'

A passing memory jolted Hugh then drifted away without leaving an impression. 'A vase you say. So where will I find it?'

'God willing, it should still be where she was laid to rest. She died at Afflighem Abbey, just a few miles from Ghent.'

Hugh nodded to the request and turned to leave the chamber. 'I wish you well in your recovery...'

'Hugh...please reconsider. Your brother in the Holy Land.'

'I am sorry for everything...so sorry.' Hugh left the room.

Chapter 38

Dover
Kent

It had been a harsh winter and the northerly winds had ripped apart last summers harvest. Famine was rife and there was even talk of a plague breaking out in the West Country. Times were as dire as Hugh could remember and he looked forward to his imminent departure from England, for what would probably be the last time.

He received a message from Count Philip saying it would be an honour to greet Hugh personally and they were to meet at St Omer in about five days time.

A boat was waiting for them at Dover and the night before the morning tide, he sat with Simon in lodgings overlooking the harbour. That night, the aide discovered he had a taste for English beer and Hugh plied him with another jug before taking the opportunity to talk about the count.

'So I understand the count is married but has no children,' he asked boldly.

Simon nodded. 'They have tried, but God does not bless them with a child. Anyway, it is probably for the best,' Simon slurped from his pewter cup.

'Oh, why do you say that?'

'The count suspects the countess is having an affair but alas he has no proof…yet.' Simon giggled. 'I should not say this but the count is so sure of her guilt, he has already planned his revenge.'

Hugh pricked up his ears. 'You mean he has found someone else to scratch his itch. Who on earth could that be?'

'Don't worry; I am sure you will find out soon enough. But not from my lips.' Simon yawned and closed his eyes. 'Oh Jesus Christ help me...my head is spinning. I must get some sleep before we sail.'

Just then, the captain of the ship walked into the inn and in deference to the status of his passengers, he shouted across the room. 'The tide has turned my lords. Your horses are stowed and we are ready to sail now, if you please.'

No one on board the ship escaped the sickness and nausea as the bow lurched precariously into the sides of the swell. Hugh barely managed to keep his stomach contents down and could spare little sympathy for Simon who was sick even before they left the harbour. By the time they landed on the coast of Flanders, the aide was so ill he found it difficult to walk and his squire had to hold him in the saddle for the twelve-mile ride to St Omer.

They were met at the town gates by one of Count Philip's stewards who led them through the streets to the Abbey of St Bertin, close to the river. By now, Simon had bravely shaken off the effects of the sea crossing and led Hugh to the abbey church where they were informed Philip was in a meeting with the abbot.

Walking through the grounds, Hugh tried to remember the last time he had been at the abbey and thought it was nearly fifty years since the dramatic events surrounding the death of his nemesis, William Cliton.

While Simon stepped eagerly down the knave towards the two men, Hugh waited at the back of the church. All those years ago, Hugh recalled the enigmatic appearance of the Knights Templar and the strange, compelling deathbed confessions of Cliton.

For a while, Simon spoke to Philip, then the count greeted Hugh warmly with a broad smile of genuine delight. 'My dear Earl Bigod, it is an honour and a privilege to meet you again. What is it...seven years since we visited Thomas Becket at Pontigny?'

Hugh was impressed by the respect shown by the count. 'I was reminiscing the last time I was here. The night, I met your father.'

'Yes, it was on the very night Thierry became Count of Flanders. Our meeting today is more than coincidence, my friend. This occasion is God-given. Please...come over to the chapel by the pulpit.'

Hugh walked with the count down the nave. 'I have asked the abbot to prepare a meal for us in the refectory but in the meantime I want to show you something.'

In the tiny chapel, next to the pulpit was a small niche that contained a statue of the Virgin Mary. Count Philip leant forward and picked it up. 'On the night you met Thierry; there were others here in the abbey. Do you remember who they were?'

'Apart from Stephen of Blois, later to be king, I presume you mean the Knights Templar,' Hugh replied, unsure of where the question was leading.

Philip nodded enthusiastically. 'Did you know they were three of the founding Knights of the Order, the Grand Master Hugo de Payen, André de Montbard and the one known as Gondermar.'

'I only really remember de Payen...'

'It is incredible. You must be one of the few people living who actually met one of the greatest men ever to have walked this earth,' he stated passionately.

Hugh raised his eyebrows. 'To me, he was just another knight.'

Philip removed the base of the statue and three tiny bones dropped into the palm of his hand. 'These bones are from the forefinger of Saint Bertin, the patron saint of this abbey. They were carried to the Holy Land by Godefroi de St Omer and his brother Hugh who were both killed fighting in the Holy Land. By a miracle, the bones were returned to this resting place by Hugo de Payen, the very night you were here with my father.'

The bones were tiny and Hugh failed to look impressed. 'So why all this interest in the Knights Templar?'

Philip put the relic back inside the statue. 'Do you know there were no more than nine or ten who rode out to Jerusalem, to guard and escort the pilgrims from the coast. No braver men than those prepared to lay down their lives for the sake of others.' Philip put his arm around Hugh's shoulder and slowly walked back up the nave of the church. 'I find the origins of the Order quite fascinating.'

Hugh listened but showed little interest.

Philip gave a humourless smile. 'The flow of knights riding out to join the Order continues unabated. You may be interested to know, I have just heard the pope has exiled the knights who murdered Archbishop Becket and ordered them to ride out to Jerusalem and serve under the Templar Rule for fourteen years.'

Upon hearing the news, Hugh paused in the corridor and Philip went on ahead to the refectory. In the flickering torchlight, a small cross that was clumsily nailed to the wall caught his eye.

'Fucking good for nothing pope.'

The abbot had laid on an impressive spread of food including a platter of trout and venison. Philip offered Hugh a chair at the head of the table and poured two goblets of wine, and then settled down next to Hugh.

After prayers, the monks filed out leaving the esteemed guests to talk freely. 'Lest I forget, I must thank you. I know that the release of the Fleming soldiers and mercenaries from Norwich Castle after the rebellion was down to your personal intervention. Many of those men were under my command and they owe you their lives.'

Hugh accepted the praise modestly. 'I wonder if things may have turned out better if you and the young Henry had joined the rebellion...in England.'

'For that I apologise, but I had no authority over the wishes of Henry the younger. But you are here now and I hope you will enjoy your time in Flanders.'

Hugh sipped his wine. 'Well, we shall see.'

Philip's next comment came out of the blue. 'My aide-de-camp tells me you wish to go to Afflighem Abbey. Something about an old vase.'

Hugh paused, suspicious of giving up the truth too readily. 'Earl Wills of Arundel has asked me to pay respects at the resting place of his wife, Queen Alice.'

'Ah yes,' Philip nodded. 'Before being married to the earl, she was married to the first King Henry of England. How strange that she should want to live out her days as a nun. I wonder why.' Philip was hoping for a response from Hugh but all he received was an enigmatic smile.

He tried again. 'There was much talk of miracles at Afflighem Abbey around the time of her death. Saint Bernard of Clairvaux witnessed visions of the Virgin Mary and the voices of angels. He dedicated his staff and chalice to the church and I promise you will see both when we arrive.'

Hugh frowned. 'Just remind me, which one was Saint Bernard?'

Philip looked across at his friend not knowing if he was teasing or not. 'The abbot was canonised two years ago.'

Hugh returned a blank stare.

Count Philip sipped the last of his wine. 'It is three days ride to Afflighem. Time enough for me to impart everything I know.'

Count Philip managed to regale Hugh with a multitude of stories about the famous abbot. He told how the tireless work of the Cistercian Saint had resulted in the building of hundreds of magnificent cathedrals and monasteries on both sides of the English sea.

The repetitive pious views of the count began to wear thin on Hugh and he was relieved when they entered the peace and quiet of Afflighem Abbey.

After greeting the mother abbess, she led them to the abbey

church where they attended a service at Nones. Throughout the service, Hugh looked around for the jar but could not see it. The last of the psalms finished and Philip suggested they spend some time alone at the gravestone of Queen Alice. Nodding her understanding, the mother abbess pointed midway down the aisle on the left and said she would leave them to their prayers while she ensured a hot stew was ready for them on the stove.

Hugh wandered up to the archway that separated the nave from the chancel, while Philip stood silently above the gravestone, reciting a small prayer.

There were a number of niches and small recessed windows around the quire and but Hugh was drawn to the raised effigy and tomb of the Duke of Louvain that lay in the apse, behind the altar. As he ran his fingers over the fine cut stone, he asked Philip. 'Why does the duke have such an monumental tomb, when his daughter the Queen of England, only qualifies for a stone slab cut into the floor?'

Philip walked to the altar and joined Hugh. 'I don't know, but look there on the effigy.' Placed on the tomb were a chalice and a wooden staff. 'There they are,' Philip spoke reverently. 'The relics of Saint Bernard.'

To Hugh, the chalice was a disappointment. It was simply a bowl on a stem with no adornments or jewels. 'I was expecting something more...expensive. Looks no different to any other cheap chalice I have seen in a hundred churches.'

'I doubt you have been inside more than a handful of churches even over your extensive lifetime. The value does not matter. You must remember this is a Holy chalice that bears witness to the miracles of Saint Bernard. He stood on these stone slabs and threw the devil out of this church, and cleansed the monks and sisters of the evil that had corrupted them. God sent a blinding light to herald the call of angels and a vision appeared...'

While Philip was caught up in his eulogy to the Saint, Hugh

strolled around the apse at the rear of the altar. He had to look twice to be sure but sat in a tiny niche, was an ancient looking jar. He picked it up and was surprised to hear a thin, metallic rattle come from inside.

Like a shadow, Philip appeared at his side. 'So is that the Holy vessel that Earl Wills of Arundel has asked you to find and return to him?'

Hugh raised his eyebrows and remembered Simon. 'Your aide-de-camp has good hearing.'

Philip stared at the jar. 'There sounds to be something inside. Don't you think we should open it?'

Feeling a sudden reluctance to part with the relic, Hugh hesitated before agreeing but the feeling soon passed. 'Very well, open it now before the abbess reappears.'

Taking a sharp blade from his belt, Philip carefully cut into the lid. The brittle wax split into a dozen pieces that scattered over the tomb. Slowly he tilted the jar and the curled up contents tantalisingly appeared.

The tinted metal scroll fell onto the stone surface of the effigy. 'What the hell is that?' Hugh asked.

'Copper, I think,' Philip replied, his hands shaking as he held the scroll up to the light. 'The writing is in an ancient language.'

Hugh reached out to touch the scroll.

'No...don't handle it,' Philip ordered. 'It is so fragile it will fall apart. Look, there are already detached pieces in the bottom of the jar. We need a specialist and I think I may be able to find one.'

Chapter 39

Gravensteen Castle
Flanders

Somehow, the discovery of the jar left by Queen Alice had stirred his imagination and dredged up long forgotten memories from decades long past. Uncomfortable as it was, Hugh's cynicism prevailed.

How could it be the same jar after all these years.

Gravensteen had been one of many seats of power for the Counts of Flanders and Hugh was disappointed by its state of disrepair. Philip conceded that the building programme was behind schedule but he would make it a priority to the improve the whole structure, once time and money permitted.

As always the unannounced arrival of the count at his castle caused great consternation for the household who immediately set about making the hall presentable and ensuring the kitchens were adequately supplied with food and wine.

Philip marched tirelessly up to his apartments, and reaching the top of the staircase, he called out for his wife.

Voices came from the chamber and he opened the door. The look of surprise on his wife's face was absolute, as was the expression on the face of Walter des Fontaines, one of his favoured knights.

Instinctively, Philip drew his sword, and stood for a moment before realising the truth of the scene in front of him. At last, he had found his adulterous wife with her lover.

He stood in the door, ensuring neither of them could pass and ordered a servant to ask his bodyguards to come up to the chamber. Moments later four guards arrived and he told them to drag Walter outside.

To hide her shame, his wife pulled the blanket around her head but it proved to be no defence. Philip dragged her screaming out of the door and threw her down the stairs.

They beat Walter with clubs and staves for half an hour and Philip ensured his distraught wife witnessed every blow. Once his temper had cooled, Philip ordered them to stop and took a more considered approach. First, he took his wife to a ledge on the edge of a cesspit and tied her to a balustrade to prevent her falling in. Then Walter was dragged to the pit and had his feet bound and the rope looped around a stave so he was suspended upside down, his head just a fingers width above the stinking excrement. Four hours later, it was nearly dark and Philip brought Hugh to a window seat to observe the final act of revenge. He signalled to one of his guards who lowered the rope holding Walter and his head slowly disappeared into the pool of excrement.

His wife screamed and fainted, but Philip's vengeance knew no bounds.

Hugh gasped in astonishment as a bucket was lowered into the cesspit and thrown over the countess to wake her up. Never before had he seen such a shameful act against a noble spouse. Thankfully, she was spared a prolonged ordeal, as the errant knight Walter did not struggle too long for his life. Once declared dead, his body was thrown into the moat and his wife was washed down with buckets of cold water by her maids.

That night, the meal in the great hall was a subdued affair. With his wife locked in another room, Philip could not to engage in conversation. 'Before I retire for the night, I suggest taking the copper scroll to Troyes. To oversee its translation by experts.'

Feeling fatigued, Hugh had showed little desire to go with him.

Philip continued. 'You should stay here at the castle and I promise you will be made comfortable until I return from Troyes.'

That night, after such dramatic events, it was a while before Hugh could close his eyes and when sleep finally came, it was restless and disturbing.

The nightmares returned. They were relentless and more vivid than ever. Like the pages of a book written long ago, his life was peeled back in layers. First, he was in the cellars at Thetford manor where he found a bundle of relics from the Holy Land that he presented to good Prior Stephen. All except the one wrapped in the bloodied cloth. Then the pathetic face of Walter de Fontaines, his mouth opening and closing. It became a blur and began to resemble the face of Bishop Herbert of Norwich, jabbering delirious words about having to find a jar...but Hugh would not listen to the drivel...then the bishop was opening and closing his mouth, as the cushion pressed out his last breath.

Waking up, Hugh threw back the blanket, shaken by the vivid visions he had experienced. A bright strip of light shone from a crack in the shutter and a servant entered the chamber to remind him that the count was already eating his breakfast and awaiting his company.

Philip was giving orders to his men to assemble for departure to Troyes, and he saw Hugh enter the hall. Philip invited him to sit opposite and a servant brought bread and a bowl of thick meaty gravy. The man sat next to the count looked like a priest.

'Hugh I am glad you are here, for I must apologise for the lurid events of yesterday. As you can see, this is my chaplain and we are preparing to depart tomorrow. Now, can you give me the old jar you found at Afflighem.'

Having had time to reconcile his nightmares, Hugh felt an inexplicable reluctance to let the jar leave his possession. 'I have slept on my decision to stay here and have decided instead to join you. I will come with you to Troyes.'

Philip was surprised at his change of mind. 'If you prefer to come with me to Troyes, my friend I must warn you, it is a long way; probably seven days ride or more.'

'I am sure we can manage to do it in six if you don't slow me down,' Hugh replied with a hint of mockery.

A glimmer of a smile passed over Philip's lips and was shared by a flicker of disappointment in his eyes. 'Then perhaps you would be good enough to show the jar to my Chaplin?'

'Of course,' Hugh replied, dipping his bread in the gravy and feeling justified at changing his mind. For now, he believed Philip was hiding something.

When they departed the next day, Hugh was surprised at how many knights and men-at-arms had appeared to join the escort. When he asked Simon, he replied that over a long journey, the count simply liked to show off. But Hugh knew that as the numbers gradually increased, there was more reasoning than simple vanity.

By the time they reached their destination, Philip's escort had grown to the size of a small army. Hugh had never been to Troyes and he was instantly struck by its joyous life and soul. The vibrancy and animation was unlike anything he had ever witnessed in England. The streets were entwined with market squares and littered with tradesmen of every vocation. Even the children were clean and well fed, and the smell of food wafted on the breeze, overpowering the usual stink of offal and sewage.

Their arrival brought many of the citizens out onto the streets and they cheered as the knights on their mighty stallions rode past, heading for the palace with its lightly fortified ramparts and moat.

At the gates, they were met by a reception party and after dismounting and meeting some of the local dignitaries, Philip was led into the palace to meet Marie the Countess of Champagne.

Hugh walked next to Simon. 'So Marie is the daughter of King

Louis of France and Eleanor of Aquataine, so she must be aged about thirty. I remember when Eleanor divorced Louis and married King Henry of England. After that I get confused,' Hugh admitted.

Simon sighed at Hugh's ignorance. 'It is quite simple. Marie is married to Henri, the Count of Champagne. Her sister Alix is married to Theobald the Count of Blois. Theobald and Henri are brothers. It is quite simple.'

'Ah, then is Theobald the one who killed the Jews of Blois, while Alix supposedly watched....'

Simon held Hugh by the arm to warn him. 'Don't ever repeat such a slander if you want to see out your final years in comfort,' he whispered.

Hugh smiled at the veiled threat. 'What a lovely family they all must make.'

Once they had assembled in the beautifully decorated reception hall, the arrival of the countess was announced. She floated down the wide flight of stairs like an elegant bird, her flowing gown cut fashionably low, giving a hint of cleavage. Her skin was pure as white snow and her smile radiated across the room making every man weaken under her spell.

Her voice purred like a cat. 'My dear Count of Flanders, what a pleasure to see you again.' She held out her hand.

Philip bowed graciously and kissed her ring. The look that passed between them made Hugh blink twice. Married or not, he had discovered the object of Philip's illicit love. He introduced Hugh to the countess. 'The Earl of Norfolk cannot trust his safety to the King of England, so I have agreed to house him in Ghent. My castle is his castle.'

Her face broke into a forced smile. 'It is an honour to meet you, Lord Bigod. You reputation speaks volumes.'

Hugh opened his mouth and was about to ask the whereabouts of her husband, but in an instant her attention had gone elsewhere and

Hugh resigned himself to the background while her gorgeous blue eyes shot amorous looks in Philip's direction.

So convenient that Count Henri was away in Provins.

The evening light fell away quickly and once the food had been served and the lamps had been lit, the household staff slowly dissolved into the palace corridors to leave Marie and Philip sat opposite Simon and Hugh around the inlaid oak table.

Philip leant across the table. 'Hugh, would you mind bringing the jar to the table as the countess wishes to see it.'

Hugh agreed and moments later he had brought the jar from his chamber and handed it to Philip. Awkward glances passed between each of them and Simon tactfully suggested that as all the food was gone, he would show Hugh around the palace, by starting at the kitchens. They left discreetly down a corridor, excusing themselves for the night.

'Don't forget I have a surprise for you tomorrow night,' Marie called out after them.'

They entered the kitchens where a cheerful cook obliged with helpings of cakes and mulled wine. Hugh gulped down a cup. 'So what will the surprise be, I wonder.'

Simon sighed. 'Usually it is a troubadour or some poet.'

Hugh smiled. 'I can see why you called her eccentric.'

'Don't be fooled by her peculiar ways. She has the utter devotion from her male subjects, none more so than her husband Henri. She insists on good manners and an elegant lifestyle. She promotes culture, chivalry and learning, and listens to the troubadours tell stories of courtly love, just like her mother used to. Her moral conduct is the most important thing to her and she expects the same of others.'

'She will be no admirer of me then,' Hugh said.

'Don't be so dismissive. Philip tells me she truly appreciated the way you rescued the Flemings from Norwich after the rebellion.'

Thank God for my bloody Flemings.

That night Hugh found himself in a large bed with soft blankets and pillows. Sleep came easily to him, but was followed quickly by the nightmares. His brother William was shouting to him on the quayside at Barfleur. The noise was intense and all around people were shoving as he tried to hear his brothers' words.

'We must find the jar...Cliton has told me the story from his father...meet me on the ship...' When he looked again though the crowd, all he could see was his brothers face behind a large door, peering through a sliding face panel...his voice pleading to be rescued from his imprisonment. Then the scream blended with his own as the knife cut out his brother's tongue...

Hugh woke up, startled by the intensity of the imagery. Splashing cold water over his face, he wondered if he would ever see the end of his night-time terrors.

Chapter 40

Troyes
Champagne

The next evening, the great hall in the palace of Troyes was filled with nearly a hundred guests from the city. The countess was renowned for her grand banquets and sophisticated style of entertainment.

This night was no different. A succession of jugglers, musicians, fire-eaters and poets delighted her audience and after a lavish feast, she announced her special guest, Chrétien de Troyes. Everyone had heard of the great poet and of his years of patronage to the countess. They also appreciated he rarely gave public performances.

At the top of the staircase he appeared, wearing a white habit with a tabard across his chest, emblazoned by a red cross. In a typical dramatic gesture, he thrust a shining sword into the air and yelled 'Beauseant!'

His audience froze in silence, all eyes looking up to the poet.

His performance had begun. 'Beauseant! The cry of the brave warriors of Christ as they charge into battle against the ungodly Saracens. The Poor Knights of the Temple of Solomon who give up everything in order to serve God. Lives without love, except for that of our Lord Jesus Christ. Lives without chattels, for God's charity provides all their needs, and obedience to none but the Grand Master of the Order. I beg all of you, to take heed of my words. For it was seventy years ago that Hugo de Payen, the first and founding Grand Master, stood on this very staircase and addressed the lords, and ladies of this fine city. Our great Count Hughes proclaimed him his 'best of knights' and lavished gifts upon him of armour, shields, and swords then to the stables to hand over horses and squires. I am not worthy to stand on the same step, nor to breath the same air as such mighty sons of Champagne. May their memory live on...forever!'

A rousing cheer erupted from the spellbound audience. Slowly descending the staircase, he regaled them with a story of romance and courage mixed with foolhardy acts of bravery, death and compassion. The visionary mix of prose that lit the imagination for nearly an hour drew long applause from everyone and when the lateness of the hour meant they were obliged to leave, they groaned in dismay.

The sound of applause stirred Hugh from his intermittent slumber, and he sidled to the fireplace as everyone filed out of the grand hall. Hugh was surprised to see the upper echelon of knights who would normally sleep on the floor rushes were ushered into other rooms with the servants. Eventually the room was cleared.

As a rainstorm battered the shutters, Philip, Marie, Simon and Chrétien joined Hugh around the warmth of the fireplace. Chrétien shook hands with Hugh. 'My lord, let me say what a great honour it is to meet you this inhospitable night.'

Marie sat down first. 'Chrétien has taken the liberty of studying the jar and will tell us his findings.'

Chrétien began immodestly. 'Well I do recognise a roman jar when I see one. The writing around the middle is Aramaic and is translated as 'the Truth according to Nicodemus,' though it was scratched on almost as an afterthought. Now as for the copper scroll, it is more of a confession rather than a Gospel. A subtle difference I agree, but important nonetheless. The words are beautiful though it is difficult to grasp their true meaning.' Chrétien paused to recall the text.

"Behold and bow your head. For on this wooden beam died our Lord Jesus Christ spread nailed and naked for all to see...here, in the dark, deep shadows, is the place of secrets...that must be kept so. Here, may

God protect the world from the truth. Here, I must hide the shame of what they did to Him. Fear not as your body trembles... fear not for your faith, for the Lord has truly risen, as sure as night turns to day the resurrection is the truth...and if in Lydda this holy sanctuary dedicated to our Lord should become a den of doubt, then God forgive me for I have let you down. The crossbeam that held our Lord by the nail should be venerated...but what else could I do? Oh the shame of it...oh the shame of Lydda..." I am afraid the end of the scroll is indecipherable at this point. There are some broken pieces, but nothing I can save.'

Only the crackling flames could be heard as they contemplated the mysterious eulogy.

Philip clasped his hands together and hardly dare ask the burning question. 'So, did Nicodemus write those words?'

'Without a doubt my lord, the jar and the scroll are authentic.'

Hugh watched awkwardly as they all closed their eyes in silent prayer. To him the words made little sense, no matter who wrote them down.

After a while, Philip lifted his head to speak. 'My grandfather, the Count Robert of Flanders was a leader of the first army of God. At Lydda, he discovered the tomb of Saint George though inside only a few big bones and the ribcage remained intact. All were covered in a layer of dust. Undeterred, he was determined to send the remnants back to the Abbey of Anchin with the Cannon Gunscelin of Lille. Gerbault his chaplain and Gerard of Buc and were to provide an escort but within a month they were all dead save Gerbault who went blind.

On the sea voyage to Italia, the ship never arrived and the relics was believed lost.'

Philip stood up to pour some wine. 'Then there was my mother the Countess Sybille. I remember she once wrote of a life-changing experience at Lydda. I never discovered what, but afterwards she took her vows at the Abbey of Lazarus.'

'And what of your father?' Marie asked. 'He ventured to the Holy Land more times than anyone.'

Philip collected his thoughts. 'He never mentioned Lydda...except once. He was witness to the last words of William Cliton. I cannot remember precisely, but he mentioned the Gospel of Nicodemus and the old jar.' Suddenly he spun round and looked at Hugh. 'You were there, were you not?'

Hugh stared into his ornate pewter goblet. 'I was there...but I only recall a jumble of delirious words. The man was dying...'

Marie stood up and the perpetual kindness in her face had disappeared. 'Lord Bigod, let me tell you of what I know of Lydda. I speak for my husband, Henri who was with the second Army of God. He was riding with the Templar Grand Master on the road up an escarpment to Lydda and witnessed the death of William Peverel...crushed under his own horse, God rest his soul. Henri heard with his own ears that Peverel was seeking a relic of Christ at the church of St George in Lydda.' She turned to look at Hugh. 'He said he met your elder brother, William Bigod that very day.'

The words were left echoing in the vastness of the great hall.

Now Hugh understood the previous indifference shown by the countess. The truth was out and Marie and Philip obviously knew of his deplorable secret. He could feel his heart racing. His only defence was to attack and with a calm smile that belied his humiliation, he stood in front of them with his head held high and sighed. 'Many accounts are told of my brother's miraculous escape to the Holy land. If they are true, then I wish him well. Many stories also tell of an imposter. I for one do not know which is the truth. Do you?'

Marie stared back at Hugh and slowly shook her head.

Before she could reply Hugh gave a yawn. 'My Lady, I shall retire for the night. Oh, as Count Henri is away, I meant to ask about the sleeping arrangements. I do not want to cause embarrassment by entering the wrong chamber by mistake...'

The uncomfortable silence was broken by Chrétien. 'This is extraordinary...altogether fascinating. All of you are unwitting witnesses to eighty years of history.' He rested his hand on Philips shoulder. 'My dear Count, when you return from the Holy Land, we must discuss writing a prose. Do you intend to depart soon?'

The reddening face of Marie had distracted Philip. 'I shall leave soon...in the spring...when the weather improves.'

'You are going to the Holy Land?' Hugh asked, startled by the news.

Philip looked at him sternly. 'Yes my Lord Bigod. But fear not, while I am away you can still enjoy the comforts of Gravensteen. In fact it is preferable to have it occupied by a nobleman, of sorts.'

Although, the following weeks of preparation for Philip's departure passed by slowly, Hugh decided to stay on in Troyes. Besides, the palace was far more comfortable than the draughty rooms of Gravensteen and the constant noise of an army of masons.

Given free rein of a large comfortable apartment, he stayed mostly within the palace walls, venturing only occasionally into the city. In the light of his indiscreet comments, he kept very much to himself, only encountering Marie when necessary.

He stayed in regular contact with Simon who kept him up to date with events. Sat one day in his expansive chamber, only one question prayed on his mind. 'So tell me the truth, why does Philip intend to go to the Holy Land?' he asked. 'He always struck me as a fighter with a sword; not a monk with a prayer book.'

'Then you are wrong, my lord. You briefly met Count Philip's father, Thierry. He was a devout Christian, journeying and fighting many times in the Holy Land.'

Hugh nodded, but found it difficult to reconcile his memory of Count Thierry whose only intention was to bed Sybille, the widow of

William Cliton, even while Cliton was still warm in its grave.

Simon continued in his pompous manner. 'I believe Count Philip wishes to be as devoted to God as his parents.'

Hugh gave the impression he was surprised. 'Oh really, is that the reason. I thought Philip was having to serve a penance for the death of Walter des Fontaines.'

'Ah Walter the poor lad…I warned him but alas he never could keep his ardour under control,' Simon said sensitively. 'The count cannot be blamed for his anger.'

Hugh sought confirmation. 'So, as I suspected, he goes to Jerusalem out of guilt?'

'I don't think it is that simple. There are many more reasons than you can imagine,' Simon said thoughtfully. 'His mother was the daughter of Count Fulk who became the King of Jerusalem. The son of Fulk was King Amalric and he is now dead, leaving his young son Baldwin on the throne. But God has struck a cruel blow and Baldwin's leprosy means he is not long of this world. Keep this to yourself, but perhaps the count has designs on taking the crown of Jerusalem for himself. Knowing full well that King Henry of England has an equal claim to the throne of Jerusalem, he would give Henry an apoplectic fit, even from the other side of the world.'

Hugh smiled and scratched his wispy, grey beard. The thought of upsetting King Henry always appealed to him. 'I had given little thought to the complex relations between Philip and Jerusalem.'

Simon continued. 'Then again, his intentions may well be compromised. You must remember that Philip has no natural heir and when his brother Matthew died, he became guardian of Matthew's two daughters aged seventeen and seven. So, if Philip stayed in the Holy land, his younger brother Peter would naturally have taken the title of count and responsibility for the children. Unfortunately, Peter died tragically last year.'

'You are one of the counts closet advisors. You really don't know why he wants to cross to the other side of the world?'

Simon paused. 'Truth be told. I don't think Count Philip even knows. His mind has been plunged into turmoil by recent events and his only solace and confidante is here in Troyes.' He looked expectantly at Hugh, deliberately leaving the ambiguous statement hanging in the air.

Raising his eyebrows, Hugh took the bait. 'So it is more than lust. He is actually in love with the Champagne Countess.'

Simon responded immediately. 'I never said that,' he insisted angrily, checking to see if anyone had heard the indiscreet remark.

Hugh ignored his concern and chuckled to himself. 'Bloody hell, they call me many things but at least I am not a fucking hypocrite. I don't suppose anyone will be drowning him in a cesspit.'

'I am simply saying that the countess has a vivid imagination and is fired by stories of valour and heroism in the name of God. Marie is patron to the poet, Chrétien de Troyes and encourages him to write tales of epic adventures, like the one you heard.'

Hugh sat back in his chair and contemplated the intricate ambitions of the House of Champagne and Flanders.

A servant gave a loud knock on the door and entered, making an announcement that surprised them both. 'Earl Wilhelm de Mandeville of Essex has arrived this morning and wishes to advise you of his intentions, my lord.'

Startled for a moment, Hugh sat up. 'Perhaps I am to be arrested after all,' he retorted. He ambled after Simon along the corridor and down the staircase, exiting into the grand hall.

Stood next to Count Philip, he saw the back of Wilhelm as he dried his rain soaked clothes in front of the roaring fire.

Wilhelm turned around. 'Lord, do my own eyes deceive me. Earl Bigod is alive and well and living in a palace in Troyes,' he quipped.

Genuinely pleased to see Wilhelm, Hugh countered. 'Don't tell me the king has sent you to keep an eye on me.'

Wilhelm grinned and shook his hand. 'You know what he is like. Whenever you and Philip are together all he can smell is rebellion.'

Count Philip raised a cup of wine. 'Wilhelm has asked to join me on my journey to the Holy Land and I have said he is most welcome.'

Hugh smirked at the folly of the young. 'At my age I can do with a little less adventure…'

'Nonsense!' Wilhelm gulped his wine and raised his goblet. 'To Hugh Bigod, the Earl who will live forever. I can feel the Holy Land shaking at the very thought of your arrival.'

'I think you are misinformed,' Hugh corrected. 'I will not be accompanying you on your adventure to the Holy land. Christ almighty, I would probably burst into flames if I set foot in Jerusalem.'

Wilhelm bowed his head. 'My apologies Lord Earl, I assumed as you were here you would be coming with us…but like you say, at your age…'

Any discomfort between Philip, Wilhelm and Hugh evaporated as the wine flowed and as the other guests arrived, the revelry continued into the night. After the food was served, Wilhelm took Hugh to one side for a quiet word. 'I saw your son Roger only a week ago. Petronella has recovered from her injuries but he remains under house arrest. I have heard his council is optimistic that all charges will be dropped. He sends his goodwill, and asks that for once you keep your promise. So tell me, what did he mean by that?'

The question put Hugh on his guard. Perhaps Wilhelm really was spying for the king. 'I promised him…one day I would go to the Holy Land to seek a renunciation of my excommunication by the pope.'

Wilhelm nodded. 'I thought as much. That is why I believed you had decided to join Count Philip.' Wilhelm sighed. 'Oh, by the way, did you hear that Earl Wills of Arundel died a few months ago. I believe it was a few days after you went to see him at Wymondham.'

Hugh looked down at his feet then took another drink of wine. He felt genuinely saddened. 'No, I did not know. Thank you for telling me the sad news.'

As the festivities continued, Hugh looked for Count Philip but could not see him in the crowd of people. Deep inside, his mind was troubled by promises made to his son and the urgings of an old childhood friend. The death of Wills meant he was no longer obliged to return with the jar to Wymondham.

Hugh took his leave of the festivities, intending to go back to his chamber. Before retiring, he visited the garderobe and sat down to his ablutions. He shook his head at the way the fireplace in the hall below warmed the walls where you had a shit, and a slit in the wall provided ventilation for the smell. And yet at night there was nowhere to place a torch.

Suddenly Hugh heard voices coming from the balcony outside. He leant against the window sill and listened through the slit. He recognised the voices of the two men and as no light shone through the slit, they were oblivious to the fact that he could hear every word.

'I tell you....I spoke with Marie at some length and she was quite determined. She left me in no doubt as to her true feelings. Indeed, she said as much. *"Don't let that perjurer Hugh Bigod know the truth. Ensure Philip is made aware of the full translation. Bigod will be none the wiser,"* were her exact words,' Chrétien quoted.

The voice that replied was unmistakably that of Count Philip 'I know much of the story already from any number of sources I have collected over the years. Tell the countess I appreciate her trust and her candour, but does it really matter at this stage?'

Chrétien continued. 'I think you will agree with Marie when I tell you the rest of the translation, that the secret must be kept from everyone, including Wilhelm and certainly Bigod.'

Hugh held his breath and listened but much of what he heard was

410

indistinct. Then he heard Philip gasp with surprise.

The two men dispersed and Hugh retired to his chamber, his mind in familiar territory as he was swept up in a whirlwind of bitterness. Now everything began to make sense.

No wonder these bastards wanted to go to Lydda.

Their only intention was to steal the Christ relic, some precious discovery made in the name of his family, not the House of Flanders or the House of Champagne but the Bigod family.

How many times, over how many years, had he dismissed the knowledge of the ancient jar found at Lydda. Well now would be a good time to discover Christianity, thought Hugh. The Holy Land beckoned and he had an unerring feeling that any number of ghosts would be looking over his shoulder every step of the way.

That night he settled on his mattress and conceded that fate had truly conspired that he should sacrifice his last days on eastern soil.

Chapter 41

Ramleh
Palestine

They all thought the voyage from Genoa to Acre to be the most arduous journey they had ever made. Twice the ship nearly capsized in heavy seas and three oarsmen were lost to the waves but it was nothing compared to the savage heat and dust of the road from the coast to Ramleh. The summer sun quickly reached its apogee and beat down relentlessly, creating a furnace of heat that scorched cloth and seared shields. Suits of chain mail became too hot to touch and were reluctantly discarded in favour of lighter clothing.

The Templar garrison at Ramleh gave a quiet yet respectful welcome. They were informed that most of the Knights Templar were in Gaza while a small troop had gone in search of a party of knights that had apparently attacked their own escort and then sped off.

Count Philip had accumulated nearly fifty knights and a hundred men-at-arms, and the empty space in the cool hall and dormitory was a relief for his heat-stricken men.

For the first time since landing at Acre, they were able to have proper food and rest. The last three nights, they had endured fitful sleep due to the guards raising the alarm at every passing Saracen, who they assumed were out to attack them. Philip became so agitated by the constant calls to attention, he ordered the guards to stand down unless fighting had actually begun.

Hugh was in a state of abject depression. When he departed from Troyes, he doubted he would have the strength to complete the journey to the Holy Land. Now in his eighties, he would surely succumb to disease or mortal injury, like so many that had gone before. Each passing day, each passing mile, brought him inexorably closer to the moment he had most dreaded in his life. After riding and sailing across the world, he would gladly die rather than experience the pain of seeing his brother again.

The Templar sergeant had confirmed that William Bigod was still alive and in reasonable health for one so old. Apparently, he had sold the horse-farm in Lydda to the Templars and settled into an annex adjoining the church.

Philip rose before dawn, looking fresh and happy. If he was in any way concerned that Hugh had belatedly decided to join him, he did not show it. In fact he insisted that the whole experience would be beneficial to Hugh's soul. But Hugh knew the real truth.

Opening the shutters, Philip urged Wilhelm and Simon to ready themselves for the detour to Lydda. Despite the relative comfort of the garrison quarters, Hugh had not slept for more than an hour.

Pacing the terrace, Philip stepped outside to join him, just in time to see the sun rise over the eastern hills. He looked to the slope that led the mile and a half to Lydda and sighed. 'It is God's Will that has kept both of you alive: longer than any other brothers in history. I have counted fifty-six years since the tragedy of the White Ship. This is a wonderful day and I pray you will learn the true meaning of redemption. In a strange way, you should be proud of this chance to redeem yourself.' Philip looked towards the stables. 'Are you ready Lord Bigod, to shake hands with your destiny?'

Hugh scowled at Philip. 'Fuck destiny. For some the road to redemption is straight and clear. My redemption lies somewhere at the end of a rocky path… to a precipice overlooking an abyss.'

As they mounted up, Wilhelm and Simon joined them begrudgingly, moaning at having missed the food being served from the kitchens.

'Where is the escort,' Simon asked.

'The least number of people that know our business the better,' Philip replied. 'Don't worry, we simply take the bridge over the ravine then we follow the track up the slope for only a mile or so. We will be back in two hours, well before the sun starts to burn.'

'At least it is cooler today,' Wilhelm grumbled. Riding through the gates of the compound, he noticed the sun disappear behind a thick cloud that was welling up from in the east. 'Pray that is rain in those clouds and not another dust storm.'

The bridge over the ravine to Lydda was no longer than fifty paces and appeared sound, but they crossed in single file, only ten paces above the flooded, mud-laden river.

At the foot of the slope, the track undulated. 'This uneven ground must be due to subsidence,' Simon commented. He looked ahead and saw the track run alongside a coppice. Nervously, he touched the hilt of his sword for comfort. He would feel happier once they had reached Lydda.

Joab Mandeville walked to the edge of the coppice, waiting patiently for the others to come to some agreement. They had been arguing for an hour over what to do next and Richard le Breton was still threatening to leave their little faction. Breton was distressed at the murder of the small escort that had been at their side all the way from Rome and told them he wanted to complete his penance alone.

'One of them was a priest...from the office of the Holy Father,' he cried, but his words fell on deaf ears.

'So what, I for one will not be handing myself over to the fucking Templars so they can tan my hide for fourteen years,' FitzUrse scowled. 'I say for the time being we hide in these hills around Ramleh. If we can avoid capture we stand to make a living from thieving and kidnap.'

'You are not in Yorkshire now,' de Tracy pointed out. 'Out here we have no castles, no estates, no squires. We have four horses and two of those are going lame.'

A crackle of thunder sounded and the storm clouds rolled in from the eastern hills. While the quarrel rolled back and forth, Joab kept watch down the slope towards the bridge. 'Shut up all of you. There are horsemen coming over the bridge.'

Keeping his head down, Le Breton left the cover of the coppice and clambered to the rocky ledge to see who was coming. Suddenly the heavens opened and the heavy rain made it difficult to see.

De Morville crawled up alongside him. 'Have they seen us,' he whispered.

'I don't know…'

'One has gone for his sword. I tell you they have seen us.'

'We can take them on…'

Suddenly le Breton leapt over the ledge and scrambled down the stony slope on his rump. Reaching the track, he found his footing and ran towards the four horsemen, calling out. 'It's a trap…turn back!'

FitzUrse, de Morville and de Tracy mounted up and galloped down the track after le Breton, but with a head start, he had nearly reached Count Philip. His mount was already skittish with the thunder and before Philip could react to the sudden appearance of the knight running towards them, his destrier charged towards the oncoming threat.

His voice lost above the sound of rain, Le Breton slipped on the rock strewn track and could do nothing to avoid the warhorse that had been trained to be a killing machine. The slip saved his life and although the muscular flank knocked him to the ground, he avoided the deadly hooves, missing his limbs by an arm's width.

With surprise and impetus, the other three knights were quickly upon the count and with drawn swords a vicious mêlée ensued. Philip was widely regarded as one of the finest exponents of the tournament and held his own against the three horsemen.

Simon and Wilhelm came alongside and immediately joined the affray. Wishing to exclude himself from such obvious danger, Hugh stopped close to the bridge and was ready to dash back to safety if necessary.

After taking a blow to his shield, de Tracy was the first to fall from his horse and although winded, he knelt on the ground keeping hold of the hilt while the fight went on around him. The ground quickly became a mud bath and inevitably, as Wilhelm took a mighty blow from FitzUrse onto his shield, he lost his balance and fell awkwardly into the mire. But he recovered faster than de Tracy and spinning around he lunged forward with his sword, hard enough to pierce chain mail and gambeson. The blade ran through the back of the kneeling knight, exiting out of the front of his mail-coat, killing de Tracy instantly.

The downpour continued and the horses were flailing around unable to respond to the pull of the rein. Philip dismounted and attacked de Morville's stallion, slashing out at the tendons. He heard the awful snapping sound as his blade struck. Striding around the fallen horse, he took no notice of the scream for mercy from de Morville and ruthlessly followed up with a mortal blow that severed his arm and cut deep into the side of his torso.

There was no time to dwell over right and wrong. Blood gurgled from his mouth as he squirmed to free himself and Philip placed his sword against the throat and pushed until his blade struck earth.

Fifty paces away, Simon yelled out for help. He had lost his sword and was on foot trying to recover it from the mud. FitzUrse steered his mount and struck a blow with his flail-mace at Simon that broke his shoulder blade. Leaving his sword, Simon ran clumsily though the mud, endeavouring to reach the bridge, but FitzUrse followed.

Both Philip and Wilhelm watched helplessly as FitzUrse rode him down, cleaving his skull in half with one blow. Somehow, FitzUrse was able to gather his horse before sliding into the ravine, and then turn around to face Philip and Wilhelm.

With swords raised and without fear they both steadied themselves to confront the oncoming stallion.

Philip glanced at Wilhelm. 'Get the horse. I shall deflect his flail.' But before they could move, both were struck by the sight of Hugh Bigod galloping fast along the side of the ravine.

From the relative safety of the rocky outcrop, Joab Mandeville watched transfixed as the bloody mêlée played out. Disregarding the old man by the bridge, he took to his horse and with a short lance in his hand, he rode out of sight down to the edge of the ravine and galloped along its banks, his lance aiming for the backs of the two warriors who stood facing FitzUrse. He only needed to hit one of them, leaving the other for FitzUrse to finish off.

Hugh had immediately seen the danger. Philip and Wilhelm were focused on FitzUrse and were unaware of the lone knight who had outflanked them and was now riding at speed towards them from behind.

FitzUrse struck first, crashing his flail into Wilhelm's shield, while Philip stepped aside to land a sword blow on FitzUrse that cut deep into his thigh. He slid from his saddle, landing heavily about twenty paces away.

At the sudden sound of a charging horse, Philip spun on his heels. Joab Mandeville was bearing down at a gallop and Philip feared the worse. Then like an apparition appearing out of nowhere, Hugh crashed into the side of the charging warhorse, sending it skidding sideways. In the collision, Hugh had dealt a lethal blow. His sword had pierced the groin of Joab, going through the saddle and pinning him to his horse. With his head sunk low, Joab slowed to a halt in the pouring rain.

Hugh appeared to lose control and as if time itself had slowed, they watched as the legs of his stallion slithered along the crumbling edge of the ravine, unable to gain a hold in the mud.

Instinctively Philip ran to help Hugh as Wilhelm guarded their rear from further attack. He slithered to within ten paces of Hugh then watched in horror as an entire section of the gully slipped away, taking the aged lord and his horse tumbling over the precipice.

Philip fell to his knees and crawled on all fours towards the edge, praying as he peered over the edge. Halfway down the side of the deep river gully, amongst the fresh slippage of mud and earth, the horse lay with its neck broken. Laying underneath the horse was Hugh. The lance had snapped in half and appeared to protrude from the deathly still body.

Wilhelm called Philip back from the edge. 'My lord, we are not out of danger yet.' Philip stirred from his malaise and shaking with fury, he strode back to FitzUrse who was trying to escape, hobbling on one leg.

'Stay where you are or die,' Philip shouted. 'Who are you?'

FitzUrse hung his head, refusing to talk.

Another voice answered nearby. 'He is Reginald FitzUrse and the other maniac is Joab Mandeville. I am Richard le Breton and we were supposed to go to Jerusalem...'

'Joab!' Wilhelm yelled out, turning to look at his half brother. Bleeding heavily, his horse had slipped onto its knees and Joab was slumped in the saddle, where Hugh's sword dangled from his groin. His hands were grasped around the blade, pulling as he gave an anguished cry.

Wilhelm walked through the mire. 'Joab, my brother...I don't understand. What is going on here...'

Joab lifted his head and grimaced at Wilhelm. All the years of evil that had devoured his soul, gave him the strength he needed. His palms bled profusely as he pulled again at the sword and giving up a final scream, the blade came free.

Unable to move, Wilhelm watched as Joab slipped from his blood-soaked saddle and staggered towards him, his sword raised high; intent on killing the half brother that had been brought up in the palace of a count.

In a flurry of clattering hooves, there suddenly appeared on the bridge a troop of six Knights Templars, galloping at full speed. Three of them leapt from their mounts to the defence of Philip and Wilhelm.

The lead Templar spoke calmly but firmly. 'We will take care of this. Follow my men across the bridge now.'

'That is my brother!' Wilhelm yelled.

No one took any notice. As they were led out of danger by three of the knights, Wilhelm looked back to witness the bloody demise of Joab.

His brother gave one final shout as the remaining Templars bore down on him. 'Father, make space for me in hell!'

Without mercy or hesitation, the Templar sword fell, slicing off half the skull and exiting through the jaw. Amid blood curdling screams, they hacked Joab and FitzUrse into pieces. Then they turned on le Breton.

Putting on a brave face, he accepted his fate and bravely knelt down in the mud. As the swords scythed into his body, he shouted his last words 'Pray God forgive me…'

The Templars quickly reassembled and hurried from the bloody scene, ignoring the indignant cries of Philip and Wilhelm. They rode hard for five miles along the road to Jerusalem, not stopping until they reached an outcrop with a small fort overlooking the road.

Both Philip and Wilhelm were shaken by the their close call with death and sat quietly as the senior Templar introduced himself. 'I am Grand Master Odo de St Armand. You must be Count Philip of Flanders and Earl Wilhelm of Essex. Your knights and troops have gone on ahead to Jerusalem, believing they were following you. The council expects me to escort you with all haste to Jerusalem.'

Philip looked blankly at the Grand Master and simply nodded.

Wilhelm stood up and faced the Templar. 'You gave my brother no chance. I could have quelled his fears and...'

'He was going to kill you Earl Wilhelm and deep down you know that to be true. We knights have no family but God, so cannot share your grief. As for saving your life, then let us praise God's will.'

Shaken and humbled, Wilhelm sat back down.

Odo continued his censure. 'These men killed their papal escorts without mercy and therefore they received no mercy. There are bandits and outlaws around every corner. Most are Saracen but some are from the west. They prey on the weak and pious, bringing to the Holy Land nothing but their immoral western values of theft and treachery. If we truly want to preserve Palestine for all Christian pilgrims, then all such devils shall receive the same treatment. I pray in future you will treat the roads with more care.'

Philip barely had the strength to respond to the harsh words. 'Sire, you did well. Those murderers killed Thomas Becket, the Archbishop of Canterbury. They also killed two brave men. Simon de Moorslede was my aide-de-camp. And I saw Hugh Bigod, the Earl of Norfolk lying half-way down the side of the ravine. He was dead,' he stated flatly.

Odo nodded and told his aide to make a note. 'Earl Bigod's family will be informed forthwith and his body collected tomorrow. Now if you are refreshed, please remount so we can reach Jerusalem before dark.'

Chapter 42

Jerusalem

News soon spread around the Holy City of the arrival of a great count and his army from the west. A count whose grandfather was King Fulk and father was Count Thierry was a pedigree far more impressive than many could have prayed for.

Despite his obvious fatigue, Philip was so troubled by the loss of Hugh Bigod and his aide Simon that he could not sleep. As dawn broke, a delegation from the Council of Jerusalem knocked repeatedly on his door. They ignored his protestations, saying it was urgent that he presents himself to the Royal Court to advise on his intentions in the Holy Land. Looking pale and drawn, he was ushered into the Royal assembly hall built alongside the great mosque.

After some obligatory introductions, the Constable of Jerusalem stood up to commence proceedings. 'For the benefit of the count, I repeat my news that a fleet of seventy Byzantine ships are stationed off Acre waiting for the word to invade Egypt.'

Philip seemed distant, even dazed by events. 'Egypt?' he said staring blankly into the distance.

'Yes my lord, Egypt,' the Constable repeated. 'This royal court wishes to formally invite you to lead the army into Egypt.'

Philip remained tight lipped and the air of anticipation around the table was replaced by nervous disappointment.

Raynald de Châtillon was one of the few council members who had been irritated by the pompous arrival of the count. He saw the Egyptian campaign as his means of securing control of the army. 'Perhaps Philip of Flanders would prefer more time to rest before responding to our impertinent questions.'

Murmurs circulated around the table. The intervention by de Châtillon was seen as a bold attempt to remove the usurper before he had even addressed the court.

Philip stirred uncomfortably in his seat. 'Many of you know that my mother and father were great adherents to Jerusalem and all that it stood for, and there is nothing more I would like than to follow in their footsteps. Yesterday, a good friend of mine saved my life...I wonder if this place, this holy place, has a way of changing even the most hardened of characters into someone who gives a damn for others...even if it means making the ultimate sacrifice...'

'My lord, can you give this court an answer,' Raynald interrupted. 'The Greek fleet awaits an answer. The Jerusalem army awaits an answer. This Royal Council of War awaits an answer. Do you intend to lead an invasion force into Egypt or not?'

Philip stared at Raynald, annoyed by his brusque manner. 'Are you asking me to oblige the Greeks? I owe the Greeks nothing and I can certainly inform you that I have no interest in Egypt.'

Mayhem broke out around the table and Raynald had to shout to make himself heard. 'Count, do you intend to fight at all while you are in Palestine. If not then why have you come here?'

'I and my colleagues have come to the Holy land as humble pilgrims and out of a duty to Christ. I prayed I would receive the privacy to honour my mother and father...then yesterday I witnessed a brave lord lose his life and I want to tell you about ...'

Wilhelm Mandeville stood up. 'I think Count Philip needs to recover from his recent ordeal before saying anymore in front of this court.'

Raynald looked pleased with himself. With the unwitting help of Wilhelm, he had succeeded in making Philip look weak and indecisive. 'I suggest we reconvene tomorrow, that is if the count is up to it.' The meeting dissolved into accusations and counter accusations, most of them aimed at Philip.

Confused and tired, Philip turned to Wilhelm. 'God Almighty, this is when I miss Simon. How the hell am I going to cope without him.' He wiped a tear from his face.

Wilhelm tried to remain positive. 'You have brought a big enough entourage. Surely there is one of them you can promote.'

'They are too young and inexperienced,' Philip said dismissively.

Outside, the sun beat down relentlessly and the room was filled with a humid heat making him feel faint. Philip's body craved sleep. 'I need to retire and take to a mattress for the rest of the day. Stay here and give my excuses.' As he left the assembly room, he could hear the chatter of voices grow louder as everyone questioned Wilhelm.

The heat made for a fitful sleep and for much of the next twelve hours, he turned around on his mattress staring at the ceiling, his mind in turmoil. Every time he closed his eyes, his heart would start thumping. He would pace around his room taking an occasional glance out of the window. A knock at the door made him jump. He stepped away from his bed, expecting a servant with food and wine.

To his surprise in walked the young King Baldwin. Wearing a light flowing gown and gloves, he sat on a chair. 'Count Philip, my cousin, you look surprised to see me. I apologise for not seeing you at the meeting today but I have been recovering from a bout of malaria...as if leprosy is not bad enough. Unfortunately, it means I must rest as much as possible.'

Philip bowed graciously and held out his hand to greet the king.

Baldwin kept his gloved hand by his side. 'You understand the disease has only affected my hands, so far.'

Despite the assurance, Philip observed the flesh on the king's nose was showing signs of deterioration as the flesh eating infection took its toll.

The king spoke in a quiet assured voice for one who had just turned sixteen. 'Before you return to the meeting tomorrow, I wish to make my position clear, without the interference of third parties. If you were to agree to the invasion of Egypt I would like to personally offer you the command of the Jerusalem army...and that of regent.'

'I am honoured by your generous offer, my lord king, but I have not come to Jerusalem to acquire power or indeed a kingdom. I doubt I will be staying long enough to make a worthwhile contribution to your war-effort. In any case, with the greatest of respect, I see little incentive in leading your army. If the campaign were to fail, I would stand accused of incompetence and if it succeeds then all the lands go to the crown or indeed the Greeks.'

The king dipped his head and sighed. Truly, like many western newcomers, the count was only motivated by the ideals of the west, where territory was fought over for personal gain. He had no comprehension of the wider implications of warfare that dictated the politics and the struggle to maintain a Christian force in the Holy Land. 'Even though I am disappointed, I understand your feelings. Jerusalem can have a strange effect on the reasoning of those who visit and I shall not ask you again. However, Baldwin of Ibelin has briefed me on another matter. He tells me the council is confused over your purpose and says you have some ulterior motive regarding marriage. Would you be good enough to enlighten me.'

'My lord king, I can assure you I am already married,' Philip retorted quickly.

'But not so happily as you should be...I am told.'

Curling his lip into an awkward grimace, Philip wondered how such personal information had been leaked so quickly.

Baldwin sighed showing obvious signs of fatigue. 'Perhaps when you next meet with the royal court, you would be good enough to explain your intentions, so this sorry mess can be put to rights.'

Philip nodded and apologised if he had caused any concern in front of the royal court and that he would feel much better after a good night's sleep.

At the door, Baldwin paused. 'I hope you recover from your malaise. I shall ensure you receive some peace and quiet and order a decent meal to be brought to your chamber. If you require anything else, just call the servants outside in the corridor.'

Try as he might, Philip's restless mood continued overnight as he tried again and again to reconcile the loss of Hugh and Simon, as well as the unreasonable expectations that had been thrust upon him. His mind was racing in a whirl trying to find the right road to take. Did he now regret his earlier decision not to join forces with the Jerusalem army and seek battle against the Saracen? Perhaps he was being naive but invading Egypt just seemed to be the wrong strategy. In any case, the truth prevailed for he knew of many reasons why he had to return to Troyes. But the most pressing was to be close to the love of his life.

The next day Philip entered the royal court, unnerved by the sound of silence. The only smiles in the room came from the four representatives of the Byzantine Emperor. Glaring at the count, Raynald de Châtillon motioned his arm towards the empty chair placed on the opposite side to Wilhelm and sitting down he wondered why his comrade would not meet his gaze.

After a long-winded preamble from the Constable, the court approved the proposal made by King Baldwin of the appointment of Raynald de Châtillon as Commander of the Army.

The floor remained open for Raynald to resume his questioning. 'Would the Count of Flanders care to illuminate us on his so-called marriage plans,' he asked in a churlish manner.

'I do not appreciate your attitude, de Châtillon. Yes I had plans to marry off two of the sons of my favoured vassal Lord Robert de Bethune to Princess Sybilla and her half sister Princess Isabella, but after recent events, that does not seem so appropriate or important...'

'Who in hell's name do you think you are?' Baldwin of Ibelin interrupted, aggrieved that Philip should interfere with his own plans to marry Sybilla. 'How do you expect this court to countenance such meddling? You come here thinking you can rule the lives of those of us who are dedicated to defending the Holy Land from the Saracen. What are you...a coward? Why don't you fight, damn it!'

Philip rose from his chair, his face red with anger. 'I find your remarks brutish and offensive. I refuse to be drawn into a response that would offend the sanctity of this court. May I remind you I have to fulfil my duty as a pilgrim and I shall pray at the holy sites as well as my mother's grave. Upon completion of my pious responsibilities, I shall be returning to the west to take up other responsibilities to my provinces and my family. I don't know what expectation leads you to believe I could be in two places at once.'

To the chagrin of some and the despair of others, Philip left the royal court in a sulk. He paused for Wilhelm to join him but then as he looked down the table he realised his companion was staying put.

As he slammed the door behind him, the four emissaries from Constantinople looked totally disenchanted by the whole exchange and stood up to leave, saying they would report their findings to the Emperor.

'Well, there goes our fleet,' Raynald mumbled dryly.

Wilhelm looked sheepishly at the faces of the council. He hoped his disassociation with the count would ease the humiliation he had endured.

Sat next to him, a Knights Templar felt obliged to comment on Count Philip's behaviour and turned to Wilhelm, speaking quietly. 'I can understand how he must feel. Sometimes it is very distressing to lose a companion in battle. I assume they were close.'

'Our companion saved the count's life. It was the bravest act I have ever witnessed. Unfortunately, in doing so he killed my half-brother, so my own feelings are somewhat mixed,' Wilhelm explained.

'And the count must be equally distressed. I am sure it explains his irrational behaviour in front of the court. Perhaps I should speak to him and offer my condolence.'

Wilhelm nodded. 'I am sure your concern is well intentioned. May I ask your name.'

'Of course, I should have introduced myself. I am commander of the garrison at Ramleh and my name is Jacques de Exemes.'

Chapter 43

Lydda
Palestine

The recent storms had turned much of the horse feed and grain stores at Lydda to mush. Gerash and Abdul rode to the church annex to tell William the bad news and together they set off to Ramleh for more stock and provisions.

As they reached the top of the road above Ramleh, they could see the carrion feeding on what looked like fresh corpses. Ever cautious, they perched on the cart for a better view.

By the time they reached the foot of the slope their worst fears were realised. At the side of the track, just before they reached the bridge, they counted the bodies of six horseman, some of them obviously knights. They were strewn around a small area, and at first sight all of them appeared to be fresh arrivals from the west. It was disturbing to see that some had been hacked into pieces.

'They were probably attacked by Kurdish bandits. Will you help me bury them in a Christian grave, ' William asked Gerash. Feeling skittish and vulnerable out in the open, Gerash nudged his reluctant son out of the cart.

William could see a fresh slippage of earth at the side of the ravine and walked over to the edge to take a closer look. Another body lay about ten paces down the side of the ravine, and William asked Gerash to bring a rope from the cart. 'We must do our Christian duty and give him a proper burial as well.'

Gerash scrambled down the shale and mud and tied the rope around the waist while William slowly pulled up the dead weight using the carthorse.

At the top of the ravine, Abdul crouched over the body and gently pulled out the broken shaft that had lightly pierced the flesh just below his ribs.

William stood at the side of the shallow grave Abdul had dug at the side of the road and he recited a short prayer as the boy wiped the mud from the nostrils and eyes of the body.

'He is very old, almost as old as you,' he quipped in William's direction. Suddenly he leapt backwards, falling onto his rear. 'My God, I swear he blinked.'

William limped over on his walking stick. Shaking his head, he looked at the mud covered face. 'Your imagination is playing tricks, young man.' He stared at the body for a while, and then yelped with shock when he saw the chest rise and fall.

'God be blessed, he is alive! Quickly, load him onto the cart and take him up to the church.'

'Is it quicker to take him to Ramleh?' Gerash suggested. Being found with the dying body of a knight was wrought with danger.

'We have better medicines and bandages.'

Placing some sacking under his head, Gerash dripped some water into the old man's mouth and was relieved to see him swallow.

As the cart wobbled slowly up the slope, William steered the horses through the mud. He looked over his shoulder. 'Pull open his tunic and push a cloth into the wound to stop the bleeding, then search his pockets and pouches to see who he is.'

Gerash stemmed the flow of blood and found nothing in the old man's clothing. 'He is very pale, Master William but he is lucky that the coating of mud prevented the sun from burning him and the rain kept his lips moist. His clothes are expensive, like that of a lord from the west,' Gerash observed astutely. 'I will go back later and retrieve the saddlebags from the ravine.'

The wheels of the cart squelched through the mud and William forced the cart around the gate. Upon reaching the church, William asked Gerash to warm some mulled wine, while he made up another mattress alongside his own.

Abdul ran off to the garrison to find the monk who could treat the wound and William took down a box of ointments and potions from a shelf. They laid the injured lord down onto the mattress and William dribbled some warm wine into his mouth. For a brief moment, he opened and closed his eyes.

The monk arrived and looked at the pale face of the old man on the mattress. Examining the wound, he tutted and shook his head. 'Although the flesh is pierced there cannot be too much damage or else he would be dead by now. I will clean it up and apply a salve. Be prepared to treat a fever when it comes. At his age it is quite likely to kill him.' While William heated some more wine, the monk rummaged around in the box, applying some salve from a flask and a herbal lotion.

An hour later, the lord was washed and bandaged. 'He is in God's hands now.' The monk crossed himself. 'Chances are he is a lord from the west. I shall pray for him and if by God's grace you discover his estate and funds, then the Order shall of course expect a donation.' He opened the door and walked across to the side gate that overlooked the square. 'Hopefully it will cover the cost of that stallion of yours…eating more than the rest of us put together.' As he watched the monk walk across the square, William could still hear him complaining about the cost of horse feed.

He looked at the empty paddock adjoining the garrison. The tactless remark did remind William to ask after the health of his pride and joy. Ever since the extra wall around the church was erected, he missed the sight of the greatest pure white stallion he had ever bred.

Jacques was the only knight he entrusted to its care and although he had taken the charger on escort duty, he had never been bloodied in battle. The small paddock was the only place he actually got to see Perseus but the stallion was nowhere to be seen.

Gerash was sat on the mattress, still washing the face of the mysterious lord.

William walked towards the door. 'No more to do here. Just need some fresh air.'

Walking across the square to the garrison, he called out to a groom asking if Perseus was in the stable or on patrol.

The groom knew of the extraordinary pedigree of the stallion and was happy to oblige the old horse farmer. 'I will get him for you sire.'

For half an hour, William watched the mighty steed as he strutted proudly around the tiny paddock, flinging his white mane from side to side. The groom held him as best he could and William rubbed his old hands along the neck and down each tendon. The horse was perfect, almost too perfect for common battle, where a stray arrow could cripple him or worse.

He decided, no matter how much Jacques complained he would never let him ride the beast into battle. Instead, he would ask that Gerash take him out of the tiny paddock and back to the horse-farm, where he could sire a new generation of stallions and mares. An entirely new breed of warhorse that would be the envy of every knight and lord in the east.

From his first sight of the Abbey of St Lazarus in Bethany, Count Philip could see it attracted the wealth of many bequests and donations. No doubt, much of the appeal was due to the hard work and dedication of his mother who had died within its precincts more than ten years ago. His escort of half a dozen knights waited outside the gates, while he and Jacques de Exemes entered bearing gifts for the abbess.

Philip was surprised at the pouch of silver bezants that Jacques handed over. 'I did not know the Knights Templar donated to other monasteries.'

'It is more out of regard for your mother than the actual monastery,' Jacques replied. 'Your mother was a highly respected abbess and when Queen Melisende died, your mother came from the abbey and in the temporary absence of the king, virtually ran the royal court as regent, as well as her other duties at the abbey.'

'She was obviously a remarkable woman,' Philip lamented. 'I know my parents felt obliged to serve most of their lives in the Holy Land; still I just wish I could have seen more...' His words faded before he sounded too needy.

The abbess took them into the small church and adjoining the southern transept was a chapel dedicated to his mother. In the centre, they knelt in prayer at her stone tomb. Philip's attention was distracted by a prayer book with a handwritten cover. 'I am sure this is my mother's writing. Look even her prayer's have extra verses written in the margins.' He turned round to the abbess. 'Do you have any of my mother's notebooks or journals?'

'No my lord, all such worldly things are disposed of. It is a sin to have pride in our own thoughts that are written down,' the abbess replied sternly.

They returned to the stables and just as they were about to mount up, a sister appeared from the cloisters. From inside the sleeve of her habit she produced a small book encased in leather containing some ten pages of notations and verse.

'She gave this to me to look after. I was to give it to no one except a family member. Please don't tell the abbess.' Without another word, the sister hurried back to the cloisters avoiding eye contact with the other nuns.

In the shade of an acacia tree outside Bethany, Philip broke the seal and read the pages of the book. Paraphrasing the text, he read the contents out loud to Jacques. 'It relates to the time when she was with Thierry, my father and they had just arrived in the Holy Land when she met someone.' He paused while he read more of the words to himself. 'She thought he was a Jerusalem Knight...but had been desperate to see him for some years. They met secretly...' Again, he read the words to himself then placed the book down, his face a picture of sheer astonishment. 'She had a secret tryst with...with this knight. My God, he took her down into the crypt...' Philip read to himself the next passage that described her euphoria at running her hand along the Cross of Christ and how she felt as if she had touched God. Her final words insisted that the cross must remain in its final resting place. Philip continued. 'Soon after this experience she entered the abbey not daring to think of her knight anymore for fear of causing retribution.'

Jacques had shown little surprise at the words and thought it best to tell what he knew of the story. 'I know much from the lips of William Bigod, my lord. There is little doubt that he was the secret knight your mother refers to, though he will vehemently deny as much.'

'William Bigod,' Philip snorted. He stood up, embarrassed that the Templar knew so much of his mother's alleged infidelity but even more upset and confused at the mention of William. 'My God, is there nothing that the Bigod name does not taint. After we have finished in Jerusalem, I must go to William. He needs to know about his brother Hugh.'

Jacques looked up, suddenly interested. 'Oh, and what is it about Hugh Bigod?'

'Didn't I tell you? Hugh was my comrade in arms who died when we were attacked between Ramleh and Lydda last week. He was going to seek forgiveness and absolution from his brother William, so his excommunication could be lifted, God rest his soul'

Jacques seemed incredulous. 'So you are saying it was Hugh Bigod that died saving your life, within a mile of seeing his brother. My God in heaven, please do not tell William. He is a good man who has led an exemplary life; a man of God and more forgiveness than any man I know. The thought of Hugh dying under such circumstances will be the end of him for sure.'

'Be that as it may, I still have unfinished business in Lydda.'

Jacques decided he would stay with Philip; just to ensure no harm came to William. From the abbey in Bethany they headed north west to Jerusalem to refresh their water skins and take a meal of bread and fruit. A messenger arrived with a letter from Raymond of Tripoli.

He read it out. 'With the consent of King Baldwin and the Commander of the Army, Raynald de Châtillon, the Lord of Tripoli has taken it upon himself to commandeer your knights in order to assault the town of Hama which threatens his territory. He left yesterday at dawn and begs your support, and asks you to join him on the road north.

Philip looked to Jacques for advice.

Jacques smiled sardonically. 'The king is quite within his rights to commandeer any knights stationed within the walls of Jerusalem. Seems as if you are in a battle, whether you like it or not. I will accompany you if you wish.'

'Well perhaps I have had my fill of piety and prayer this last week. Time to engage the enemy, I think.' Philip replied. 'How in God's name do we get to Hama, anyway?'

'Well I presume Raymond has taken the route north through Galilee to avoid Saracen incursions along the coast. We can catch him up in two days if we leave now.'

Somehow, Philip felt relieved that the decision to go to battle had been taken away from him. Of course, he would lead his own army or he would become the laughing stock of Palestine.

Chapter 44

Lydda
Palestine

After only three days, the fever was finally beaten. Taking the wet cloth from the face of the unknown lord, Gerash was able to see the extent of his recovery. Occasionally he regained consciousness only to slip back into oblivion. He decided to stop administering the fever remedy and went to put it back in the box, on the shelf behind the door.

Suddenly the door opened and William entered, accidentally knocking the flask from the hands of Gerash. The glass shattered on the stone floor.

Gerash apologised and in the tiny annex built for one, it had become apparent that there was insufficient space for three of them.

'I shall move back to the horse farm for a few days,' William conceded.

Gerash agreed, saying he would continue to care for the recovering lord. 'Abdul is more than capable of looking after the farm as well as seeing to your needs.' He handed a small flask to William. 'Better you take this poppy juice back to the farm before it is also broken.'

William put the flask in his pocket and wondered if Gerash was aware of his occasional use of the sedative. His aching body and tired limbs were becoming more burdensome and the juice provided much relief. Now the damp cloth had been removed, he saw the clean face of the nameless lord for the first time.

Gerash handed over the saddlebag. 'Master I have recovered this from the ravine. There was nothing inside that helps to identify him.'

William put his hand the inside the bag and pulled out the jar. 'How strange...' William commented. 'The writing around the middle appears to be ancient...' He stared for a moment at the jar as his words drifted away.

'Probably an urn that contains the ashes of a loved one,' Gerash said dismissively. 'Many pilgrims bring them.'

William placed the oddment on a shelf.

Later that afternoon, William was back at the farm and he took to his bed. Normally sleep came quite easily to him, but now he was annoyed at being tired and unable to sleep. He remembered the poppy juice still in his pocket and he took a dose out of pure frustration, something he had never done for a week or more. Anything to make him sleep.

Sleep was no longer a pleasure or even a normal bodily function. It became a test of endurance, to see how long he could tolerate the plethora of nightmares that fought over every fibre of his frail body.

The loud shouts were only the start. Was he arguing with himself or was someone else shouting back at him. They were bitter words that hurt. Then a ship...a sinking ship, and he was drowning, flapping his arms in the waves trying to stay afloat. Murder and mayhem followed and then held by the devil's chains in the dungeons where he lost endless years in the dark...and then his tongue.

At every beat of his heart, at every breath that he drew, a face began to form. Sometimes it was a young face, then became blurred and gnarled with time...until it was old. And now he recognised to whom it belonged.

The anguished screams from William's chamber ripped through the walls. The terrified servants burst into his chamber as Abdul came running from the stables, thinking that someone had been murdered.

They crowded into the room and peered as one over the bed onto the floor.

William was sat with his back against the wall, tears streaming down his face. The dappled light from the setting sun, lit the sorrowful scene as he raised his hands to cover his sobbing and hide the deep consternation that twisted his insides. He begged everyone to leave him alone.

Noticing the bottle of white juice on the side of the bed, Abdul thought it best to let William recover in his own time. No doubt, his mind was numb and reliving outlandish dreams, as he had once experienced himself. He too had only wanted to be left alone.

To be on the safe side, he thought it best to inform his father. Telling the servants to make sure William came to no harm, he mounted a horse and rode down the track towards the town. He had gone only a hundred paces when his father came galloping towards him. Slowing down he waited for his father to stop and speak, but instead he kept racing on by as if he wasn't there.

Gerash had seen Abdul pause on the track but deliberately sped on by, his mind fixed on riding to the farmstead as quickly as possible. Dismounting outside the front door in a cloud of dust, he pushed his way through the servants and entered William's chamber. Coming in from the bright light, it took a moment to see William crouched in the corner, crying like a baby. 'Master William, are you all right?'

William continued to stare into space. He spoke in a flat dull voice that was difficult to understand. 'You have come to tell me who he is, haven't you.'

'Master, it is your brother.'

'I know,' William replied softly. 'I know.'

Once William was comforted and strong enough to face his brother, they took him on horseback down the track to the church. Outside the gate, William paused to steady himself, then asked Gerash to wait outside. Walking through the gate into his annex was like walking into a dream where reality had ceased. Taking a deep breath, he opened the door. In the poor light he saw someone sat on the bed with his back to him. His first words seemed ridiculous but at the same time perfectly normal. 'Hello Hugh,' he said.

The reply came from his right and startled him. 'My God William, it is you.'

The figure on the bed turned round and it was the physician, packing up his bandages into a bag. 'Gerash tells me you accidentally broke a flask. Such a shame.' The physician smiled. 'Well, you two have a lot to talk about,' he said hurrying out of the annex, leaving William and Hugh alone.

For what seemed an age they took in each other's appearances, like two sponges soaking up a lifetime of memories that were etched within their craggy faces. William sat down on the bed and Hugh seemed content to stay in the chair.

'How are you feeling?' William asked, feeling stupid for asking.

'Fine, just a little tender. That monk has the skills of seamstress.' Hugh lifted his shirt to show the wound.

William rocked on his heels. 'My God, you were lucky. That lance took out quite a slice of flesh. And you spent all night lying in a muddy ravine, underneath your horse.'

'The monk said the warmth of the horse kept me alive. Load of sodding rubbish.' Hugh gave a thin smile and sighed. 'Your man did a good job of looking after me; that is until I told him who I was. Then he was out of here like lightening, but not before calling the monk to attend to my wounds.'

Both of them fell silent. The occasion had become bigger than anything they could say and they stared into the empty space that echoed unconsciously between them. Shaking his head, William found it difficult to come to terms. Try as he might, he could not hold his eyes on Hugh and both of them looked away. The long forgotten sentiments, the hardened memories that had faded over the years: all their feelings began to overwhelm them both. Neither of them wanted to break the spell that simply held them in the same room, so the battle continued over who could hold back the emotions, locked deep inside.

It took all his strength for Hugh to break the highly charged deadlock. His voice started off strong, then wavered. 'I have come a long way to say I am sorry. I don't want to spend my next life in purgatory...so I have come to beg your forgiveness.'

William could have been forgiven for thinking his brother was asking too much of him but the slight tremble in the voice had the effect of making the words sound genuine. Although he wanted to say something profound, he suddenly felt the loss of his tongue and lost all confidence to speak.

Hugh lifted himself from the chair and approached William. Kneeling in front of his brother Hugh buried his head in his hands. 'Please forgive me. My sins are so many and I do not deserve your sympathy. But I do need your forgiveness.'

Lifting his head, William saw the way ahead and forced himself to speak. 'Come inside the church to pray with me. If God thinks you deserve forgiveness then who am I to deny you.'

Hugh followed his brother through the side door and into the aisle, where they knelt side-by-side facing the altar. Moments later William saw Hugh was shaking and wondered if he was having a fit. But he was simply sobbing. He put his arm around his brother's shoulder to comfort him and before long, they were both crying. Like a grief-stricken lament, they cried for everything they had lost and never shared.

They clung on to each other, afraid now of their own mortality and of what the future held. Drained of all emotion, they retired to the rear of the church under the tall pillars and the cool vaulted ceiling of the nave.

William felt it was time to say something. 'Time is short for both of us. You must not feel under any obligation to go over old misdemeanour's and misunderstandings. In fact I would rather we did not discuss our past at all. Is that agreed?'

Hugh concurred. They sat for a while gazing at the altar.

'Did you have children,' Hugh asked.

'Only one son, by the name of Gabriel,' William sighed. 'Let me tell you something I have never told another soul. He was the bravest soul I knew. He killed Zengi, one of the most evil Sultan's ever to have lived, and paid for the heroic act with his life.'

'You must be very proud of him,' Hugh acknowledged.

William looked away, his eyes betraying the pain he felt. He kept his reply simple. 'He died fighting for his freedom.'

'Some ways of dying are better than others,' Hugh granted. They sat in silence reflecting on personal memories of life and death.

'What about your children?' William asked.

Hugh raised his eyebrows. 'I have two sons, one with each wife. No doubt they will be fighting over my estates as we speak.'

William kept the first words that entered his head to himself.

Your estates…

Moving a little closer, Hugh held on to his brother 's arm. 'Tell me the truth, has your life here been free of pain.'

'I don't know what you mean.'

Hugh tried to explain. 'If your life here has been filled with despair and melancholy...I would feel responsible.'

Like listening to an errant child.

William smiled, grateful that all the pent up resentment he felt against Hugh, had disappeared long ago. 'I don't think I could have had a fuller life. I have so few regrets, I should actually be grateful for the life I have led.'

Hugh dipped his head, acknowledging the gracious attitude of his brother. 'Thank you for saying that. My whole life has been one massive regret.' Hugh rose unsteadily to his feet and stretched his limbs. 'But you will be heartened to know that I made the lives of three Kings and an Empress an absolute misery.'

They both raised a chuckle at Hugh's admission. So many memories came flooding back it was impossible to cope with them all at once.

Staring at the ceiling, Hugh made a suggestion. 'You should show me around Jerusalem.'

'Of course…but you must regain your strength. Both of us have had a shock and we are not getting any younger.'

Helping William to his feet, Hugh felt as if an enormous weight had been lifted from his shoulders. He handed his brother his walking stick and they left the coolness of the church.

Walking out of the main doors into the square they were astonished to be greeted by a hundred people or more. Gerash and Abdul had spread the word around Lydda that the elderly brothers had been reunited for the first time in over fifty years.

Cheers greeted the two men as everyone celebrated the two lords finding each other after so long. Many of the women who had known William for many years, openly wept at the sight of them supporting each other, arm in arm. Joyful shouts filled the air. 'Allah be praised!' and 'God bless you!'

Chapter 45

Hama
Syria

The siege of Hama reached a stalemate and Count Philip soon became restless. He hated long sieges at the best of times, but the oppressive heat of Syria made for a gruelling ordeal.

Raymond of Tripoli had proved to be a good ally mainly because he distrusted Raynald de Châtillon and the others who had spoken so provocatively against Philip at the royal court.

'Don't let them fool you into thinking they are all do-gooders,' he advised Philip. 'They are all power hungry maniac's who think only of selfish gains. All of them would gladly slit the throat of the king today, if they were certain the crown would be theirs tomorrow.'

The more he heard of the machinations of the Jerusalem court, the more he was dissuaded from spending any more time than necessary in the Holy Land.

'How much longer should we lay siege this town?' he asked Raymond, his patience running out.

Raymond yawned, for he to felt jaded by the lack of impetus. 'I suspect they will raise troops from Damascus any day now. Then we can retire back to Tripoli.'

'But we will have achieved nothing,' Philip complained.

'True, but sometimes it is best to let the enemy know its limitations. Fighting out here is often about keeping the status quo.'

Philip had given up trying to understand. 'I think I shall return to the south. I have to go to Lydda before I leave.'

'And so you shall, but first we must complete the campaign. While Damascus prepares to bring a force from the south, we shall move further north to besiege the town of Harenc.'

'But again we achieve nothing,' Philip repeated his exasperation.

'It keeps the enemy occupied and makes it difficult for them to raise a serious attack against Tripoli and Antioch. They can never drop their defences,' Raymond explained. 'Try and appreciate, there are no victors in Palestine. Everyone knows their place.'

Philip shook his head in dismay at the stalemate then turned to see the Templar Jacques de Exemes riding fast next to a messenger.

'My lords, I am afraid I must take my leave of you,' Jacques told them breathlessly. 'There is a rumour that Saladin is assembling a massive invasion force and I have been ordered back to the Templar stronghold at Gaza. If you agree, my lord, I shall take your fastest ship from Tripoli.'

'Of course and I wish you God's speed,' Raymond said sincerely

Jacques turned to Count Philip. 'The messenger also has a message for you my lord.'

Breathless from his journey, the messenger took a drink of water before addressing the count. 'I have been told to give you this message personally. It is from the garrison at Lydda. Earl Hugh Bigod of Norwich is alive and well, and in the care of his brother William.'

Philip stared in disbelief at Jacques. 'Hugh is alive…' He turned to Count Raymond. 'Listen, I want to go with Jacques on the ship, as far as Jaffa. From there, I shall make the ride to Lydda. And before you ask, I will agree that my men stay under your command to besiege Harenc. Tell no one of my departure and in two weeks time, I will meet up again in Tripoli, to sail back to the west.'

Raymond appeared taken aback by the idea. 'So this Earl Bigod is the friend you thought was dead. And I thought the urgency of your visit to Lydda emanated from the strange stories from that church.'

'Why do you say that exactly,' Philip asked.

Raymond did not answer but looked at Jacques. 'Perhaps he is better placed to answer that,' he said.

Jacques hesitated, unsure of what to say. 'For hundreds of years, stories of St George's church have echoed around the Holy Land and beyond. Celebrated as the birthplace of Saint George and also his martyrdom, and final resting place. Countless numbers swear they have seen ghosts and dragons of all shapes and sizes.'

Raymond concurred. 'That's right. Only last month I met a Greek pilgrim called Phocas. He told me that the Bishop of Ramleh recently entered the tomb of the saint and a flame burst forth, burning one of his men to death and severely injuring another. Only a fool dare enter the crypt to be incinerated without warning.'

Philip looked unconcerned at the dire warnings. 'I was aware of everything you say. But tell me what you know of the relics and the Cross of Christ?'

Jacques was reluctant to continue. 'There was a skull found in the crypt...and was supposed to be the head of Christ.'

Philip looked surprised. 'The head of Christ!' he repeated. So what happened to this head..?'

'The Templars took it. That is all I know.'

'And what of William Bigod? What does he know of the relics?'

Jacques looked straight at Philip. 'I don't know and I have never cared to ask. The man is eighty-three years old; probably the oldest man living in the whole of Palestine. For his sake, let him live out his life in peace.'

Philip wanted to ask more but he could tell from Jacques belligerent expression that he was in no mood to answer. 'Well now he has finally met with his brother, I think it is time to congratulate him on becoming the new Earl of Norfolk.'

Jacques was adamant. 'He will not want it. Not William.'

'You are probably right,' Philip conceded, his eyebrows raised. 'Time waits for no man. I suggest we make preparations for our departure as discretely as possible.'

Chapter 46

Petra
Palestine

In the glow of the blue desert radiance seen before dawn, the two dark figures made their way through the once thriving city of Petra. The only sound came from a breeze whistling around the ghostly rock-cut tombs that lined the sheer sides of the dramatic red gorge. Edom had never seen a canyon of such natural beauty, capable of engulfing his soul from above.

As they walked in the footsteps of Moses and the Hebrews, they glanced at the weathered ruins of a roman amphitheatre cut into the left side of the gorge. Muzawi gestured towards an indistinct line of steps that quickly disappeared into the murky heights of the mountain side. 'Up here.'

Encumbered by the girl's body over his shoulder, Edom looked up and sighed at the task before him. Ahead, the steeply cut path was unyielding and Edom dare not stop for fear of losing sight of his master. Given his advanced years, he wondered how Muzawi could keep up such a relentless pace, for his strength seemed to defy all natural laws. Then again, there was little about his master that appeared natural. Thankfully his lifeless load seemed slight and weighed next to nothing.

Muzawi paused as if preoccupied by the stars that were dotted like luminous pinpricks across the sky. Behind them an eerie luminosity bathed the barren wilderness all the way to the horizon.

Edom shifted his weight and tossed the small body over his other shoulder. Before long the ground levelled out a little then started climbing again.

Two monolithic obelisks, the height of a church, dominated the view over the ancient landscape. After a few more steps they reached the platform on the mountain top and Edom paused while Muzawi stood on the sacrificial podium. The ancient High Place of Sacrifice, as old as time itself, his master had said. In the poor light, the sheer sides of the peak troubled Edom as he gazed below at the winding Wadi.

Muzawi made his way solemnly towards two ancient altars carved out of the rock. Three steps led up the first altar where he knelt on the well-worn stone and raised his arms in supplication while whispering ancient incantations. He nodded to Edom who was grateful to divest himself of his burden as he draped the body across the second altar, her limp form easily fitting within the shallow cut bowl. As the sky began to lighten he noticed her simple beauty and delicate innocence. He offered a quiet incantation.

Sitting at the foot of the altar, Edom remembered his instructions to prepare the altar with the lighting of incense. Feeling detached from his emotions, he watched and waited for his next orders. Cut into the centre of the altar he noticed the deep inner bowl and the channel that drained the sacrificial blood through a spout cut into a channel. The channel ran around the base of the altar and eventually out over the sheer face of the gorge.

Muzawi tore his gaze from the horizon and descended the steps, pausing in front of the second altar to mumble ancient words and breathe in the sweet fumes of incense. Many years had passed since the last time he had stood with his father Tammuz and young Shishak in front of the altar dedicated to Baal. In the light of their failings, he was now secure in his belief that he alone deserved to receive the blessing of Baal.

Taking the stone stele of Tanit from its protective cloth he settled the base into the channel, next to the girls face. Reverently, he laid the precious single sphere upon the altar and waited.

Fixing his eyes upon the ancient stone stele, he studied the ancient engraving. A triangular symbol of a priest or shaman held the two sceptres apart. Above the sceptres floated the two spheres and in the centre the crescent moon cradled the circle of the sun. Satisfied that everything was perfect, he waited for the miracle to begin.

Controlling his anticipation, he spoke to Edom. 'Thousands of years ago, the shaman would stand at this altar to sacrifice an innocent child. Can you not feel the ghosts that have stood here before? Their power runs through my blood.'

Over a crystal clear horizon, Muzawi watched in sheer amazement as the thin crescent of the sun rose above the mountainous horizon.

Muzawi whispered. 'Look…it is time.'

He drew back his black hood and in a voice that resonated around the sterile platform, he read out the names of the Sky Gods. 'Anu, Enlil, and Enki. You are the immortals who once walked amongst primitive men. Chosen to breed with the women of the earth to create a race of Earth-Gods. Those who commanded fire, the wind and the sea, and all natural wonders. One such God was named El and his son was named Baal, the Sun God.'

Catching his breath, Muzawi glanced up at the horizon and smiled nervously then proceeded with the ritual. 'Baal procreated with Astarte, the mother of abominations, the goddess of war and sex. Her beauty dazzled as does the light of the sun. Baal ordered the building of enormous Temples of sacrifice where they would be deified as living Earth-Gods. A thousand years passed. To keep the blood strong, the Sky God's generated the 'time of promises'…a secret that can only be recognised by their descendants.'

Panting from his state of elation, Muzawi gathered his senses, his hands shaking as he lit more incense. The moon moved inexorably over the face of the sun leaving just a sliver of light visible above the horizon. For the next few moments, the sun sparkled like a ring of jewels then in an instant the moon extinguished the last speck of light.

Holding his breath, he drew the gold, bejewelled dagger from his belt and held it aloft. He called out to the Gods. 'As a baby in my mother's arms I suckled on her blood. You saved me and now I repay you. I call upon all the priests of the underworld that have gone before. "Gehenna, Gehenna!"'

Staring up at his master, Edom had little understanding of the ancient ritual. He gasped as the girl opened her confused eyes, her mouth unable to utter any sounds of distress. The intensity of the moment froze Edom to the spot. There was nothing he could do as his willpower drained away and his soul was undeniably claimed by the devil holding the dagger.

In the ethereal light of the eclipse, Muzawi felt for the girl's throat, drawing the blade deep across the arteries. Air bubbled from the tiny windpipe and made a faint whistling sound as the blood sprayed onto the altar, spilling over the sphere, making it hiss and spit.

A spark of light pierced the dark as the sun reappeared. 'The sun is reborn, now I am reborn. A new dawn rises over the land of Moses. May the Gods hear my call! Fulfil the 'time of promises.' Your return is nigh. Let me kneel at your feet and together we can rule the world! '

Muzawi was wise enough to realise that lesser mortals would find themselves drawn unwittingly into the web. Once they had witnessed his power, all opposition would crumble. Defeated, they would soon come to him as allies, eager to form client kingdoms and be a part of the new world order.

Elated by the perfect timing of the sacrifice, he warmed his tongue with the blood of the innocent, its taste as sweet as nectar. In the absolute stillness, the earth held its breath.

He watched the blood run down the altar and over an engraving of two pillars, chiselled into the base of the altar. The sunlight struck the altar to show him the way. Underneath the engraving, letters appeared as if by magic. They were ancient, but with his heightened senses he translated them in an instant. His heart soared. Now he knew the location of the two sceptres.

They left the corpse of the girl exposed on the altar, as it would have been in ancient times, and started down the steps.

Pausing at the emergence of the sun, Muzawi felt the growth of his heightened perception. Saladin's army progressing up the coast towards the Templar stronghold of Gaza. The last thing he wanted was Saladin interfering in his plans.

'Saladin is moving north. We must reach Lydda before him.'

Edom looked surprised. 'But you told me the entire Order of the Knights Templar have been called as one to hold Gaza at all costs. Any siege of the city walls could take a week or more.'

'But now I know what Saladin wants. He will continue up the coast and will not be diverted, even by the prospect of killing a few Templars. Lydda will be his objective.'

Chapter 47

Gaza
Palestine

The annoying distraction of unseen assassins and the strange encounters with the 'old man of the mountain' were long behind Saladin. Now with a campaign underway to take back Jerusalem, he was determined to concentrate his efforts on fighting the Christians in their own territory.

After months of preparation, his army had finally crossed the border from Egypt into Palestine and soon they reached Gaza.

It was tempting to linger and enter into a prolonged siege against the large Templar force within the city. Nothing would please him more than to see them suffer from starvation and beg for relief.

Saladin pointed out his good fortune. 'King Baldwin lies on his sickbed and sends reinforcements to the north to Harenc. He is blind to any threat from the south.'

But Maimonides was quick to counter. 'Yes, but if this new adversary, Count Philip were to return south with his army, he could be here in just a few days.

Saladin thought for a moment. 'But what if I could convince them that Gaza was under siege. We could set up a defensive position with just a few troops and a mangonel to batter the walls.

Maimonides was not convinced. 'Well that would only work if the deception was well planned and the siege of Gaza holding...'

'Why are you so negative? You know nothing of military matters. A small infantry force and just two mangonels could keep the Templars in Gaza. Meanwhile I take the army twenty miles north to Ascalon and once outside the walls, I could repeat the exercise. Two mangonels and a some young but willing infantry. They will believe the whole army has been utilised, while I will lead twenty-five thousand men to take back Jerusalem.'

An over-sized camp was set up on the outskirts of Gaza and manned by only a six hundred men and two mangonels. Meanwhile, the rest of Saladin's army proceeded north.

Just a few miles later the scouts reporting seeing a small troop of Templars riding along the coastal path in the direction of Gaza.

'There was no mistaking the white tabards and red crosses', one scout reported.

Twenty horse archers were immediately dispatched, but Saladin countermanded the order. 'Keep discipline within your ranks,' he told his general. 'Don't waste your time and men chasing them. We have six hundred men outside Gaza to prevent them entering the city.'

The remaining miles were quickly covered and as they arrived at the walls of Ascalon, a captain from the vanguard sped forward to report. 'Sultan, we have seen King Baldwin arrive from Jerusalem. He turned to confront us but when he saw he was outnumbered he scurried like a whimpering dog to hide behind the walls of Ascalon.'

Saladin could barely hold back his pleasure and offered a ruby ring to the captain.

'What strength was his army?' he asked.

'About four hundred knights and a hundred other horses my lord, including Raynald de Châtillon, Baldwin of Ibelin and many other distinctive lords.'

'What of the army of the Count of Flanders?' Saladin urged.

'There was no standard of Flanders, my lord sultan. He must still be in the north, besieging Hama or Harenc. There was something else, my lord. On a cart I we saw a bishop carrying what looked like the Christian Holy Cross.'

Saladin held up his arms. 'Allah be praised. Even accounting for the permanent garrisons at Gaza and Ascalon, we outnumber them ten to one. And they hobble themselves with ornamental blocks of wood with a few studded jewels. Well I will have their precious cross.'

Sharing his glee, his councillors and generals surrounded him, offering advice as to the next course of action.

Maimonides could not believe how the Christian army appeared so ill prepared. Perhaps it really was Saladin's day, he thought as he rode off to find something to eat.

Eventually the impromptu meeting broke up and Saladin had made his decision. He found Maimonides eating a hastily prepared rabbit stew. 'We shall establish a perimeter around Ascalon tomorrow, and the day after we attack Ibelin. Four days from now, we shall be in Ramleh and Lydda. You will be pleased to know the towns have no walls and I shall take great delight in pillaging every coin from every village between here and Jerusalem.'

'And what of the Christian civilians?' Maimonides enquired.

Aware that his generals were listening, Saladin spoke up. 'The usual practise of course. The women and children shall be taken as slaves and the men of fighting age will be killed.'

'Slaughtered you mean.' Maimonides bit his tongue knowing he had spoken out of turn.

'Yes, so be it, slaughtered! Is that all right with you?'

Maimonides paused for a moment and tugged his beard before speaking, giving the impression of wisdom. 'I don't wish to criticise my lord sultan, but are you in danger of losing momentum. I am worried at the advice you receive. Sometimes it seems Muzawi...'

'Do not mention that name!' Saladin looked furious. He took a moment to recover his poise. 'I want you to be my Shaman. Think of the power we can wield...the whole world will kneel at our feet. I shall destroy every Christian shrine throughout the east and I shall kill or enslave every Christian.'

Maimonides gave a more considered response. 'With all the honour I can bestow I shall be as a guiding light by your side. But only for good. I would not have it any other way.'

Saladin spat out. 'You expect me to lay down the instruments of the Gods and behave like some godforsaken holy man! I will carry the power of the ancient God's in my hands and I will use that power, with or without your help. All will kneel before me...including the Jews. Unless you know of someone who can stop me?'

The anger suddenly fell away from Saladin's face. 'Come on my friend, be happy for once. I have enough to worry about when I look at the long face of my wife.' Everyone gave a nervous laugh.

Maimonides tried to cheer up but as the day ended, he began to feel vulnerable so far away from Cairo and the reason slowly became obvious. There was no vanquished enemy, no victorious battle. They had beaten no one.

Gaza was now to the rear of Saladin's army and home to a full fighting garrison of Knights Templar, the most feared warriors on the battlefield. Less than a mile away, the King of Jerusalem sat in conference with his most feared and experienced generals. Maimonides felt every right to be nervous.

The ship from Tripoli made good progress down the Syrian coast until an offshore wind slowed it down some five miles off the coastal port of Jaffa. The captain explained the problem to Count Philip. 'This wind makes no sense. Whichever way I try, I cannot steer for Jaffa. We have been blown off course to the south and it may take another two days to reverse our position. However, if you wish we can carry on down the coast and make landfall at Ascalon before tomorrow afternoon.'

Though disappointed both Philip and Jacques agreed it was the best option, and they kept up an impressive rate of knots going south. By the time they had reached the harbour at Ascalon, the wind had died down and they disembarked with their horses and squires just three hours before sundown.

'There is of course a problem,' Jacques said. 'You are now some forty miles from Lydda and you cannot risk travelling alone at night. You will have to ride with me to Gaza. If we leave straight away we can be there by nightfall.'

Philip felt as if he was being drawn away from ever seeing Lydda. Always so close then inexplicably pulled away yet again.

Jacques could see his disappointment. 'I am sorry but there really is no alternative. But I swear I will do everything to get you to Lydda as soon as possible.'

They set off down the coast road and after fifteen miles at an even pace they spotted Gaza around the next headland.

'Is it a sandstorm?' Philip asked, pointing inland. A dust cloud over a ridge made them pause.

Jacques did not know and they rode on a little further while the dust cloud headed inland. As they reached a knoll, they paused again.

'My God, it's the Egyptian army! 'Jacques yelled. 'Ride as fast as you can.'

Philip and his squire galloped on ahead while Jacques and his two squires followed on behind. They galloped a further mile before they were able to see if anyone was following.

His order to return to Gaza with all haste now made sense to Jacques. Reports of the Egyptian army had proved to be true but what of Gaza? Within half an hour, they came to a rise and could see the city walls. The shock of seeing Egyptian troops milling around outside the walls filled him with foreboding.

Philip began to wonder if his journey to Palestine was destined to become a disaster. 'Someone's plans were a little inept. I thought we were supposed to invade Egypt, not the other way round.' He observed dryly.

Jacques paid no heed to the remark. He dismounted and climbed a small outcrop on the side of the road to better gauge what was happening.

The demeanour of the infantry seemed out of place and the two siege engines were unmanned. Having learnt all he could he descended the rocks to find Philip watering the horses.

'I can hardly believe my own eyes,' Jacques said panting from his exertion. 'The city is not under siege. But for one unit of men nearest the walls, the rest of the infantry are sat out of sight under the trees. They have no one in charge and no stockpile of boulders for the mangonel…the whole siege is a subterfuge.'

Philip was beyond caring. 'Like I said, your leaders are inept.'

Jacques continued. 'Even so it is too risky to try a direct approach. There is a way into the city through a passageway that is known to a few and can only be reached at low tide. I suggest we make our way to the shoreline and wait there until dusk.'

Philip's mood was not lightened by the proposal. 'Oh please tell me why we would want to break into a city under siege, or should I say…surrounded by Saracen layabouts.'

'Once I tell the Grand Master the truth behind the deception, then believe me, there are enough Templars within the walls of Gaza to break out through that collection of Saracen conscripts.'

Philip smiled. 'Now that is what I like to hear.'

The Egyptians saw no reason for lookouts along the rocky northern shoreline and Jacques was able to lead Philip through the secret entrance without being seen.

Jacques ran through the corridors with Count Philip and along the wall until they ran into a startled sergeant. Introducing himself, he demanded to see the Grand Master Odo St Armand immediately.

The Grand Master gave an air of incredulity over the true state of the army beyond the walls and Jacques explained why. 'Saladin has taken advantage of your strategy to stay behind the walls. The Saracen army is driving hard up the coast and will be within sight of Jerusalem within the week. Outside these walls there is but a row of runts that should be treated as such.'

Within an hour, Odo St Armand had organised a front line of all the fully-fledged knights into battle order with two lines of sergeants and novices behind them. Philip sat on his destrier next to Odo, fascinated by the training exercise. He looked across the impressive lines and counted. 'Where are the rest of the Templars?' he asked naively.

'This is all of them,' Odo stated. 'We have received word that the king has taken the army into Ascalon and is surrounded. We leave at dawn.'

Philip swore under his breath. 'But we saw an Egyptian army of thousands. I pray God and all His saints and angels are watching over us at dawn, or we may be in trouble.'

Chapter 48

Lydda
Palestine

Over the last few days the nervous tension between Hugh and William had broken and despite their extra sensitive past, they happily engaged in normal conversation.

The night was particularly humid and they sat on the bench outside the main door of St George's church catching the miserly breeze. People gathered with torches in the square, just to catch a glimpse of the renowned brother from England who had enlivened much of the gossip in the town over the past weeks.

'So Hugh, what is it like to be famous?' William asked with a sardonic smile.

'They smile only because they are gambling on which of us drops dead first.'

They both laughed, totally at ease in each other's company.

'Why did you really come all this way?' William asked solemnly.

Hugh lowered his head. 'First I must tell you that Wills Albini died last year. He insisted I come to find you...to seek forgiveness.'

'Seems as though the three of us have lived enough lifetimes for an entire family,' William said. He barely remembered what Wills even looked like.

Personal memories filled the silence.

Then Hugh sighed as if coming to a decision. 'I don't know how much you know...but for quite a few years this old church of Lydda has been the subject of much talk all across England, Normandie and Champagne. I told you I arrived here with Count Philip of Champagne, didn't I.'

'Yes you did,' William nodded. 'And I briefly met with his father, Count Thierry...and his wife Sybille...some years after the death of William Cliton.'

Hugh sighed, unsure of how to continue. 'What you need to know is that Philip is after...whatever is in the crypt. The chamber of 'the shame' they call it.'

'William's face dropped. 'Who calls it that?'

'There is a group of elites made up of Marie of Champagne, the writer Chrétien de Troyes and Count Philip. Those three I know for definite but there will be others. I think they are dangerous and will stop at nothing to lay their hands on the holy relic. I don't think they should steal what is ours.'

'What do you mean, *ours*,' William queried.

'Ours because Ilger Bigod first discovered the cross of Christ when he was with the first army of God. Therefore it is a Bigod family relic.'

William did not reply; he let the words hang in the air. There were no more secrets. Hugh was right; the cross must to be moved. He tugged at a chain around his neck and leaned over to show Hugh.

Hugh nearly fell off the bench. 'Shit and hell...is that Ilger's piece of the true cross. But how did you find it...did he come back here?'

'Hugh, you have never been so right. I don't know how all this time I could have been in self denial. If you are up to it, we have to go into the chamber and recover the cross.'

'It's the middle of the night. Can we get help from this lot?' Hugh asked looking around the square.

'They are good people but are easily swayed in the wrong direction. It's better if Gerash made sure no one follows us inside.'

Leaving the porch, they appreciated the cool air of the church and lit a single torch and some candles by the altar. 'I must tell you; there is gas everywhere that is highly toxic and volatile. The skeletons scattered around the crypt are...'

'Yes, yes, blood, guts, shit and gas. I should feel at home. Now come on.'

In the face of their biggest challenge together, William chortled at Hugh's dry sense of humour. He started to prise open the first slab and was surprised at how strong Hugh appeared as he heaved up the second one, single-handed.

William wandered over to the font and handed Hugh a damp cloth to wrap around his face. 'Believe me, you will need it. Leave the torch here and make your way down four more steps till you reach the floor. I will follow,' William instructed, panting at his exertion and wrapping a cloth around his own face.

Hugh disappeared into the crypt and William followed. He saw him standing by the scree slope that led into the secret chamber.

'Christ, what a fucking stink.' Hugh pointed to a skeleton. 'Who was that?'

'That was Pagan Peverel, aide-de-camp to Duke Robert of Normandie. I watched him burn to death.'

'Peverel! God almighty, I remember the name from somewhere...'

'Breathe slowly. Whatever you do, do not panic. Now wait for your vision to improve...'

Hugh ignored Williams' words of caution and slowly slid on his bottom down the slope.

William quickly followed behind and immediately noticed the walls were more luminous than he could ever recall, giving a distinctly eerie feeling to the chamber.

Hugh walked under the first beam and saw the sword impaled into the solid earth. On the floor, around the blade were the scattered remains of a skeleton.

William said just one word. 'Ilger.' If Hugh showed any emotion, he could not tell.

Impatient for more, Hugh disappeared under the beams. William was about to call him when he heard a faint voice echoing from above. Moving back a few steps, he listened again and heard Gerash calling in a distressed state, into the crypt.

William called out at Hugh. 'Follow me now!' and signalled he was going back up. He climbed out of the chamber and across the floor of the crypt.

Without warning, his vision began to blur and he stumbled against one of the columns. The face of a man appeared on the stone and a bloody hand print appeared underneath. His nightmare was coming to life. He forced himself to move and stumbling up the steps, he felt the outstretched hand of Gerash.

'The Egyptians. They are here.' Gerash pulled him up the stairs. 'There are thousands of them running through the streets, killing everyone…burning the houses. They will find us here…we must try and escape now.' Grabbing his arm, Gerash steered William to the door of the church.

'Stop pulling me!' William paused and pulled the cloth from his face, gasping for breath. He looked behind him at the chancel.

Where on earth is Hugh?

Shouts were coming from the square and Gerash was shaking with fear. With one last effort, he virtually carried William through the door onto the porch.

They got no further before two men with curved swords blocked their way. One of them looked at William. 'Not that one.' He then looked at Gerash. 'Kill that one.'

Edom sliced his blade across the chest of Gerash, cutting through bones and flesh, his internal organs held together by fine sinews of muscle. William tried to hold him up and was instantly covered in blood for his effort. He let the body slip to the ground.

Muzawi stepped forward and pulled his shoufa from his face. The flames that burnt through a nearby roof lit up Williams face. 'You!

The old Templar and father of Yarankash, the assassin of the great Sultan Zengi.'

Even for one so old, the hatred he felt for Muzawi ran deep in William's veins. 'You killed my lovely wife and family. You strung them up like animals for the slaughter...'

Without warning, Muzawi struck William's face with his hand. 'That is nothing compared to what I have planned for you, old man! Hearing your screams after all these years, shall be an honour afforded only to a God.' His eyes blazed brighter than the flames behind him. There was an evil madness within his stare that made William shiver and his hair stand on end.

'Where is the other old man you were with?' he shouted.

William kept silent and stiffened as Muzawi swung his mace lightly.

'You are not too old to lose your balls, my friend.'

'He is in the crypt... dead. The gas killed him.'

Shaking his head, Muzawi picked up the wooden coffer containing the sphere.

'No matter.' He gave an order to Edom. 'Tie him to the church door while I collect the second sphere.'

'Do you want me to come with you?' Edom asked.

Muzawi hesitated. 'No. But make sure no one follows me.' He strode down the nave, gripping the mace in his right hand. He stopped to dip his scarf in the font of holy water.

Apart from feeling a little light-headed, Hugh continued his search for the beam that held the cross of Christ. He looked towards the shale slope for William but he had obviously retreated back to the church, probably affected by the gas. There was no light other than the glow coming from a pool.

Touching each beam as he passed under he watched the strange pool of luminous bubbling water and guessed it was the source of the deadly gasses. Anyone wanting to enter the inner sanctum would come with a torch that would ignite the gas. Without the torch, you cannot see where you are going, so you suffocate. Of course, it was the perfect defence mechanism.

At the sound of someone sliding down the shale, he turned around expecting to see William. Instead, he saw a menacing figure in black holding a small coffer and a mace. A pair of yellow eyes glared though a slit in the scarf .

A trickle of real fear struck Hugh. 'I am just an old man and I promise that if you let me by...'

The dark figure moved closer, his mace swinging at his side. Then he looked beyond Hugh towards the pool of water. He took another two steps until he was alongside Hugh. His words were difficult to understand under his scarf. 'You...his brother?'

Hugh lifted his arms upwards and grasped the beam above his head to steady his failing legs. 'Yes, William is my brother, may God forgive me. Look, I have no weapon.' For the first time in his life, Hugh prepared to die.

'Whose sword is that?' The man pointed to the blade stuck in the stone floor behind him. 'Why won't it come out of the ground?'

'I don't know...'

The man took a step forward, then dropped the mace and shook his head.

Hugh imagined the devil had smiled under the scarf.

With one swift movement of the arm and wrist, Muzawi buried a dagger into Hugh's side.

Clinging onto the beam, Hugh fought to keep standing. He gasped as Muzawi pulled the blade out.

Not wanting to waste any more time on the old man, Muzawi wiped the blood from his dagger and knelt beside the pool. He opened the ancient coffer and quite suddenly, the sphere held within the metal claw began to glow an iridescent colour, like the shimmering of a pearl. The water in the pool began to glow brighter and he dipped his fingers into the water.

Was the second sphere waking from a long sleep?

As his arms stretched under the surface, the stench from the bubbles became made him light headed. The depth was more than he anticipated but he thought nothing of what he had to do next. He knew where his destiny lay. Holding his breath, he put his head under water and reached out as far as he could. He was not surprised when his hands touched flesh and bone. For thousands of years the pool had been a place of pagan sacrifice.

He surfaced and drew in a deep breath before thrusting the top half of his body through the stinking green water once more. This time his fingers danced delicately along a submerged shelf, probing to the right until he found what he was looking for. The other sphere.

Gasping for air, a sense of euphoria and utter ecstasy overwhelmed his body as he brought the ancient artefact of the Sky Gods to the surface. How he admired the shaman who had placed the sphere in such a place. Muzawi stared at the translucent beauty of the spheres as the colours coalesced and gave a sound like a bee humming. Sensing someone else was in the crypt above, he listened and heard the voices coming nearer. He took out a dagger, looking intently towards the scree slope.

With their horses tied by the gate, Maimonides and Saladin approached the doors to the church, keeping to the shadows. Maimonides surprised Edom, recognising him immediately.

Frozen to the spot, he appeared to be guarding an old man who was tied to the church doors.

'Who are these two?' Saladin asked.

Maimonides explained who Edom was, and an inner rage took

hold of Saladin. Holding Edom by the throat, Saladin pinned him against the doors then ripped open his guts with a dagger.

Edom barely had time to reconcile what had happened to him before sinking to the ground. Wiping his blade, Saladin stared at William as if trying to place him in the distant past.

Maimonides grimaced and shook his head at the wanton murder. As Edom spilled his entrails over the porch, Saladin tugged at the rope securing William to the church door before ordering his captain. 'Keep this one here. I think we have unfinished business.'

Alone, Saladin opened the door and disappeared into the church. He walked purposefully down to the chancel and in the flickering torchlight, he saw the opening to the crypt.

He was about to descend when Maimonides appeared holding a torch, running down the nave toward him. 'You are about to meet the sum of every nightmare you have ever endured. You may need my help.'

Saladin paused then nodded his head. They both walked slowly and silently down the steps and across the floor of the crypt. As they reached the lip of the underground chamber, Maimonides could smell the gas. Suddenly he realised he was carrying a burning torch. 'Saladin, we must retreat a little while I throw the torch down into the gas. There will be an explosion but afterwards it should be safe for a while. Saladin was about to disagree, when he saw the flame begin to brighten. Perhaps he should err on the side of caution. They both took a few paces back.

'Turn your back or the blast could blind you.'

'Throw the damn thing...' Saladin ordered. The torch disappeared down the hole.

Hugh knew it was imperative to keep hold of the beam. If he fell, he would die on the spot. He tried to pull himself along the beam towards the wall, using the twisted bits of rope that held it in place. If he could make it as far as the wall, he may be able to prop himself up and shuffle along to the scree slope. His hand reached the point where the beam met the wall and he placed his hand into the gap where the mortar had crumbled. There was a stiff leathery object attached to the beam and he held on, hoping it would keep him steady.

The upright stance seemed to ease the pain and for the first time, he thought he could make it out of the hell-hole. He pulled on the unknown object and it came away in his hand.

With barely a glance, he fought through the mists of swirling madness trying to understand its importance. Tucking it into his tabard, he had to take both hands off the beam. Without the support, he lost his balance. He was only vaguely aware of the sensation of falling and in the back of his mind he saw a searing whiteness, accompanied by a deafening explosion. As all his senses dimmed, there was nothing left to feel.

That is when he saw the vision.

Chapter 49

Jerusalem
AD 33

Joseph of Arimathea hurried down the steps of the Governor's Praetorium and out into the pouring rain. With his head lowered, he tried to avoid stepping into the rivulets gushing into the streets. He had never seen the roads around the palace so empty; perhaps even the holy city was holding its head in shame.

At his age, it was impossible to run far but he was anxious to let Nicodemus know that he had succeeded in obtaining permission to have the body of Jesus taken down from the patibulum. Short of breath, he paused to feel in his pocket again for the all-important document with Pilate's seal.

Pulling the cowl of his cloak over his face, he took a deep breath and slowed to a walking pace through the city gate. Keeping his head down, he passed the guards and turned up the hill to Gol Goatha, the place of executions.

The muddy track to the rocky outcrop, proved the most difficult to keep his footing and when he reached the plateaux at the top he called out to the forlorn figure of Nicodemus who was stood beside the upright stanchion. 'Where are the others?' he asked.

'You were taking so long...I told Mary and James to take his mother to wait at the tomb.'

Joseph understood. It would take time for the family to recover from the horrific ordeal of that day.

'I have Pilate's seal,' he gasped. 'Do you have the linen and the myrrh?'

Shivering and soaking wet, Nicodemus nodded to the bundle at his feet then pointed to a tarpaulin shelter under a thorn tree about thirty paces away. 'The captain is over there. You must show him the document.'

Darkness had fallen earlier than usual but through the rain, he perceived three guards playing dice by lamplight. Joseph approached them slowly so as not to startle them.

'Who the fuck are you old man, and what do you want?'

Even though he was a respected member of the Sanhedrin, Joseph was accustomed to the gutter language of the Roman soldiers. Fumbling with the tie around the scroll, he passed it to the captain. 'Sir, this document gives me permission to have the man taken down from the patibulum. You understand tomorrow is the Sabbath.'

The captain carried on playing. 'Oh is it. And what makes you think I am going to get off my arse in this weather to please you and your fucking Sabbath.' His two cohorts laughed.

Joseph persevered. 'Sir, the permission is signed by Governor Pilate and carries his seal.'

One of the men glanced at the scroll and nodded.

The captain sneered. 'I appear to be losing this game because you are distracting me. Well…?'

Joseph understood the silent language of the Romans and handed over a few coins.

The captain gestured to the rear of the hut. 'There's a ladder around the back. Help yourselves but you better be quick because I am off duty soon. And the next guy is a real bastard.' Again, his men laughed.

Joseph was about to ask for help when he saw Nicodemus pick up the ladder. He followed and helped tilt the ladder until it was propped securely against the left side of the patibulum. They looked at each other and Joseph went up the ladder, grateful that the women were out of sight. He tugged at the nail that pierced the joint between the hand and the wrist, and it came away without too much effort. Both arms were loosely tied to the patibulum and he called down to Nicodemus. 'Hold on to the legs while I unwrap the rope.' As the rope went slack, the right side of the body twisted and came forward. Now the rope and nail on the other side took all the weight. He pushed the nail back into the hole then climbed back down the ladder.

Joseph looked into the ghostly tear-stained eyes of Nicodemus as he hung on to the legs, as if his life depended on it. No words of comfort could possibly have sufficient meaning. He placed the ladder against the other side of the crossbar and climbed to reach Jesus' left hand, but this time he noticed the tip of the nail had been turned over and no amount of pulling and twisting would loosen it.

Exhausted by his efforts, he paused to look down. 'I can't loosen it. Will you try?'

Nicodemus agreed and exchanged places. Once up the ladder he too pulled at the nail, trying to bend it straight. In desperation, he told Joseph. 'It is too dark and I can't see what I am doing. I am going to untie the rope and pull the hand through the nail. Please God help me.' Pulling with all his strength, he could not release the hand through the capped nail. Suddenly the ladder swayed and he thought he would fall, but managed to grab onto the crossbar.

Joseph clutched at the ladder but slipped in the mud, leaving the legs without support. The whole body swung away from the crossbar, suspended only by one nail in the left hand and two pinned through the anklebones.

The sound of raucous laughter came from the tarpaulin. The captain had gone and the two guards had been watching them make fools of themselves. 'Get down from there and I will give you a hand,' one of the guards shouted out. Striding over with a hammer, he took the ladder around the back of the crossbar and climbed up. He took two hefty swings at the bent nail but it failed to come free. 'Well you have buggered it up, haven't you,' he said looking at Nicodemus and dropping the hammer to the ground in frustration. 'Only one thing for it.' He took his sword from his belt and leant over the crossbar. It took one firm strike to sever the hand above the wrist.

Frozen to the spot Nicodemus cried out as if the sword had struck him. All Joseph could do was close his eyes and utter a prayer.

The guard replaced his sword and let the body fall as he shouted out. 'Catch!'

The body of Christ lurched forward before they could move and their cries were drowned out by the loud crack of a breaking leg bone. Joseph turned away in revulsion, looking to the rain sodden sky, begging God to put an end to such wretchedness.

Now the second guard appeared and he picked up the hammer and successfully hit out the two nails from the bottom of the stanchion. 'Fucking dozy idiots. You should have taken out the bottom nails first.'

The body at last came free and Joseph helped take the strain as they both lowered Jesus onto the ground.

Handing the hammer back to the guard up the ladder, he advised the two old men to move back, while they took down the crossbar. 'Have to get it down for the next lucky bastard tomorrow,' he grinned. The pin that held the pivot came out with just two hammer blows and the guards lowered the crossbar from its notch with well-practised ease. The guards hurried back to their shelter paying scant attention to the two men.

Joseph laid out the linen cloth and wrapped it around the body of Jesus three times. Nicodemus glanced over at the crossbeam lying on the ground next to them. 'We can't just leave it for the Roman's to feed to the dogs.

'But it is impossible to remove. We have both tried,' Joseph replied, eager to leave the hill as soon as possible.

'The guards aren't watching. If we place the beam next to Jesus and wrap the extra linen around both of them before putting them on the cart. God willing, they will not even suspect the beam is missing until the morning.'

Joseph glanced up and confirmed the two guards were still playing dice. He nodded and they lifted the wrapped body over to the beam and lifted them together. The weight was more than expected and they urged each other to reach the cart before they were spotted. If they were stopped now they would be arrested and charged with any number of crimes.

Nicodemus flicked the reins and the cart pulled away down the track, just as the rain eased. The rock-cut tomb was in sight and they could see Mary Magdalene stood in the doorway.

Nicodemus had to think quickly. 'No one must see the mutilation, not even Mary. We will carry the body inside the tomb and I will apply the aloes and myrrh while you pray together.'

'And what of the crossbeam? The cart will be searched…' Joseph asked nervously.

'Keep it covered for now. Before we leave the city we will disguise it with a pile of firewood and a tarpaulin.'

Joseph nodded as the cart drew to a halt outside the tomb. Mary looked distressed as she ran out to meet them, holding a jar in her hand. 'The aloe juice has dried up…I am sorry…'

Nicodemus gave Mary a reassuring hug. 'Don't worry, I have brought enough to wash the wounds and prepare his body.'

A single oil lamp lit the interior of the tomb and while Joseph and Mary knelt in prayer Nicodemus unwrapped the body of Jesus. Laid on the anointing stone he gasped at the extent of the injuries that covered the body. With trembling hands he began to wash around the bloody wounds, wringing out the sponge on the ground.

Suddenly Mary stood up and handed Nicodemus the empty jar. 'Please, wring out your cloth in here.'

After much deliberation, they agreed it was too dangerous to stay in Jerusalem. Joseph told Nicodemus of a small house in Lydda he used for storage. To ensure her safety, Mary was ushered back to her house and with the beam hidden underneath a load of firewood, they steered the cart to the city gates. The guards were questioning everyone entering or leaving and they nervously waited in line, only to be waved through with the minimum of fuss.

On the journey, Joseph described his house. 'It is enclosed by a walled courtyard, with a cellar where I used to store grain and perishables. There is only one problem. Workmen in the cellar, digging out a well, but I can ask them to leave. We can take the beam down there and prise the hand from the nail.'

That night they slept in a small inn and arrived in Lydda the following evening.

Making sure they were not followed, they entered the courtyard and closed the gate behind them.

'Wrap the tarpaulin around the beam,' Nicodemus said, unable to have the shameful sight visible. They carried the beam from the cart to the rear of the house where Joseph nodded to a wooden trapdoor.

'It's just so heavy.' Joseph dropped the crossbeam and it hit the ground with a thump. He gasped trying to catch his breath. Joseph opened the trapdoor and peered inside. After a few moments he signalled he would try again. They carried the beam down the cellar steps and dragged it across the floor placing the beam next to a pile of shale.

Even though they faced a grim task ahead, it was the first time for some days they had felt safe,hidden from the world.

Joseph lit some lamps and looked around the cellar. 'These six columns must have been a foundation,' he told Nicodemus, who was sat on the bottom step. 'Upstairs the staff have all gone. When I return from the market, I will find the means to extract the nail.'

'How long will you be?' Nicodemus asked.

'Half an hour at the most.' Joseph waited a moment at the top of the steps then crossed the courtyard and shut the gate behind.

Two hours passed, and then another. Joseph was nowhere to be seen.

Nicodemus had gone all day without food and decided to risk walking across the square to a small shop. Under the cover of darkness he mixed with shoppers queuing for fresh fish and bread. There was only one topic of gossip and that was the mysterious arrest of Joseph of Arimathea, a good patron of Lydda. Rumours were repeated of his involvement with a Nazarene prophet who was crucified.

Keeping his head down, he paid for the food and turned to leave the store when a man burst into the square shouting. 'He is risen...Jesus is risen!'

The man was ignored by most of the people, while others laughed scornfully, saying he was drunk. But some had recognised the name and were more sympathetic, asking what had happened and who had seen what.'

'She said he was the Son of God and would rise in three days. They are calling it the resurrection…the tomb is empty and all his disciples witnessed his ascension. Soldiers are everywhere.'

Nicodemus hurried across the square and into the courtyard, his heart and his head pounding. All he had planned to do must happen now before it was too late. He returned to the house and eventually found everything he needed.

Outside it was dark and from the street he thought he heard roman voices. Working fast, he climbed onto the cart and gathered the rope that held the firewood together and put it inside the bag of tools. His hand brushed over the Titular.The prophetic inscription chiselled in three tongues would also have to be hidden.

Silently he entered the cellar and closed the trapdoor behind him. The next voices he heard were unmistakable. The Sanhedrin security officer was walking across the courtyard but it was Roman soldiers who gave the orders. 'Search every room and arrest any collaborators.'

Gripped by panic, Nicodemus looked around the

cellar. If he barred the trapdoor, they would know he was inside, so he had to hide. His torch fluttered as he ran down the length of the cellar past shovels, lamps and various other implements, towards the crossbeam leaning against the mound of shale.

Behind the shale he looked into a hole. Closer inspection revealed the well that was being dug out by Joseph's workmen. Peering over the edge, he could see the floor to the well was dry and a short ladder rested against the side.

The guards could be outside at any moment and his mind saw only one option. He climbed down the ladder. Dousing the torch, he waited in the dark in total silence, not daring to move. In a flash of light, the trapdoor to the cellar opened. Footsteps and muffled voices came closer and he heard two soldiers standing by the mound of shale. After what seemed an age, the one of them called out. 'There's no one down here!' Moments later, the footsteps receded and the trapdoor slammed shut.

Nicodemus started breathing again.

His mind drifted, seemingly unable to grasp recent events. What had happened to Jesus? Was he dead or not?

He climbed the ladder until he could peer over the edge. He stared at the crossbeam and an overwhelming emotion fixed him to the spot. A feeling of utter guilt and shame. Whatever would become of the world of men? It should never have happened. In the great scheme of things, it was never supposed to happen, but it did. No! God did not ordain this travesty, this utter indescribable shame.

No one must ever set eyes upon the hand, but it would be impossible for him to destroy. Did the well hold the answer? Lighting a lamp, he climbed back down and to his left he noticed the workmen had created a space in the side of the well.

What he discovered next baffled him to such an extent; he had to light another lamp to believe what he had seen. The workmen had begun to dig out a cavity that was filled with shale, not earth. The shale was loose and filled the floor of a large chamber. He stared at the ceiling in utter amazement. Beams of wood held up the ceiling. They looked old. Very old.

Who on earth could have put them there?

A path to the end wall had been cleared where he could see a pool of water. Touching the closest beam, he felt the age and wondered again at the ancients who lived in such a cave.

Then the solution struck him. He climbed back up the ladder into the cellar and dragged the beam to the opening, sliding it down to the chamber below. First, he found the strongest beam then cut a niche in the wall, clearing out a hole big enough to fit the crossbeam. Two ropes were tied to Christ's crossbeam and these were wrapped around the roof beam. Pulling with all his strength he managed to slowly lift the crossbeam, until the two beams were tight together. He pushed the end with the hand into the niche in the wall then tied the two beams together. The 'shame' was no longer visible and only God was witness.

Exhausted, he lay down and drifted into a light sleep. He felt little satisfaction in his work, just numbness and a deep, unshakable guilt. Whenever his mind crossed into that dark space where he dared to think of Christ in heaven, he felt a gnawing in his stomach. But even more shameful was the thought that the resurrection could be condemned as a lie. The hand...the shame, must never be found.

Either way, he and Joseph were the only ones to know a terrible secret and they would have to carry that burden until their dying days.

Waking a few hours later, he inspected his work. All that remained was to mortar the crossbeam into the wall. It was clumsy but he was confident no one would ever see his handiwork. To finish, he hammered home the titular with a large nail.

Now, he had to pass on a relevant message to Joseph, assuming one day he would return. From the sack he pulled out a roll of copper and some inscribing tools. Over the years, Joseph had inscribed verses from the Torah onto copper scrolls for the Sanhedrin, where he had once taught the art to Nicodemus.

Turning the lamp wick up he prepared the tools and began to inlay the words with a tiny chisel and hammer onto the small reams of copper. Hopefully he was hidden deep enough in the earth so no one to hear the tapping.

The scroll was an explanation of what he had done with Christ's crossbeam, written in a way that only Joseph would understand. He paused as he reached the final words, trying to ignore the tears that fell down his face.

"The crossbeam that held our Lord by the nail should be venerated...but what else could I do? Oh the shame of it...oh the shame of Lydda. They cut off the hand of God. How can we, your servants, ever be forgiven? Within the bowels of the earth I leave His hand for all eternity and I pray that in your infinite wisdom, oh lord, you will forgive me for this shame. Amen"

Carefully he rolled up the scroll and from his bag he took out the embalming jar left over from the tomb. Then he remembered the jar contained the blood and water from the washing of Jesus. Without a thought, he walked just a few paces away to the green pool and tipped the liquid into the pool, then placed the scroll inside the jar, ensuring it was a good fit.

Using the chisel, he roughly scratched the words, *"The True Testimony of Nicodemus."*

To his surprise the pool began to bubble fiercely and emit a stinking odour. Working quickly he replaced the seal on the jar. He dare not leave the jar in the house, in case he was arrested in possession of the scroll but had to leave it where it could easily be found by Joseph, if and when he were to return.

He stood the jar carefully against the wall.

To his surprise he noticed one of the nails had fallen out of the crossbeam and he pushed it back into its receptacle. To his horror, blood squirted from the hole onto his hand. Not daring to touch anything, he held his breath and sped as fast as possible up the ladder into the cellar. The smell of gas was beginning to effect his balance. Stumbling against a stone column, he was unable to prevent his hand from touching the column, leaving a bloody imprint.

The risk of being killed by the gas outweighed the risk of capture. He crept silently back into the house and for the rest of the day he listened out for soldiers but heard nothing. A walk around the courtyard confirmed they had gone. Now he took stock of his chances of escape.

He decided he would stay with his brother in Damascus, hoping it was far enough away from Jerusalem to grieve without interference. As a diversion, if it were needed, he left a written note stating that he had gone to Ascalon.

Leaving the house, probably for the last time, he knew the memories of the last few days would serve as a penance for the rest of his life.

Joseph of Arimathea spent three months under house arrest in a small room next to the prison. All charges were dropped. He was not a young man anymore and the hardship was not to his liking.

When he arrived back at Lydda, a crowd soon formed in the square, some relieved to see him alive while others scowled disapprovingly. Closing the courtyard gate behind him, he entered his house and was relieved it appeared unscathed. Everything was as he left it except for his writing desk. All his inscribing tools had gone.

His first concern was for Nicodemus but upon reading the note, he thanked God. Joseph had known his friend long enough to know he did not have any relatives south of Jerusalem. Clearly, it was a lie to deter anyone who suspected his sympathies and wanted to question his loyalty to the Sanhedrin.

Inside the cellar, he immediately noticed that the workmen had been very busy, as a large pile of shale loomed out of the darkness next to the well he had discovered years ago. The beam was nowhere to be seen, so he assumed Nicodemus had disposed of it in the underground cavity.

The next day a surprise lay in store when a group of six men from Jerusalem turned up at his gate. They wanted to give thanks to the man who had looked after the body of Jesus in his time of greatest need. A spokesman stepped forward. 'We were told you fought for permission from Pilate and donated your own sepulchre to the Lord. Is there anything we can do for you by way of our gratitude, Master Joseph?'

Joseph invited them into the courtyard and sat them down with some refreshments and made a proposition. 'All of you have reverence for Jesus Christ. What if we rebuild this house and turn it into a holy chapel where like-minded students of His teachings can gather. We can listen to those who have stories to tell and hold services to celebrate His resurrection. Let us make it a fitting tribute.' All the men agreed enthusiastically and appointed the stonemason Anthony as supervisor.

Joseph led Anthony into the cellar and showed him the pile of shale and the hole. 'First, I would be grateful if you would tip all this shale back into the hole, then seal it with a marble slab from the merchant.'

'I can understand why. That stink smells like the breath of Baal,' Anthony said, screwing up his face.

'What a strange expression. Why do you say Baal?'

'Oh I don't know, it was something my grandfather always used to say.'

They left the confines of the cellar to discuss his ideas for the new chapel. Joseph was keen to see the project completed as soon as possible so he could continue with his plans to escape Judea with Mary. His boat at Sidon was ready to take them across the Great Sea, to a beautiful island he knew off the coast of the Antibes. There they would be safe and have access to the mainland, when the time was right.

Later that day, Anthony returned with two young men to shovel the shale into the hole, though there was never enough to block it up completely. It simply formed a slope into the cavern below.

As instructed, they dropped a massive slab of expensive marble over the hole. Looking at the pure white slab, he shook his head. He was an experienced builder and stonemason, and his clients had a habit of changing their minds. Just as a precaution, he fixed a metal eye into the ceiling lintel above one end of the slab, and screwed in a hasp to the opposite end of the marble slab. Then he ran a chain from the eye to the hasp and was pleased that the fulcrum was perfect. The slab pulled up without too much effort.

Lowering the heavy slab of marble over the hole, he lay the chain against the cellar wall.

Anthony smiled to himself. If Joseph were ever to think about accessing the cavern below, he would be pleasantly surprised by his skill and forethought.

Chapter 50

Lydda
Palestine

Muzawi lay crumpled against the wall and turned to look down at his legs, fearing he had been badly injured. He felt no pain even though his arms and face were badly burnt. The old knight had taken the brunt of the gas explosion and now his body lay face down in the pool. There was no sign of life.

Slowly, the feeling returned below his waist. Shaking his head, he looked around for the small coffer and saw it in pieces around the floor. Thankfully the two spheres were undamaged and rested at his feet. Instinctively, he picked up the spheres, nestling them like babies in his arms. Then his senses prevailed as he remembered the spheres must be kept apart.

Suddenly he realised someone else was in the chamber. He stood up and spun round to see who was there.

Saladin let out an audible gasp. 'Muzawi, it is you. How on earth did you '

Fortunately, Maimonides saw the glint of metal and the flash of a blade spinning through the air, aimed at Saladin. Instinctively, he pushed him out of the way and heard the dagger clatter harmlessly against the wall.

Muzawi laughed abruptly then stopped to look down at his other hand. In throwing the dagger, the two spheres had come together.

An expression of sheer horror passed over his face as he held them in one hand, tight against his chest. For a while he did not move, as a loud humming sound emitted from the spheres. He pulled them apart, keeping his arms outstretched but the spheres began to take on a life of their own.

Saladin saw the expression on Muzawi's face change to one of utter terror. He shouted. 'Let go of the spheres!'

Something was happening to Muzawi and it filled him with dread. Still he stood quite still, not daring to move.

Maimonides sensed a great calamity was about to occur. 'I don't like this; we should get out of here now.' He pulled ineffectually at Saladin's arm, afraid that the nausea building up in his stomach had riveted him to the spot. One look at Muzawi told him why he could not drop the spheres. The metal was melting his hands and unbelievably, his feet began to lift imperceptibly from the floor.

Having just come to terms with Muzawi being alive, Saladin was now watching him die. Very quiet at firstly, a low guttural sound came from the throat of Muzawi. A primal sound, almost animal like. Gradually it rose in volume. With his eyes fixed on Saladin, the sound became an ear-splitting scream.

Maimonides was mesmerised by the spectacle before him. As his eyes watered and his stomach churned, he shifted his gaze to the lower half of Muzawi's body. His waist seemed to be moving uncontrollably then a putrid smell overpowered them as his bowels vacated into the pool. This was followed in quick succession by large pieces of large and small intestine. It looked as if his body was liquefying from the inside.

'Put the spheres down!' Saladin shouted above the appalling noise.

Muzawi gave no earthly response. By now his mind must surely be so damaged by pain. For what seemed an age, they all stood their ground. Standing in the pool amongst his own innards, Muzawi let out a deep groan. He pulled the spheres close to his stomach. 'The power shall be mine.' Copious amounts of blood shot from between Muzawi's legs and some of his organs now began to protrude, making it impossible for him to move. He screamed again as he realised the end was in sight and he tried in vain to tuck his spleen back into the huge orifice that had erupted between his legs. Conciousness finally deserted him and he sat upright in the pool as mysterious forces dragged him by his intestines into a murky, greenish hell. Tiny bolts of lightening shot between the spheres.

Saladin stepped forward momentarily thinking he could save the spheres, but they and Muzawi were gone. As if caught in a trance, he turned to Maimonides. 'I can excavate this whole cave…and find the spheres…'

Maimonides pulled him back. 'Remember what we have just witnessed. Remember what happened to Arius. Don't you see. Leave it Saladin. Bask in your glory, then have a hundred men bury this place forever. Nothing good can come from this hole to the underworld. Let the curse take its final victim.'

Saladin brought himself back from the brink as the hypnotic pulse from the spheres was quelled and he watched as they finally disappeared under the water and silence prevailed. As the water violently effervesced, he stood over the pool, wondering what could have been.

After a while, he bent down to pick up the mace and noticed Maimonides glaring at him. It seemed heavier than he remembered and felt cumbersome and unwieldy in his hands. For a moment he wanted to keep it…then the moment passed. He looked into the bubbling pool and dropped the mace into the maelstrom. The green pool seemed to part and swallow it with hardly a splash.

Saladin grunted and turned his attention back to the old dead Frank. He placed his foot under his torso and turned him onto his back. There was not a mark on him.

A thin, tired voice called out from behind. 'Master, if you value our lives we must get out of here now.'

Stirred into action, Saladin looked at Maimonides. 'Yes, of course.' Under the effects of the poisonous gas, his head was pounding and his stomach ached with nausea. Taking a stride towards the shale slope, Saladin pushed past Maimonides, anxious now to leave the hell hole.

Maimonides hesitated and looked over his shoulder. He stumbled over to a double beam on the ceiling and pushed his hand into a recess where it had once been mortared into the wall. Nothing was there. He looked forlornly at the beam and paused rocking from side to side. Unable to place one foot in front of another, Saladin grabbed him to support his legs. 'When we reach the surface, you shall receive the best attention from my finest physicians.'

'I am your finest physician, my lord Sultan.'

The smile from Saladin was wasted on Maimonides. Climbing awkwardly out of the chamber they sucked in the acrid air of the crypt and once back inside the church, they were grateful to fill their lungs. Through the windows, the fires around Lydda shone brighter than the rising sun and the screams of the innocent provided an ignominious dawn chorus.

Saladin lay Maimonides on a bench where he could rest and drink some water. Walking out of the church doors, Saladin looked across the rooftops. Most of the town was in flames and the stench of burning did nothing to help his pounding headache. The captain of his bodyguard was still stood next the old man tied to the door.

Saladin grabbed William by the throat. 'What was your brother doing in the chamber below the crypt?'

'No doubt stealing relics,' William replied.

'I thought as much.' Saladin stared at William.

He had accepted his fate at the hands of Saladin.

'You are the one with no tongue that I have heard so much about. I do not like assassins and you and I my friend have a promise with destiny. Do you remember…?'

'I will never forget you and your shaman…excreted by the devil himself. You do not deserve to breath the air or walk the earth…'

Saladin shook his head unable to understand every word. He crouched down and looked into the eyes of the old man.

'Is Muzawi dead?' William asked.

Saladin was taken aback by the question. 'Oh, if only you had seen it with your own eyes. Life has come full circle and your retribution is complete. Like I said, we all have our destiny...'

With a flick of the wrist, Saladin produced his stiletto and drove it twice into the eyes of William. He pulled out the serrated blade and inspected the eyeballs.

The scream of shock and agony was long and hard but Saladin was unmoved. 'I foresaw this moment when I was a boy. So now, you have no tongue and no eyes.'

One of his general's stood nearby with an urgent need to speak to his master. 'My lord Sultan, your army is in disarray, scattered around the towns and villages. The light is upon us and we must start reinforcing some discipline if we are to march on Jerusalem.'

Standing up, Saladin took one last look at the pathetic figure tied to the church door. He was close to death. 'Very well, there is little more to be achieved here. Clear everyone out then burn down the church. Gather the army as best you can and tell them we ride into Jerusalem tomorrow.'

Feeling the worse for wear, Maimonides walked from the side door and joined Saladin as the horses were brought up from the gate. The thought of riding the mare made Maimonides vomit.

The next few hours passed slowly for William. With so much pain came the realisation that he was dying. The shock of having his eyes torn out and the subsequent loss of blood was too much for his frail body to take. Tied to the door of the church, Saladin had left him to die, though ironically the warmth from the burning aisles probably kept him alive.

Distant voices came and went until someone shouted out his name. Abdul was running across the square in a panic. 'Master, are you all right…oh no!' He turned away at the Williams disfigurement. 'They have blinded you,' he sobbed.

'Abdul, you must be strong when I tell you the truth. Before they took my eyes, I saw your father killed. They left his body near the door.'

Abdul peered behind William and saw what he thought was a pile of ragged clothes. Abdul uncovered the headscarf and saw what they had done to his father. William placed a gentle hand on his arm and squeezed. As Abdul quietly wept, he could feel the utter despair of loss.

Suddenly the flames burst through the roof and Abdul hurriedly untied the rope tying William to the door then led him away from the church to the shelter of a wall on the opposite side of the square. He then recovered the body of his father.

Abdul tore a strip of linen from his shirt to wrap around William's blood soaked eye sockets.

As his will to live began to ebb away, William wondered if he would survive the day. All his strength, all his spirit had deserted him. 'Abdul my young friend, I am close to death. You must tell me; what of the people of Lydda?'

'Saladin killed everyone who was left in the garrison and burnt it to the ground. I passed many bodies lying in the streets; woman and children hanging from trees…all the houses have the smell of death. All the buildings have been burnt. I hope the sun hides its face in the smoke.'

'And the church?'

Abdul looked to the other side of the square. 'Your room was crushed when the roof collapsed. Nearly all of the walls are fallen. Abdul saw some movement between the columns. 'Master, someone is coming this way…'

Out of the thick pall of smoke billowing in the dawn breeze, there appeared a man. 'Is he armed?' William asked, holding on tight to his arm.

'Yes...it is a knight with a mighty sword.'

'Be brave my boy...we face death in the knowledge that God...'

'Master, it is your brother...but he looks different. He is here now.'

Through his agony, William raised a smile as he sensed the man crouch opposite him. 'Hugh you are alive...is it really you?'

A hand reached out and touched his face. 'Do not be alarmed my brother. The one who fills your heart with hate has been taken into the underworld, where he will die a thousand times a day.'

'Hugh, you sound so different. Are you hurt...?'

'William, don't fret so. I have the great sword. Here, you can feel the power it holds.'

William felt the hilt and ran his hand down the blade. 'Hugh, it is the sword from the crypt. How did you...?'

'We should be proud of Ilger. In the end, he found the redemption he sought...as did I. Perhaps we are all part of some greater purpose...some greater force...or was it just fate that has brought us to this moment.'

William relaxed and sighed, his breathing becoming shallow. 'Hugh...the ancient jar rests on the shelf in my little annex in the church...'

Hugh glanced at the pile of rubble alongside the church. 'Then it has turned full circle and rests where it was always meant to be.'

William could barely be heard. 'Did you see the hand of God?'

'More than that...much more.'

William tilted his head at the sound of approaching hooves. A sound he instantly recognised. 'Perseus...it is Perseus come to see me. Oh my lord...thank you for saving him.' The great while stallion trotted across the smoke filled square and stopped to lower his head. William could feel the breath on his face. 'Hugh, meet Perseus.'

'I feel we know each other already. He too has his part to play, for Perseus and I have a great and heroic battle to fight, which is only fitting for such a mighty steed. You should be very proud of him.'

William gave a faint smile, then his face fell still.

Hugh stroked his brow. 'I must go now, but have no fear. Abdul will take your body back to your beloved farmstead. Sleep forever in peace my brother, and remember this. There is no shame. There never was any shame. Sometimes, things just happen and it is up to us to choose to believe what we see. Good or bad…we have always had a choice.'

Am I at peace now?

'Yes my brother, you are at peace.'

Perseus and his new master rode as one towards the gate of Lydda. For as long as anyone could remember, the gate had stood in the same place and no one could make any sense of it. Why such a strange looking gate, just two pillars the height of a man, with only enough width for one horse to pass through. Such a useless gate that for many years the road was diverted around the pillars. Some recalled the stories of those who tried to destroy the gate, with battering rams and oxen. But the crusty old pillars were impregnable. All had failed.

But now the ground shook and the pillars began to vibrate and hum.

With barely a pause in his step, Hugh struck the left pillar with his mighty glistening sword. The ancient stone crumbled. Again he struck; lower down this time. The blow jarred heavily and the vibration reverberated along the full length.

With the stone sheath gone, the true structure inside was revealed.

Now he attacked the second pillar and after two blows, the outer stone shattered. The world seemed to shake.

For the first time in aeons, the metal sceptres were exposed to the light of day. As if by magic, they grew, doubling in length, until they seemed to pierce the sky. Inside the sceptres lay the most precious gems on earth. The Stones of Heaven. Stones that came from the stars.

The 'time of promises' reached its peak. The thinnest sliver of a new moon rose above the horizon only to be burnt out in an instant by the rays of the rising sun.

Then the metal clicked again and now an intense beam of light shot from the Stones of Shamir into the sky. It was written long ago that if the spheres had been in place, the world would have seen the 'end of days.' Or perhaps the world could have been a better place. The choice was always there.

The sword did not ask nor was an answer given. It simply cut through the sceptres, dissolving the metal until nothing was left. Except for the two Stones of Heaven.

They were picked up, fitting neatly into the palm of the hand, before being put away for safe keeping.

They would need to be safe. For the master and stallion rode off fast, on the heels of Saladin and an army of twenty-five thousand.

Outside his tent, Saladin spun on his heels to see the two fingers of light pierce the dark skies above Lydda. 'The time of promises,' he muttered, taking a step forward. 'I must go…'

Maimonides grabbed him by the arm, stopping him in his tracks. 'No. For once, listen to the goodness that comes from within and choose your destiny wisely.'

Saladin looked again at the lights. 'It was foretold. That is where my destiny lies. …'

Suddenly the shards of light disappeared. Maimonides gave a sigh of relief. 'Too late, my sultan. Now prepare yourself for worldly matters.'

Chapter 51

The Battle of Montgisard
Palestine

In the hours before sunrise, the Knights Templar charged through the gates of Gaza, surprising the Saracens that languished outside the walls. Instead of stopping to fight, the knights were under orders to ride out through the enemy line and keep going as far as Ascalon.

Two hours later they were riding across the coastal plains and were in full view of the walls of Ascalon. The Muslim ranks stood up as one, terrified at the reputation of the white knights that charged inexorably towards them. The Saracen general belatedly turned his men around to face the oncoming charge but they were slow to gather weapons and form defensive ranks. Without warning, the gates of Ascalon opened and King Baldwin emerged with his army of knights squeezing the Saracens onto a small ridge where they immediately offered surrender.

Raynald de Châtillon rode up to the king, his sword already well bloodied. 'My lord, we cannot waste time discussing terms for the surrender of these Saracens, when Jerusalem is under threat from Saladin.'

Baldwin could read the wild look in Reynald's eyes. He wanted to gorge himself on the slaughter of two thousand infantry and take whatever loot he could lay his filthy hands on. But who could blame him after spending seventeen years of hell imprisoned in Aleppo.

His generals gathered, impatient for a decision.

'I agree we cannot risk leaving them to take Ascalon while we try to catch up with Saladin. We must protect our rear. Châtillon and his knight's shall quickly disarm and neutralise these Saracens before rejoining us. My scouts report that Saladin's army camp is being prepared a mile from Lydda. That is where we shall meet. Don't be late.'

It was a cold, calculated decision and King Baldwin took no pleasure in giving Raynald free reign to solve the problem. As he headed for the road, his nobles formed ranks alongside.

Count Philip of Flanders spoke up. 'You know he will kill them all don't you?'

King Baldwin snapped back. 'So the famous Count has seen fit to join us in battle. What irks you so? Is it the sight of blood or your pricked conscience that troubles you?'

Realising he had spoken out of turn, Philip turned his horse away. The screams of men running in terror, travelled far across the plain.

Châtillon led his knights into the midst of the unarmed Saracens and only then did Philip notice who was riding alongside Raynald. Wilhelm de Mandeville was excitedly swinging his sword across a sea of throats and necks, like a fox gorges itself on chickens. To take such pleasure in death defied his senses and made him wonder if all men truly followed their own father.

By all accounts, Saladin's army numbered as many as twenty-five thousand Arabs, Kurds and Sudanese as well as a thousand Mamelukes sworn to protect the Sultan.

As King Baldwin's army marched north, news began to reach them that throughout the night, Saladin's army had broken into raiding parties, in the belief that the Christians were already defeated. In the early hours, Ramleh had been sacked and Lydda burnt to the ground.

King Baldwin turned his army inland, keeping discipline and ignoring small parties of Saracens that would scatter as they approached. Scouts were reporting hourly on Saladin's position and as the sun approached middle day, it seemed as though the Sultan had made little progress and was still trying to reassemble his army.

An hour later, Saracen infantry were spotted on the horizon scaling the side of a shallow ravine at the foot of Montgisard, only a short distance from Lydda. As Baldwin waited for his scouts to report, he ordered his nobles and generals to assemble into formation.

His face lit up with hope. The scouts reported remarkably good news. 'This was Saladin's last reported position. I think he is still in the ravine. The Saracens are still arriving at the ravine with over laden donkeys and carts full of pillage.'

'My lord king, we should attack now,' Baldwin of Ibelin urged, still smarting from Saladin's rampage through his estates only two days ago.

Odo de St Armand kicked his destrier forward and the king acknowledged the Grand Master of the Order. 'Sire, I agree but I can see a way to win this battle. Advance with three long lines of infantry. Saladin will turn to engage and when they do, your knights can break through on the left flank. In the meantime, my knights will traverse along that shallow gully that runs into the right side of ravine. We will be on top of the Saracens before they see us. Together we will entrap them.'

King Baldwin knew Odo to be a good tactician and instantly agreed with his strategy. 'Very well, but take your knights now while the infantry are still assembling into ranks.'

The banners of black and white fluttered in the hot breeze as they watched Odo lead his knights along the lea that curved round into the ravine.

'How many Templars does Odo have?' Baldwin asked his seneschal.

'Eighty, my lord king,' came the answer.

'My God in heaven, they will face twenty thousand Saracens in that ravine.

Our left flank is late in moving forward. Pray that Saladin attacks the infantry first or the Knights Templar will be no more.'

It was like watching everything happen in slow motion. Still Saladin's army did not move from the ravine.

'I cannot stay here and watch. Get everyone on a horse. The left flank must move forward before it is too late.' He turned to the Bishop of Bethlehem. 'Pray with me. We need God with us this day like non before. Make the cross shine brighter and hoist it high so that everyone can see the glory of God.'

Every noble and general felt proud of the spirited young king, who despite his painful condition, rode out amongst his knights, encouraging them and pushing them on. 'Know that every Christian on earth is fighting by your side. This is a battle ordained by God, under the banner of His Holy cross. This is a battle to tell your wives, your children, and your whores for years to come. This is a battle for Jerusalem itself.'

As they marched ever closer towards the ravine, the sky turned ominously black and a sense of trepidation spread through the infantry. But as the king rode amongst his nobles and knights, the mood lifted and they cheered loudly.

Then, at the precise moment that the Knights Templars steadied their steeds to charge into the ravine, the whole world seemed to grind to a halt. Every man looked up at the apparition on the slopes of the ravine.

At first, it was the burst of sunlight against the blackened sky that that caught the eye. The hooves of the pure white stallion kicked up a cloud of dust as he descended an impossible trail. Never putting a hoof out of place as he rode into the heart of the Saracen army. A blinding flash of light took the breath away as the sun caught the the metal blade of the sword.

'Saint George!' went up the cry from the knights on the left flank.

Then the infantry took up the call. 'Saint George!'

When the Templars charged into the ravine, every single Saracen was looking up at the sole knight that sliced his way through the outer ranks. Suddenly the white clad Templars were charging in tight formation towards them as one. There was no time to react.

Every Templar lance found a target. Swords were drawn and they began the task of scything through the outer ranks of Saracen infantry. The disturbance from the right of the ravine began to filter through the army like a ripple...and then became a wave. Many of the Saracens ran up the side for a better look, only to see lines of infantry marching towards them.

Panic struck home, and it was more deadly than any blade. With the white tabards of the Templars sending a murderous shock-wave from one end of the ravine and the first wave of spearmen breeching the top, Saladin's troops only had one way to go. They massed as one towards the open end of the ravine where it was less steep and easier to climb the sides. Then out of the dust appeared King Baldwin with nearly four hundred knights, he charged down the slope, cutting a massive swathe into the fleeing Saracens. The cries of 'St George!' echoed even louder.

In the middle of the mayhem, Saladin ran out of his tent where he had been recovering during the heat of the day. He could see nothing of the fighting but assumed rightly that Baldwin had sallied out of Ascalon and was now on the offensive. Two of his generals ran past him and he shouted out. 'Stop running you fools. You are scaring everyone.'

The generals paused, then carried on running.

Saladin studied the scene for a few moments to see what they had seen. His army was being attacked on all fronts. On the side that skirted Montgisard, he glanced up the slope and was astonished to see a lone knight on a white horse and wondered how the stupid knight had come to be separated from his army.

Looking to his left and right, for the first time he began to worry. More of his men were running instead of fighting. 'Stand and fight you fools. They are but a few men on horses. Stand and fight!'

Something made him look behind again. This time the sole knight was much closer. No matter how many stood against him, he was able to cut a swathe through them all. Just twenty paces away from his tent, Saladin called out to his personal bodyguard who were stood beside him. 'If that man gets within ten paces of me I shall have all of you skinned!' The threat worked and a line of elite guards quickly formed between him and the knight.

'Saladin, I don't like this,' Maimonides said nervously. 'There is something wrong with this man. Look, he kills two and three at a time with every stroke of the blade.'

It was true, and he was hardly slowing. 'The guards will have him, just wait and see.' But Saladin's words carried little conviction. He glanced again to the left and right, only to see more of his army running away.

Maimonides saw the fear of failure flash across Saladin's face. 'Enough. We have to go now. We can reorganise…'

'No!' Saladin yelled. 'We still outnumber them.'

'But they hold the initiative.'

Saladin was staring at the lone knight as he reached the ranks of his bodyguards. He spoke quietly, almost in reverence. 'He has no helmet and his horse has no chain mail. Is it the white devil who comes…?'

'Whether he is a devil or a saint, no one has the better of him,' Maimonides replied while looking around for the horses. But they were gone. He ordered a guard to bring two fast camels immediately.

'There!' Saladin cried. 'He has taken a blow to the leg…and now the horse has a spear in the flanks. That will slow them down. Kill him now! Kill him!'

But the knight did not slow down. The sword still shone silver and Saladin could see the blood run from the blade without staining it. A glancing blow from a double-edged axe hit the knight in the back and he crumpled forward in the saddle, only to rise and skilfully strike back at the Mameluke guard, slicing open his head from ear to ear.

Blood covered much of his body and yet he still fought from the saddle, coming ever closer; his flailing blows seemingly inexhaustible.

'My lord sultan all your council have fled,' Maimonides reported, trying to instil some urgency. For the the first time in his life, he carried a sword. Now he gripped the hilt ever tighter.

'So be it. If this is to be the will of the Gods, then so be it. He has sent his greatest demon against me. And I shall stand!'

Neither of them could take their eyes from the knight. Only four bodyguards now stood in his way, but he was tiring and they were fresh. The first guard struck with a thrust of a long spear into the stallion's throat. Rearing up, the horse crushed his skull with his hooves. But there was still one last act of bravery for Perseus.

Although covered in blood and unable to move from its terrible injuries, the stallion still refused to fall to the ground. The horseman struck another guard across the throat then as he paused to turn, the two remaining guards moved in against him on either side. One smashed his axe into the horse's head and the other slashed aimlessly at the knight. Under the hail of blows, the massive stallion finally keeled over, and the knight landed on his knees and groaned. Inexplicably, the guards found themselves blind-sided by the fallen horse and failed to see the knight stand up. Taking one step and then another towards Saladin, he lifted his sword and pointed it at Saladin's chest.

Frozen to the spot, time stood still and Saladin could not find the will to move. In that moment of complete resignation, he recognised the old man from the crypt.

'You! I saw you dead.' His mouth opened but no words came out.

Wavering under the weight of the sword, the knight could barely stand up. But the silver blade stayed straight and true, the tip resting against Saladin's chest. Closing his eyes, the razor sharp metal grazed Saladin's skin and then a spark jumped between them. From another place he heard a voice.

'I am done...'

Maimonides blinked as if from a dream. The two guards quickly recovered and climbed over the bloody carcass of the horse to attack the knight with a blind fury, hacking off the arms and legs.

'Stop it now!' Saladin ordered.

The guards looked up from their belated, bloody success, knowing they had let Saladin down. They looked at each other and ran.

Maimonides pulled open Saladin's tunic, expecting to see a fatal wound. Instead, all he saw was a tiny smudge of blood from a cut no bigger than his smallest fingernail. 'How did he miss killing you?'

'He did not miss. What you see is what was meant.'

Maimonides shook his head, affording one last look at the bloody remains of the aged knight. 'It was a high price to pay, just to prick your conscience.' He pointed to a line of camels. 'Let us get out of here now, while we can.' Seizing two camels from the tether line, Maimonides stirred Saladin from his malaise. 'If we leave now we live to fight another day. Stay and we die.'

Saladin looked up at the state of his failing army and nodded. They set off across the slope, riding past all of the knight's victims and away from the fighting. Neither of them looked forward to the long and difficult ride back to Egypt.

Chapter 52

Redemption

The battle was over and the Christian army had a decisive victory. They kept pace with the retreating Saracens, harassing them at will and robbing them of every coin and gem. Those that escaped the Christians were mercilessly assaulted by the Bedouin tribes who sensed easy pickings.

To the sound of cheering, the young leper king left the scene of his great triumph on a litter, alongside the true cross. Around his face he wore a shoufa to hide the growing infection on his face and despite the pain, he managed an occasional wave. Watching him go, Count Philip wondered if he would ever see the king again.

In the aftermath of the battle, only one story was on everyone's lips. The sight of the knight on the white warhorse that inspired the entire army and led them on to victory. Many truly believed the knight was the reincarnation of the martyred Saint George, who was no stranger to joining the Christians in battle, especially when victory was in the balance.

As the fog of battle cleared, Philip and the Knights Templar scoured the dead looking for the mystery knight. Odo de St Armand spotted Saladin's fallen tent in the lea of the ravine and found the knight hacked to pieces. He knelt down beside the knight to pray.

Philip broke through the ranks of Templars, desperate to see the identity of the knight. When Odo pulled the torso and head onto its back, Philip could not conceal his shock. 'Oh Jesus Christ…my Jesus,' he gasped unable to speak coherently.

Odo ordered everyone to stand back while he and two other Templars collected the grim remains of the arms and legs. It was not the dismembered parts that shocked him, but the age of the knight. 'Does anyone recognise this heroic old knight?'

Philip knelt solemnly next to the remains. 'Hugh Bigod, Earl of Norfolk. He was my companion...I thought he had died...'

Odo was surprised at the rank. 'An Earl! We will take good care of him now,' he scowled at Philip. He made no secret of his dislike of the Count of Flanders. He then ordered his men to cover the body in the shade and ride into Lydda to bring a coffin.

'What do you plan to do?' Philip enquired.

'He will be taken immediately to Jaffa to the salt stores. There his body will be wrapped in an ox hide filled with salt. Then his coffin will be filled with the preservative and sealed before being taken back to England. No doubt his family will want a shrine to honour his deeds this day.'

Philip looked at the body, still unable to take in what he had witnessed with his own eyes. 'But...but all he wanted to do was meet his brother...the man had no honour as such...'

'I think you have said enough,' Odo interrupted. 'If he sought redemption for his sins then the Lord will truly forgive him this day. His glorious death was something we should all aspire to. Perhaps now you will be on your way back to Flanders. And don't forget your army at Antioch. I am sure they will want to thank you for omitting them from one of the greatest victories ever fought in the Holy Land.'

Philip heard the Templars grumble their disapproval and felt their eyes eat into his back. Not wanting to endure any more discomfort, he decided to leave. As he rode out of the ravine, he spotted Wilhelm de Mandeville riding towards him.

'My God, I wish I had stayed with you,' Wilhelm said. 'There must be thousands dead.'

'Where is de Châtillon?' Philip asked quietly, ignoring de Mandeville's misplaced zeal.

'He rode off long ago looking for more plunder.'

Philip nodded. 'Can you believe it; Hugh Bigod was alive after all and joined the battle. I saw him from a distance and to my shame, I never recognised him. He appeared so strong and...somehow different.'

'What! Are you sure it was him?' Wilhelm sounded doubtful.

'I have just been with the body, as close as I am to you. I don't know how he could have lived...never mind fight in a battle.'

Wilhelm looked at the circle of Templars in the distance. 'Do they know what he was really like...I mean about his brother and everything,' he said tactfully.

'I don't think they want to know. They have their hero this day and that is all they will want to believe,' Philip concluded. Then he lifted his head. 'Do you want to join me in Lydda? Hopefully we will meet his brother, William. Then we might get some answers.'

'By all accounts, I think we will be lucky to find anyone left alive in Lydda,' Wilhelm said gravely. 'Apparently the Saladin's army killed everyone and burnt the town.'

As Philip and Wilhelm rode into Lydda, they were humbled by the pitiable efforts of the survivors searching for loved ones amidst the destruction. The great church was burnt through and only two walls survived the fire. Along the side of the square, a young Muslim was covering a row of bodies with blankets.

They dismounted and Philip walked over to him to asked what he was doing.

'Who else is going to bury them? There is only me.' Abdul looked like he had been crying for hours.

'Do you know William Bigod?' Philip asked.

'Yes, he was my master, now he lies next to my father.'

Philip asked to see his face.

'They took his eyes out,' Abdul warned before pulling back the

499

blanket.

Philip steeled himself but was astonished to see the smile on William's face, considering the pain he must have endured. His age immediately struck them.

Wilhelm leaned over to see for himself. 'So he was older than his brother. I have never known anyone as aged as that.'

'There is too much work for one man. If you take us now into the church crypt, we will help you dig the graves. Agreed?'

Abdul thought for a while. 'I will not descend into the pit of the dragon. But I will show you where it is.'

'Lead the way.'

It took half an hour just to clear a path through burnt timbers and fallen stonework and another half hour to find the opening to the 'dragon's lair'. Philip descended with utmost reverence and Wilhelm followed cautiously behind.

'I will stay here on guard,' Abdul said with false bravado.

Philip took the lamp to the edge of the scree slope and watched the flame. 'The air seems good,' he said taking a long breath. A little stale, but otherwise breathable.

Wilhelm nodded in agreement. 'Well what are you waiting for? This place is giving me the shits.'

They scrambled down the scree slope and peered around the walls and beams. Philip could not contain himself and threw caution to the wind. Turning to his right, he went under the beams inspecting each of them, looking for one that was different.

Following Philip, a glint of metal caught Wilhelm's attention and he picked up a gold and ruby encrusted knife lying against the foot of the wall. The hilt had an elaborate design of an eight-pointed star with a sun disc in the middle. He would show it to Philip in daylight.

Philip found the beam he wanted and saw Wilhelm had his back to him. He placed his hand inside the gap between the beam and the wall. There was nothing. 'Damnation and buggery!' Philip snorted.

He had waited more than a lifetime to discover the hand of Christ, and now it was gone. Nothing else remained except for a puddle of water against the far wall.

'Have you found anything?' Wilhelm asked.

'Nothing.' Philip rejoined Wilhelm.

'Well see what I have found.' Wilhelm showed Philip the ornate knife.

'Very nice...only I have seen a hundred knives like it before. You can buy one on most street corners for a few bezants. But look at the design; they have not even bothered with the Holy cross. Instead, there is a stupid star with points. What use is that?' Philip climbed the scree slope without looking back.

Wilhelm was surprised at Philip's outburst. He was about to throw the knife away but thought King Henry may find it an interesting memento of his adventure.

Upon reaching the surface, the air reeked of burning and death, far worse than the smell inside the chamber. They spotted Abdul sifting through an annex to the church. Very little appeared to have survived the destruction.

'My lords, I did not realise you had finished so soon. This was my master's room and I thought I would see if anything survived. He must have taken everything back to the farm when his brother came here to recover from his injuries.'

'Hugh Bigod slept here? I thought he lived with William on his horse farm.'

Abdul sifted through the debris on the floor. 'My father and the physician from the garrison cared for his brother Hugh. There was little space so my master returned to the farm. We can go there to eat if you wish. Pray it is untouched by the stench of death.'

Wilhelm face lit up. 'That is the best suggestion I have heard. There is nothing to eat in the town.'

Philip agreed and as they left the annex, he stepped onto a broken pot. Behind him, he glanced at Abdul, bending down to pick up the pieces. 'I am sorry Abdul, was the pot something special?'

'It was a gift...just an old pot I think. It doesn't matter now.' He threw the shards of pottery and the broken pieces of copper onto the pile of debris then wiped his hands. 'I will take you to the farm now.'

The horse farm was untouched though many of the household were busy burying dead relatives in the town. Philip and Wilhelm cooked over the fireplace and enjoyed their first good meal in ages.

Philip asked how long William had lived at the horse farm.

'Many years I think. My father said his family were murdered in the barn. Then he travelled for a long time but eventually he came home. Everything he did he wrote down in his book. I will see if I can find it. You may as well take it to remember him by for I cannot read his words.'

While Abdul searched, Philip spoke of the time when his grandfather, Count Robert of Flanders, had ridden in the vanguard of the first army of God. 'He witnessed the destruction of Lydda wrought by the spiteful Saracens. And now nearly eighty years later, I have witnessed the same. Time makes a mockery of our lives as events seem to repeat themselves. As if it was meant to be.'

'Those are the words Master Hugh said this morning. "It *was meant to be*," Abdul said.

Philip was stunned. 'You saw Hugh Bigod this morning?'

'I was tending to my master as he lay dying. His brother walked towards him and comforted him in his last moments. Then he rode off on Perseus, the white stallion.'

'Was he carrying anything?'

'Only a sword...a big shining sword. So strange...' Abdul seemed lost for words. 'He looked and sounded different...younger and stronger, and his hair was white...like Perseus...'

502

'This is very important, Abdul. Did he come from the church crypt?'

'Yes…he came through the smoke from the church…'

Philip quickly thanked Abdul. 'We must take our leave of you young man. God be with you in your time of need.'

'I have found his book. Do you want it?'

Philip looked down at the cumbersome pages stuck inside a leather wallet and bound up with braid. 'Yes, of course.' He strode over to his horse and tucked the book into his bulging saddlebag.

'Why the hurry,' Wilhelm asked. He was looking forward to his wine and his bed. 'I need to pay my last respects to Hugh before he leaves these shores. We can catch them up on the road to Jaffa.' In a cloud of dust, they galloped off down the track towards the escarpment.

Darkness had fallen by the time Philip entered the garrison at Ramleh and asked to see whoever was in charge. He was told that everyone was attending prayers so he agreed to wait. Nearly an hour passed as he paced the floor of the refectory, while Wilhelm lay on a bench and slept. There was some movement coming from the Templar church and he was surprised to see Odo St Armand come through the door.

'Count Phillp, my apologises but my prayers for the souls of the fallen are important. I am told you wish to see inside the coffin of Earl Bigod. Why is that?'

'He has something of mine,' Philip lied. 'Probably under his tunic.'

'I can assure you, that if Earl Bigod has something of value then it will be as one with the glory of God.'

'No, you do not understand, I must just look…'

'You are after the sword aren't you.' Odo stepped forward, his face red with anger. 'How dare you question my authority? Your presence in the Holy Land has been a disgrace. I pray your father and

503

your grandfather can forgive your selfish manner and deeds that are unworthy of the name of Flanders. Perhaps on your journey back to the pleasures of Champagne you can reflect on that.' Odo slammed the door behind him.

With his head hung low and shrouded in disappointment, Philip left the garrison. Bitter words meant for Hugh hissed from his lips. 'I was the only friend you ever had you bastard. And all you can say is, *"it was meant to be"*. What was meant to be?'

Wilhelm overheard his muttering. 'Stop talking to yourself and let's go home for God's sake. I am missing my comfortable life in Henry's court.'

Just as they were about to enter the stables, a figure appeared in another door to the dormitory and limped towards them. It was Jacques de Exemes. 'My lords, I thought I recognised your voices.'

They shook hands and Philip asked if Jacques was staying long.

'No, I am only here to have my wounds bandaged before I return to the garrison at Lydda.'

Wilhelm was surprised. 'What good will come of living in such a godforsaken place?'

'There is a church in need of rebuilding. The least I can do for William.'

'And what of Hugh?' Count Philip wondered.

'I know the Knights Templar well enough. Hugh will be honoured more than he could ever have imagined.'

Philip smiled and wished Jacques well as he turned to leave with Wilhelm. About to mount their horses, they felt a shudder beneath their feet. Doors and shutters rattled and the horses kicked out pulling at the reins. Then the tremors stopped as quickly as they had started.

Wilhelm settled his palfrey and mounted up. 'I hate this country.'

Many days passed before Philip had time to open the book given to him by Abdul. On the first calm day on the quiet waters of the Great Sea, he flicked over the pages of William Bigod's journal. Gradually it dawned on him that he was reading a fantastic tale of brotherly love and hate; of betrayal and loyalty. The untold story of the Knights Templar made his heart race as the pages dripped with sheer bravery and heartfelt emotions that few could endure. Towards the end, he was suddenly struck when the name of his mother leapt off the page.

The next ten pages spoke of the undying love William had held for the Countess Sybille. Philip was reduced to tears as he read every word of the love William had felt for another man's wife. Each sentence laid bare his soul as the doomed relationship was inevitably torn apart.

In understanding the heartache felt by William, he began to appreciate the feelings he had about Marie. And laden with coincidence, she too was another man's wife, and a countess.

After reading the last few pages again, it irked him that the story was incomplete. Was he not a witness to the heroic and tragic end of the Bigod brothers? Surely he had a duty to conclude the story.

With a long journey ahead of him, Philip began to weave together the final chapter on to one extra page. Nothing would be left out. All the secrets would be laid bare for all to read.

Then it suddenly struck him. What would Chrétien de Troyes make of such epic tale? Upon his return, he would present the accomplished author with William's book, assured that it would inspire in him a great prose.

Satisfied with his ending, Philip inserted the page into the leather binding, then noticed William had transcribed a passage from the scriptures. .

Reading the transcript from the Gospel of Luke, he urged the boat to sail quicker and prayed to have a favourable wind to send him home.

"When you see Jerusalem being surrounded by armies, you will know that its desolation is near...for this is the time of punishment in fulfilment of all that has been written. How dreadful it will be in those days for pregnant women and nursing mothers! There will be great distress in the land and wrath against this people. They will fall by the sword and will be taken as prisoners to all the nations. Jerusalem will be trampled on by the Gentiles until the times of the Gentiles are fulfilled. There will be signs in the sun, moon and stars. On the earth, nations will be in anguish and perplexity at the roaring and tossing of the sea. People will faint from terror, apprehensive of what is coming on the world, for the heavenly bodies will be shaken. At that time, they will see the Son of Man coming in a cloud with power and great glory. When these things begin to take place, stand up and lift up your heads, because your redemption is drawing near."

Luke 21:20-28

Epilogue
Thomas Martin

Five hundred and ninety two years later…
1769

"On the twenty-seventh day of November 1095, Pope Urban II preached to the masses on the fields of Clermont, promising absolution for those that would join the Army of God and deliver Jerusalem from the Saracens.

On the very same day, Bishop Herbert de Losinga laid the foundation stone of Norwich Cathedral, and Lord Roger Bigod rejoiced in the birth of his second son, whom he named Hugh.

Chroniclers of the day who lived at the heart of such times were ignorant of any connection between these events and the lives that would become so inextricably entwined. I keep asking myself. Did the Will of God pull the strings of such a grand scheme? And does the everlasting truth lay buried in the choir of Thetford Priory, waiting to be discovered.

Today I will open the grave of Hugh Bigod, the first Earl of Norfolk, and pray the contents will reveal the answers I seek."

Extract from the journal of Thomas Martin
September 22nd 1769

Chapter 53

Palgrave
Thetford

Thomas carefully replaced the floorboard and cocked his head to listen to the voices coming from the kitchen below. Indistinct words wafted up the staircase and he hurried as the sounds became louder. Twice in two days he had given his wife implicit instructions not to be disturbed in his private study, but the stranger had persisted and her will appeared to be weakening.

Footsteps now...coming up the stairs.

Looking into the hollow space, he tapped the short piece of floorboard back into its grooves just as the stranger suddenly emerged at the top of the stairs. Unable to hide his discomfort, he cursed at the effort required to rise from his knees.

The stranger smiled, then spoke with a French accent. 'Monsieur Martin I presume. I caught you at an inopportune moment...'

Wiping his hands on his trousers, Thomas grunted and straightened his stiff back, ignoring the handshake offered by the other man. A tall gentleman, well dressed with a continental flair, aged about fifty; his complexion burnished by the sun. Hoping his advanced years excused his dishevelled appearance, Thomas tightened his starched collar. 'I was just...tiding up. So many books to keep tidy.'

The stranger gave an appreciative nod. 'I have seen your collection of books. One of the finest I have seen assembled in all Europe. Particularly the ancient manuscripts from the East.'

Thomas raised his eyebrows. 'Oh, you are interested in the Arab writings.'

The man glanced left and right at the mountain of over laden shelves stacked with books and folders. 'I am interested in all ancient writings, of all faiths, all denominations. I believe they hold the key to everything we have learnt...everything we think we know.'

'I see.' Thomas cleared a pile of papers from a wooden chair and invited the man to sit down while he sank into his favourite armchair and poured himself a cheap brandy. 'They said the drink would kill me but here I am in my seventieth year. He inspected the bottle. 'Oh, not much left I am afraid...'

'You are too kind Monsieur, but it is a little early in the day for my delicate stomach, but I shall take some water from the pitcher.'

Thomas reluctantly placed his glass back on the bureaux and poured his guest some water. For a moment they sat eyeing each other up.

Thomas offered a weak smile. 'After your visit yesterday, my wife told me you have a bookshop in London and you are here for the auction. I pray you have deep pockets,' .

'Yes, I can see myself parting with a quite a few sovereigns. I have two shops...but I consider myself more of an adventurer than a simple collector and bookseller.'

'An adventurer, you say. Pray tell me more.'

'I have travelled far and wide over the Middle East and the Holy Land, mostly with my father. He died ten years ago but his spirit remains in me. Like him, I have a thirst for knowledge.'

The man reached into his waist pocket and handed Thomas an ornate business card.

Placing his reading glasses firmly on the bridge of his nose, Thomas read the card out loud. 'Thomas Payne...oh, my namesake I see. Are you related to young Tom Paine from Thetford town?'

'Indeed, I am a distant cousin. However, I consider myself his...how you say...his mentor.'

Thomas Martin grunted. 'Tom Paine went to Thetford Grammar

school...my old school, built on the grounds of the Church of Saint Mary, opposite the ruined priory on the other side of the river. I suppose he must be thirty by now and from memory something of an ordinary young man. I would not expect him to have an exotic mentor such as yourself.'

'Tom has progressed well in recent years. He is on the governing body for the town of Lewes and carries influence with the local church and the parish vestry, with responsibility for taxes and tithe distribution to the poor. Small beginnings I know, but he learns fast. He is due to be married soon...in fact I am to be at his engagement dinner. Rest assured, his day will come.'

'Well Mr Payne, I wish you luck with that.' Thomas looked again at the card. 'Strange. I see your surname is spelt differently to his.'

'You are very astute, sir. I am named after the town of Payen in France. The environs of my ancestry.'

Gazing into the fireplace Thomas Martin muttered the name to himself. 'Payen...Payen, where have I heard that name? Of course, Hugo de Payen, the founder of the Knights Templar.'

'Ah! Just as I anticipated, your knowledge is boundless. I am indeed a descendant of Hugo de Payen.'

Martin guffawed and leaned over to take a gulp from his glass on his bureaux. The brandy was cheap and his glass was rarely empty. 'Now I know you are mistaken. I have studied the history of the Templars and I know for a fact that Hugo de Payen had no children.'

Payne pulled his seat a little closer. 'Hugo had a manor at Montigny where he lived for a short time with his young wife. Tragically, she died giving birth to his son. When a priest eventually arrived, Hugo was found unconscious and his wife dead from blood-loss. Naturally, Hugo was grief-stricken and believing the baby to be stillborn, he immediately 'took up the cross' on the first crusade. You see, the priest kept the truth from him deliberately.'

'What truth?'

He lowered his voice. 'That his son survived the birth of course. The priest never explained why...perhaps he thought it best that Hugo seek redemption on crusade for his wife's death. Whatever the reason, the baby boy was taken into the care of the local nunnery.'

Martin was dumbstruck. 'Go on. What happened to the boy?'

'By the age of nineteen, he was listed at Clairvaux Abbey as Gilbert, under the sponsorship of Saint Bernard. So favoured by Abbot Bernard, he was promoted to be the Abbot of Sens.'

Martin waited while Payne took a sip of water. 'Later, there was a scandal. A letter written by Abbot Gilbert was discovered that implied he had sired a son born to a noblewoman. This led to the abbot seeking absolution in the Holy Land, from where he never returned.'

'And how do you know all this?' Martin asked, intrigued by the unlikely story.

Payne gave a confident answer. 'I have seen the ancient church records in Montigny and Clairvaux. The priest was good enough to record the birth and the adoption in the monastery registers.'

Martin sat back in his chair and stared into the bottom of the glass. 'Fascinating. I mean to find such a record from so long ago. You must have been surprised.'

'Not at all. My family have known of the secret for many generations, and we wish to keep it that way.'

'Indeed. So Monsieur Payne, are you also a Knight's Templar?'

Payne gave a thin smile. 'I am sure you are aware of the dissolution of the Templars by the papacy in the year thirteen-o-seven. Although, some people mistakenly believe the Freemasons to be Templars, but nothing is further from the truth.'

'Somehow I don't believe you are a simple London bookseller, are you?' Martin asked.

'Actually, my father was a Sabian and so am I.'

Martin could not hide his surprise at such an outlandish

revelation. 'Sabian, you say. Am I right in thinking that was an old Arab cult?'

Payne seemed wounded by the term. 'The origins of the Hurran Sabians go back as far as the seventh century but there is evidence of influence as far back as the time of Solomon. The wise men that became the Sabians existed when the first civilisations were being formed in Anatolia and Mesopotamia. They were the first astronomers and scientists and were probably responsible for the greatest advancements in human history, as well as restraining many of its excesses. No sir, not a cult. More an institution of the mind.'

'Yes, all very interesting. But I must ask myself, why is a man of such great wisdom and learning, sat in my study in Palgrave. Your curiosity extends to more than just the upcoming auction.'

'And you would be correct in thinking so. Though please, do not belittle your book collection. You are a famous antiquarian of great character and standing. You are…how you say…a gentleman. That is why I want to be totally honest with you.' Payne took another sip of water then stroked his chin, deep in thought.

'I have been on a quest as great as that of the Holy Grail, looking for one particular book. I eventually found a copy a few months ago when the library of Chrétien de Troyes was being demolished. You know he was one of the greatest twelfth century prose writers and an advocate of courtly chivalry.'

Martin nodded and stiffened slightly. Carefully he placed his glass on the bureaux, pausing to pick up the bottle of brandy. 'Well Mr Payne, your stories are quite remarkable, but I am in need of my afternoon nap. If you don't mind…'

Payne took the brandy bottle away from Martin, his face narrow and solemn. 'You don't need any more of this. You need to hear the rest of my story, old man.' He sat so close their faces were almost touching. The words he uttered were almost reverential. 'It is the story of William Bigod.'

At the mention of Bigod, the atmosphere of the meeting changed. The blood drained from Martin's face and his hand began to tremble.

Payne lowered his voice. 'Despite what history tells us, William survived the White Ship disaster. But you know that don't you?'

Martin did not answer. His heart had skipped a beat and he licked his lips, longing for the brandy that seemed to be floating further away by the minute.

Payne continued. 'You also know William Bigod kept a journal that describes in detail his covert involvement with the Knights Templars and of his unrequited love for a married woman, Countess Sybille of Flanders. What started as a simple journal became a leather-bound book brimming with astonishing encounters and incidents. This much you know, n'est-ce pas?'

Giving the slightest nod, Martin extended his hand to the bottle, and this time Payne nodded his consent.

Sitting back in his chair, Payne rested his head and sighed. 'Monsignor Martin, there is plenty of evidence that Count Philip of Flanders, the son of the Countess Sybille, went with Earl Hugh Bigod on pilgrimage to the Holy Land. Alas Hugh died in the Holy Land, at the Battle of Montgisard. Incredible, at his age.'

Martin nodded, eager to deflect the conversation away from Bigod. 'Saladin was something of an enigma. Some say he was a monster and yet there are many accounts of great compassion and chivalry.'

Payne gave a knowing smile. 'Monsignor, I have tried to understand the change in his character as a result of losing that battle. And not just his character but also his appearance. Apparently, a scar that was visible across his face, faded away within a month. You realise if Saladin had won the battle, then Jerusalem was at his mercy. He had sworn to destroy every Christian shrine and kill every

Christian and Jew across all Palestine. Christ could have been written out of history. Only with God's grace, he left with his tail between his legs; a much wiser and more tolerant man for the experience. But there are enigmas within enigmas. At the time, the earl's death was documented in Norwich in 1176, yet this is contradicted by a Templar account of the battle in November 1177.'

'One wonders how many times a man can die,' Martin smirked trying to make light of the story.

But Payne remained focused. 'The final pages of William's book describe an emotional reunion between William and Hugh and could only have been written by William. And I have no doubt that his book inspired one of the great masterpieces of French literature.'

Payne took a sheath of paper from inside his waistcoat and showed it to Martin. 'It is the prologue to a most famous prose, 'Perceval' or 'The Story of the Grail,' written by Chrétien de Troyes in the late twelfth century. I have had the relevant passages translated into passable English so let me read it to you.'

"He is the Count Philip of Flanders, the man about whom such greatness is told…

The count is such a man that he listens to no senseless jokes, nor haughty words and if he hears others slandered suffers for them. Whoever they may be. The count believes in firm justice, loyalty to the Holy Church and hates all vile acts.

He is more generous than one can imagine and gives, without hypocrisy or guile, as the bible tells, saying "Let your left hand ignore the good done by your right." Why does the bible say, "Hide your good deeds from your left hand?" The left, tradition says, means vainglory that comes from false hypocrisy. And what does the right mean? Charity that from its good works seeks not to boast but to hide so well that no one knows of it, except he whose name is God and Charity. So he who receives God, who sees all secrets, and knows all that is hidden deep

514

within our hearts.

Yes, there is no doubt about it. So, my labours will not be in vain, as I follow the count's wishes. From a book given to me by the count, I put into verse the best story ever told in a royal court: the Story of the Grail."

Payne waited for a reaction but Martin gave no response and for the first time wondered if the old man even understood the importance of what he was saying.

He continued. 'Count Philip was always trying to impress Marie, the Countess of Champagne. Chrétien was patron to Marie but upon receiving what was described as a wonderful gift from Philip, he changed his patronage to Philip. Reading this prologue, Chrétien seemed extremely grateful to the count. The rest is history. For a hundred years after Chrétien's death, "The Story of the Grail" became the source for all the Arthurian legends.' Payne stood up and ran his hand through his dark hair. 'William's book finishes quite suddenly, with a brief transcript from the Gospel of Luke. So, imagine my frustration upon finding an additional page that was written in a different hand but was damaged by damp and mostly indecipherable, except for a few tantalising words…Bigod's corpse, cross of Jesus, the hand of God…nothing that made sense.'

The profound silence was broken by Thomas Martin's wife at the door. 'I thought your guest might like a glass of wine. It's all right sir, I'll pour. Now where have you put that nice tablecloth you had on your desk? You know you are always spilling…'

Martin shook his head. 'I don't know. It doesn't matter,' he snapped. He hated his wife fussing over him.

Payne sat back down in his chair and smiled at Martin's wife. 'Thank you madam, you are most kind.'

As the wine trickled into the glass, she studied her husbands face and saw how pale he looked. 'You don't look well, Thomas. Is your stomach playing you up again?'

'No, I am fine. Monsieur Payne will be leaving soon. You can go now.' He dismissed her with a small hand gesture and her skirts swished against the banister rail as she descended the stairs.

Payne took a sip of wine and grimaced imperceptibly before continuing. 'Monsieur Martin, have you ever made a jigsaw puzzle and felt the frustration when confronted with a missing piece? The spoilt page is the missing piece I have been searching for. There is little doubt in my mind that the fate of Hugh Bigod holds the key to solving this puzzle. What is even more bizarre is when William refers to mysterious artefacts and relics...even the head of Christ is mentioned...

'Stop there!' Thomas Martin cried out. He thumped the table so hard the glass of wine splashed over the bureaux. 'Stop it now.' For a few seconds, the awareness of discovery hung silently in the air. 'This has gone far enough. Tell me...how did you know I had a copy of William's book?' he asked angrily.

Upon hearing the admission, Payne visibly relaxed. 'Two things came to light. I recently established that a copy of William's book was in the hands of Peter le Neve, President of the Society of Antiquaries. Upon his death, you married his widow, thereby inheriting his vast book collection for yourself. Then just a week ago I read that you had excavated the grave of Hugh Bigod from under the choir in the ruins of Thetford Priory. Was it just a coincidence, I asked myself? I think not.' He took a drink of the sour wine. 'Now, Monsieur, I must know what you found in the grave.'

Martin gripped the side of his armchair and began to show his irritation at the constant questioning. 'Is that so. Tell me Monsieur Payne, what treasure do you think I found buried in the grave of Hugh Bigod?'

The mention of treasure made Payne sit up. 'It is interesting you say treasure. In the thirteenth century, there were relics from the Holy Land found in the hollowed out head of a statue of the Virgin

Mary. Someone had gone to a great deal of trouble to wrap and label every relic. Do you know that the relics originally came from the other side of the river? From the old church of St Mary, the ruins you mentioned on the site of your old school. After the relics came the miracles and yet no one knows how the relics came to be there…'

'There was no treasure in the grave!' Thomas Martin interjected. 'And there is no point in looking, for I am sure that in his wisdom, the astute King Henry the Eighth will have secured all religious valuables for himself.' He walked a few steps before crouching down and tugged at one of the floorboards. It came loose in his hands and with his back to Payne, he reached into the space, pausing for a moment before replacing the floorboard. 'You must understand, I love my books. They are my life.'

As he turned to face Payne, a tear ran down his cheek. 'This auction is a disgrace, but my creditors…well, I have no recourse in the matter. I intend to keep one or two books and documents I consider priceless but only for sentimental reasons…not because they are worth any money. I would appreciate your silence on the matter. Give me your word and I will show you what you came all this way to see.' He sat down again and settled his stiff bones into his chair, letting out a deep sigh. 'This is the copy you are looking for.' Martin unfurled a wallet to reveal a small, leather bound book. 'Your quest has not been in vain, Monsieur Payne and I will fill in the missing piece of your puzzle.' Again, his attention turned to the bottle.

This time Payne stood up to empty the remaining brandy into the old man's glass. 'I give you my word that this meeting shall remain just between the two of us.'

Martin seemed satisfied and nodded. 'It appears as though Count Philip recovered the book from Lydda and indeed presented the tome to Chrétien de Troyes. Of course it was Count Philip who wrote the additional page you refer to, no doubt as he was returning from the Holy Land. He wrote of his attempt to retrieve something from the interred body of Hugh Bigod but in his own words, the Templars refused him access.'

'So what did Count Philip want to retrieve?'

Martin stroked his chin. 'There was some mention of a sword belonging to Saint George. No doubt a great prize for relic hunters like the count. But for whatever reason he failed. Count Philip returned to the court of Champagne and after presenting the book to Chrétien he wanted to fulfil his own heroic destiny. He departed on a later crusade with King Richard and was killed while scaling the walls of Acre.'

'And what of the remains of Earl Bigod?'

'The believe the salted body was first taken to London...and before you ask, I do not know why. However the Earl was eventually buried at Thetford Priory with only his wife and family present.'

Payne could not hold back any longer. 'And you dug up the coffin only a few weeks ago. Please, tell me what did you find?'

'There was a Latin inscription on a metal plate attached to the lid that confirmed the remains of Earl Hugh Bigod lay within. I found the pieces of his skeleton. It appeared all his limbs had been dismembered. Believe me, there was nothing else worthy of your misplaced and rather unethical excitement. I must say I don't appreciate treasure hunters.'

Payne hung his head, hiding his disappointment and ignoring the barbed comment. 'I can't believe all this was for nothing. You must show me the final words written by Count Philip. Perhaps they will shed some light...'

Martin gave a thin smile. 'I was shown the loose 'extra' page by Peter le Neve some twenty years ago. Yes, the count described his regret at not returning with any important relics as well as being unable to pay his proper respects to his friend, Earl Hugh. It seems Peter le Neve removed the page because it was obviously written in a different hand to William's and did not belong in William's book. I read the page once and have never seen it since.'

Thomas Payne stared at Martin then put his head in his hands, his face screwed up in disappointment. 'All this time I believed the page would reveal a clue to something, something...unique. To find a priceless relic of Christ perhaps, A fragment of the True Cross or maybe the Holy Grail itself. Even Chrétien refers to secrets in his prologue.'

A profound silence fell between the two men.

'Well...there is always the London Temple,' Martin offered. 'Have you never wondered on the identity of the anonymous knights buried there? Like I said, you have to ask why the Templars would take a respite for six days in London Temple before laying the body of Hugh to rest in Thetford Priory. That is where I would look...but at my age...'

Payne leapt to his feet, his face suddenly brimming with anticipation. 'Alors! So you think the Templars may have taken something from the coffin and buried it at the London Temple?'

Martin tried to appear enthused. 'Anything is possible. I read that an impressive escort of twenty knights in all their finery escorted the corpse to London. Later, the coffin arrived in Thetford on just a simple ox cart, with just two squires.'

Payne weighed up the promise of taking his search even further. Yes, the Templars would want to keep any important relic for themselves. For the first time that day, Thomas Payne afforded himself a sardonic smile. 'Perhaps I shall pay a visit to the London Temple before I see Tom Paine next week.'

Stood at the front door, Thomas Martin wished Thomas Payne well on his quest and jovially asked him to keep the bids high for the coming auction of his collection.

Telling his wife that he did not want to be disturbed, she replied she was going to the nearby farm to collect some eggs and would lock the outer door.

After ensuring that no one was downstairs, Martin returned to his study and lit two candles and an oil lamp. Again, he removed the floorboard and placed William's book back in its hiding place. Reaching a few inches to the side he picked up the the page written by Count Philip of Flanders and replaced it in the back of the book.

Kneeling, he paused to listen again for any signs of movement from downstairs before reaching even deeper under the floorboards until he felt the tablecloth. It was wrapped around an object about nine inches long and he carefully placed it on the bureaux, making sufficient space. With trembling hands, he unfurled the tablecloth.

His voice was but a whisper. 'Oh God, Oh God...what shall I do with you. I knew they would come looking for you but they will never take you from me.' Apart from a fearful, perfunctory look some two weeks ago, it was the first time he dared to remove the cloth. He pulled up a stool and perched like a hawk with his glasses balanced precariously on the end of his nose. The cut had been clean, severing bone and sinew just above the wrist. The thumb and fingers were only a little stiff though perfectly formed. In fact, the whole hand felt supple as if made of soft leather and there was no deterioration of the perfectly formed skin.

As each minute passed, he felt slightly braver. Holding the hand up to the light, he could see a jagged hole in between two bones, just where the palm met the wrist. The nail had left its mark. He knew now without any doubt it was the hand of Jesus Christ. The moment he had seen it lying amongst the skeletal remains of the Earl, he knew what he had found.

For the last few weeks, he had read every page of William's book, as well as the last page inserted by Count Philip. While sitting at sea, Count Philip had laid bare all his personal beliefs about the crypt at Lydda.

Philip surmised that the hand of Jesus Christ had been attached to the Holy Cross for a thousand years. He believed that by some miracle, Hugh had taken the hand and rode the white stallion into battle, carrying a great sword. The spirit of the army were lifted by such a vision and yet the miracle was short lived. Hugh Bigod was brutally hacked to pieces by Saladin's bodyguard.

In all their arrogance the Templars must have taken the sword but amongst the detached limbs in the coffin, they had failed to notice the holiest relic in all Christendom. The hand of Christ.

There was no guilt in lying to Thomas Payne. How could he trust a man who was no more than a French treasure seeker? Oh, others were sure to follow and he would have no qualms in telling as many lies as was necessary to keep the most important secret in the world between himself and God.

After all Jesus knew all about secrets.

He held the hand close to his chest and closed his eyes in prayer. 'I will keep your secret Lord and I shall await my reward in heaven.'

Wrapping the hand again in the cloth, he placed the precious relic back under the floorboard.

There was only one pressing notion that continued to plague his thoughts. According to the New Testament, Jesus ascended to heaven with the nail holes present in his hands.

But if Jesus only had one hand, what does that say about the resurrection? Does Jesus sit next to God in heaven with one hand or two? Thomas anticipated many sleepless nights and wondered how many souls had gone before, pondering the same unfathomable question.

The End

"The story of the redemption will not stand examination. That man should redeem himself from the sin of eating an apple by committing a murder on Jesus Christ, is the strangest system of religion ever set up."

"Among the most detestable villains in history, you could not find one worse than Moses, who gave an order to butcher the boys, to massacre the mothers and then rape the daughters. One of the most horrible atrocities found in the literature of any nation. I would not dishonour my Creator's name by attaching it to this filthy book."

"It seems the bible is more the word of a devil than a god. It is the book of demons, and people have no clue what they are worshipping."

Thomas Paine
The Age of Reason 1794

522

Historical Notes

Every effort has been made to keep the actual characters inside genuine events and real locations. Some are well known, but in the face of any confusion between fact and fiction, I recommend investigating the historic details on-line or in the library.

The mythological content of the narrative describes two gems as *Lapsit Exillus* or 'the Stones from Heaven'. The Talmud and the Midrashim contain many references where they are also named *Shamir*. Both Rabbi Rashi and Maimonides described *Shamir* in Talmudic commentaries as 'living creatures like a worm', though this was later disputed in preference to an active mineral. The most precious possession of Solomon, his *Shamir* did not survive and apparently with time it became inactive.

In many countries, I was struck by the number of stele of the goddess Tanit, also known as Astarte the consort of Baal. The most elaborate design usually showed the priest under a crescent moon, with arms outstretched holding onto two upright sceptres, stuck into the ground. Suspended above each sceptre appears a round sphere. This created a formidable 'fantasy' weapon, something that could be contained within the Ark of the Covenant. I combined an interpretation of the image with the mythology of *Shamir*.

The trials and tribulations of King Henry and Thomas Becket are well documented and in the context of this saga, there was no need to detail their convoluted relationship. However, Hugh Bigod and Philip of Flanders were both asked to intervene in their reconciliation, though with little success. What contributed to Hugh's paranoia in his later years? No doubt his excommunication by Becket will have incensed Hugh and the construction of Orford Castle was seen as a threat to his power and an insult to his status.

The little known Battle of Fornham, near Bury St Edmunds, decided the fate of Henry the second and the English crown. As with all such battles luck played an enormous part in the royalist victory and proved again the ineffective use of mercenaries in battle.

The second instance of 'Blood Libel' occurred as described in Blois 1171. Like the murder of the Norwich boy, William, the retribution was catastrophic for the Jewish community. The accusation of murder was the first known case outside England, leading to the town's population of thirty-one Jews being burned to death.

Despite evidence to the contrary, I would like to believe that Hugh had no intention of burning Norwich when he entered the city in 1174. Perhaps events quickly spiralled out of control and he was powerless to prevent a disaster, though I omitted to say he took hostages.

The reasons why Count Philip, William(Wilhelm) de Mandeville and Hugh Bigod undertook the arduous journey to the Holy Land in 1176 are difficult to understand. Apparently Philip simply intended to marry off two of the sons of Lord Robert de Bethune to his cousins, Princess Sybilla and her half sister Princess Isabella. His pilgrimage probably honoured his father as well. There is some evidence that de Mandeville's intention was to deliberately embarrass Philip on the orders of King Henry. As to why Hugh should join them to the Holy Land at the age of eighty, remains a mystery. Did he conclude he needed redemption for his guilty past or was he simply bored with his enforced and powerless retirement?

The death of Nuradin enabled Saladin to claim the rule of Egypt and Syria. Around the time of the solar eclipse in the spring of 1176, Saladin was engaged in a campaign against Rashid ad-Din Sinan and the assassins. Once satisfied with his accomplishments, he returned to Cairo establishing defensive walls against the Christian forces.

After so much instant success, perhaps Saladin was over confident and believed he could seize Jerusalem at any time? Why did he allow Baldwin's army to lie untouched in Ascalon while his undisciplined soldiers ran rampant? The numbers suggest he had the upper hand.

William of Tyre documented Saladin's army at Montgisard as *"26,000 soldiers, of which 8,000 were elite forces and 18,000 were black soldiers from Sudan. The army raided the countryside, sacked Ramleh and Lydda, and dispersed themselves as far as the Gates of Jerusalem."*

Lucky to escape with his life, Saladin perhaps felt humbled by failure. There is no reason to believe that Saladin had an epiphany after the battle of Montgisard, although he was later recognised as a wise and merciful leader, capable of great acts of compassion.

Placing Hugh's wife Gundred in the care of the nunnery in Bungay was a little unfair. The collapse of her mental state provides another reasonable excuse for Hugh to seek redemption in the Holy Land. Although she patronised the nunnery at Bungay, there is no evidence she suffered from any illness. She actually outlived Hugh, dying at the age of sixty-five, in the year 1200.

Another mystery is well documented and remains unexplained. For some reason, Hugh's death was reported in March 1176, some eighteen months before his actual death at the Battle of Montgisard. In the face of appeals from his wife Gundred and his son Roger, King Henry II actually took advantage of the news to try and seize the late Earl's vast estates for himself. Reports of his death appeared premature hence my interpretation that describes the contradiction in dates.

The relics hidden by Prior Steven, inside the sculpted relief of the Virgin Mary gathered dust for many years in a corner. Around 1250, reports of miracles and visions of the Virgin Mary were widely circulated and the prior was persuaded to build a Lady Chapel adjoining the nave. In doing so he placed the old relief in the new chapel, employing a painter to beautify the image. A metal plate was revealed and removed, whereupon the relics were discovered inside, wrapped in lead. According to Blomefield, these were listed by the prior as follows:

The robe of our Lord, the girdle of our Lady, the rock of Calvary, some grave-clothes of Lazarus and relics of many Saints including Saint George. Apparently, a letter by Hugh Bigod and the monk named Ralph, was also found. The Lady Chapel subsequently became an important pilgrimage site and the scene of miraculous cures. The ruins of Thetford Priory, the Lady Chapel and the choir can still be visited today.

Significantly, the Christian army at the Battle of Montgisard were reportedly heartened by the sight of Saint George riding into battle. The death of Hugh Bigod at Montgisard, aged eighty-two, was one of the main inspirations for writing this saga. However, the discovery of two further events were equally important.

One was the account of Count Philip of Flanders presenting a mysterious book of unknown origin to Chrétien de Troyes, that inspired Chrétien to write "Perceval, the Story of the Grail." The book was dedicated to his patron, Philip of Flanders as described and was ultimately transformed into the Arthurian legends.

The second was the story of Thomas Martin, the eighteenth century antiquarian, who excavated the bones of Earl Hugh Bigod from the choir of Thetford Priory, as described by Francis Blomefield in "The History of Norfolk". Thomas Payne from London acquired much of his book collection at auction and by coincidence the infamous Tom Paine lived in Thetford as described.

If the Knight Templars brought back Hugh's body from the Holy Land, they would have stopped en-route in London. Nine effigies of knights were buried in the London Temple Church, five of which have been attributed to recognised Lords, including William Marshall and surprisingly, Geoffrey de Mandeville. However, a clumsy restoration in 1841, and subsequent bomb damage in the blitz made determining their identity rather arbitrary.

Of the remaining 'anonymous' four effigies, two of these are cross-legged indicating they have visited the Holy Land. One of these effigies has a sword in the scabbard.

The other does not.

Bibliography

The prologue to 'Perceval: the Story of the Grail'

          Translated by Kirk McElhearn 2001

Rashi, Pesahim 54a;   *Maimonides, Commentary on Abot 5.6.*

The History of the Crusades   *Steven Runciman*

The History of Norfolk   *Francis Blomefield*

Historical Atlas of the Crusades   *Angus Konstam*

The Crusaders   *Norman Housley*

The Rise and Fall of The Knights Templar *Gordon Napier*

Jerusalem   *Simon Sebag Montefiore*

The Templars History and Myth   *Michael Haag*

The Revolt of 1173-74   *Roger of Hoveden circa 13[th]Century*

          Translated by Henry T Riley 1853

The Works of Thomas Martin (1696-1771) known as 'Honest Tom Martin of Palgrave'.

Many texts referred to in the novels are viewable on the 'Internet Medieval Source Book'.

Seventeen years of researching medieval history and genealogy sites on 'The Internet,' and still continues.

Made in the USA
Las Vegas, NV
22 November 2022

60044979R10295